WOMEN AND SLAVERY IN AFRICA

Women
and Slavery
in Africa

Edited by

Claire C. Robertson

Martin A. Klein

THE UNIVERSITY OF WISCONSIN PRESS

Published 1983

The University of Wisconsin Press
114 North Murray Street
Madison, Wisconsin 53715

The University of Wisconsin Press, Ltd.
1 Gower Street
London WC1E 6HA, England

First printing

Printed in the United States of America

For LC CIP information see the colophon

ISBN 0-299-09460-X

Contents

Part III. The Slave Experience: Case Histories

Part IV. Women as Slave Owners, Users, and Traders

Maps and Figures

Maps

Figures

Foreword

The editors of this volume are to be congratulated, for it will surely be a landmark in the fast-growing literature on slavery and the slave trade both in Africa and elsewhere. Not only does it provide new information on a vital and hitherto neglected aspect of the subject, but it yields some surprising evidence. Thus it seems that women slaves were often valued more for their manual labor than for their reproductive role as the bearers of children. Furthermore, it highlights the many functions of female slaves, who could serve as field hands, artisans, mothers of rulers, breeders of lineage members, rewards for warriors, wives for male slaves, or simply as domestic servants—a versatility which explains the preference for women on the African slave market. Although female slaves were often the lowest of the low—suffering male dominance as well as servitude—women do not emerge from these pages merely as victims. They played an active part in the exploitation of slaves—as owners and overseers, as slave dealers, and as the chief beneficiaries from slave labor.

This is a wide-ranging book, containing a mix of theoretical analysis and empirical research. It is illustrated with valuable case studies, in which the slaves themselves speak, adding the poignancy and human interest all too often missing from scholarly works.

Doubtless the conclusions and the theories in this volume will be tested and contested, for whereas in some areas they confirm existing beliefs, in others they open a range of new questions, and radical reassessments not just of slavery but of other features of African societies. This is, therefore, one of those invaluable seminal works which stimulate further research and debate among scholars, thus enriching our knowledge and refining our perceptions.

This book owes its inspiration to Claire Robertson. The idea germinated from a lively discussion I had with her at a hectic but fruitful meeting of the African Studies Association in the mid-1970s. Fresh from coediting *Slavery in Africa* and busy planning a companion volume on the suppression of slavery, I had been struck by the key role played by women in African slavery, an aspect not explored in the existing literature. Claire Robertson had not only been thinking along the same lines but was in the midst of research in Ghana which provided an important case study. It was thus that I had the rare privilege of playing a part in the very inception of someone else's work, for Claire subsequently set out to fill this gap in our knowledge with an enthusiasm fueled by her concomitant interest in Women's History. Martin Klein, with his long interest in slavery, particularly in the western Sudan, his various articles on the subject, and his experience in editing—he was then in the throes of his important *Peasants in Africa*—was a natural choice for coeditor. I now look forward to the rich and fruitful debate which this work will provoke and which will reward their efforts.

Suzanne Miers

INTRODUCTION

1 *Claire C. Robertson & Martin A. Klein*

Women's Importance in African Slave Systems

Most slaves in sub-Saharan Africa were women. But many accounts of African slavery are written as though the slaves were exclusively men. Thus, we are frequently told that the master owed his slave a wife, rarely that he was obliged to provide her with a husband.[1] Likewise, many accounts assume that the owners and users of slaves were male. It may be that most slave owners were male, but a large percentage of the users were female, and the distinction between ownership and usage rights is important (see Wright, this volume; Kopytoff 1979:63). Assimilation of these two propositions inevitably changes one's perspective on African slavery and slave systems. This volume establishes the importance of women's roles in African slave systems and explores the resultant implications.

Most of the papers fall within the period from the early nineteenth to the early twentieth centuries (Broadhead and Thornton excepted), and thus cover the period after the abolition of the Euro-American slave trade. The effort to abolish the slave trade often began with conquest or soon after, but most colonial regimes only tried to regulate slavery itself beginning in the early twentieth century.

The word *slavery* has been used for a wide variety of relationships. It has been variously defined in terms of property relationship (Tuden and Plotnicov 1970:12) or in terms of the slave's kinlessness (Kopytoff and Miers 1977:3–76). Whichever definition is used, the slave is involuntarily servile, has a marginal position within her social unit, and is subject to the

---

1. See Wright paper, this volume, fn. 2; Nwachukwu-Ogedengbe 1977:144; Horton 1954:315; Nwulia 1975:112. Even as good an article as that by Cooper (1979:106, 119) does not make the critical sex distinctions, despite its focus on the use of slaves by particular groups in striving for wealth and power. Patterson (1979:37) even included in his definition of slave status loss of manhood.

control of another. This definition encompasses a whole range of servitude that is reflected in these papers, which draw on West African evidence in nine cases, and East and Central African in nine.[2] Most of the societies described are patrilineal by descent, but where matrilinearity is involved (Wright, Harms, Olivier de Sardan, Alpers, Brooks, Broadhead, Thornton), no particular uniform differences are evident regarding women slaves. In effect, unity comes out of diversity when considering women and slavery. The first question we must ask is why most African slaves were female. The answers to that question are usually sought in the functions of women slaves. Here we will seek them also in the functions of free women. Certain of our answers are speculative due to the paucity of evidence on some points, but together we feel that they form a body of thought that sums up a wealth of evidence gathered from different kinds of sources and methods used by the authors. Above all we hope that this volume stimulates new questions and answers about African slavery and societies.

Before going into the reasons why most slaves were female, we must establish that they were. For this we have a considerable body of evidence. On the African continent there were three different slave markets in terms of sex ratios. The European export market purchased male slaves by a margin of at least two to one (H. Klein and Thornton, this volume; Curtin 1975:76). The somewhat smaller Muslim market of the Arab world absorbed primarily female slaves (Austen 1979:44; Campbell 1981:225). The internal African market, which may well have been the largest of the three, absorbed mostly women and children.[3] This was true not only on the mainland, but also on Madagascar. Campbell (1981:209–10, 225) described the intersection of the three markets there. The expanding Imerina state killed all male captives over the age of ten and absorbed primarily female slaves. The European planters purchased mostly male "contract" labor, and the Arabs bought mostly women and children.

The ratio of male to female slaves seems to have varied depending both on the uses of slave labor and the nature of external demand. Thus, on the

2. Unfortunately, recruitment efforts over three years of work on this volume failed to yield either contributions on southern African or substantial African participation. We did not attempt to include North African contributions.

3. Most of the papers in this volume support this assertion. See also Nieboer 1900:141, 145, 147, 151; Klein and Lovejoy 1979:188; Cooper 1977:221; Meillassoux 1975a:226; Holsoe 1977:297; Harries 1981:314; Thornton 1980:422–23; Smith 1954:252; Curtin 1975:175–77; Curtin 1969:19, 28, 41, 46; Ross 1979:421. MacCormack in this volume asserts that on the Sherbro coast and hinterland women slaves were worth no more than men slaves, while giving fragmentary price data supporting the opposite view and describing a pattern of slave raiding which netted more women and children than men, leaving us with the impression that the raiders were either economically inefficient or incompetent in not getting more men. The European market included Cape Town, where a ratio of 344 male slaves per 100 female slaves prevailed in the eighteenth century (Ross 1979:412).

Zaire River, there was almost equal demand for men as canoe paddlers and for women as food producers, and the male-female ratio seems to have been close to parity (Harms, this volume). The ratio in Zanzibar was also close to parity, largely because of the high value placed on male labor, though as in the Americas, women were overrepresented among field laborers (Cooper 1977:221–23; H. Klein, this volume). In areas where the indigenous market and the American market were both active, it is probable that African societies absorbed very few men, and those mostly for military purposes (M. Klein, this volume; Manning 1981). By contrast, in areas serving North African or Middle Eastern markets, the male-female ratio was probably closer to parity (Manning 1981). It also seems fairly clear that women and children predominated among those enslaved through warfare. Male prisoners were often killed (M. Klein, this volume; Keim, this volume). Patrick Manning has recently expanded the discussion of the impact of various slave trades on African demography, and John Thornton picks up the discussion in this volume.

Not only were women more common in the African internal slave trade, but they were also in higher demand. They consistently brought higher prices. Austen noted that in Cameroon adult male slaves commanded the best prices in the 1790s, but from the 1860s to the 1890s twice the price was paid for women and children (1977:320). Nachtigal reports prices for the Kuka market which indicate that women were more valuable at all ages (Fisher and Fisher 1970:164). Harries reports a similar price differential for South Africa (Harries 1981:322, 326). This preference for women seems to have existed throughout Africa (Kopytoff and Miers 1977:62; Piault 1975:334–35; Uchendu 1977:125; Dunbar 1977:162; Goody 1980:38; Tambo 1976). Furthermore, the price differential reflected African demand. Curtin remarks that the European traders in Senegambia were willing to pay the same price for women and men, but that in the interior, women cost twice as much as men (Curtin 1975:176). This price differential eventually declined somewhat, but persisted up to the end of the internal slave trade (M. Klein, this volume). In Africa, then, slave women were generally more highly valued than slave men. Why?

The major debate over the function of female slaves centers on production and reproduction, the subject of Part 2 of this volume. Many scholars have assumed that African women were preferred as slaves because of their value for reproduction. Augé (1975) writes that "if male slaves constituted a labor force, a means of production, female slaves constituted a means of reproduction."[4] Goody, one of the few to raise the issue, had

---

4. Bohannan and Curtin (1971:265) and Piault (1975:335) made reproductive functions the sole explanation for the higher prices for females than males, and Bourgeot (1975:83) tended the same way, even though he said that the sexual division of labor did not apply to slaves, which would indicate that men and women were used for the same *productive*

much difficulty explaining the phenomenon because he assumed that women slaves were valued only for reproduction (1976:37–39). Reproduction in this context is often defined as biological reproduction, or expansion of the owner's lineage. Many writers also stress the ease of women's assimilation, and the benefits to men of acquiring kinless wives or concubines. In patrilineal societies, so the argument goes, men could acquire a slave concubine more cheaply than a wife, and build up their lineages with the free offspring of these unions (Cooper 1979:117). In matrilineal societies, as Broadhead shows (this volume), the advantages for men were even greater, since they could achieve direct control over their offspring with slave concubines, instead of relying on the uncertain loyalty of their sisters' children (Miller 1973:25; Rattray 1929/1969:43–44; Poku 1979:35). Furthermore, slave wives could be doled out to cement alliances with neighbors, or to ensure the loyalty of subjects, as Bay and Keim show (this volume; see also Austen 1977:319).

The greater ease of assimilating women slaves as opposed to men slaves is not only attributed to structural factors and women's reproductive functions, but also to their submissive socialization (see M. Klein, this volume). In many societies women were and are taught to obey men unquestioningly. Kopytoff and Miers emphasized the assimilation of African slaves as the chief problem, "the 'rehumanization of the [trade slave] nonperson in a new social setting." They stressed the necessity of attachment to a kin group or a patron for individuals in African societies (Kopytoff and Miers 1977:17, 23). In his essay in this volume, M. Klein notes that male slaves often preferred the acquisition of a slave or a second wife to the purchase of their own freedom. For women slaves fuller incorporation often came as a result of bearing a child to the master or a member of his family, as many essays here show (Kopytoff and Miers 1977:31–32; Grace 1977:422; Meillassoux 1975a:240; Smith 1966:158).

Stressing assimilation of slave women and the expansion of lineages is useful as one perspective on slavery, but in the case of women slaves it distorts their position in several ways. First, the assumption is common that families or lineages were not stratified. Rey, Meillassoux, and others have argued elsewhere that African societies were stratified by age and sex, which determined the division of labor.[5] Labor recruitment was the basis of African wealth, and kinship often set the terms for that recruitment. Lovejoy (1979:26) noted that among the facilitators of African slavery were "kinship structures which allowed the transfer of rights over people

purposes. Cooper (1977:195n) emphasized the role of female slaves as concubines, implying that concubines did not do any work outside the home.

5. The use of these divisions to apportion labor and surplus can be called a lineage or corporate kin mode of production. Rey 1975:27–80; Meillassoux 1975b and 1981; Robertson forthcoming, ch. 1.

and which permitted the development of dependent relationships that in certain situations could lead to slavery." Thornton (this volume) cites a number of cases of relatives being sold for petty violations in the Guinea-Bissau area in the seventeenth century. It was, in a sense, the very lack of opposition between kinship and exploitation that often allowed slavery to exist. "No woman or girl in Ibuza was free," Emecheta tells us, "except those who committed the abominable sin of prostitution or those who had been completely cast off or rejected by their people for offending one custom or another" (1977:157). The sexual division of labor exploited women in many instances, and was justified by an ideology which assumed female inferiority.[6] Thus, even being completely assimilated into a society as a free person did not necessarily ensure equal status for female ex-slaves. Second, even when free, the children of slaves or ex-slaves often bore a stigma from their origins and had inferior inheritance rights.[7] An Asantehene, ruler of a kingdom which absorbed many slaves, made it illegal for people to inquire into a person's antecedents (Rattray 1929: 43–44).

If women were sometimes freed through their reproductive functions, they were also trapped by them. Women often refused to abandon their children. The mother of Swema chose to sell herself into slavery along with her daughter, rather than be parted from her (Alpers, this volume). In most societies, slave women could not legally marry, though they did form regular unions with either freeborn males or male slaves.[8] MacCormack in this volume tells us that slave women were not valued for making alliances because of their kinlessness. Adukwe, the Accra slave whose history is given by Robertson, spent much of her adult life in a futile search for a man who would perform a full marriage rite for her in order to assure her social respectability. Adzo, the Ewe slave mentioned by Nukunya (appendix to Robertson, this volume), had no marriage rite done for her. She was also threatened with supernatural sanctions if she ran away, a common phenomenon indicating that slave owners were un-

---

6. Smith (1966:159, 162, 164) pointed out that families are not exempt from stratification, which "consists in the restriction of access to positions of varying advantage," and that a major defect of current sociology was to assume a consensual basis and integrative function of the family even if the stratification was forcibly imposed, as under colonialism or slavery.

7. For a contrary case, see Brain 1972:14–15. "It is part of Bangwa dogma that a person's female ancestress, traced matrilineally, was a slave, bought in a grassfields market. . . . There is no feeling of shame linked with slave parentage, no notion of guilt about the slaving days."

8. Bourgeot 1975:90; Klein 1977b:347; MacCormack 1977:187; Meillassoux 1975a:228. Héritier (1975:489–90) cites the most telling case for not allowing free-slave marriage (as opposed to liaisons): "you cannot eat the slave twice," her informants said, referring to its value and its fruit.

sure that physical coercion and/or "assimilation" would be enough to assure the slave's loyalty.

A last point is that the slave person's social status in his or her society of origin could affect the ease of assimilation positively or negatively. This was true in Adzo's case, and Wright cites the case of Meli, a woman from a chiefly family, whose former high status prevented her from being completely assimilated and perhaps made her treatment more harsh.[9] Conversely, the Dahomean rulers mentioned by Bay in this volume were routinely descended from slave wives of their predecessors, who were often from areas newly incorporated into the kingdom. Such wives brought with them and contributed substantial cultural innovations, as both Bay and Keim (this volume) point out. With the Bangwa their contribution of Bamileke culture was so valued that they became the wives of chiefs and givers of high social status (Brain 1972:14). Another function of female slaves, then, was as transmitters of culture in some cases.

Stressing reproduction and assimilation also distorts the position and functions of female slaves by underestimating their productive functions.[10] Arguments which attribute the high prices paid for women to their biological reproductive function do not hold up very well under the impact of the fertility data available. In his essay Meillassoux uses data culled from other chapters of this book to argue that slave women were subfecund: "slave reproduction took place mostly through purchase or capture" (p. 54, below). Furthermore, their masters or mistresses did not further the women's reproductive functions. Although Ross (1979:424–26) speaks of masters being solicitous about their slaves' reproduction and fecund women fetching high prices in Cape Town, the ratio of children per slave woman in 1749 was 0.9, for free black women 1.6, and for white women 2.9. In medieval Muslim Spain, advanced pregnancy was even a cause for depreciating the value of a female slave (Verlinden 1955:235). Slave women themselves, of course, often lowered their own fertility by using various birth control methods, as Harms shows (this volume; see also Cooper 1977:225; Cooper 1980:82).

We would like to suggest, then, that the analysis of the status of slave women suffers from an overweening emphasis on the so-called biological functions of reproduction. This is not to deny that the reproductive functions of women led on occasion both to their enslavement and manumission, but this emphasis has often obscured rather than clarified their func-

9. Wright 1975:813–15. Meli eventually had a full marriage because the missionaries who took her in acted as her parents.

10. Austen (1979:44n, 47) assumes that "males would be preferred for military or *rural labor roles*" in North Africa (our emphasis). There is little basis for this assumption.

tions and socioeconomic status. Nieboer (1900:22) even distinguished wives from slaves because wives' "relation towards their husbands is wholly bound up with the sexual and family life." Even Meillassoux here makes the mistake of saying that concubines were not really slaves, as if compulsory sexual relations somehow ameliorated rather than reinforced slavery for women. Strobel (1979:48) has a more accurate vision, in our opinion: "Slavery and male dominance converged in the institution of concubinage." Nwulia (1975:196) noted that the British Anti-Slavery Society strongly objected to a provision of the Zanzibar 1897 slavery abolition act, which said that concubines should remain in their current position unless cruelty could be proved, because they felt that as a result the majority of the female population would remain in slavery. Was it a *privilege* that, as Cooper (1977:195) states it, "any female slave was legally at the sexual disposal of her master," or that the freedom of concubines on Zanzibar was delayed until twelve years after that of other slaves?

Women's reproductive functions have often been seen only in biological terms. Strobel has suggested in this volume that there are three different kinds of reproductive labor: biological reproduction, daily reproduction (i.e., the servicing of workers), and the reproduction of relations of production by the transmission of the ideology supporting the whole social structure. All of these functions are predominantly performed by women in many societies.

Whatever definition of "productive" we use (Eisenstein 1979; Gerstein 1973; Robertson, forthcoming), African women slaves performed mostly productive labor, just as most free women did. Thornton describes the multiple productive functions of Bissagos Islands women in the seventeenth century (this volume). Estimates of the proportion of agricultural labor currently performed by women in sub-Saharan African hover around 60 to 70 percent (Boserup 1970; United Nations Food and Agriculture Organization 1979:110). This proportion obviously varies today, and it varied greatly from society to society and was possibly smaller in the nineteenth century. The immigration of more men to towns and their greater access to education have disproportionately reduced male agricultural participation in many areas. However, there is no reason to suspect that in precolonial times women did not perform most of the agricultural work. The sexual division of labor often dictated that women perform the more labor-intensive tasks, not only in agriculture but in craft work. Thus, slave women weeded rice, or spun thread for male weavers' use (see Brooks and M. Klein, this volume). On Zanzibar, men picked cloves, but women picked, separated, and dried them (Cooper 1977:157). Men might have been more productive individually because, like the Baule weavers, they used higher technology (Etienne 1977), but women probably did much

more of the work. Increasing production, then, depended more on acquiring female labor.[11] Meillassoux argues below that "in slavery, women were
valued above all as workers" (p. 49). We concur. This is the fundamental
reason why most African slaves were women.

This was especially true in many Muslim areas. The seclusion of upper-
class women removed them from productive labor outside the home. Thus
they needed slave women to do women's work: trading, farming, building
homes, porterage, and so on. On Pate Island off East Africa, women complain now about having to build houses themselves; in the past their female slaves did it for them (H. Brown, pers. comm. 1982). Hausa women
in Kano are now dependent on child labor for their trading activities
(Schildkrout 1978); in the past, freeborn Hausa women undoubtedly used
female slaves to trade for them. Cooper (1977:171) commented that on
East African plantations "All slaves worked, men and women alike," five
days per week.

One of the arguments which has been used to deny the validity of making a distinction between men and women in analyzing slavery is that
under slavery the sexual division of labor broke down. Certainly, in the
United States and the West Indies masters used women slaves in the fields
for hard labor which they would never have inflicted on their free female
relations. H. Klein points out in this volume that female American slaves
were overrepresented in fieldwork.[12] However, in Africa if the sexual division of labor broke down under slavery the pattern seems to have been
reversed. Men did women's work, as Olivier de Sardan and MacCormack
point out below (see also Prins 1980:70). Nieboer (1900:391) even said
that slaves usually do women's work. The explanation for this is that
women's work in Africa was generally the less desirable labor-intensive,
low-status work. In some cases slave women relieved free women of agricultural labor (Meillassoux 1975b:233; Smith 1954; Harries 1981:325),

11. M. Klein notes below that women worked at least as long as men, though their
domestic responsibilities probably kept their productivity lower.

12. Leveen (1975:75–76, n. 39) made the mistake of assuming that women were less
productive than men because they could not do the same hard labor, and because they would
not work for six months if they bore a child. He deduced from this that the slavers wanted
to buy more men than women and only increased the proportion of females if the planters
wanted "homegrown" slaves. In contrast, Knight (1970:75–82) says that Cuban slave women
were only allowed forty-five days' leave after birth, that many of them induced abortions
to avoid giving birth under such conditions, that their terrible punishments sometimes brought
on miscarriages, and that the infant mortality rate among their offspring was high. Neither
in Africa nor in the New World, then, did slave owners usually value women slaves chiefly
as biological reproducers, although the New World situation may have changed somewhat,
in various areas, after the abolition of the slave trade put a higher premium on "homegrown"
slaves.

but there is no evidence that slave women performed jobs reserved other-wise for men only. The dominant sub-Saharan African pattern was for women slaves to do the same things that most free women did, which meant most of the agricultural and virtually all of the domestic work. The value of women slaves was based on a sexual division of labor which assigned much of the productive labor to women.

A last function of female slaves needs to be mentioned. Women, usually girls, served more frequently as pawns than did boys. They were also used to reward soldiers, as part of the booty of war, as payment of fines, and even as bridewealth, on occasion (Brain 1972:99, 121; Holsoe 1977:295–94; Dunbar 1977:162; Keim and Bay, this volume). In many cases little distinction was made between pawns and slaves, as shown with Swema (Alpers, this volume) and the women mentioned by Wright (1975). As Wright and Alpers have suggested, low-status women may have become especially vulnerable in times of social dislocation to being sold into slav-ery in order for men to raise capital.[13]

In all of this, the female slave appears primarily as victim. As the bi-ographies of Bwanikwa and Swema make clear, the slave was often totally powerless, the abject instrument of the will of others. At the same time, slaves were actors. Wright, who depicts female slaves in their most des-perate straits, also stresses their strategies. The slave trade could and usu-ally did reduce human beings to things. They were stock, investments. In contrast, slavery had to recognize their humanity. The slave did not neces-sarily like her condition, but her acceptance of it was necessary to slav-ery's effectiveness. There is a poignance to Bwanikwa buying her free-dom—as many slaves did. She was already effectively free, but by buying her freedom, she made clear that de facto freedom was not enough. This acceptance was produced by a combination of coercion, rewards, and ide-ology (Cooper 1977, ch. 1; Davis 1966:31–35; Genovese 1972; Lovejoy 1981). It is this acceptance of the slave's humanity and frequently the exploitation of her dependence that gave the slave some room for maneu-ver. Expressions of gratitude, flattery, begging, and providing entertain-ment were all ways of wheedling money or gifts out of owners (Meillas-soux 1975a:230; Klein 1977b:356; Baldus 1977:446; Wright 1975:819). Given the demand for labor, however, running away was probably the most effective way for slaves to combat ill treatment. Flight to mission sanctuaries, to towns, to *villages de liberté,* or just to other societies, was common. Some slaves' life histories include multiple owners, not only from being sold, but from running away. Bwanikwa influenced her fate

---

13. Wright 1975:818–19. This was true as late as the 1930s, when French West Africa saw a radical upsurge in pawning, usually of women, by families unable to pay their taxes.

positively by running away at a critical juncture. Adukwe ran away from her old mistress to join a master who ultimately became her lover. But the demands of having several owners simultaneously caused some slaves problems, Wright tells us.

Because slaves were often taken as children and removed far from their homes, flight usually meant enslavement to another owner, but there was always the hope of better treatment. Bowdich noted in Asante in 1873 that: "The good treatment of slaves is in some degree provided for by the liberty they have of . . . transferring themselves to any freeman, whom they enjoin to make them his property, by invoking his death if he does not. . . ." A slave could accomplish the same goal by giving him or herself to a god, although the owner could invoke a sort of fugitive slave act by paying a fee to the priest to prevent his runaway slaves from claiming sanctuary.[14] Some slaves accumulated enough money to buy their freedom. Such strategies, however, were probably less available to women than to men slaves; Alpers, Broadhead, and M. Klein tell us that opportunities for social mobility were more restricted generally for slave women than for men. Commerce was most likely to offer those opportunities, as Harms shows.

If women slaves were circumscribed in their ability to act, this was not the case with the female slave owners, users, and traders dealt with in Part 4. This subject engenders unease on several fronts. First, some believers in female solidarity do not like images such as that presented in a letter from a British Indian subject in Zanzibar in 1889 (Collister 1961:124): "Often I have seen a slave girl tied to a post and unmercifully flogged for some supposed or petty delinquency, while the mistress of the house would enjoy the sight and join in a hearty laugh with her other domestics at the heartrending cries of the wretch flogged." Nor would they be enthusiastic about Hutchinson's account (1875:315) of two women attempting to sell him their three children (two boys and a girl) in exchange for bottles of gin near Calabar in 1854. In this female-centered approach, the primacy of class over sex allegiance may be ignored. Second, some persons adopting a male-centered approach are more comfortable with the idea of women as victims of, or at least passive participants in, slavery. This tradition is especially alive among some adherents of Lévi-Straussian principles who view women as pawns to be sent back and forth between lineages by men.[15] In both views, women are seen simply as the victims of male

---

14. Bowdich (1873:211). We use "he" here for the owner because Bowdich did so; however, in Asante women could also own slaves and presumably take the same measures.

15. Lévi-Strauss 1969. A useful corrective to such views is Bourdieu's (1977) demonstration that women can sometimes *act* to perpetuate their own subordinate position.

control. Third, some scholars of various persuasions find it uncomfortable to study stratification and exploitation within African societies. This reluctance often reflects a romantic view of an egalitarian Africa.

For these reasons, then, the topic of women as the controllers of slave labor has been almost completely ignored. It is probable that free women derived much of the benefit from slave labor in sub-Saharan Africa. There are several reasons for this. First, most slaves were women, and the sexual division of labor was largely maintained for women slaves; second, the majority of free women kept their property separate from men's; and third, the main functions of female slave labor were productive rather than reproductive. Fage (1975:398) has said,

> slavery and the making, buying and selling of slaves were means by which certain privileged individuals in West African society, or persons who wished to gain or to extend positions of privilege in that society, sought to mobilize the wealth inherent in the land and people on it. . . . [T]his process had already gone some distance before the Europeans arrived.

Women were not exempt from ambition or ingenuity. The only question was whether they had the opportunity to indulge their ambitions. They did so in situations where there was a tradition of female commercial entrepreneurs (Robertson, Strobel, Harms, this volume), where women participated in political power (Bay, Broadhead, MacCormack, this volume), or where women could exploit their position as mediators between two different cultures (Mouser, Brooks, this volume).

Women, especially in commercially developed societies, utilized the slave labor of their less fortunate sisters. Even if the free women were not the legal owners of the slaves, they were likely to be their users, as Keim, Wright, and Harms note. In many societies women had greater difficulties than men did in recruiting male labor through the lineage system. The situation was definitely asymmetrical. Men could call on women relatives for help relatively easily, but not vice-versa. Thus male slaves may have offered to free women the great advantage of subservient male labor, while female slaves offered the same benefits to women as to men. Bujra (1977:36) noted that even recently a wealthy freeborn woman on an East African coastal island who married a man of ex-slave descent ensured for herself labor for her farm and control over its produce. Furthermore, even male and female slaves sometimes developed a vested interest in perpetuating the institution, because the only labor they could control was that of less assimilated slaves. The marginal utility of slave labor went up as the users themselves became more marginal. Hutchinson (1875:315) noted what he called "a sort of democratic sliding-scale" of the institution of slavery where "a boy, who is my property, may be owner of another boy, or several boys, each of whom may be owner of boys in his turn," thus blurring the distinctions between owners and slaves (see also Cooper 1977:223).

At this point, some will protest that women did not control the biological reproduction of female slaves. Slavery was, in fact, one way in which female owners could profit from reproduction, as Strobel's case study shows. The owner of a female slave in most cases was the owner of her offspring. Reproduction is not only a biological process. It is also a social one, and slavery is only one way of accomplishing it. As the discussion of demography makes clear, it was not always the most effective way.

Another was woman-marriage. Woman-marriage, or female husbands, as the institution has been called, is widespread in sub-Saharan Africa. O'Brien (1977:110–13) listed thirty-three societies in different parts of Africa which had it, and commented, "Political and economic power are concomitants of the female husband role in many populations." She distinguished several different functions performed by the institution. In some cases (Zulu, Pedi) it served only to perpetuate a man's lineage, his widow acting as his proxy. More commonly, however, a woman assumed the legal role of genitor by purchasing or paying bridewealth for a younger woman. The children of the latter belonged to her female husband and were fathered by a male recruited by her female husband. The institution in this form was more likely to be present where women had political and/or economic power. Bohannan (1949:282–84) commented that woman-marriage in Dahomey enabled a wealthy woman "to found a compound, acquire control of people—everywhere an essential to native wealth—and to establish an estate held in trust for the next heir by the person who inherits the founder's name." Such a woman could become the main object of an ancestor cult. Obbo mentions a similar situation among Luo women, and Bryson among Bamileke women in Cameroon.[16] However, as Bohannan suggests, woman-marriage can be seen as chiefly a mode of labor recruitment, with productive rather than reproductive functions,[17] which brings us back to the productive functions of female slaves for their female users.

"Those who have people are wealthier than those with money," goes an old Igbo saying (Emecheta 1977:151). Women who had people were not as widespread as men who had people, but they were not uncommon either. In addition to the women who not only owned but traded slaves mentioned by Bay, MacCormack, Brooks, and Mouser, we find Iyalode Efunsetan, a

16. Obbo 1980:93; Bryson 1979:23. Bryson and Evans-Pritchard mentioned woman-marriage as mainly a way of compensating barren women for childlessness, probably a too restricted view. See also Krige 1974:11–37.

17. Obbo (1976:313–14) gives a number of examples which support this view.

trader and owner of over 500 slaves in Ibadan, Nigeria, in the late nineteenth century (Awe 1977:152). Then there was Madam Yoko, a Kpa Mende chief, described by Carthew (MacCormack [Hoffer] 1974:181) in 1885 as

> the possessor of many slaves, who live in small towns owned by her, near and around Sennehoo. These work her farms, and she is supported solely by their labor and industry. About her person is a train of female attendants—about twenty in number—who are her ladies-in-waiting, and minister to her wants and wishes.

Harries (1981:323) mentions wealthy African women in Lourenço Marques in the late nineteenth century, who "bought female slaves to sell as concubines or employ as prostitutes in the town." Other examples are available of elite women profiting from female slave labor (Nwachukwu-Ogedengbe 1977:141; Broadhead, this volume; Swan *ca.* 1909:58; Baier and Lovejoy 1977:400; Prins 1980:76).

In some societies slavery was so widespread that even nonelite women possessed slaves, and some women slaves possessed slaves. In societies that were decentralized and relatively small-scale but involved in commerce, such as the Ga and the Baule of West Africa, many ordinary women had slaves (Robertson, this volume; Etienne 1977). According to Strobel, Bi Aisha, a woman from the middle level of Mombasa society, owned at least twenty-eight slaves, most of whom were female. In Ahafo in Asante male traders kept women slaves who were a by-product of Samory's wars in the 1890s and awarded them to their favorite wives (Arhin 1972:37). Many Igbo women had pawns working for them as servants in the 1930s (Leith-Ross (1965:226). Madame Tinubu, a Yoruba woman of commoner origin, was a trader in slaves, palm oil, and guns, who rose to become a power behind the throne in both Lagos and Abeokuta, and a key engineer of the Egbas' decisive defeat of Dahomey in 1864 ("Madame Tinubu," 1960). Many more examples could undoubtedly be found. Women slaves owning slaves are noted in this volume by Harms, Bay, and Brooks. Brooks suggests that Mãe Aurélia Correia and others like her may once have been slaves themselves.[18] Some of the slave wives of the Dahomean rulers owned slaves.

What functions, then, did female slaves perform for their female users? The labor of female slaves freed their female users for leisure, as in Mombasa, or to increase their productivity, as in the trading towns along the Upper Zaire or Accra. Maraka slave women grew indigo, made dye, and

18. Swan *ca.* 1909:107; Horton 1954:332; see Harms, this volume. M. Klein notes in this volume that it was often seen as more desirable for a male slave to buy a female slave "wife" than to buy his freedom. It was probably more common for a male slave to own other slaves than for a female slave to do so.

helped their mistresses with dyeing cloth. They also spun the thread for the male weavers to use (Roberts 1978, ch. 7). In Ahafo they mined alluvial gold, and collected rubber and snails (Arhin 1972:37). With the Gaza Nguni they served as cultivators, maids, and porters (Harries 1981:321, 325). In Imerina women slaves served as porters and drove cattle (Campbell 1981:210). Slave women, then, did domestic, craft, and/or agricultural work—the same things that free women did (Baier and Lovejoy 1977:400; Uchendu 1977:127). Quite possibly another reason so many African slaves were women was that so many free women needed help with labor-intensive productive and reproductive functions. By starting with female slaves we may have put the cart before the horse; female slave labor was often tied to female free labor.

Another question which arises out of the use of female slave labor is the allocation of the surplus value created by their work. Bi Aisha's slaves worked for others, earning wages which they turned over to her, and Adukwe gave her earnings from trade and wages for hauling sand in construction work to her mistress.[19] The Lourenço Marques prostitutes presumably turned over their earnings to their mistresses (in Cape Town they turned them over to male slave pimps; Ross 1979:430). If a significant proportion of the value of slave labor went in this manner to women who had no obligations to turn their earnings over to men, then the abolition of slavery may have damaged female slave owners more than their male counterparts. In fact, Brooks (1980:78) blames abolition for the decline in the economic power of *signares* (wealthy women traders) on nineteenth-century Gorée.

A last function of female slaves requiring discussion is that of trusted retainers. Izard (1975:291) noted that Mossi kings usually trusted slaves more than their free subjects and often married their children. Many rulers were descended from slave wives, as Broadhead and Bay note (see also Brain 1972:15). These "marriages" must often have had an element of convenience. The ruler got a person who was doubly dependent, as woman and as slave, whose loyalty was ensured by her kinlessness. In exchange, the slave got the possibilities of influential position for herself and her children and of manumission. Ross (1979:429) speaks of women slaves achieving upward mobility by virtue of judicious liaisons which sometimes became legal.

But slave women could also sometimes attain high position on their own, like the ward chiefs mentioned by Harms. Such influential slave women were likely to have gained economic status from trading, and be

---

19. "Koelie geld" earned by Cape Town women slaves went to their masters (Ross 1979:424), as did money earned by seventeenth-century West African coastal slave women prostitutes (see Thornton, this volume).

the owners of other female slaves. Hogendorn (1977:373) mentions female slave overseers working for male overseers in Zaria. In fact, sex segregation in some Muslim societies made slave women's freedom from seclusion practices an asset in attaining influential positions. Dwyer (1977:48) tells us that the only female court official in the Taroudannt area of Morocco must be a descendant of a slave (and used to be a slave). Thus, she could talk freely with men as well as women, an impossibility for a woman of free descent. It is very important, then, as Cooper has pointed out, to focus on the use of slaves by particular groups in the struggle for wealth and power. We need more research efforts on the topic of women controlling other women in order to further explore intra- and extrafamilial stratification.[20]

Another issue on which these papers shed light is the relative ineffectuality of European abolition efforts (Robertson, Keim, this volume; M. Klein 1977a:6–21; Swan *ca.* 1909:29; Nwulia 1978:89–101; Suret-Canale 1964:85–89). Once securely in power, colonial regimes often moved swiftly against the slave trade, which threatened European commercial interests, but they tended to be hesitant in dealing with slavery itself, in part because they feared social disruption. Even where they moved against slavery, they were often reluctant to undercut the control by men of slave wives and concubines (Cooper 1977:223). But slave labor was also important to them for the production of wanted commodities. The process of change was generally slower than a superficial reading of official reports and legislation would suggest. Official abolition of slavery in most areas preceded the changes in the mode of production which made slavery obsolete.[21] The rate of change was often more rapid for male slaves. Men more often had formal education and wage-paying jobs open to them, whereas women remained in labor-intensive work. Thus men were more rapidly and completely integrated into capitalist relations of production, while women had more incentive to keep utilizing female slave labor.

Slavery as a relation of production remained important in many areas

20. Cooper 1979:104. Schlegel (1977b:17) says that it is important to examine areas in a society where men and women exert power and authority and how those areas of control stand in relation to one another.

21. Klein and Roberts 1980:375–94. Nieboer (1900:166ff.) posited a positive connection between the existence of slavery and of free land (p. 348), and a negative one between slavery and capital intensity: "Where subsistence is dependent on capital, slaves are not wanted" (p. 255). Meillassoux (1975a:236): "The amelioration of the condition of the slave is intimately linked with transformation in the relations of the production they were engaged in." (See also Robertson forthcoming, ch. 1.) Goldin (1975:428) has noted in the American context the adverse effect on slavery of exposure to the urban wage economy. Kilkenny (1981:169) noted that "new job opportunities and new avenues for social mobility arising out of the colonial economy probably were the major factors in effectively ending slavery" in Dahomey, where it was not until 1905 that slavery was abolished by the French.

into the interwar period.[22] In some economically marginal areas, it is significant to this day. The issue was an important one for several radical parties in the 1950s, most notably Modibo Keita's Union Soudanaise in Mali, and Sekou Touré's Parti Démocratique de la Guinée (Morgenthau 1964). As late as 1978, Mauritania abolished, or rather reabolished, slavery, thus confirming the widely known existence of the institution.[23] In such areas, female slaves were more likely to remain because they had fewer options and fewer marketable skills, and remained in a subordinate corporate kin mode of production.

If the imposition of colonialism broke the power of the elders to control the young, it did not necessarily lessen the control of men over women (see Olivier de Sardan, this volume).[24] It rather reinforced that control by giving many men the tools to participate more successfully in a capitalist mode of production. The labor recruitment skills of women entrepreneurs became irrelevant as the skills imparted by formal education, whether academic, agricultural, or artisanal, gave men an increasing advantage. With independence, the men regained political power, but the women's political power was dissipated by colonial disregard (Awe 1977:144–60; Van Allen 1974; Sosne 1979). Their ability to recruit and control labor inevitably also weakened.

In dealing with women and slavery, then, we are standing at the intersection of intra- and extrafamilial stratification. A Swahili proverb goes, "There is no freeborn woman" (Strobel 1979:43). A missionary cited by Wright (below, p. 247) claimed, "Add slavery to polygamy, and reduce a woman to the status of a slave, then you have the sum of human degradation, the lowest creature on God's earth—a slave woman." In many cases both free and slave women were exploited, making their status similar, as many contributors to this volume note.[25] Being a slave of a wealthy person was undoubtedly a better choice for some women than being a

22. Nwulia (1975:202) noted that as late as the 1920s many slaves remained on the plantations. Hopkins (1979:91) noted that the rise of legitimate commerce actually increased the demand for slave labor in Nigeria in the late nineteenth century for collecting, preparing, and transporting the new export crops. In some areas, because of the dominance of men in the cultivation and sale of export crops, the demand for male slaves increased with the rise of "legitimate" commerce (Austen 1977:324).

23. The British Anti-Slavery Society issued a report recently that made a "conservative" estimate that 100,000 slaves existed in Mauritania (Anti-Slavery Society 1981; see also Colvin 1981:256–57). A reliable witness recounted to Robertson the existence of a slave market active in the 1970s in Niger not far from Niamey.

24. A number of sources have noted this phenomenon with relationship to slavery, among them Hopkins 1979:84; Horton 1954;326; Kopytoff and Miers 1977:27; Cooper 1979:155n, 119.

25. Nieboer (1900:396) said, "As soon as [the slavery of women] exists it renders slavery less necessary than it would otherwise be." See Wright, this volume, in particular.

free, but vulnerable, low-status woman.[26] The degree to which women profited from this exploitation is the degree to which women had control over significant resources and authority structures.

With colonialism, the female labor recruitment structure still remained necessary for women, but men developed alternative routes to power. It is not surprising, then, that both slaves and low-status women often became insubordinate after the imposition of colonialism. It was no accident that among the British laws most disliked by Ga men were both the law against cruel treatment of wives, which allowed wives to leave their husbands, and the law freeing ill-treated pawns or domestic slaves.[27] Questions concerning women and slavery, then, ultimately involve a consideration of the marginality of both free and slave women; if slaves were incorporated into African societies to varying degrees, then so were and are women as secondary citizens.

References

Unpublished Sources

Klein, M. A. 1977a. "From Slave Labor to Migrant Labour in Senegambia: Southern Saalum 1880–1930." Paper.
McSheffrey, G. M. 1977. "Slavery, Indentured Servitude and the Impact of Abolition in the Gold Coast: 1874–1901. A Reappraisal." Paper presented at the Canadian Historical Association Conference, Fredericton, New Brunswick.
Roberts, R. 1978. "The Maraka and the Economy of the Middle Niger Valley: 1790–1908." Ph.D. thesis, University of Toronto.

Published Sources

Adamu, M. 1979. "The Delivery of Slaves from the Central Sudan to the Bight of Benin in the Eighteenth and Nineteenth Centuries." In *The Uncommon Market,* ed. H. A. Gemery and J. S. Hogendorn. New York.
Anti-Slavery Society. 1981. "Slavery in Mauritania in 1980." *Anti-Slavery Reporter.* Series 7, vol. 13:15–19.
Arhin, K. 1972. "The Ashanti Rubber Trade with the Gold Coast in the Eighteen-Nineties." *Africa* 42:32–43.

---

26. MacCormack 1977:91. Mary Kingsley noted that a master controlled his slaves as an absolute monarch, and his wives as a constitutional monarch (cited in Grace 1975:16). Prins (1980:76) attributes the failure of abolition among the Lozi to this phenomenon: "If working for the Princess chieftainess was hard it was also hard, although less conspicuous to the blinkered gaze of Native Commissioners, to be a woman at home."

27. Reindorf *ca.* 1890/1966:323. The latter law actually outlawed all domestic slavery regardless of treatment, but it is significant that Reindorf, a Ga man, interpreted it in this manner; it was usually the ill-treated (and very few of those) who sought their freedom.

Augé, M. 1975. "Les Faiseurs d'ombre. Servitude et structure lignagère dans la société alladienne." In *L'Esclavage en Afrique précoloniale*, ed. C. Meillassoux. Paris.

Austen, R. A. 1977. "Slavery among Coastal Middlemen: The Duala of Cameroon." In *Slavery in Africa: Historical and Anthropological Perspectives*, ed. S. Miers and I. Kopytoff. Madison.

Austen, R. A. 1979. "The Trans-Saharan Slave Trade: A Tentative Census." In *The Uncommon Market*, ed. H. A. Gemery and J. S. Hogendorn. New York.

Awe, B. 1977. "The Iyalode in the Traditional Yoruba Political System." In *Sexual Stratification*, ed. A. Schlegel. New York.

Baier, S., and P. E. Lovejoy. 1977. "The Tuareg of the Central Sudan. Gradations in Servility at the Desert Edge (Niger and Nigeria)." In *Slavery in Africa*, ed. S. Miers and I. Kopytoff. Madison.

Baldus, B. 1977. "Responses to Dependence in a Servile Group: the Machube of Northern Benin." In *Slavery in Africa*, ed. S. Miers and I. Kopytoff. Madison.

Bloch, M. 1980. "Modes of Production and Slavery in Madagascar: Two Case Studies." In *Asian and African Systems of Slavery*, ed. J. L. Watson. Oxford.

Bohannan, L. 1949. "Dahomean Marriage: A Revaluation." *Africa* 19:272–87.

Bohannan, P., and P. Curtin. 1971. *Africa and the Africans*. Garden City, N.Y.

Bonnafé, P. 1975. "Les formes d'asservissement chez les Kukuya d'Afrique centrale" In *L'esclavage en Afrique précoloniale*, ed. C. Meillassoux. Paris.

Boserup, E. 1970. *Women's Role in Economic Development*. London.

Bourdieu, P. 1977. *Outline of a Theory of Practice*. Cambridge.

Bourgeot, A. 1975. "Rapports esclavagistes et conditions d'affranchisement chez les Imuhag." In *L'esclavage en Afrique précoloniale*, ed. C. Meillassoux. Paris.

Bowdich, T. E. 1873. *Mission from Cape Coast to Ashantee*. London.

Brain, R. 1972. *Bangwa Kinship and Marriage*. Cambridge.

Bridge, H. 1845/1968. *Journal of an African Cruiser*. London.

Brooks, G. E. 1976. "The Signares of Saint-Louis and Gorée: Women Entrepreneurs in Eighteenth-Century Senegal." In *Women in Africa: Studies in Social and Economic Change*, ed. N. J. Hafkin and E. G. Bay. Stanford.

Brooks, G. E. 1980. "Artists' Depictions of Senegalese Signares: Insights Concerning French Racist and Sexist Attitudes in the Nineteenth Century." *Genève-Afrique* 18:75–89.

Bryson, J. C. 1979. "Women and Economic Development in Cameroon." United States Agency for International Development report.

Bujra, J. 1977. "Production, Property, Prostitution. 'Sexual Politics' in Atu." *Cahiers d'études africaines* 65:13–39.

Burnham, P. 1980. "Raiders and Traders in Adamawa: Slavery as a Regional System." In *Asian and African Systems of Slavery*, ed. J. L. Watson. Oxford.

Campbell, G. 1981. "Madagascar and the Slave Trade, 1810–1895." *Journal of African History* 22:203–27.

Collister, P. 1961. *The Last Days of Slavery: England and the East African Slave Trade 1870–1900*. Dar es Salaam.

Colvin, L. 1981. "Mauritania." In *The Uprooted of the Western Sahel: Migrants' Quest for Cash in the Senegambia*, ed. L. Colvin et al. New York.

Cooper, F. 1977. *Plantation Slavery on the East Coast of Africa.* New Haven.

Cooper, F. 1979. "The Problem of Slavery in African Studies." *Journal of African History* 20:103–25.

Cooper, F. 1980. *From Slaves to Squatters: Plantation Labor and Agriculture in Zanzibar and Coastal Kenya, 1890–1925.* New Haven.

Coquery-Vidrovitch, C. 1976. "The Political Economy of the African Peasantry and Modes of Production." In *The Political Economy of Contemporary Africa,* ed. P. C. W. Gutkind and I. Wallerstein. Beverly Hills.

Curtin, P. D. 1969. *The Atlantic Slave Trade: A Census.* Madison.

Curtin, P. D. 1975. *Economic Change in Precolonial Africa: Senegambia in the Era of the Slave Trade.* 2 vols. Madison.

Davis, D. B. 1966. *The Problem of Slavery in Western Culture.* Ithaca.

Dunbar, R. A. 1977. "Slavery and the Evolution of Nineteenth-Century Damagaram." In *Slavery in Africa,* ed. S. Miers and I. Kopytoff. Madison.

Dwyer, D. H. 1977. "Bridging the Gap between the Sexes in Moroccan Legal Practice." In *Sexial Stratification,* ed. A. Schlegel. New York.

Eblen, J. E. 1975. "On the Natural Increase of Slave Populations: The Example of the Cuban Black Population." In *Race and Slavery in the Western Hemisphere: Quantitative Studies,* ed. S. L. Engerman and E. D. Genovese. Princeton.

Edholm, F., O. Harris, and K. Young. 1977. "Conceptualising Women." *Critique of Anthropology* 3:101–30.

Eisenstein, Z., ed. 1979. *Capitalist Patriarchy and the Case for Socialist Feminism.* New York.

Emecheta, B. 1977. *The Slave Girl.* London.

Engerman, S. L., and E. D. Genovese, eds. 1975. *Race and Slavery in the Western Hemisphere: Quantitative Studies.* Princeton.

Etienne, M. 1977. "Women and Men, Cloth and Colonization: The Transformation of Production-Distribution Relations among the Baule (Ivory Coast)." *Cahiers d'études africaines* 17:41–64.

Fage, J. D. 1969. "Slavery and the Slave Trade in the Context of West African History." *Journal of African History* 10:393–404.

Fage, J. D. 1975. "The Effect of the Export Slave Trade on African Populations." In *The Population Factor in African Studies,* ed. R. P. Moss and R. J. A. R. Rathbone. London.

Fage, J. D. 1980. "Slave and Society in Western Africa, c. 1455–c. 1700." *Journal of African History* 21:289–310.

Fyfe, C. 1981. "A Brief Note on the Demographic Effects of the Transatlantic Slave Trade on West Africa." In *African Historical Demography,* ed. C. Fyfe and D. McMaster. Edinburgh.

Fyle, C. M. 1978. "The Idea of Slavery in Nineteenth Century Sierra Leone: The Career of Bilali." *Journal of the Historical Society of Sierra Leone* 2:57–61.

Gemery, H. A., and J. S. Hogendorn. 1979a. "The Economic Costs of West African Participation in the Atlantic Slave Trade: A Preliminary Sampling for the Eighteenth Century." In *The Uncommon Market,* ed. H. A. Gemery and J. S. Hogendorn. New York.

Gemery, H. A., and J. S. Hogendorn. 1979b. *The Uncommon Market: Essays in the Economic History of the Atlantic Slave Trade.* New York.

Genovese, E. 1972. *Roll Jordan Roll.* New York.

Gerstein, I. 1973. "Domestic Work and Capitalism." *Radical America* 7:101–28.

Goldin, C. D. 1975. "A Model to Explain the Relative Decline of Urban Slavery: Empirical Results." In *Race and Slavery,* ed. S. L. Engerman and E. D. Genovese. Princeton.

Goody, J. 1976. *Production and Reproduction: A Comparative Study of the Domestic Domain.* Cambridge Studies in Social Anthropology No. 17. London.

Goody, J. 1980. "Slavery in Time and Space." In *Asian and African Systems of Slavery,* ed. J. L. Watson. Oxford.

Grace, J. 1975. *Domestic Slavery in West Africa.* London.

Grace, J. 1977. "Slavery and Emancipation among the Mende in Sierra Leone, 1896–1928." In *Slavery in Africa,* ed. S. Miers and I. Kopytoff. Madison.

Hair, P. E. H. 1978. *The Atlantic Slave Trade and Black Africa.* London.

Harries, P. 1981. "Slavery, Social Incorporation and Surplus Extraction: The Nature of Free and Unfree Labour in South-East Africa." *Journal of African History* 22:331–48.

Héritier, F. 1975. "Des cauris et des hommes: production d'esclaves et accumulation de cauris chez les Samo (Haute-Volta)." In *L'esclavage en Afrique précoloniale,* ed. C. Meillassoux. Paris.

Herskovits, M. J. 1952. *Economic Anthropology.* New York.

Hoffer, C. P. (see also MacCormack). 1974. "Madam Yoko: Ruler of the Kpa Mende Confederacy." In *Woman, Culture and Society,* ed. M. Z. Rosaldo and L. Lamphere. Stanford.

Hogendorn, J. S. 1977. "The Economics of Slave Use on Two 'Plantations' in the Zaria Emirate of the Sokoto Caliphate." *International Journal of African Historical Studies* 10:369–83.

Holsoe, S. E. 1977. "Slavery and Economic Response among the Vai." In *Slavery in Africa,* ed. S. Miers and I. Kopytoff. Madison.

Hopkins, A. G. 1979. "The Lagos Strike of 1897: An Exploration in Nigerian Labor History." In *Peasants and Proletarians in Africa,* ed. R. Cohen, P. C. W. Gutkind, and P. Brazier. New York.

Horton, W. R. G. 1954. "The Ohu System of Slavery in a Northern Ibo Village-Group." *Africa* 24:295–336.

Hoselitz, B. F. 1966. "Interaction between Industrial and Pre-Industrial Stratification Systems." In *Social Structure and Mobility in Economic Development,* ed. N. Smelser and S. M. Lipset. Chicago.

Hutchinson, T. J. 1875. "The Social and Domestic Slavery of Western Africa, and Its Evil Influence on Commercial Progress." *Journal of the Society of Arts* 23:310–18.

Izard, M. 1975. "Les captifs royaux dans l'ancien Yatenga." In *L'esclavage en Afrique précoloniale,* ed. C. Meillassoux. Paris.

Johnson, M. 1966. "The Ounce in Eighteenth-Century West African Trade." *Journal of African History* 7:197–214.

Kilkenny, R. W. 1981. "The Slave Mode of Production: Precolonial Dahomey."

In *Modes of Production in Africa: The Precolonial Era,* ed. D. Crummey and C. C. Stewart. Beverly Hills.

Kilson, M. 1971. "West African Society and the Atlantic Slave Trade, 1441–1865." In *Key Issues in the Afro-American Experience,* ed. N. I. Huggins, M. Kilson, and D. M. Fox. New York.

Klein, M. A. 1977b. "Servitude among the Wolof and Sereer of Senegambia." In *Slavery in Africa,* ed. S. Miers and I. Kopytoff. Madison.

Klein, M. A. 1978. "The Study of Slavery in Africa: A Review Article." *Journal of African History* 19:599–609.

Klein, M. A., and P. E. Lovejoy. 1979. "Slavery in West Africa." In *The Uncommon Market,* ed. H. A. Gemery and J. S. Hogendorn. New York.

Klein, M. A., and R. Roberts. 1980. "The Banamba Slave Exodus of 1905 and the Decline of Slavery in the Western Sudan." *Journal of African History* 21:375–94.

Knight, F. W. 1970. *Slave Society in Cuba during the Nineteenth Century.* Madison.

Kopytoff, I. 1979. "Indigenous African Slavery, Commentary One." *Historical Reflections* 6:62–77.

Kopytoff, I., and S. Miers. 1977. "African 'Slavery' as an Institution of Marginality." In *Slavery in Africa,,* ed. S. Miers and I. Kopytoff. Madison.

Krige, E. J. 1974. "Woman-Marriage, with Special Reference to the Lovedu—Its Significance for the Definition of Marriage." *Africa* 44:11–37.

Leith-Ross, S. 1965. *African Women.* New York.

Leveen, E. P. 1975. "A Quantitative Analysis of the Impact of British Suppression Policies on the Volume of the Nineteenth Century Atlantic Slave Trade." In *Race and Slavery,* ed. S. L. Engerman and E. D. Genovese. Princeton.

Lévi-Strauss, C. 1969. *The Elementary Structures of Kinship.* Boston.

Lombardi, J. V. 1974. "The Abolition of Slavery in Venezuela: A Nonevent." In *Slavery and Race Relations in Latin America,* ed. R. B. Toplin. Westport, Conn.

Lovejoy, P. 1979. "Indigenous African Slavery." *Historical Reflections* 6:19–61.

Lovejoy, P., ed. 1981. *The Ideology of Slavery in Africa.* Beverly Hills.

MacCormack, C. P. 1977. "Wono: Institutionalized Dependency in Sherbro Descent Groups." In *Slavery in Africa,* ed. S. Miers and I. Kopytoff. Madison.

MacCormack, C. P. 1979. "Sande: The Public Face of a Secret Society." In *The New Religions of Africa,* ed. B. Jules-Rosette. Norwood, N.J.

"Madame Tinubu." 1960. In *Eminent Nigerians of the Nineteenth Century.* Cambridge.

Manning, P. 1979. "The Slave Trade in the Bight of Benin, 1640–1890." In *The Uncommon Market,* ed. H. A. Gemery and J. S. Hogendorn. New York.

Manning, P. 1981a. "The Enslavement of Africans: A Demographic Model." *Canadian Journal of African Studies* 15:499–526.

Manning, P. 1981b. "Two Comments on Manning and a Response." *Canadian Journal of African Studies* 16:137–39.

Meillassoux, C. 1975a. "Etat et conditions des esclaves à Gumbu (Mali) au XIXe siècle." In *L'esclavage en Afrique précoloniale,* ed. C. Meillassoux. Paris.

Meillassoux, C., ed. 1975b. *L'esclavage en Afrique précoloniale.* Paris.

Meillassoux, C. 1981. *Maidens, Meal and Money*. Cambridge.

Miers, S., and I. Kopytoff, eds. 1977. *Slavery in Africa: Historical and Anthropological Perspectives*. Madison.

Mill, J. S. 1869/1970. "The Subjection of Women." In J. S. Mill and H. T. Mill, *Essays on Sex Equality,* ed. A. Rossi. Chicago.

Miller, J. C. 1973. "Slaves, Slavers and Social Change in Nineteenth Century Kasange." In *Social Change in Angola,* ed. F. W. Heimer. Munich.

Mintz, S. W. 1975. "History and Anthropology: A Brief Reprise." In *Race and Slavery,* ed. S. L. Engerman and E. D. Genovese. Princeton.

Newbury, C. 1960. "An Early Enquiry into Slavery and Captivity in Dahomey." *Zaire* 14:53–67.

Nieboer, H. J. 1910. *Slavery as an Industrial System*. The Hague.

Nwachukwu-Ogedengbe, K. 1977. "Slavery in Nineteenth-Century Aboh." In *Slavery in Africa,* ed. S. Miers and I. Kopytoff. Madison.

Nwulia, M. D. 1975. *Britain and Slavery in East Africa*. Washington, D.C.

Nwulia, M. D. 1978. "The 'Apprenticeship' System in Mauritius: Its Character and Its Impact on Race Relations in the Immediate Post-Emancipation Period, 1839–1879." *African Studies Review* 21:89–101.

Obbo, C. 1976. "Dominant Male Ideology and Female Options: Three East African Case Studies." *Africa* 46:371–89.

Obbo, C. 1980. *African Women: Their Struggle for Economic Independence*. London.

O'Brien, D. 1977. "Female Husbands in Southern Bantu Societies." In *Sexual Stratification,* ed. A. Schlegel. New York.

Orde-Brown, G. St. J. 1933/1967. *The African Labourer*. New York.

Patterson, O. 1979. "On Slavery and Slave Formations." *New Left Review* 117:31–67.

Piault, M. H. 1975. "Captifs du pouvoir et pouvoir des captifs." In *L'esclavage en Afrique précoloniale,* ed. C. Meillassoux. Paris.

Poku, K. 1979. "Traditional Roles and People of Slave Origin in Modern Ashanti—A Few Impressions." *Ghana Journal of Sociology* 5:35–38.

Postma, J. 1975. "The Origin of African Slaves: The Dutch Activities on the Guinea Coast, 1674–1795." In *Race and Slavery,* ed. S. L. Engerman and E. D. Genovese. Princeton.

Prins, G. 1980. *The Hidden Hippopotamus*. Cambridge.

Rattray, R. S. 1929. *Ashanti Law and Constitution*. Oxford.

Reindorf, C. C. Ca. 1890/1966. *The History of the Gold Coast and Asante*. Accra.

Rey, P.-P. 1975. "The Lineage Mode of Production." *Critique of Anthropology* 3:27–79.

Robertson, C. C. Forthcoming. *Sharing the Same Bowl, A Socioeconomic History of Women and Class in Accra, Ghana*. Bloomington, Ind.

Ross, R. 1979. "Oppression, Sexuality and Slavery at the Cape of Good Hope." *Historical Reflections* 6:421–33.

Schildkrout, E. 1978. "Age and Gender in Hausa Society: Socio-Economic Roles of Children in Urban Kano." In *Sex and Age as Principles of Social Differentiation,* ed. J. S. LaFontaine. New York.

Schlegel, A. 1972. *Male Dominance and Female Authority: Domestic Authority in Matrilineal Societies.* Human Relations Area Files, Inc.

Schlegel, A., ed. 1977a. *Sexual Stratification: A Cross-Cultural View.* New York.

Schlegel, A. 1977b. "Toward a Theory of Sexual Stratification." In *Sexual Stratification,* ed. A. Schlegel. New York.

Smelser, N. J., and S. M. Lipset, eds. 1966. *Social Structure and Mobility in Economic Development.* Chicago.

Smith, M. G. 1954. "Slavery and Emancipation in Two Societies." *Social and Economic Studies* 3:239–90.

Smith, M. G. 1966. "Pre-Industrial Stratification Systems." In *Social Structure,* ed. N. J. Smelser and S. M. Lipset. Chicago.

Sosne, E. 1979. "Of Biases and Queens: the Shi Past through an Androgynous Looking Glass." *History in Africa* 6:225–52.

Strobel, M. 1979. *Muslim Women in Mombasa, 1890–1975.* New Haven.

Suret-Canale, J. 1964. *Afrique Noire Occidentale et Centrale. L'Ere Coloniale (1900–1945).* Paris.

Sutton, C., and S. Makiesky-Barrow. 1977. "Social Inequality and Sexual Status in Barbados." In *Sexual Stratification,* ed. A. Schlegel. New York.

Swan, C. A. *Ca.* 1909. *The Slavery of To-Day.* New York.

Tambo, D. 1976. "The Sokoto Caliphate Slave Trade in the Nineteenth Century." *International Journal of African Historical Studies* 9:187–217.

Thornton, J. 1977. "Demography and History in the Kingdom of Kongo, 1550–1750." *Journal of African History* 18:507–30.

Thornton, J. 1980. "The Slave Trade in Eighteenth-Century Angola: Effects on Demographic Structures." *Canadian Journal of African Studies* 14:417–27.

Tuden, A., and L. Plotnicov. 1970. *Social Stratification in Africa.* New York.

Uchendu, V. C. 1977. "Slaves and Slavery in Igboland, Nigeria." In *Slavery in Africa,* ed. S. Miers and I. Kopytoff. Madison.

United Nations. Food and Agriculture Organization. 1979. "Women in Food Production, Food Handling and Nutrition." Food and Nutrition Paper No. 8. Rome.

Van Allen, J. 1974. "Women in Africa: Modernization Means More Dependency." *Center Magazine* 12:60–67.

Verlinden, C. 1955. *L'Esclavage dans l'Europe Médiévale.* Vol. 1. Bruges.

Watson, J. L., ed. 1980a. *Asian and African Slavery Systems.* Oxford.

Watson, J. L. 1980b. "Slavery as an Institution: Open and Closed Systems." In *Asian and African Systems of Slavery,* ed. J. L. Watson. Oxford.

Wright, E. O., and L. Perrone. 1977. "Marxist Class Categories and Income Inequality." *American Sociological Review* 42:32–55.

Wright, M. 1975. "Women in Peril: A Commentary on the Life Stories of Captives in Nineteenth-Century East-Central Africa." *African Social Research* 20:800–819.

I. DEMOGRAPHIC AND THEORETICAL PERSPECTIVES

2 _Herbert S. Klein_

African Women in the Atlantic Slave Trade

African women did not enter the Atlantic slave trade in anything like the numbers of African men. At all ages, men outnumbered women on the slave ships bound for America from Africa. As both contemporaries and later commentators have pointed out, far fewer women entered the slave ships of the Europeans than would have been the case if the Atlantic slave trade had operated randomly. Ever since the slave trade began, this disparity has elicited comments from all observers, and in recent years scholars have begun to pay serious attention to determining both its cause and its consequences.

In this short essay, I would like to examine the actual rates of participation of African women in the slave trade as seen from the experience of several European controlled trades, and to speculate on both the causes and consequences of this sexual disparity. As the reader will quickly realize, many of the hypotheses that I set forth are highly speculative because of the tentativeness and incompleteness of available records. Nevertheless, enough progress recently has been made on this problem so that some broad general features can be established even if the causes and consequences of these factors are still subject to extensive debate.

What recent research has now established is that contemporaneous observations of the slave trade, based upon limited experience, in fact hold for the entire history of the Atlantic slave trade. Women did not participate in the trade as fully as men; this was true of every period and every trade for which records are available. Only beginning in the late seventeenth century were systematic records kept of the sexual and age divisions among some African slaves. Fortunately for the purposes of this study, these records coincide with the most important phase of the Atlantic slave trade,

29

Table 2.1
African Slaves Transported by Dutch Slave Ships, 1675–1795

Period	Men	Women	Boys	Girls
1675–1740[a]	22,682	10,132	2,442	865
1730–1795[b]	11,488	8,135	3,314	2,114
TOTAL	34,170	18,267	5,756	2,979

SOURCE: Postma 1979:257.
[a]Seventy-three shipments by vessels belonging to the West India Company.
[b]Ninety shipments by vessels belonging to free traders.

when over three-quarters of the African slaves were shipped to America (Curtin 1969:265).

One of the earliest of the trades keeping sexual breakdowns was that of the Dutch at the end of the seventeenth and beginning of the eighteenth centuries. Among the over 60,000 slaves shipped from Africa to the West Indies in this period by both the West India Company and free trader ships, females were only 38 percent of the forced migrants. Even when slaves are examined by age group, the same disproportionate representation of males is apparent. Thus the adult sex ratio was 187 men for every 100 women, and the child ratio was 193 boys for every 100 girls.

This same pattern can be seen among the slaves carried by the Danish slave traders in the second half of the eighteenth century. In the two decades of recorded trading, the Danes shipped from their own Guinean forts and from areas on the Guinean coast to the west of them some 15,000 slaves, of whom only 36 percent were females. Just as in the case of the Dutch, this sexual imbalance appeared among both adults and children, with 186 men to 100 women and 145 boys to 100 girls.

In the last decade of the eighteenth century, the British took some 83,000 slaves from the entire western African coastal region. But even in this more broadly based sample of African slaves, the same discrimination against women which was evident in the more geographically limited Dutch and Danish trades is apparent. Among the British slavers, females represented only 38 percent of the slaves, with both adults (165:100) and children (164:100) showing the same bias toward males.

Table 2.2
African Slaves Transported by Danish Slave Ships, 1777–1789 (49 ships)

Origin	Men	Women	Boys	Girls
Danish African Possessions	5,289	2,660	1,077	653
Non-Danish African Possessions	2,333	1,438	984	769
TOTAL	7,622	4,098	2,061	1,422

SOURCE: Green-Pedersen 1971:192–95.

Table 2.3

Age and Sex of Slaves Carried from the African Coast in English Ships, 1791–1798

African Region	Men	Women	Boys	Girls
Senegambia	4,319	2,143	817	519
Sierra Leone	517	243	55	29
Windward Coast	4,526	2,414	383	215
Gold Coast	2,539	1,321	188	117
Bight of Biafra	14,375	10,971	435	384
Bight of Benin	304	189	9	10
Congo-Angola	11,596	6,144	968	509
Unknown	10,113	5,822	992	556
TOTAL	48,289	29,247	3,847	2,339

SOURCE: G.B.L., July 28, 1800. Figures are from the 272 ships (out of 332 listed) for which age and sex breakdowns were available.

Finally, in the last trade for which we have extensive data on age and sex among the slaves, the same pattern emerges. Of the approximately 182,000 slaves arriving in Havana, Cuba, at the end of the eighteenth and beginning of the nineteenth centuries, only 29 percent were females. Especially among adults, women were severely underrepresented, with 251 men for every 100 women. Among the teens and children the rates were considerably less lopsided, being 153:100 and 200:100.

Table 2.4

Age and Sex of Slaves Arriving in the Port of Havana, Cuba, 1790–1820

	Males			Females		
Period	Adults[a]	Teens[b]	Children[c]	Adults[a]	Teens[b]	Children[c]
1790–1794	14,985	1,587	3,885	3,531	1,173	2,062
1795–1799	11,805	1,537	2,846	2,662	763	1,031
1800–1804	18,344	2,548	4,320	6,218	2,004	2,334
1805–1809	6,727	1,172	2,405	1,738	520	931
1810–1814	8,712	2,133	3,711	2,494	1,289	1,823
1815–1819	22,606	7,910	12,558	9,171	5,251	6,603
1820	69	127	73	57	105	105
TOTAL	83,248	17,014	29,798	25,871	11,105	14,889

SOURCE: S.A.I., legajo 2207.

[a]Adults were listed in the traditional *piezas de indias* slave trade terminology, which means an age of eighteen or older.

[b]Teenagers, or *mulecónes* (f. *mulécas*), were defined as imported slaves aged eleven to seventeen years.

[c]Children, or *muléques* (f. *mulecónas*), were defined as imported slaves aged about seven to ten years.

Being of both intra-Caribbean and African origin, the slave trade to Cuba presents special distortions which should be taken into account before these figures can be compared to those of the other African originated trades. To distinguish the origins of the slaves, unfortunately not listed by Spanish royal officials, I have taken African originated slaves to be any slaves who arrived on ships carrying 200 or more slaves per voyage. This procedure is based on a series of hypotheses about the trade and is supported by some alternative sources (H. Klein 1978, ch. 9). If these vessels are isolated from the totals, we are left with an estimated 102,000 slaves who arrived directly from Africa on some 322 vessels. The ratio of males to females among the Africans, 221:100 (with a much higher ratio among adults than among the two child categories—see table 2.5), was slightly lower than among slaves of mixed African and intra-Caribbean origins. But what the disaggregated figures show is that there was an even more pronounced lack of women in the local interisland trade. Evidently, West Indian planters were reluctant to part with women now that the trans-Atlantic slave trade was coming to an end.

Thus in all trades, between two-thirds and three-quarters of all slaves arriving in America were males. But this general trend obscures some interesting internal variations. In some periods and from some regions more women were sent than was the norm. In analyzing the sources of the slaves bound for the West Indies on English ships in the 1790s, for example, it is evident that the Bight of Biafra supplied a much higher percentage of women than was common to the rest of the African exporting regions.

Interestingly, table 2.6 does not support the correlation that might have been expected between the movement of women and of children. Thus Biafra, while contributing a very high percentage of women, was nevertheless contributing only an average percentage of children to the trade. This may be an accident of time and place, or it could mean that the factors influencing the flow of women were quite independent from those affecting the flow of children.[1] While no definitive pattern may be seen over time and across trades, the data do suggest that the very earliest (seventeenth-century) and very latest (nineteenth-century) periods of the mature slave trade may have been times of unusually low participation for women, or conversely that the mid- to late eighteenth century was a period of unusually high participation. But given the relatively nonrepresentative nature of the currently available samples of the trade which provide infor-

---

1. That this particular case may not have been the norm is seen in figures gathered for slaves seized off the Biafran coast in the 1821–39 period. Of some 24,000 slaves whose age and sex were known, the ratio of females to males remained a relatively high 100:195, but the ratio of children had now increased to 39 percent. Northrup 1978, appendix D.

Table 2.5

Sex Ratio and Percentage Children and Teens, by Route of Origin, of Slaves Arriving in Havana, Cuba, 1790–1820

	Routes[a]			
Age Category	*Caribbean*	*Mixed*	*African*	*All Routes*
Adults	479	302	283	322
Teens	229	160	139	153
Children	255	197	187	200
All Ages	376	244	221	251
(N =)	(38,629)	(41,652)	(101,644)	(181,925)
Children and Teens (%)	32	41	43	40

SOURCE: S.A.I., legajo 2207.

[a]The routes were defined as follows: Those ships carrying from 1 to 99 slaves were assumed to be engaged in an intra-Caribbean trading; those with 100–199 could be either smaller African shipments or vessels engaged in broken voyages and mixing slaves from several sources; while any ship arriving with 200 slaves or more was considered to be coming directly from Africa to Cuba.

Table 2.6

Average Sex Ratio and Percentage of Children Carried per Shipment in the English Slave Trade to the West Indies, 1791–1798

African Region of Origin	Sex Ratio	(Number of Shipments)	Children (%)	(Number of Shipments)	Mortality (%)[a]	(Number of Shipments)
Senegambia	210	(5)	10	(5)	3	(5)
Sierra Leone	210	(29)	22	(24)	4	(37)
Windward Coast	208	(15)	14	(9)	4	(15)
Gold Coast	184	(26)	12	(21)	3	(26)
Bight of Benin	187	(2)	6	(1)	4	(3)
Bight of Biafra	138	(79)	14	(22)	11	(105)
Congo-Angola	217	(60)	14	(39)	4	(63)
Unknown	188	(56)	12	(43)	2	(47)
Average	183		14		6	
(Total Shipments)		(272)		(164)		(301)[b]

SOURCE: G.B.L., July 28, 1800.

[a]These are average mortality figures. There was a high degree of variance among the voyages in terms of mortality, thus the coefficient of variation for the 301 shipments for which complete data existed was 1.27. Individual regions ranged from .70 to 1.38. Biafra, which will be of concern later on in this essay, was at the lower end with a coefficient of variation of .91, which implies that its spread of mortality experience was on average lower than for the entire sample, and for most regions as well. Thus its high average mortality is not due to an unusual concentration of ships with high mortality experience.

[b]Only 272 shipments had complete age and sex breakdowns (of which only 164 carried children); the others simply gave total slave figures. This accounts for the discrepancy between the mortality sample and the sample from which the age and sex breakdowns were taken.

mation on sex, such hypotheses can only be offered on the most tentative basis.

If, as now seems proven, women were disproportionately underrepresented in the Atlantic slave trade, the question remains why. Was this due to demand or supply considerations? Was there a planter preference for males which was based on labor, productivity, or other factors and reflected in price differentials? Or could it have been that women were more costly to transport than men and thus were less desired by the slave captains who made their purchases on the African coast? Or, finally, were the Africans themselves keeping women off the market despite demands for them from American planters and European slave captains?

As early as the eighteenth century, administrators and analysts of the trade were concerned with this question and offered all possible answers, from explanations based on supply or demand considerations to speculations about differential mortality and costs of transport. Thus qualitative support for every possible causal model can be found in the eighteenth- and nineteenth-century records.

To deal with this crucial issue systematically, it is essential to outline the relevant variables. One of the more general concepts in the qualitative literature is that planters preferred men over women and paid higher prices for them. In the Parliamentary reviews of the trade, several experienced captains stressed this theme, along with the belief that the planters preferred men because women were useless in field labor.[2]

After some two decades of systematic analyses of slave prices and studies of working conditions of slaves in many American slave societies, it is evident that the perception of the captains on this point does not agree with the reality of the American experience. Several recent studies have shown that the earnings of male and female slaves differed little during the years of productive labor (Fogel and Engerman 1974, 1:75–77; Carvalho de Mello 1976, ch. 2; Fraginals et al., forthcoming). This was reflected in quite similar prices paid for male and female slaves in almost all major slave societies in the Americas. Prices for male slaves were usually somewhat higher than for female slaves, on the order of 10–20 percent in the prime working years. In almost all such societies, however, women were denied access to skilled occupations, and all skilled slaves were more highly priced than unskilled ones (Fogel and Engerman 1974; Carvalho de Mello 1976, appendix). Controlling for this differential access to skills, and comparing just unskilled fieldhand labor, the price differential between males and females is reduced almost to insignificance (Higman

---

2. G.B.C., Report on the Slave Trade, 1789, part I. While many captains stressed differential American prices and other demand-related factors, some two-thirds of them also spoke of the difficulty of procuring slave women on the African coast.

1976:192). Women's prices in the prime years reflected a positive price for unborn children, and therefore may have compensated for whatever differences in physical potential might have existed.

Even if price differentials were not significant, is it possible that women could not be used in the harsh physical labor of plantation agriculture and were therefore needed less than men? Again on the contrary, all recent studies reveal that planters showed little or no sexual preferences in labor use, with women performing all the basic unskilled manual labor tasks that men worked at. Women in most American plantations were, in fact, overrepresented in all the brute force fieldhand labor occupations, and in mature plantation areas they tended to be the majority of actual field gang plantation workers. Thus, in both the sugar and coffee estates of early nineteenth-century Jamaica, the majority of women were found in field labor, and made up at least half of the gangs on most plantations (Higman 1976). In Worthy Park, one of the best studied of the larger sugar planta-tions, for example, from the late 1780s until 1838, women were never less than 54 percent of the total of the field hands, with two-thirds being the average ratio; and unskilled field labor—clearing, planting, weeding, and harvesting—occupied on average close to two-thirds of the women on the plantation (Craton 1978). A similar division of labor was found in nineteenth-century United States cotton plantations, and in late nineteenth-century Cuban sugar plantations and Brazilian coffee fazendas (Gray 1932, 1:547–49; Fraginals 1978, 2:42–43; Stein 1957:71).

Thus in terms neither of prices nor labor needs can the sexual imbalance of the African slave trade be explained by the actions of the American planters. Alternatively to explanations based on demand, could it be that transportation problems caused ship captains to take fewer females than males? The few studies available on the relationship between mortality and sex in the Atlantic slave trade make it evident that mortality rates of females were the same as or even less than those of males of the same age group.[3] Nor do any of the studies of the costs of transportation show any bias against women. Both men and women were allotted the same space between decks—though women were usually segregated from men for policing purposes—and both were fed the same foods on the trip. Since few infants were transported, there were no special transport problems or costs related to nursing mothers. In short, neither demand nor transporta-tion factors can explain the sexual disparities in the trade.

That fewer women entered the Atlantic slave trade market than would

3. See, for example, Postma 1979:258. According to the House of Lords listings for the English Atlantic slave trade in the late eighteenth century, mortality among adult Africans averaged 6 percent for women and 5 percent for men. Among the children the mortality rates were higher, but differed little sexually, with females averaging 11 percent mortality in the Atlantic crossing and males 13 percent.

have been purchased by the Europeans if the supply had been totally elastic is the obvious conclusion. But why they were kept out of this market can only be speculated upon. Women were enslaved within Africa itself. Also, there is now general agreement that a major internal slave market existed within Africa to supply local demands for slave labor. Some fragmentary price data which Philip Curtin has gathered from the interior of Senegambia suggest that there was a much higher local price paid for female than for male slaves.[4] If this was the case, then Africans could have been outbidding Europeans for females on the African markets. Or it could be that the higher prices reflected a much more limited supply of slave women, who in turn were being kept off the slave market either by their own societies or by their captors.

In support of this hypothesis of African demand for women, scholars talk of the vital importance of female agricultural labor in West Africa, while some also stress that in those societies where polygyny was important, the role of slave wives was crucial. Children born to such women were usually incorporated into the local society, and women in general were highly prized for their social and economic importance. Thus it has been suggested that the role of women in the economy and society gave them a higher value, especially as slaves, than men. In contrast, it has been suggested that male slaves were not easily absorbed into the local labor systems, and thus represented a potential threat in terms of access to women and arms. They were therefore more easily put up for sale in the Atlantic slave market. If these various hypotheses ultimately prove to have some validity, it might be suggested that an indication of the viability of a given African region or state in the epoch of the Atlantic slave trade was its ability to retain women and keep them from the trans-Atlantic trade. The shipping of more women than normal might indicate a fundamental breakdown in the economic or social viability of the state. Some support for this position can be found in the English slave trade data for the 1790s, which show that the region of Biafra was then exporting the highest number of women of any African region, and also that the ships leaving from these shores experienced by far the highest rates of slave mortality at sea (see table 2.6). Moreover, this mortality was consistently the highest of any region for every single age and sex category of slaves being shipped.[5]

In terms of the impact on American slave populations of the sexual

4. Curtin 1975:175–76. Recent demographic studies of Africa during the slave trade period have stressed the predominance of women on the coast and in so-called raider societies in the interior. See Thornton, this volume.

5. Both men and women leaving Biafra suffered 10 percent mortality on average, with boys having 28 percent and girls 33 percent. For girls only Congo-Angola, at 44 percent (5 ships), had a higher rate. For all other categories, the Biafra region was unique.

distortions apparent in the trans-Atlantic slave trade, the implications are clearer. Since fewer women than men were arriving, and since those fewer women were already well into their adult years and brought with them few children, African populations in America were incapable of reproducing themselves. Most women had already used up some of their potential fecundity by the time they had arrived in America, and the problems of changing nutrition and cultural adjustment further reduced potential births. Supposing that there were on average only some fifty women for every hundred men, and the number of their children was also reduced, then African slave populations in America could only have experienced a negative growth rate.

The historical record of American slave populations, in fact, supports this finding. Every slave state with heavy direct importation of African slaves had a difficult time maintaining its servile laboring population. Only as the trade lessened and the creole slave populations grew were positive growth rates finally achieved. Thus negative growth rates of American slave populations are highly correlated with heavy rates of direct African importations.[6]

From this brief survey, it is apparent that determining the incidence of female participation in the slave trade is only the beginning of a long-term process in explaining its cause and understanding its impact. If it is primarily African supply considerations which determine the movement of women and girls into the trans-Atlantic trade, then the incidence of such females is an important, if indirect, index of African social and economic conditions. How that index is to be interpreted will differ from region to region, as the extreme fluctuations from the western African regions demonstrate. But that fewer women than men entered the trade and that Africans exercised a direct control over this movement cannot be doubted.

References

Unpublished Sources

Carvalho de Mello, P. 1976. "The Economics of Slavery in Brazilian Coffee Plantations, 1850–1888." Ph.D. dissertation, University of Chicago.
G.B.C.: Great Britain, House of Commons, Parliamentary Papers.
G.B.L.: Great Britain, House of Lords, Record Office, Papers.
S.A.I.: Spain, Archivo general de Indias, Audiencia de Santo Domingo.

6. Klein (1978:243–46) provides detailed information on this issue for most American societies.

Published Sources

Craton, M. M. 1977. *Searching for the Invisible Man: Slaves and Plantation Life in Jamaica.* Cambridge, Mass.

Curtin, P. D. 1969. *The Atlantic Slave Trade: A Census.* Madison.

Curtin, P. D. 1975. *Economic Change in Precolonial Africa: Senegambia in the Era of the Slave Trade.* 2 vols. Madison.

Fogel, R. W., and S. L. Engerman. 1974. *Time on the Cross: The Economics of American Negro Slavery.* 2 vols. Boston.

Fraginals, M. M. 1978. *El Ingenio, complexo económico social cubana del azucar.* 3 vols. 1978.

Fraginals, M. M., S. Engerman, and H. S. Klein. Forthcoming. *Nineteenth Century Cuban Slave Prices in Comparative Perspective.*

Gray, L. C. 1932. *History of Agriculture in the Southern United States to 1860.* 2 vols. Washington, D.C.

Green-Pedersen, S. 1971. "The Scope and Structure of the Danish Negro Slave Trade." *Scandinavian Economic History Review* 19:150–97.

Higman, B. W. 1976. *Slave Population and Economy in Jamaica, 1807–1834.* Cambridge, Mass.

Klein, H. S. 1978. *The Middle Passage: Comparative Studies in the Atlantic Slave Trade.* Princeton.

Northrup, D. 1978. *Trade without Rulers: Pre-Colonial Economic Development in South-Eastern Nigeria.* Oxford.

Postma, J. 1979. "Mortality in the Dutch Slave Trade, 1675–1795." In *The Uncommon Market: Essays in the Economic History of the Atlantic Slave Trade,* ed. H. A. Gemery and J. S. Hogendorn. New York.

Stein, J. 1957. *Vassouras: A Brazilian Coffee County, 1850–1890.* Cambridge, Mass.

3 *John Thornton*

Sexual Demography: The Impact of the Slave Trade on Family Structure

In the past few years, the study of the Atlantic slave trade has shifted emphasis from measuring its volume to judging its effects in Africa. In the recent seminar in African Historical Demography held in Edinburgh, the four contributions dealing with the slave trade assessed its effects on African population size, structure, and density (Diop, Inikori, Manning, Thornton 1981). Emerging from this new concentration on the African side of the slave trade has been the realization that the slave trade had a significant impact on the role and life of women, and researchers are increasingly pointing out that the study of women, both as slaves and as free people in areas where slaving occurred, is a necessary corollary to the study of the slave trade as a whole (Manning 1981a).

The fact that the slave trade carried more men than women to the Americas, about two to three men for every woman according to those statistical series that are available, has long been seen as the cause of the inability of the slave population to grow in America. Low birth rates were largely a product of an extremely unbalanced sex ratio on American plantations, which when coupled with bad nutrition, few incentives to reproduce, and high abortion rates meant that slave populations could not keep ahead of their own mortality except by renewed imports from Africa (Sheridan 1975; H. Klein, this volume).

My own work on the Angolan population of the late eighteenth century suggested what were the effects of the very differently altered sex composition in Africa (Thornton 1980). In Angola, women outnumbered men by nearly two to one in the population left behind after the slave trade. However, unlike in the Americas, the skewed sex ratio did not result in a marked decline in population. Because of the established institution of polygyny, the almost undiminished numbers of women were able to coun-

39

terbalance some of the losses to the slave trade by continued reproduction. In a study presented at the Edinburgh conference, I charted the probable effects of the slave trade on age and sex distribution in a model population with characteristics similar to those of the population of Angola (Thornton 1981). Then, operating on the assumption that the rest of western Africa had similar population structures, I tried to suggest what would be the effect on such a model population of withdrawing a number of slaves equal to the number known from studies of the volume of the slave trade. Working independently, Patrick Manning created another model, which, while differing in approach and assumptions, nevertheless arrived at similar conclusions (1981a and 1981b). Both models supported the conclusion that the population, although showing no long-term growth, suffered little long-term net loss. However, in both models the population, while not shrinking, did undergo fairly substantial alteration in structure, such that the group of males of working age was substantially reduced as a result of the specific demands of the slave traders and American purchasers for slaves in that age and sex group (Thornton 1980; Manning 1981b). In my own model, in which I tried to establish the minimum population densities necessary to support the known volume of slave exports in the interior behind each of several slave-exporting centers and then compared these densities with probable densities based on modern population size, I found that at the peak period of the slave trade in the late eighteenth century the demand for slaves must have come close to matching the maximum ability of all these regions to supply them. Moreover, in every region, the sex ratio in the age bracket 15–60 would have been only 80 men per 100 women, and in the hardest-hit area, Angola, as low as 40–50 men per 100 women (Thornton 1980).

The older debate on the slave trade had concentrated in one way or another on quantitative assessments of the population changes in Africa caused by the slave trade. Thus in Fage's many papers on the subject he insisted that the total volume of the trade was insufficient to offset natural growth and Africa was not depopulated (Fage 1975). Criticisms of Fage's approach, such as those of J. E. Inikori and L. M. Diop presented at the Edinburgh conference, maintained simply that Fage had underestimated the total number of slaves exported and that depopulation *had* occurred, with its most important negative effect being a less favorable land-to-labor ratio in the remaining population. The approach to the problem suggested by Manning and myself, on the other hand, involves investigation of the quality of the population left behind, and not simply its quantity. This approach supports an argument that the major impact of the trade was not so much the reduction of the total number of people remaining in Africa as fundamental alterations in the ratio of working to dependent populations or of male to female labor. In this reexamination, the position of women is highlighted, since it is they who suffered the most from the trade in Africa.

The alteration in the age and sex ratios affected women in Africa in two ways, both results of the age- and sex-specific nature of the demand for African slaves by the traders. First of all, since they retained their normal fertility, the burden of child care imposed on them was not lessened by the loss in population—all the more so since children younger than age fifteen or so were rarely taken by the slave traders. At the same time their own numbers, and more important the numbers of males who played a vital role in child support if not in child care, were declining. This can be clearly seen if we examine the change in the dependency ratio of a hypothetical population in which the working group aged 15–60 has been depleted by 10 percent (the effect of having a sex ratio of 80 men per 100 women in this age group). Before the onset of the trade, according to the model life table from which my work was constructed, about 60 percent of the population fell into this age bracket, while the other 40 percent were either younger and required child care, or older and were unable to participate in productive labor. Thus there were approximately 67 dependents for each 100 working people. After the distortion introduced by the slave trade, however, 54 percent of the population fell into the category of able-bodied workers, while 46 percent were dependent, giving a dependency ratio of 85 dependents for each 100 working people. Thus the burden of work falling on the productive members of society was greatly increased, forcing more and more of their time to be spent in purely subsistence activities and reducing their ability to produce surplus for commerce or to maintain an efficient division of labor.

Women were hit in another way as well, however, and this was due to the alteration of the sex ratios among the producers just at a time when the work load of all producers was increasing. The model suggests that there must have been 20 percent fewer males to perform work allocated to men during the slave trade era, work which would then have had to go undone, or be done by females, or compensated for by purchased items. For example, in central Africa women did agricultural work, but men did heavy clearing of the fields, chopping down trees and digging up roots. Without this clearing labor, the women would have had to plant less or move their fields less often, both of which would tend to reduce production (Thornton 1983:28–31). Likewise, because hunting, fishing, and the rearing of livestock were activities which many traditional African societies left to men, the loss of males resulted in a less protein-rich diet for the remaining people.

This model is, of course, an average calculation based on rather crude assumptions. The actual adjustment of particular African societies is much more difficult to determine. The model is a global one applied to all re-

gions of western Africa that supplied slaves, and is based on data obtained
from a few rather large areas. How the slave raids affected the population
in smaller regions within these larger areas is not considered. For example, a society subjected to raids might lose men and women in equal
numbers and the raiding society incorporate the women while selling off
the men. Alternatively, slave raiding which matched military forces against
each other might result in all the slaves procured by the victor being males
of saleable age, since armies select for the same age and sex criteria as
plantation managers. My model suggested that the societies that procured
slaves selected men ahead of women, and left the societies which gave up
slaves with unbalanced sex ratios, while Manning's model assumed that
the victims of slave raiding lost men and women in equal numbers, and
the unbalanced sex ratios affected the societies that did the raiding. In fact,
a variety of different methods were used to procure slaves, from large-
scale wars to small-scale kidnapping, including judicial enslavement and
raids of organized military forces against disorganized villagers. Each of
these methods might have resulted in a different mix of ages and sexes for
both the aggressors and the losers, and hence a whole distinct constella-
tion of resulting demographic structures.

In Angola, for example, slaves were procured by major wars between
military powers, a method which would probably favor the acquisition of
males by the group that sold the slaves (da Silva Corrêa 1782; Birmingham 1966), and smaller-scale kidnapping and raiding against villagers which
would have resulted in the acquisition of both men and women (A.P.F.
1705). Moreover, the census data from Angola show unbalanced sex ratios and distorted age structures for both slaves and free people, suggesting that the depletion of males among victims and the incorporation of
females by the groups that acquired slaves were going on simultaneously
(Thornton 1980). Equally diverse means of slave procurement were probably being used in other regions as well, which future research may do
much to clarify.

Although a focus on the age and sex distribution of affected African
populations does not tell us as much about the qualitative social effects of
the slave trade as we would like, it suggests some lines of research that
could reveal more about those effects. For example, one result of the unbalanced sex ratios would be an alteration in the institution of marriage.
Since the institution of polygyny was present in Africa at the time that the
slave trade began (Fage 1980), the general surplus of women in the marriageable age group would have tended to encourage it and allow it to
become much more widespread, driving down the bridewealth that women's
families could demand and weakening the stability of the marriages in
existence. It might also have favored men building up large households of
wives through the purchase of female slaves; these slaves and their chil-

dren, unprotected by their kin, would have been subject to abuses. This in turn might have had a detrimental effect on the status of marriage even for free women. These effects might vary according to whether the surplus of women was caused by an influx of female slaves, as in a society that was capturing slaves of both sexes but only selling the males to the Atlantic trade; or by a shortage of men, as in a society in which men were being drained off by warfare to the trade, leaving the women behind.

We can examine such qualitative changes in more detail by looking at one region, that of modern Guinea-Bissau (the Upper Guinea coast), for which descriptive data are available. By the early seventeenth century the region had become one of the foci of slave exporting from the western end of West Africa. Witnesses of the time commented on this fact, as for example the memorial submitted by the Jesuit priest Baltasar Barreira in 1606 (Brásio 1958–79, 4:190–98), or the group of Spanish Capuchins who submitted an open letter to the Pope and several other European rulers in 1686 (Labat 1728, 5:215–20; Texeira da Mota 1974:121–33). Extensive slave trade activity is confirmed as well by surveys of the ethnic origins of slaves landing in the New World, such as those compiled from notorial records in Peru by Frederick Bowser (1974:40–43). A fairly large percentage of the slaves leaving Guinea-Bissau were from the numerous small political units in the area (Texeira da Mota 1974:124–28). From the written observations of many visitors to Guinea-Bissau, we can form some idea of the social ramifications of the slave trade there. It was the wealth of written evidence, much of it from residents hostile to the slave trade, that enabled Walter Rodney to write so poignantly and effectively about the distortion of life and justice caused by the slave trade in the region (1970:112–51). These hostile witnesses were mostly missionaries to the coast, which possessed a substantial settlement of Portuguese and Afro-Portuguese residents and was in need of clerical ministrations, and, as a non-Moslem zone, was open to attempts to missionize the African population. The Jesuits worked in the country from the start of the seventeenth century, and were joined by the Capuchins in mid-century (Brásio 1958–80; Carrocera 1957). Unlike lay residents, whose writing is also quite extensive, the missionaries took pains to describe daily life and customs, and were not indisposed to denounce the slave trade since it interfered with their successful proselytization as well as offending their sense of justice.

This corpus of writing allows us to see some of the ways in which women were affected by the Atlantic slave trade. Writing in 1684 in an enlarged recension of a manuscript he originally composed in 1669, Francisco de Lemos Coelho, a Portuguese resident of the area, made some interesting notes on the Bissagos Islands. Although he does not mention unbalanced sex ratios as such, Lemos Coelho noted that polygyny was so widespread there that "there are blacks there who have twenty or thirty wives, and no one has only one," and moreover, "the children in their villages are [as numerous as] a beehive" (Lemos Coelho 1953:178). Given the heavy slave trade in the area, the disproportionate number of women and children remarked by Lemos Coelho is not surprising. This unbalanced age and sex structure may also account for the very large share of work done by women on the islands, which astonished Lemos Coelho. After describing their complicated work in making cloth for clothes, he goes on to say: "They [the women] are the ones who work the fields, and plant the crops, and the houses in which they live, even though small, are clean and bright, and despite all this work they still go down to the sea each day to catch shellfish . . ." (Lemos Coelho 1953:178). Lemos Coelho was not the only observer to comment on the burden of work falling on the women of the Bissagos Islands. Over half a century earlier, André Álvares d'Almada made almost identical observations, noting, "they [the women] do more work than men do in other places" (Brásio 1968–79, 3:317). The men, it seems, were absorbed largely in war, which in this case meant slave raiding, while the women had to engage in production and perform more than the normal share of work. In the case of the Bissagos Islanders it seems probable that the real burden fell upon the extra women, those who had arrived as slaves, although Lemos Coelho's report does not distinguish between slaves and free women.

Elsewhere in the area, other witnesses explicitly drew a connection between slavery, an influx of women, and the peculiar status of slave wives. The Spanish Capuchins, who complained of the state of affairs in the region around Bissau in 1686, believed that the plenitude of female slaves encouraged concubinage (Texeira da Mota 1974:125, 131–32). Manuel Alvares, a Jesuit who wrote of conditions in the same area in 1616, observed, "All have many wives," again suggesting the generality of concubinage. Alvares also noted the special vulnerability of slave women: "If a noble takes his own slave for a wife, and she gives him some displeasure, he will sell her along with her child, even if the child is small, without any regard for the child being his own" (Texeira da Mota 1974:59–60). Others who had lived in Guinea noticed the ease with which subordinate family members might be sold for petty violations of custom (Texeira da Mota 1974:125), although Alvares added that upper-class women were protected from such dire measures. Much of this testimony was used years ago by Rodney to support his thesis that the slave trade had led to substantial legal distortion, and certainly this particular social custom would allow members of the upper classes to hold or sell subordinates at will and according to other needs or the demands of the trade (1970:106–10). Thus slaves held in marriage arrangements such as those described by Alvares could be mobilized for sale without costly wars or risk of retribution. Of course, most witnesses agree that warfare was still the major source of slaves (Texeira da Mota 1974:124–26), and one cannot help but suspect that the marriage customs were reported more for their shock value (and perhaps from isolated cases) than for the importance of their incidence.

Nevertheless, the slave trade brought many surplus women into coastal society in Guinea, and the Spanish Capuchins even noted that housing was inadequate, forcing male and female slaves to share quarters during peak periods of the trade (Texeira da Mota 1974:131). Inquisition authorities were aware that large numbers of slave women were affecting the Portuguese residents as well; in 1589, one Nuno Francisco da Costa was denounced to the Inquisition for having many *mulheres* (an ambiguous word in this case, meaning either women or wives) and reputedly saying that he cared more "for the fingernail of [a particular] slave woman than all the masses and confessions" (Baião 1906:251; Texeira da Mota 1976:15–16). Slavery and surplus women might even have altered the marriage patterns of theoretically monogamous Christians.

These scattered observations on female roles and marriage customs might be taken for no more than passing remarks of writers who were somewhat unsympathetic to African culture, were it not for their close agreement with our expectations based on demographic trends in the area. Just as Rodney's generalizations about the effects of the slave trade on class structure and the institution of slavery have been criticized as being atypical of West Africa (Fage 1980:289–91), so too might these remarks on women's roles and the status of marriage. The data are not quantifiable, and were obtained from observers who were antagonistic toward the slave trade and hence anxious to highlight its ill effects. But they do fit some predictions based on a knowledge of the demography of the slave trade, and as such must be taken with new seriousness.

Scholars interested in understanding the slave trade must undertake an investigation, covering as many areas and time periods as possible, of the status of women (both slave and free) and the institution of marriage in the context of our understanding of the population structure of societies participating in the slave trade. Similarly, it is an urgent task of those interested in the social history of Africa to investigate the nature and dimensions of the internal slave trade, and the strategy of its agents. To what extent did this internal trade involve the transfer of women from interior districts to the regions of the slave-trading states? Can we guess at the volume of this trade in females, which was fairly extensive in some regions? To what extent did the displacements of women within Africa and the siphoning off of men to the trans-Atlantic slave trade affect the pre-colonial population distribution, and what is the legacy of those effects today? We also need further exploration of how male and female roles were affected by the change in sex ratios.

In addition, more study of slave trades not involving shipment to the Americas might yield interesting results. For example, Olifert Dapper noted in the mid-seventeenth century that in every village along the Gold Coast from Allada to the Ivory Coast there were "three or four whores," recruited from female slaves, whose earnings went to the ruler of the village. To what extent was this widespread prostitution (prevalent in spite of the polygyny which Dapper also noted) a product of the trade in female slaves between Benin and the Gold Coast? (Dapper 1670:471). Was it due to the region's role as an importer of slaves (from the interior and other points of the coast), its growing role as an exporter of slaves (just beginning as Dapper wrote) (Rodney 1969), or the general concentration of strangers in the area brought about the area's position as a marketplace between the zone controlled by interior merchants and that controlled by European traders? (Vasconcellos 1639:85).

We must accept that the full story of the effect of the slave trade on women in western Africa is well beyond the range of the sources available to us. Travelers' accounts, local chronicles, and even reports of residents often neglect descriptions of women's work and women's status, or present these in categories that are either an "ideal average" or a series of horror stories like those of the missionaries in Guinea-Bissau. Statistical evidence for any period save the very end of the precolonial era is likely to elude us. But we can learn considerably more about this aspect of Africa than we know now by reading over the sources available to us with a critical eye, informed by a knowledge of probable and possible effects of the slave trade. We can also try to develop models with greater predictive power than is possessed by the ones now in existence, models which, though perhaps not testable statistically, can be effectively tested by the documentation we do have.

References

Unpublished Sources

A.P.F.: Archivio de Propaganda Fide (Rome). Bernardo da Firenze to Propaganda Fide, June 22, 1705. Scritture originali riferitenella Congregazione Generale, vol. 552, fols. 64v–65v.

Published Sources

Baião, A. 1906. *A Inquisção em Portugal e no Brazil. Subsídios para a sua história.* Lisbon.

Birmingham, D. 1966. *Trade and Conflict in Angola.* London.

Bowser, F. 1974. *The African Slave in Colonial Peru.* Stanford.

Brásio, A. 1958–79. *Monumenta Missionaria Africana*. 2nd series. 5 vols. Lisbon.

Carrocera, B. de. 1957. *Missiones Capuchinas en Africa. II. Missiones al Reino de la Zinga, Benin, Ardra, Guinea y Sierra Leone*. Madrid.

Dapper, O. 1670/1967. *Umbeständliche und Eigentliche Beschreibung von Africa*. Amsterdam.

Da Silva Corrêa, Elias Alexandre. 1782 (1937). *História de Angola*. 2 vols. Lisbon.

Diop, L. M. 1981. Méthode et calculs approximatifs pour la constitution d'une courbe representatif de l'évolution de la population de l'Afrique noire." In *African Historical Demography*, ed. C. Fyfe and D. M.~Master. Edinburgh.

Fage, J. D. 1975. "The Effect of the Export Slave Trade on African Populations." In *The Population Factor in African Studies*, ed. R. P. Moss and R. J. A. Rathbone. London.

Fage, J. D. 1980. "Slaves and Society in Western Africa, c. 1455–c. 1700." *Journal of African History* 21:289–310.

Fyfe, C., and D. McMaster, eds. 1981. *African Historical Demography*. Vol. 2. Edinburgh.

Inikori, J. E. 1981. "Underpopulation in 19th Century West Africa: The Role of the Export Slave Trade." In *African Historical Demography*, vol. 2, ed. C. Fyfe and D. McMaster. Edinburgh.

Labat, J. B. 1728. *Nouvelle relation de l'afrique Occidentale*. 5 vols. Paris.

Lemos Coelho, F. de. 1953. *Duas descrições seiscentistas da Guiné*. Edited by Damião Peres. Lisbon.

Manning, P. 1981a. "A Demographic Model of Slavery." In *African History Demography*, ed. C. Fyfe and D. McMaster. Edinburgh.

Manning, P. 1981b. "The Enslavement of Africans: A Demographic Model." *Canadian Journal of African Studies* 15:499–526.

Rodney, W. 1969. "Gold and Slaves on the Gold Coast." *Transactions of the Historical Society of Ghana* 10:13–28.

Rodney, W. 1970. *A History of the Upper Guinea Coast, 1545–1800*. Oxford.

Sheridan, R. 1975. "Mortality and Medical Treatment of Slaves in the British West Indies." In *Race and Slavery in the Western Hemisphere: Quantitative Studies*, ed. S. L. Engerman and E. D. Genovese. Princeton.

Texeira da Mota, A. 1974. *As Viagens de Bispo d. Frei Vitoriano Portuense a Guiné e a cristianização dos reis de Bissau*. Lisbon.

Texeira da Mota, A. 1976. "Alguns aspectos da colonização e do commércio marítime dos Portugueses na África ocidental nos séculos XV e XVI. *Centro de Estudos de Cartográfia Antiga. Series Separata* 97:15–16.

Thornton, J. 1980. "The Slave Trade in Eighteenth-Century Angola: Effects on Demographic Structures." *Canadian Journal of African Studies* 14:417–27.

Thornton, J. 1981. "The Demographic Effect of the Slave Trade on Western Africa, 1500–1850." In *African Historical Demography*, ed. Christopher Fyfe and David McMaster. Edinburgh.

Thornton, J. 1983. *The Kingdom of Kongo: Civil War and Transition, 1641–1718*. Madison.

Vasconcellos, Agustin Manuel y. 1639. *Vida y acciones del Rey Don Juan el Segundo*. Madrid.

Vogt, J. 1973. "The Early São Thomé–Principe Slave Trade with Mina, 1500–1540." *International Journal of African Historical Studies* 6:453–67.

4 *Claude Meillassoux*[1]

Female Slavery

While the capacity of the free woman for hard work is often cited to explain the female condition in the domestic community and such institutions as bridewealth,[2] it is the feminine capacity to procreate which is usually given as an explanation for the greater value of women than of men on the African slave market (Fage 1980). I believe that these propositions should be reversed. On the first point, I have argued elsewhere that in the domestic society a woman's reproductive capacity is what is most expected from her (Meillassoux 1981). Her submission as a laborer follows from her submission as a procreator. In slavery, on the other hand, women were valued above all as workers, mostly because female tasks were predominant in production. Consequently the demand for female labor was greater than for male labor. But female slaves were not sought for the reproduction of the slave class. Progeny issuing from slaves mating among themselves were a comparatively scarce by-product of servile labor. It was within the masters' class that slave women were introduced as reproducers, but more for qualitative than quantitative reasons.

Female labor is general in Africa. There are few communities where women are exempt from heavy physical tasks. Still, the Western attitude toward female labor is shaped by the Christian image of female fragility. The assignment of heavy tasks or military activity to women is considered incongruous or incompatible with the "nature" of women, though that assumption is peculiar to the dominant classes of the West. This might be why Western ethnology has generally interpreted the preference of African

1. Translated by Martin A. Klein.
2. Some authors consider bridewealth as a compensation for the loss of "labor" by the wife's family or as a "price" for the "purchase" of the wife.

49

and Asian enslavers for women in terms of specifically "feminine" qualities such as beauty or fertility. But such a hypothesis contradicts the economic rationale of slavery (Meillassoux 1979 and 1980).

Slavery creates an economic and social agent whose virtue lies in being
outside the kinship system. On the economic level, the genetic reproduction of the slave and the recognition of the rights of the slave to his or her
offspring would limit the profitability of slavery. On the social level, the
absence of these parental rights, and consequently of the rights of citizenship, creates a class of desocialized individuals who can be entrusted with
confidential tasks which, in a kinship or dynastic society, could only be
assigned at a certain risk to kin or full citizens.

One approach to African slavery, which stresses its benevolent character
by comparison to American or West Indian slavery, tends to play down the
differences between slaves and other dependent or dominated social categories, such as pawns, serfs, or even married women. It emphasizes, for
instance, cases of "assimilation" of the slave into the kinship system of
the master. But this process operated truly only in societies where slavery
was not institutionalized and systematized. The existence of captured or
bought people in a society is not enough to make it a slave system. Slavery
exists where the slave class is reproduced through institutional apparatus:
war or market. In such enslaving societies, "assimilation" amounts to a
limited emancipation or simply to some degree of intimacy with the master's family. In an actual slave system the taint of slavery—specifically,
prejudice against slaves or those of slave descent—usually persists indef-
initely. Actually, as Robertson and Klein note (above, p. 9), the slave is
kinless, that is, deprived of the protection that comes from belonging to
kinship groups. The offspring of slaves, being unrelated both to their be-
getters and to their owners, also find themselves in the situation of being
orphans. Even the children of concubines can only be related to their father's lineage since their mother is without kin. Hence, although these
children may be free, they are not protected by the possible arbitration
that would come from belonging to two lineages. Hence, they are excluded also from common law and citizenship. This inferior *estate*[3] char-
acterizes the slave's entire existence no matter what his or her *condition* is
or how that condition changes. The *estate* of slaves is linked to their origin
and remains constant. Their *condition* is linked to their function in the
slave society and varies according to each individual and, also, to time. It
is precisely the social weakness of slaves and of their offspring which
explains why genetic reproduction might be wanted by the master, while
the same social weakness also sets limits to it. This is observable both

---

3. I distinguish *estate* from *status* because the jural situation of the slave stands on
negative criteria whereas *status* defines people on positive jural grounds.

within the framework of the kinship system (in domestic societies) and within the framework of a dynastic system (in aristocratic class societies).

The Infertility of Female Slaves

Female slaves were more numerous and more expensive than male slaves. The hypothesis that they were preferred because of their potential for reproduction is not supported by objective data. Neither statistics nor any other kind of evidence demonstrates the maintenance or growth of slave populations by the reproduction of slaves among themselves. On the contrary, in slave societies where women were preferred, such as in sub-Saharan Africa and the Maghreb, the importation of slaves was constant, just as it was in the predominantly male slave societies of America and the West Indies.[4] In both cases, slavery was sustained by the continued acquisition of new slaves by purchase or by capture and not by genetic reproduction. Numerous statistical data for American and West Indian slavery confirm this. Figures are less abundant for Africa, but still convincing.

Thanks to the papers edited in this book, we now have more accurate data on slave fertility. If such data are still too scarce to make generalization safe, it is clear that in each case reported here, female slaves had very few children, and contrary to what we would expect if women were preferred to men for their reproductive potential, they didn't even ensure simple reproduction[5] of the slave population. Martin Klein gives evidence of this in his paper (below, table 5.2, p. 69). According to these figures, there was less than one child for each slave woman. If we suppose that half of these children were girls, the "gross rate of reproduction"[6] of the slave population falls below 0.5. Strobel reports that at Mombasa, at the beginning of the twentieth century, a group of fifteen adult slaves she studied, which included ten women, had only eleven living children of both sexes (below, p. 121). Many of these women, Strobel adds, never married (below, p. 120). Thus, not only the rate of fertility, but also the rate of nuptiality was low. Strobel notes also that "there is no evidence

4. The statistical data available for West Indian slavery show clearly that the reproduction of slaves was not the concern of the slave owners. See Curtin 1969; Martin 1948:114, 128. The slave states of North America are given as a counterexample (Gutman 1981; Engerman 1981), but this may need further investigation. The growth of slave populations by reproduction may be due to a change in the nature of their exploitation or to a decline of the farming enterprises.

5. Reproduction of one slave for one slave. This is not even a rate of reproduction equal to one, which supposes one female birth for each woman.

6. Properly speaking, the "gross rate of reproduction" is the proportion of female births to the total and constant number of women of procreative age. The figures used here don't give the age distribution of the women, which means therefore that the ratio of 0.5 is a maximum.

that slaves who had children[7] were favored over those who did not" (below, p. 121). Strobel assumes that this low level of fertility was disappointing to the masters (below, p. 120), but the repetition of this situation in other slave societies throws doubt on this interpretation.

The commercial towns of the Middle Zaire in the nineteenth century described by Harms (this volume) presents an even clearer case. Although these towns counted, on the average, 140 female slaves for every 100 males, there was no natural reproduction. Travelers were struck by the lack of children in the streets. An 1889 inquiry indicated 384 adult slaves (hence about 205 women if the proportion indicated above is valid) and only 50 children. This amounts to 0.13 children per adult slave, compared to 0.73 at Mombasa; or per woman, 0.24 in the Middle Zaire and 1.10 at Mombasa. (Our "gross rate of reproduction" would be 0.12 and 0.55.) Harms thinks that slave sterility was contrary to the intentions of the masters' class, but for two reasons which he confuses. Is it because their slave *concubines* did not give them offspring? In this case these offspring would not be slaves, and would not reproduce the slave *class:* "Men expressed anger at their wives for failing to bear children." Or is it because the slaves did not reproduce *among themselves* as a class? "The traders were forced to continually buy new slaves in order to keep up the population of their villages."

This last quotation expresses clearly that in practice it was the economic law of slave reproduction which operated, independent of any assumed intention of the masters: "The Bobangi didn't bear many children. They just bought people" (below, p. 109). The low level of natality was not due to some peculiar sterility of slave women, but to the fact that they aborted or practiced infanticide (below, pp. 106–7). Quite probably, the conditions of existence of slave women and the social climate within which they lived did not encourage them to procreate or to keep their children. If the masters wanted children so strongly, would they have welcomed them with aloofness, as reported by Harms? If we consider this sterility as a form of resistance to the slave condition, how do we explain that the behavior of these women was marked in other ways by complete acceptance of their condition if not of their alienation? The idea of widespread resistance of female slaves by voluntary sterility is backed up by neither evidence nor testimony. On the other hand, the descriptions of the way of life of slave women show well enough why conditions were not favorable for childbearing. The story of Adukwe, for example, as told by Robertson, indicates a life of wandering and instability, a succession of poor living conditions. Her relations with men were precarious, often illegitimate. Her

---

7. This refers to slaves who had children among themselves, not to concubines who bore children for their masters.

children were not generally recognized or supported by their genitors. She was never taken care of by any of her lovers. She miscarried several times. Only two daughters survived past infancy. The case of Bwanikwa (Wright, this volume) also illustrates the poor conditions of life that were unfavorable to maternity.

The precariousness of relations among Nzakara slaves is also underlined by A. Retel-Laurentin (1960): "A marital union between two slaves does not prevent the master from removing one of the two partners to conclude an exchange or to endow a relative or a client with a wife." Such conditions (which amount to no marital life) were favorable neither to maternity nor to the raising of children. Bridewealth not being paid, female slaves were in practice never "married." As a rule, their children belonged to her master even when he was not the genitor. The male slave with whom she had these children was not the "father" and had, as a result, little or no interest in them. When the master tolerated or even imposed the union of two slaves, it was not a marriage properly speaking. If it had been, the genitor, not the master, would have had paternal responsibility for the children. Women did not wish to attach themselves to children who could be taken from them at any moment. If they feared to be separated from their male companions and left alone in charge of the children, they were probably tempted to abort. Neither was it to the master's advantage for mated slaves to have too many children, because at the low level of agricultural productivity characteristic of these economies the support of numerous offspring would have absorbed most, if not all, of the agricultural surplus product. Conversely, if the masters levied a large share of the slave household's food supply, the number of nonproductive people, hence of children, had to be reduced proportionately by abortion or infanticide. The attitude of the masters toward slave children does not indicate a real concern for reproduction. Hogendorn (1977) reports that when female slaves worked on the plantations of Sokoto, young children were gathered under a tree and mothers could only approach and nurse them with permission of a guard. At Gumbu, where the same thing was done, difficult children were often buried up to their necks in the sand to keep them quiet.[8]

Thus it does not seem that maternity was as desirable for the female slave as for the free woman. Let us not forget that in a society with a lineage ethic, the wellborn woman prides herself on her fertility. It is not likely that such a society could accept high fertility among slave women, even among the master's concubines. "It is not proper that the slave be comparable to the master," goes a Soninke saying. On the other hand, cases reported in this book show that the fertility of female slaves in-

---

8. At Rome, the exposure of slave children by their masters was widespread until Constantine.

creased when their condition was transformed, when they enjoyed a form
of emancipation or more stable "unions" either with men of their own
class or with their masters. Slave concubines were often freed after conception or the birth of a child, and their offspring were legally free even if
they remained dependent. But there was no genetic reproduction of slaves
in this case.

Thus, whatever intentions are attributed to the masters, the facts reported in this book show that slave reproduction took place mostly through
purchase or capture in accordance with the economic laws of slavery. The
slave class was renewed essentially by the introduction of individuals brought
in from outside the society. In the merchant societies, the sole agent of
reproduction was money: "If you had no more money, the people were
finished for good" (Harms, this volume). Thus was the economic law of
merchant slavery perfectly expressed by Harms's informant.

The resentment which the masters felt at not having children from their
slave women was in contradiction with their general attitude towards slave
reproduction. It was convenient to believe that the curse according to which
wealth led to sterility was actualized through the infecundity of slave women,
inherent anyway in their condition. Lamenting about it helped them to
believe that it was due to fate and not to their policy of reproducing slaves
by acquisition rather than by marriage as prescribed by the Koran (Sourate
XXIV:32).

The low fertility of slave women was observed also in the royal courts.
The palace of the King of Dahomey, where a large number of women
lived, many of them slaves, was not a fertile place. The offspring of kings,
though very numerous for each of them, were few considering the number
of women to whom the kings had access. Glele had 129 children, Gbehanzin 77 (Bay, this volume, p. 350), while they had access to 5,000 to
8.000 *ahosi* (spouses or dependents) most of whom were in principle prohibited from having any other sexual relationship. In this case, we must
speak not of fertility, but of the "sterility" of female slaves.

Other examples confirm the low rate of reproduction in African slave
societies. In the Bamum kingdom, where two-thirds of the population was
servile, "thousands of slaves remained unmarried" (Tardits 1980:466). Only
those who distinguished themselves received wives as a reward. Their
families, however, remained small (Tardits 1980:467). Now the Bamum
sovereigns made constant war to accumulate slaves for their own use more
than for sale. Certain sources suggest a policy of encouraging the reproduction of servile labor, but it obviously was without effect.

In the Sokoto caliphate, Hogendorn's data suggest that 60 percent of
slave reproduction was by acquisition (Hogendorn 1977:373). Thus, it
seems that the primary value of the female slave was not in her reproduc-

tive capacity, unless we assume that slavery functioned everywhere on the basis of a misunderstanding.

The Female Slave as Worker

Swema, a very young girl, after being captured was bought and then transported by an intermediary, who had apparently received an order and payment in advance for this type of merchandise. Swema's mother did not want to be separated from her daughter, and thus gave herself as a slave to the trader. Both were taken away by a caravan, but during the trip each carried a load. When the mother, worn out, could go no further, she was left to die: no work, no food. Swema, also worn out by her heavy burden, was nevertheless brought to her destination, where, sick and comatose, she was considered dead by the consignee and buried alive. She was saved by a passerby. In this case the slaver treated these two women as sheer laborers without sparing them for their reproductive capacity. From that point of view, they had no value. "I do not think that Swema's predicament was affected by her being female," writes Alpers in describing this case (below, p. 200). It was thus only in their capacity for work, which did not distinguish them from males, that the female captives were in this case appreciated or rejected.

If the labor that a woman could perform was what determined her price, that was because the demand for female slaves was related to the sexual allocation of tasks,[9] that is, to the fact that in African societies, women's participation in labor was greater than that of men. This is noted by Robertson (below, p. 223) in connection with pawns, but it is valid for all servile labor: the greater demand for girls than for boys "had to do with the sexual division of labor."

In most African societies, women perform a greater number of tasks than men and work longer hours. They are involved in most forms of agricultural labor (sometimes sharing tasks with men) and in all domestic tasks.[10] If we admit that the economy of slave societies was based on a sexual allocation of tasks similar to that of the societies from which the slaves came and that the slaves were intended to perform the same kind of labor, then we should expect a higher demand for women than for men.

Nevertheless, this allocation of tasks was strictly conventional. Certain female tasks which did not demand any apprenticeship, as for example the gathering of wood or water, could be performed by male slaves, though

9. Allocation of tasks is predominantly based on individual status and fitness; division of labor is based on economic and technical considerations.

10. Strobel notes the importance of female labor for the physical reproduction of society.

it was humiliating for them to do so. Both men and women were equally well prepared for agricultural tasks. It was different with cooking or with the raising of children, and with certain crafts. It is not that men could not perform these tasks, since there was no question of social standing for slaves, but women were better prepared because they received knowledge which passed from woman to woman. On the whole, women were thus generally preferred to men. If men could sometimes replace women, women more often replaced men, even in the most painful tasks for which there was hardly any apprenticeship. In about 1840, Duncan said of Dahomey that "women were usually preferred as porters, because it was agreed that they could carry heavier loads of merchandise for longer distances than men who were notorious for desertion" (Obichere 1978:7). Not only were women in this case considered physically superior to men, but they were also assumed to be more docile. Hence there were no reasons why women would not have been in demand for the "manly" tasks.

In fact, the demand for female slaves was so strong that slave hunters often neglected men or massacred them on the battlefield.[11] The price of men on the African market was generally distinctly lower than that of women. But this situation seems to have evolved with the transformations of the slave economy within Africa. To better understand the choice of men or women and its evolution, we must scrutinize the demand for labor in the different societies with which we are confronted. We will distinguish between self-sustaining domestic societies, merchant societies, and aristocratic societies.

Self-Sustaining Domestic Societies

In the absence of a commercial network which would provide a continual supply of slaves and an outlet for the products of their labor, the domestic community generally enslaved only wandering victims of war or famine, asocial individuals driven from their communities, or sometimes prisoners taken in local wars and held for ransom or exchange.

In patrilineal societies, the integration of men was difficult because they found themselves immediately in competition with other men for access to women. They were as likely to be sacrificed as to be used or integrated.[12] Women and children were more likely to escape death. Female prisoners were assigned to the same tasks as were performed by free women, to assist them or do work in their place. They were thus integrated as servants, as wives, or as both. They could also perform masculine tasks

11. This was particularly true after the decline of the European slave trade, which involved mostly male slaves.

12. It is different in matrilineal societies, where the insertion of men in the kinship network seems to pose fewer domestic problems.

from which free women were normally exempt (as, for instance, the cultivation of millet in savanna societies). In societies that had not developed activities capable of producing a surplus product to be sold, the use of slaves was of limited interest. The renunciation of agricultural tasks by men and by free women may have clashed with ethical considerations. Among the Bamana, for example, no activity was more noble than agriculture, and the wellborn male could not imagine giving it up. The presence of individuals without kin ties and thus desocialized sometimes presented drawbacks rather than advantages. Keim shows the problems raised by marriage with a slave woman in such a society (below, p. 147). When there was integration, it took place within the framework of prevalent social relationships, that is to say, kinship. The female captive was thus sometimes destined to become a concubine, that is, a low-ranked wife, poorly protected because she lacked family ties, but nevertheless integrated into the community. Her children were legally "sons" and "daughters," whose social condition was weak because they lacked a maternal lineage, but who were cognates nevertheless.

Merchant Societies

The situation of a domestic community changes when it comes into contact with an external market capable both of supplying it with slaves and of absorbing the merchandise they produce. Such is, incidentally, one of the requirements for the formation of a productive class of slaves. The case of Gumbu is an example of this (Meillassoux 1971 and 1975b). Situated on the edge of the Sahara, this Soninke town was populated by families with a rustic and military tradition. It had been part of sahelo-saharan trade networks for the previous two or three centuries, but slavery seems to have expanded during the wars of Al Hadj Umar and Samory at the end of the last century. At the time of colonization (1902), slaves were about 50 percent of the population. More than 80 percent of the free families owned slaves; some families had several hundreds, for the most part purchased. According to a 1904 census, female slaves outnumbered males. Slaves fulfilled two major economic functions: they provided all or part of their masters' needs for agricultural products, and they produced merchandise sold through Saharan trade networks, especially millet and strips of cotton cloth. In addition to working as servants, female slaves cultivated millet (which was not traditionally done by the free Soninke woman), as well as cotton and indigo. They carded and spun the cotton. Thus, in the division of tasks, there was a partial substitution of women for men in agriculture, which increased the demand for women and resulted in a sex ratio among workers different from that in free society. The demand for women was still stronger, as M. Klein notes, in textile production (below,

p. 85). At Gumbu it took eight times as many slaves to spin than to weave the same amount of thread. Since weaving was done by male slaves among the Soninke, it would have been necessary to have eight female spinners to keep one male weaver busy full time. Although this situation was due to an allocation of tasks inherited from domestic society (not the most efficient organization of work), and although the ratio 8:1 was never reached, the demand for female slaves was certainly affected. The price for slave women was always higher than that for men. Again, the natural reproduction of slaves did not explain this demand for women, since the census of 1904 counted only one or two children for every three slave women.

In merchant communities like Mombasa or those described by Harms in the Middle Zaire, inhabited by a class of traders whose transactions were with distant markets, other economic and social factors influenced the sex ratio of slaves. The needs of this itinerant merchant class created a demand for cooked meals for those about to leave on expeditions and for traders passing through. The sale of cooked food led to that of ingredients and utensils, and thus to a development of vegetable gardening and pottery, which were female activities. Female labor remained particularly important for the preparation of food. This increased the domestic work load. It also led to the growth of a trade in prepared food run by free women or sometimes even by female slaves employing other female slaves. Above all, urbanization contributed to an increasing differentiation between an urban population, which no longer produced its own subsistence and depended increasingly on the market for its food, and a rural sector to supply it. We can assume that women were employed in growing manioc and in gardening, both traditionally feminine activities. According to M. Wright (below, p. 253), women "formed the backbone of the agricultural labor force which was augmented during the critical periods of the agricultural cycle by teams of men." In the cities of the Middle Zaire, women were indeed more numerous than men. But here Harms reports that there was scarcely any difference in the price. The principle which regulated the purchase of slaves was: "Don't buy men, don't buy women, just buy people" (below, p. 99).

If there was no a priori preference for one sex over the other, it was because slaves were sought as *asexual agents of work*. The procreative potential of women did not figure in the determination of their value. If, in spite of this, women still were more numerous, it was because the sexual allocation of tasks was still in favor of women. But the equivalence of price indicates a possibility of substituting men for women. Harms tells us nothing about the sexual composition of servile agricultural populations. Although cassava was grown by women in domestic societies, we can conceive, in the merchant societies, of a form of exploitation in which

agricultural labor would be performed by slaves of both sexes living together. This would tend to equalize the sex ratio. At Mombasa, Strobel
indicates that men participated more in the production of commodities:
food by agriculture, meat and ivory by hunting, and slaves by raiding. It
is perhaps thus that male slaves came to acquire a value equal to that of
the female, by a change of their activities and of the sexual distribution of
labor.

Data provided by Cooper for the east coast of Africa describe such a
transformation (Cooper 1977). Here, information indicates an average sex
ratio of fifty-two men for fifty-two women. Still, the cities had more male
than female slaves, while the latter were more numerous in some rural
areas. Since the ratio of urban slaves to rural slaves was between 1:10 and
1:15 (Cooper 1977:182, n. 130), that cannot be the only reason for the
reestablishment of an equilibrium. Cooper also reported that among slaves
purchased between 1874 and 1888, 52 percent of the adults and 61 percent
of the children were male. One can thus hypothesize a high enough number of male slaves on the plantations of some rural regions to counter-
balance the high proportion of women in other regions. Unfortunately, the
data are not available to support this hypothesis. In any case, this change
in the sex ratio of slaves indicates either new uses for male slaves or the
substitution of men for women in ancillary or agricultural tasks hitherto
assigned to female slaves. What is suggested here is that through the plantation system, the social division of labor tended to overcome the sexual
allocation of tasks. From that time, the organization of labor no longer
imposed the social choice of one sex over the other. With men selling at a
lower price, male slavery tended to increase. The system came to re-
semble that of the West Indies and America, probably for the same economic reasons and still in conformity with the laws of slave reproduction.

Aristocratic Societies

If merchant slavery tended little by little to erase female functions[13] in
favor of functions of production, in dynastic societies the female slave
kept a specific value for being a woman. Her capacity for work was combined with her use both as a neutral political vector and as a means of
social domination.

The demand for women as workers, though not easily measured, remained high in dynastic systems where a slave plantation economy operated to provide the court, the army, and the aristocratic families with food
products. Reports of such a system exist for seventeenth-century Songhay,

---

13. With the exception of a small percentage bought for their physical attractiveness or
as concubines, and whose price remained high.

eighteenth-century Dahomey, the nineteenth-century Bamum kingdom, and the nineteenth-century Sokoto caliphate. In the first two cases, we lack precise information on the dominant relations of production and thus on the use of women. We are better informed on the Bamum of Cameroon and on Sokoto thanks to the works of Tardits (1980), Hogendorn (1977), and Lovejoy (1978).

The ruling class of Bamum lived in the head town, but they possessed domains in the country which were worked by settlers, slaves, and descendants of slaves of mixed ethnic origins. The latter could be identified as slaves to the extent that they could be sold at the will of the master. They could also be seen as serfs because they had their own plots and were attached to the land which was sold with them on it.[14]

The slave was allotted a piece of land whose product provided his subsistence even during the time when he was working his master's land. Men, women, and children worked together on the master's land under the direction of an overseer of slave origin until completion of the cropping labor—and not for fixed periods. Women were responsible for weeding, cleaning, and harvesting both the private plots and the master's land, as well as for the arduous weekly task of carrying the domain's product to the master's residence in the head town. Going to and from the head town sometimes took the whole week. The portion of the agricultural work done by women in this non-trading agricultural economy seems to have been considerable, though we do not know how the woman's share compared to the man's.

The Sokoto caliphate provides an example of an aristocratic society within which a merchant economy developed and where some plantations were, as in Bamum, devoted to supplying the ruling class and others to providing commodities for export. The former were owned by nobles employing slaves by the thousands, the latter by merchants, each possessing from 100 to 500 slaves. Hogendorn (1977) describes two caliphate villages. Within them, each slave worked on his or her own plot and the master's field. If the master was a noble, his slaves produced food crops; if a merchant, cotton and tobacco. They cultivated the master's land at predetermined times of the day and during certain parts of the year. They worked in teams of twenty-five persons of both sexes and under the control of an overseer of slave origin. Although the male-female ratio is not indicated, Hogendorn tells us that women were freed from some tasks to devote themselves to others, which they performed under a female slave overseer, an assistant to the male overseer, who had the right to dispense rewards and punishments. Women prepared the food provided at noon by the master for the workers. Lovejoy indicates that in the northern part of

14. The servile class represented two-thirds of the population of the kingdom.

the caliphate, the textile industry employed "countless women who spun and carded raw cotton" (Lovejoy 1978:356). As a matter of principle the master had to provide a mate for each of his slaves, but this obligation, if followed, does not seem to have had a great effect on fertility, since only 40 percent of the slaves were born in slavery.

The use of plantations to feed the court was not unknown in Dahomey. According to Le Hérissé (1911:90), "The greater part of the king's slaves . . . were parked on cultivated lands" by the thousands to feed the palace and the army. These slaves were working on the king's field while waiting to be exported. Some slaves were also captured, according to some informants, to "repopulate the kingdom." Again this could only be a limited demographic enterprise, because the exploitation of slaves was reserved to the royal family, to certain aristocrats, and to high officials of the kingdom. Dahomey does not seem to have known generalized slavery, that is, use of slaves by all the free classes of the society as in the merchant communities. As a result, the domestic demand for household slaves was limited, since it was the needs of the court and of the dominant clans which prevailed.

The role of Dahomey in international trade was to supply slaves for export. Political, social, and economic organization, and thus Dahomean slavery, developed around this function. Dahomey was primarily a warrior state dominated by a military aristocracy and supported by a powerful army. The dominant class was organized on the basis of a slave economy and a slave administration, both supports of the military strength which imposed itself on the Dahomean populace and on the foreign people raided for slaves. The instruments of this inner and outer domination were the army, the palace, and the plantations. Within these three institutions, both executives and laborers were essentially recruited from slaves, and it was within the palace that women played the major role.

The palace, the seat of power, was marked by classical contradictions at this stage of dynastic development. Since aristocratic power evolved out of the domestic society and was directed towards domestic communities, kingship tended to express itself in terms of domestic ideology. The king was the "father" of his subjects. The people owed tribute to the king as the junior members of the community owed labor to the elders. The country was governed by one "family" among others. What was valid for the lineage went for the kingdom.

But in practice the exercise of power and of class domination did not follow the strict rules of domestic society. Keeping the dynastic power within a single aristocratic line reduces *social* kinship to *genetic* kinship. Collateral succession opens bloody quarrels between brothers and cousins. Royal polygyny dilutes the notions of eldership and filiation into arbitrary rules of succession. In contrast to what takes place in domestic societies, the fact of belonging to an aristocratic or to a royal family creates a rivalry between relatives and not solidarity. A brother, a son, or even a wife becomes a potential or active foe. In order to protect himself from their eagerness to succeed, the king had to keep them away from the levers of power and thus govern without if not against them. In denying family collegiality, the king was driven to surround himself with dynastically *neutral* councillors, people unable, because of their status, to claim the throne or to present themselves as potential successors.

In a system of masculine filiation, slaves (especially eunuchs) and women have the virtue of being "neutral" in terms of dynastic succession, hence safe for the sovereign. But in surrounding himself with "non-kin," the king exposed himself to another threat. His private council, which should have stood around him as a protection, became a wall isolating him from his family, from his class, and from the people. Behind the mask of a king who was increasingly paralyzed by rituals imposed by this entourage, bundled up in stiff ceremonial garb, and encumbered with heavy regalia, the courtly bureaucracy reigned. It selected the information the king received, chose the people he met, and channeled the sovereign into symbolic or ceremonial activities. The actual exercise of power shifted toward the council. The king only sporadically succeeded in recovering part of that power by imposing his royal image or by manipulating the instruments of matrimonial control which were left to him. This body of courtesans, sometimes of servile origin and/or female, would not use kinship as a means of recruitment for fear of falling itself into the dynastic contradictions which paralyzed the king and to which they owed their existence. It thus used co-optation to recruit other individuals who were, like themselves, socially "neutral," i.e., other slaves, other eunuchs, and other women. In such a context, to be both a slave and a woman was to be doubly set aside from any dynastic claims. Hence this double incapacity became a double virtue, which explained the appearance of female power at the royal court of Dahomey (Bay, this volume). Women of the palace were counterparts of masculine agents acting for the king in the country. The administration of the kingdom was controlled from inside the palace by neutral agents without exposing the government to the pressure of the royal family, which was as dangerous for the king as for his entourage. But the women who exercised these administrative functions did not stand as representatives of women in general and did not owe their positions to any kind of female emancipation. Even if they appeared emancipated as slaves, they remained alienated as women.

Thus, at the court, the demand for slaves in general and for female slaves in particular remained high. Bay helps us to understand how "harems," often thought to exist only for the pleasure of the kings, could have a political function. At the Dahomean court there were few activities to which women were not assigned. Their responsibilities went from household tasks, pottery, and clothing all the way to spying and warfare. Some were the concubines of the king, and their role was indeed to provide entertainment, pleasure, and children.[15] But because of their status, these slave women even when emancipated generated a "social species" of half-breed, parallel to that of the kin and capable of rivaling them, but more docile. Among this "species" could be safely recruited the queen "mother" of the sovereign, his spouses, and his heirs. A fictitious kinship was re-created between them and the king, which allowed co-optation or choice to prevail over birth.

Besides being used as agents of political and administrative power, palace women could also be used as matrimonial instruments of social control. This was one of the ways the court assured the loyalty of those who served it and who could threaten it by turning their delegated power against their king. The confiscation of female captives by the king and the use of such institutions as convents for unmarried girls—many of them slaves— limited the availability of nubile women and gave greater efficiency to the royal policy of social reproduction. The harems and the convents were the pools from which the court gave wives to men who served it and who could not, because of their status or the scarcity of women, have access to a wife by their own means. The number of these women may have been very high. At the court of the Bamum king "there were hundreds who benefitted from the gift of women, which implies a right of disposal over several thousand women" (Tardits 1970). Such arrangements, for instance, provided wives and offspring to the royal servants and to the military guard. The system operated usually on a self-regenerating basis, with the firstborn from such unions returning to the sovereign. If the firstborn was a boy, he was trained to become a servant or a guard, thus guaranteeing the reproduction of this body. If it was a girl, she was destined to mate within the body of servants or guards (Tardits 1970; Keim, this volume).

In addition to this institutional method of perpetuating the dependence of a social group, the sovereign or the court could also give away female slaves as a reward to those who pleased it. Thus, "Glélé distributed women to Agouli's men who built the palace of Jegbe" (Glélé 1974:161).

This system of distributing wives and their offspring was even more widespread than the use of palace women such as that described by Bay at the Dahomean court. The distribution of wives by the king was assimi-

15. This type of concubine was the object of a specialized trade in the Near East up to the beginning of the century. Girls caught in their early youth were educated, trained carefully, and conditioned psychologically to the role by skilled slave traders who followed them up during their entire "careers." See Kouloub (1958) and Toledano (1981), who also describe the alienation of these women.

lated to the way elders married their dependents in domestic society. It was as "wives" that these slave women were exploited.[16] Thus, in contrast to merchant society, there was at the level of the court a policy of reproduction which preserved some characteristics of the slave as a woman, but as an alienated woman. But beyond this function, it was as slaves and not as women that they surrounded and protected the king, as warriors that they were defeminized into Amazons, and as hands that they worked the plantations.

In slave society, the slave class was mainly reproduced by taking captives from other societies. The "procreative" function was assumed by the warrior or the merchant. With arms or money, they "begot" the human beings needed to reconstitute the exploited class. They even outdid women in controlling the composition of this class by sex and age and in accelerating the rate of demographic reproduction. Accordingly, the reproductive role of the slave woman lost its importance. She was more and more remote from the role of mother.

Already in domestic society, this role was subordinated to that of spouse. The husband or the brother arrogated the filiation of her progeny, and by virtue of this right he oriented the social reproduction under male domination. Nevertheless, the woman remained the essential and sole instrument of the production of human beings to make up the kinship unit. The future of the community depended on her fertility. As a result, even though she did not enjoy legal maternal filiation, she was appraised and valued as a mother, honored and even worshipped as such in regard to the community's expectations.

In slavery, femininity loses its sacredness. The data and descriptions we have analyzed show that the slave was a "non-kin" and that a woman of this status could not be a "mother." She was not recruited for procreation, but to work at female tasks or to be an instrument of social or political manipulation. If she was mated to a fellow slave, she was not married. Should she beget, she was reduced to the role of a breeder: her offspring belonged to her master and could be taken from her at any time. When she grew old, she had no claim or legal authority over her children by which she could expect to be taken care of. On the contrary, the case described by D. Rey-Hulman (1975:319) shows that sorcery accusations could be used to send aging female slaves back to hard labor. The cases of the master's concubines and of women used as matrimonial pawns cannot be considered as standards of female slavery. Even there, the "married" condition of slaves was tied to an alienation unknown in domestic

16. This is not, as in domestic society, an exchange of a wife for a wife. Between classes, matrimonial relations are predominantly hypergamous.

society, inasmuch as without the protection of her lineage the slave wife or concubine was under the single and unchecked authority of her husband's family. Her children entered into a class to which she did not belong and where they depended on the master who disposed of them at his will. If she was promoted to important administrative functions, it was not because of her active femininity but because of the social neutrality which was conferred by slavery. Her alienation as woman was joined to class alienation. The depersonalization and the desocialization which were the fate of slaves in general go along here with a joint process of desexualization.

Retel-Laurentin reports that among the Nzakara, a very young slave girl had eaten on the sly a few pieces of meat (a delicacy forbidden to this kind of being). Her mistress ordered that her hand be cut off. Being a female and a child did not absolve her from the taint of slavery, nor protect her from class repression coming from another woman.

Paris, February 1, 1981

Published Sources

Cooper, F. 1977. *Plantation Slavery on the East Coast of Africa.* New Haven.

Curtin, P. D. 1969. *The Atlantic Slave Trade: A Census.* Madison, Wis.

Engerman, S. L. 1981. "L'esclavage aux Etats Unis et aux Antilles anglaises: quelques comparaisons économiques et démographiques." In *Esclave = facteur de production,* ed. S. Mintz. Dunod.

Fage, J. D. 1980. "Slave and Society in Western Africa, c. 1455–c. 1700." *Journal of African History* 21:289–310.

Glélé, M. A. 1974. *Le Danxome.* Paris.

Gutman, H. 1981. "Familles et groupes de parenté chez les Afro-americains en esclavage dans les plantations de Good Hope (Caroline du Sud), 1760–1860." In *Esclave = facteur de production,* ed. S. Mintz. Dunod.

Hogendorn, J. S. 1977. "The Economics of Slave Use on Two 'Plantations' in the Zaria Emirate of the Sokoto Caliphate." *International Journal of African Historical Studies* 10:369–83.

Kouloub, Out el. 1958. *Ramza.* Paris.

Le Hérissé, A. 1911. *L'ancien royaume du Dahomey.* Paris.

Lovejoy, P. 1978. "Plantations in the Economy of the Sokoto Caliphate." *Journal of African History* 19:341–68.

Martin, Gaston. 1948. *Histoire de l'esclavage dans les colonies Françaises.* Paris.

Meillassoux, Claude. 1971. "Le commerce pré-colonial et le développement de l'esclavage à Gumbu du Sahel (Mali)." In *The Development of Trade and Markets in West Africa,* ed. C. Meillassoux. London.

Meillassoux, C. ed. 1975a. *L'esclavage en Afrique précoloniale.* Paris.

Meillassoux, C. 1975b. "État et conditions des esclaves à Gumbu (Mali) au XIXe siècle." In *L'esclavage en Afrique précoloniale,* ed. C. Meillassoux. Paris.

Meillassoux, C. 1979. "Historical Modalities of the Exploitation and Over-Exploitation of Labour." *Critique of Anthropology* 13:7–16.

Meillassoux, C. 1980. "Correspondance." *Economy and Society* 7:321–31.

Meillassoux, C. 1981. *Maidens, Meal and Money.* Cambridge.

Mintz, S. W., ed. 1981. *Esclave = facteur de production. L'economie politique de l'esclavage.* Paris.

Obichere, B. I. 1978. "Women and Slavery in the Kingdom of Dahomey." *Revue francaise d'histoire d'outre-mer* 65.

Retel-Laurentin, A. 1960. "Nzakara Women." In *Women of Tropical Africa,* ed. D. Paulme. Translated by H. M. Wright. Berkeley and Los Angeles.

Rey-Hulman, D. 1975. "Les dépendants des maîtres tyokossi pendant la période pré-coloniale." In *L'esclavage en Afrique précoloniale,* ed. C. Meillassoux. Paris.

Tardits, C. 1970. "Femmes à crédit." In *Echanges et communications: Mélanges offerts à C. Levi-Strauss.* Paris.

Tardits, C. 1980. *Le Royaume Bamoum.* Paris.

Toledano, E. R. 1981. "Slave Dealers, Women, Pregnancy and Abortion: The Story of a Circassian Slave Girl in Mid-Nineteenth Century Cairo." *Slavery and Abolition* 2:53–68.

5 *Martin A. Klein*

Women in Slavery in the Western Sudan[1]

A proprietor acquires male slaves in order to have servants and
workers on the land; female slaves in order to help his wives in
the work of the household and in the fields during the harvest
season.

(ANG, Kouroussa)

The introduction to this volume stressed two known aspects of female
slavery in Africa: female slaves were more numerous than male slaves,
and a higher price was paid for them. The preference for women has been
explained by their greater ease of assimilation[2] and by their role in reproduction.[3] In his chapter, Claude Meillassoux has taken issue with the reproduction argument and put forward instead the argument that the greater
value placed on female slaves was rooted in their capacity for work. This
chapter will assess Meillassoux's argument and describe the situation of
women in slavery in the western Sudan.

The western Sudan is an area dominated by Mande- and Fulbe-speaking
peoples, which includes Senegal, most of Mali, upper Guinea, Upper Volta,
and the northern Ivory Coast. It was a fairly homogeneous area, criss-
crossed by trade routes, marked by similar social structures, and dominated by Islam. It was also an area where slavery had existed since early

1. I would like to thank Paul Lovejoy, Richard Roberts, Patrick Manning, Frederick
Cooper, Joseph Miller, and Joel Gregory for their comments on earlier drafts of this chapter.
The research was supported by the Social Science Research Council (U.S.) and the Social
Science and Humanities Research Council of Canada.

2. Baldé 1975. Meillassoux recognizes (see above, pp. 56–57) that within patrilineal
societies, women were more easily assimilated than men.

3. Miers and Kopytoff speak of "a marked preference for the more pliable children and
for women as reproducers of children, rather than for men." Miers and Kopytoff 1975:162.

Table 5.1
Estimates of Slave Population (1894)

Area	Men	Women	Children
Bougouni	329	197	84
Djenné	6,000	7,000	2,000
Kankan	50%	33.5%	16.5%
Medina	197	433	56
Nioro	25%	40%	35%
Segou		Women outnumber men 4½:1	
Siguiri	2,495	2,357	2,604
Sokolo		Women outnumber men	
Timbuctu		Women outnumber men 2:1	

SOURCE: A.N.S., K 14.

medieval times, if not earlier (Meillassoux 1976; Levtzion 1973). Two types of slave system recurred across this zone. The first was characterized by a *household mode of production*. Slaves made up a small percentage of the population, lived within the household, worked alongside free members of the household, and participated in a network of face-to-face links. This system provided for the gradual integration of the slave's offspring into the kinship system as junior branches of the dominant lineage. The second system, which clearly evolved from the first, was marked by a high slave population. Slaves lived in separate settlements, and their labor was the source of sustenance for a ruling class that did not engage in physical labor and lived off the surplus produced by the slaves (Klein and Lovejoy 1978; Lovejoy 1979). I refer to this as a *slave mode of production*, not in an effort to impose a preconceived evolutionary scheme, but simply because slave labor was the major source of both sustenance and surplus.[4]

Demography

The estimates made by French administrators in 1894 and 1904 (see tables 5.1 and 5.2) would suggest that about 60 percent of all adult slaves were female at the time of conquest.[5] To be sure, these data are suspect,

4. My use of the phrase "slave mode of production" differs from that of Meillassoux, who would apply it only to those enslaved during their lifetime. The structural position and the mode of surplus extraction sometimes differed between first- and second-generation slaves, but both were involved in the same relations of production. (Meillassoux 1979.)

5. These two inquiries are a major source of the data for this paper. See A.N.S., K 14 and K 18–22. The responses differ radically in quality, but they provide the most complete source of information on Sudanic slavery at the time of conquest. The statistical data should, in particular, be treated with caution. Most are only estimates. Many administrators refused even to try to guess ratios. Only rarely did an administrator actually try to count. Only one

Table 5.2
Estimates of Slave Population (1904)

Area	Men	Women	Children
Bafoulabé	4,825	6,540	3,455
Bandiagara	2,356	3,161	1,108
Bougouni	1,700	1,640	1,186
Buriya	2,000	2,500	3,500
Diebougou		Women in the majority	
Dinguiraye	3,114	4,388	3,415
Djenné	3,961	7,981	4,039
Dori	15,300	24,565	
Dounzou	3,000	3,800	1,200
Gao		Women and children are 2/3 of slaves (about 8,000)	
Goumbou		Women and children outnumber men 3:1 (18,000 to 6,000)	
Kadé	5,000	6,000	2,000
Kaedi	10,000	8,000	18,000
Kolen	1,250	1,750	2,000
Kouroussa	3,600	4,200	3,200
Koury		Women outnumber men 2:1	
Koutiala	4,050	4,020	1,630
Lobi	2,000	4,000	2,000
Louga	2,696	3,629	2,615
Maasi	1,200	1,800	2,000
Matam	3,831	6,161	10,008
Medina Kouta	5,389	5,437	2,276
Mediné	125	400	125
Podor	6,234	10,166	2,209
Raz el Ma	440	500	600
Satadougou	545	380	575
Ségou	9,172	8,805	7,184
Siguiri	4,097	3,480	4,410
Sokolo	6,152	4,002	3,198
Sumpi	2,036	2,131	1,918
Tenkodogo	2,000	4,000	9,000
Timbi-Medina	1,300	4,000	2,200
Timbi-Tunni	1,500	1,100	1,400
Tivouane	2,951	4,236	4,447
Touba	2,400	2,720	2,880
Yatenga	2,573	2,436	1,994

SOURCES: A.N.S., K 18–20; A.N.S.O.M., Guinee XIV 3; Balde 1975:197.

---

administrator, J. C. Brevié, seems actually to have talked to slaves. His study of Bamako indicated a radical discrepancy between the numbers reported by the masters and the numbers reported by slave informants. A.N.S., K 19. If Brevié was right, the total figures represent a radical underestimate. The data in table 5.3 are, in contrast, based on actual censuses. Though not completely reliable, they are more dependable. Interestingly, they give ratios similar to those reported in tables 5.1 and 5.2.

Table 5.3
Assorted Census Data on Slave Populations

Cercle	Date	Men	Women	Children
Bandiagara[a] (Fulbe)	1911	205	217	169
Bamako[b] (2 cantons)	n.d.	165	288	286
Bamako (Malinke cantons)	n.d.	92	149	181
Banako (Beledugu)[c]	1900	682	783	55
Kerouane[d]	1894	73	68	83
Alkina	1894	95	158	158
Mediné[e]	1898	217	624	213
Djenné[f]	1911	490	491	384

[a]A.N.M., 1 D 35.
[b]A.N.M., 1 E 19.
[c]A.N.M., 5 D 20.
[d]A.N.M., 5 D 46.
[e]A.N.M., Mediné: 1 E 60.
[f]A.N.M., 5 D 24.

but I am inclined to think that, if anything, they minimize the number of women. I find it difficult to explain the few districts that report a majority of men. Certainly, women made up a considerable majority of the adults enslaved during any period.[6] As warriors, the men were likely to resist and be killed.[7] In addition, male prisoners were often killed and were more likely to be sold off. Almost two-thirds of those shipped across the Atlantic were male.[8]

The ratio is even more dramatic for Senegambia, which got most of its slaves from the heart of the western Sudan. The ratio of men to women in exports from the Gambia River approached 8:1 or 9:1 during selected periods, and a sample from the Senegal River was over 4:1 (Curtin 1975). These statistics would suggest that vast numbers of women and children

6. It is difficult to explain those few cercles that reported more men than women. It is also difficult to explain differences between 1894 and 1904. In Djenné, the number of men reported declined and the number of women increased. Ségou reports just the opposite change in ratio. Richard Roberts (1978) shares my skepticism about the Ségou data. If the model suggested by Meillassoux and myself is correct, there should be a tendency for the percentage of children to decline in stable slave populations and for the male-female ratio to move towards parity but never reach it until recruitment is ended. The degree of female predominance suggests a high rate of enslavement.

7. Raids often took place in early morning hours. The raiders would surround a village and then attack at daybreak as women were starting to prepare the first meal. Accounts suggest that the men often resisted while women and children sought refuge. See, for example, Villeneuve 1814, 4:35–37.

8. H. Klein 1978. The trans-Saharan trade involved mostly women, but its numbers during the peak period were significantly smaller than those for Atlantic exports. Furthermore, the trans-Saharan trade was more significant from Timbuctu east. Austen 1979.

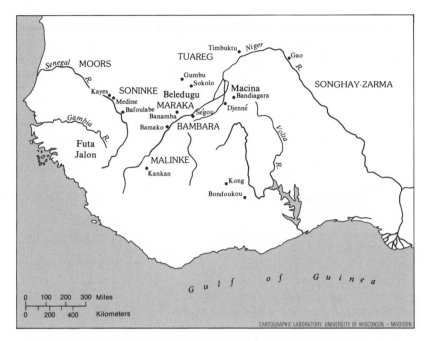

Map 5.1. Precolonial West Africa

were absorbed as slaves within the Sudan even during the period of the Atlantic slave trade. We can best illustrate this by drawing a model. Let us assume that two-thirds of those old enough to interest European slave traders were female, that 90 percent of the men were exported, and that the ratio of males to females among the exports was 2:1. All are reasonable assumptions. If they are correct, then 45 percent of those in prime ages were exported and 55 percent were kept within Africa. Furthermore, those kept within Africa were almost 95 percent female. Even if we alter our assumptions or feed into them the trans-Saharan trade, we end up with two clear conclusions: first, that a high percentage of those enslaved during the period of the Atlantic slave trade were kept within Africa; and second, that this number consisted almost exclusively of women and children (Manning 1981). We can infer from this that the major concern of African slave systems during the centuries up to the closing of the Atlantic trade was the integration of women and children, and that this explains the killing of male prisoners.

Herbert Klein has argued above that the predominance of male exports was in the absence of any strong preference for men in the Atlantic trade. European planters in the New World were willing to pay almost as much for a strong woman as for a man. Except for certain skilled tasks, men and women did the same work on American plantations. In the Americas as in Africa, women were disproportionately represented in field labor. Klein makes a similar suggestion to explain the relatively small number of children in the Atlantic trade (H. Klein 1978:242–43). They too were desired in Africa, at least in part because they were more easily assimilated than grown men (Baldé 1975).

Oral sources also indicate a clear preference for women and children. In fact, with the decline of the Atlantic slave trade, the killing of male prisoners seems to have increased. Roberts reports that Umarian armies often killed male prisoners (Roberts 1978:286). Ma Ba's forces also did so (Klein 1968:73–74; Gray 1940:419). So too did Samori's army on occasion, especially when resistance or revolt was involved (Person 1968, 2:967–69, 1009; Rey-Hulman 1975:308). The killing of male prisoners probably declined as commodity production increased and the price differential between male and female captives dropped, but it did continue (Person 1975, 3:1885), though the number of men traded undoubtedly increased. Slave caravans continued to show a higher percentage of women, as table 5.4 makes clear. In 1894, under a civilian governor determined to end the slave trade, 604 slaves were freed—125 men, 231 women, and 248 children. This number includes some runaways, but mostly slaves freed when their caravans were interrupted (A.N.S.O.M., 1894). Toward the end of the century, when the trade became illegal, it focused largely on children, with a small number of women. Men virtually ceased to be traded.[9]

Price data confirm the greater value placed on women (see table 5.5). Around 1690, Jakhanke slave traders paid twice for women and boys what they paid for men, though the price on the coast was nearly the same (Curtin 1975:176). Over a century later, Mungo Park reported a similar 2:1 ratio between female and male prices (Park 1815:278). This was gradually reduced towards the end of the century, but prices of women remained higher until the very end and wherever reported. Thus, it would seem that women generally cost up to a third more.

In opposition to the notion that female slaves were valued primarily for their childbearing potential, Meillassoux argues that they were sought primarily for their work potential, and in particular because of the wider range of tasks that could be allocated to them. Meillassoux is not alone in this. Roberts argues that among the Maraka both male and female slaves

---

9. The major sources of slaves had been closed off by 1898 when Samori was captured, though some slaves were coming from desert-side areas and from what is now Upper Volta. Presumably, children were enslaved in an approximately equal male-female ratio. Thus, with time, some women were absorbed into the mass of the free, and those born within the society divided almost equally between men and women.

Table 5.4
Some Slave Caravans

Cercle	Date(s)	Men	Women	Children
Bamako[a]	October 1886 to April 1887	404	570	—
Djenné[b]	November to December 1893	26	136	—
Kayes[c]	1894	1	0	5
	1 caravan, January 1899	20	41	41
Mediné[d]	1894	1	5	3
	February 1, 1895	7	32	32
Bandiagara[e]	April 1895	7	23	32
St. Louis[f]	1894		7	7
Ségou[g]	1895	7	23	32

[a]A.N.M., 1 E 18.
[b]A.N.M., 1 E 29.
[c]A.N.M., 1 E 44 (1899), 1 E 173 (1894).
[d]A.N.M., 1 E 56 (1895), 1 E 174 (1894).
[e]A.N.M., 1 E 56.
[f]A.N.S., K 13.
[g]A.N.M., 1 E 56.

"were valued above all for their role as commodity producers" (Roberts 1978:294). I concur with this argument. The incorporation of a slave into a community was based on an act of sale. The trade would not have persisted if there were not people willing to pay the price. The use of slave labor would not have expanded as much as it did had there not been enough of a return to finance the purchase of new slaves. I do not think, however, that the wider range of tasks allocated to women adequately explains the price differential.

Meillassoux's argument is reinforced by a second argument, that slaves did not reproduce themselves. Data from his own research at Gumbu are reinforced by data from other areas. His assumption is that if the masters had been concerned with reproduction, they would have more actively encouraged it. This argument is sound. Statistical evidence on the percentage of children is less clear than it is for women. There are two reasons for this. First, there was not always a clear definition of "child."[10] Second, the slave trade involved large numbers of children, and in its

10. Children under eight were not taxed. As a result, this came to be the definition of "child." During the early years, however, census and tax collection methods were very crude. In most cases, it is not clear how the administrator in question was defining "child," but the term was probably used for anyone not sexually mature.

Table 5.5
Prices of Male and Female Slaves

Date	Area	Slave Description	Price
1690	Near Nioro	Male	1 ounce of gold
		Female	2 ounces of gold[a]
1805	Middle Niger Valley	Man	40,000 cowries
		Woman	80,000–100,000 cowries
		Boy	40,000 cowries[b]
1894	Bissandougou	Healthy male	150 francs
		Nubile woman	200–300 francs
	Bougouni	Man	80 francs
			200 francs
		Boy	120–150 francs
		Girl	150–175 francs
	Kankan	Man	200 francs
		Boy or girl	250 francs
	Kissi	Ordinary slave	200 francs
		Young girl	250 francs
	Kouroussa	Man	200 francs
		Woman	250 francs
		Boy	125–175 francs
		Girl	125–150 francs
		Children	45–50 francs
	Nioro	Man, 20–40 years old	180 francs or 18 pieces of guinea
		Adult woman	200 francs or 20 pieces of guinea
		Children	10–15 pieces of guinea depending on age
	Sokolo	Male	150 francs
		Female	200 francs
	Médine	Healthy female	250–300 francs
	Ségou	Male	150 francs
		Female	200 francs[c]

[a]Curtin 1975, 1:176.
[b]Park 1815:278.
[c]A.N.S., K 14.

Table 5.5
(cont'd)

Date	Area	Slave Description	Price
Before conquest	Yatenga	Male	40,000 cowries
		Female	40,000–60,000 cowries
		Young man	50,000 cowries
		Young girl	80,000 cowries[d]
At conquest	Macina	Male	100,000–200,000 cowries
		Female	Up to 400,000 cowries[e]
	Dyahunu	Male, 30 years old	200 francs or 20 pieces of guinea
		Female, 20 years old	30 pieces of guinea[f]
		Boy or girl	100 francs or 10 pieces of guinea
1904	Touba	Old man	1–2 cows or 50–100 francs[g]
		Adult	5 cows or 250 francs
		Child	3 cows or 150 francs
	Tenkodogo	Male	100 francs
		Female	150 francs
	Faranah	Male	150 francs
		Female	150 francs
	Sumpi (redemption)	Man	150 francs
		Woman	350–400 francs
	Bandiagara	Male	250–300 francs
		Young woman	300–400 francs
		Boy, 12 years old	200–250 francs
		Girl, 12 years old	200–300 francs[h]
	Kouroussa	Healthy male	250–300 francs
		Sickly male	150–200 francs
		Septuagenarian	100–125 francs
		Girl under 14	150–180 francs
		Woman to age 25	250–350 francs
		Woman, 25–55 years old	60–100 francs
		Old woman	30–50 francs[i]

[d]Tauxier 1917:264.
[e]Gallais 1967:129–30.
[f]Pollet and Winter 1971:239.
[g]A.N.S., K 18.
[h]A.N.M., 1 E 23.
[i]A.N.G., 2 D 185.

declining years focused almost exclusively on children. Children grow up quickly, but at the time of the 1904 census, there were still many children who had been enslaved. In spite of this, data in tables 5.1 to 5.3 would suggest that in most societies, the number of children was below replacement. Some of the data are especially striking. The figures for Djenné are particularly important because they refer largely to *rimaïbe*, a fairly stable population of second-generation Fulbe slaves, who were clearly not reproducing themselves. Equally striking was a census in Beledugu, which reported that 37 percent of the free, as opposed to only 23 percent of the slaves, were children.[11]

Meillassoux may go too far in hypothesizing a slave law of reproduction. The slave mode, as he conceives it, involves the reinvestment of surplus extracted from slaves to buy more slaves. Purchase or capture has the advantage that it is cheaper than the cost of raising a slave and it permits a more rapid rate of accumulation.[12] In this situation, slave owners were not likely to encourage reproduction at the expense of productivity; or as I shall argue below, they were likely to pass the costs of reproduction on to the slaves themselves. This situation did not prevail everywhere, but it did prevail within the area that concerns us. Slaves were cheap and easily available. With the decline of foreign markets, slave raiding increased.

Meillassoux's argument looks very persuasive, but there is a flaw. Most slaves "born in the house" were permitted after marriage to farm for themselves. A fixed sum was paid every year for each man, woman, and child. At Gumbu, this obligation was the same for male and female (Meillassoux 1975:236–37), though the woman's productivity was lower according to Meillassoux's calculations (see appendix). In other parts of the Sudan, this lower productivity was reflected in a reduced obligation. Generally, the woman paid half what her mate paid (A.N.S., K 19 Djenné, Dori, Bandiagara). This lower obligation clearly reflected the woman's domestic

11. A.N.M., 5 D 20. On the trade during the last years, see the report of Lieutenant Colonel Millard, which suggested that in 1901, caravans from the Volta River region were almost exclusively made up of children under twelve (A.N.S., 2 G 1/19). Even for earlier periods, table 5.4 may well underreport the importance of children. There are numerous references to caravans which have no statistical breakdown, but which refer to children. For example, a caravan of seventy slaves from Samori was stopped at Bafoulabé in 1887. The slaves were reported to be mostly children between the ages of four and ten (A.N.M., 1 E 168). Similarly, two years later, caravans coming north were reported as largely made up of children (A.N.M., 1 E 168; see also Gallieni 1885:317–20).

12. Curtin makes a similar but simpler argument for the Americas (Curtin 1975:165). Curtin's data also suggest that under some conditions masters might have encouraged reproduction, and that slave systems could show an increase. See Curtin 1969:92–93.

responsibilities. She had to cook and take care of children. Because of that, she produced less and paid less to the master.[13] If this was true, we are still left with the problem of explaining the higher price. Even if we introduce textile production into our analysis, it is clear that women did not produce more than men.

Slave owners faced two major problems. The first was escape. In spite of severe penalties, escape was a persistent phenomenon, which threatened the profitability of slave systems.[14] The second problem was motivating slaves to work. Here too there were substantial sanctions. The refractory slave could be sold or punished. Parallel to these sanctions were institutions designed to integrate the slave more fully into the community and motivate him or her to produce. At the heart of the problem is the contradiction underlined by David Brion Davis between the slave as chattel and the slave as person. Ideologically, the system was based on the notion that the slave was a thing, property of the master; but the slave was also a human being with will and intelligence. To function efficiently, the system had to recognize this (Davis 1966:31–35, 58–61; Lovejoy 1981). My argument is that women were valued not only because they were easier to integrate, but also because the creation of domestic units integrated and motivated male slaves.

Stages of Incorporation

To understand the position of female slaves, we must look briefly at the way in which slaves were incorporated into the society. As Curtin has suggested, slaves had no value at the point of capture because they could easily escape. It was therefore important for the slave to be moved to an area where he or she had no links (Curtin 1975:155). During this process, the slave had no social identity. He or she was a thing, who could be worked or beaten. The female slave could be exploited sexually. The slave who faltered on the trail and could no longer proceed was either ex-

13. There has been a debate within women's studies about whether the status of women is related to their role in reproductive rather than productive labor (see Strobel, below, p. 128; Fox 1980). I find the debate a bit artificial. Certain kinds of work had to be done. Food had to be grown and cooked, firewood had to be gathered, huts had to be built. Life, for those we are studying, was a harsh struggle for survival. Much of the reproductive labor was as necessary for survival as was the work in the fields.

14. Slave escapes were a major source of correspondence between African rules and the French after the abolition of slavery in 1848 (see Renault 1971). In spite of harsh conditions in the so-called "villages de liberté" and the possibility of slaves being reclaimed, there was no lack of escapees. For a typical tale, see Pietri 1885:303–27.

changed for a healthier slave or killed. Men, women, and children were treated with equal harshness. (Park 1807 and 1815; Caillié 1830; Mollien 1820; Soleillet 1887.)

At some point, the slave was purchased and introduced into a new social unit. A new name was given, and the slave underwent some kind of ceremony in which he or she pledged not to escape. Legally, however, the new slave's status remained different from that of those born into slavery. The literature usually makes some kind of distinction between the trade slave, purchased during his lifetime, and the domestic slave "born in the house" (*woloso* or rimaïbe).[15] The usual distinction is that the trade slave was more likely to be harshly treated and was subject to sale. The woloso could not be sold and was part of the domestic unit. In time of famine or other natural disasters, there was often no choice but to sell slaves—and sale was also a threat that could be used against a refractory woloso (Meillassoux 1975:227). In many cases, a domestic slave could only be sold if the other domestic slaves approved (Moore 1738:33). Both famine and debt were widespread occurrences, and the sanctions against sale were very limited. The most important of these was the attitude of the other slaves.[16]

While the woloso might be sold, the purchased slave could rapidly integrate. If purchased young, the slave might soon forget his or her earlier life. The slave was watched carefully during the first years, and if escape was tried, the slave was flogged or put in irons. Rebellious slaves often had to sleep in irons. Women were at an advantage here. Escape by them was less feared, though women did run away.[17] Furthermore, the mature female was likely to find herself someone's consort. She could become the concubine of her master or of one of his sons. Her position was always insecure because she could not turn to her own lineage for support, but it also depended to some degree on her own qualities and on the nature of the master's family. A male slave could become a trusted retainer and had a variety of privileged roles available to him.[18] A female slave was more limited in her options, but she could become wife, mother, lover, companion, or friend.

15. *Woloso* or *Woroso* is the Mande term. *Rimaïbe* is Poular.

16. The role of the slave collectivity in protecting slaves from the arbitrariness of masters is one that has not been fully explored. For an interesting example of collective action, see Roberts 1978:313. See also Monteil 1923:191.

17. There were probably more women than men in the villages de liberté, though the ratio was less than in the larger society. (A.N.S.O.M., Gov. Grodet to Minister, Soudan XIV 1; Bouche 1968.)

18. These options depended on the nature of the owning family. In a merchant family, he could become a trader or a caravan leader; in a planter's household, the head of a slave village; at court, a military leader or administrator. See Monteil 1923:178.

Slave Systems and Modes of Production

There was a significant difference between the household mode of production and the slave mode. In the former, the slave speedily became part of the family unit. The number of slaves in a given household was small. Descriptions of the household mode generally stress that the master did the same work as the slaves. Thus, one account reported that: "With the Malinke there is no visible difference between master and slave, no disdain of one for the other, no rancor, they eat the same food and work side-by-side."[19] Thus, the female slave spent much of her time on domestic labor within the household. If she were taken into the house of her master or one of his male dependents, she could become a favored spouse. If married to a slave, she and her husband had their own hut within the larger complex. Thus she lived with, worked alongside, cooked for, and even nursed free members of the household. One British administrator tells of an old female slave complaining that her master flogged her. He offered to place her in a free slave village, and she was ready to accept until approached by the master's son, whom she had nursed (P.R.O.B., Gambia 1899). As Olivier de Sardan makes clear (this volume), the milk tie could be a very important one.

Where the slave mode of production prevailed, the masters supervised, but did not work themselves. Paul Guebhard, the administrator cited above, reported that the slaves were ". . . poorly nourished, poorly treated and poorly rewarded . . . they only work as long as their masters are present to watch them, as a result of which the latter are forced to remain close to them, seated under a tree reading the Quran or chatting with friends . . ."[20] Within such a society, female slaves could be taken into the master's house, but most slave women were married to male slaves. They were worked much harder, often fed less well, and not involved in face-to-face relations with their masters, who formed a distinctly different class.

Slaves were used within these societies because they were the cheapest and often the only readily available source of additional labor (Hopkins 1973:24–25). Thus the societies that were accumulating slaves were those societies that could pay for them. A major difference between the household mode of production and the slave mode was that within the household mode, there was limited expropriation of surplus commodity production, whereas under the slave mode, expropriation and accumulation increased dramatically. The flow of slaves is perhaps the best index of

19. A.N.S., 7 G 84/1. The difference was more economic than ethnic. In some areas, Malinke were large slave exploiters. In some, they were not. The same goes for the Fulbe.

20. A.N.S., 7 G 84/1. Roberts (1978:299 and 1981:182) argues that the exchange of food for labor was "the nexus of the master-slave relationship." Brevié describes serious under-feeding among the Maraka (A.N.S., report on Bamako, K 19).

where economic growth was taking place within West Africa. The drop in prices that resulted from the end of the Atlantic trade simply facilitated this growth. Slaves went into the desert-side cities, where they produced grain and wove cotton for sale to nomads, who brought salt and cattle south. Slaves went into the coastal areas that produced commodities like peanuts and palm oil for European markets. Slave plantations developed around the Juula cities, such as Kong, Boundoukou, Bouna, Banamba, and Kankan. Each had a belt of land intensively cultivated by slave labor, as the free peasantry were pushed out to more distant and less safe areas. (Bernus 1960:253; Boutillier 1969:9–10 and 1975:268–69; Baillaud 1902: 294; Caillié 1830, 1:281). In some regions, like the Futa Jalon, political elites were important in expanding slave production, but in most regions the decisive influences were the commercial elites.[21] The expansion of the slave sector involved primarily diversification from trade into production (Lovejoy forthcoming, ch. 9).

The Price of Female Slaves

During the crucial years of the Atlantic slave trade, it is probable that relatively few adult males were absorbed into African communities as producers. The system, as it evolved, was primarily concerned with absorbing women and children. With the closing of the Atlantic trade, the number of men increased and the price gap decreased. The majority, however, remained female, and the price of women remained higher.

To understand the reason, we have to return to the demography of slavery. We must remember that we are dealing with patrilineal and polygynous societies. They had a capacity to absorb an indefinite number of women. Extra wives were desirable at all levels of the system. And they were cheap. In the Futa Jalon, the bridewealth for a female slave was a rooster, a mat, and several loads of wood.[22] But we can go further. A surplus of female slaves became essential to the functioning of the system. Let us look at three levels: the masters, the slave warriors, and the agricultural slaves.

For the masters, increase in the number of dependents was not only a source of status, but also the basis of the perpetuation and expansion of the social unit. Ruling lineages, maraboutic households, and merchant

21. In an earlier article, I linked the expansion of slave use within Africa in the nineteenth century to the development of commodity exports (Klein 1970:5–28). I would now revise this to give greater importance to the growth process within Africa, though it is probable that the ultimate stimuli for most of the nineteenth-century economic growth, and thus for the increased exploitation of slave labor, came from the growth of exports.

22. Fonds Vieillard, Cahier 92. In Siguiri, it was ten kolas, a hen, and a rooster (A.N.S., K 14). In Dyahunu, it was a bundle of firewood and a rooster (Pollet and Winter 1971:244).

families all sought increase through the accumulation of wives and concubines. The virtue of a slave wife was that she had no family. She had no brothers to support her if there was conflict. She could not divorce her spouse. And her children looked to no matrilineal kin for backing. At the same time, she was part of the cement. Rich and powerful lineages tended to be very large, numbering generally in the hundreds, and sometimes more. The existence of a large patrimony became a factor of cohesion, dissuading the restless from splitting. The largest part of that patrimony was an accumulation of slaves. The female slave also relieved the wellborn woman of the burden of domestic work.

Slave warriors represent a different case. Throughout the Sudan, they provided the bulk of the various armies, and the source of key administrative personnel. Slave chiefs were generally well remunerated. The slave warriors were not. Few rulers could afford to feed a large force of warriors: the question becomes how these warriors fed themselves. Jean Bazin reports that the Bambara *tonjon* cultivated very little (Bazin 1975:151). My informants suggested that the Wolof *tyeddo* cultivated, but they probably did little work on their fields. Wars were generally conducted during the dry season. Warriors were clearly free to work during the rainy season, but they were generally contemptuous of sustained agricultural labor. They often went on raids during the dry season and spent much time drinking. Booty is an inadequate source of sustenance. It is not regular enough. Furthermore, there were restraints on free-lance military activities. Kidnapping was frowned on, and in some societies punishable by the death penalty because it threatened the stability of the society. Raiding within the borders of a kingdom was also frowned on (Bazin 1975:146–47; Klein 1972). Warriors probably brought home some food, but it is likely that most of their sustenance came from the labor of their wives. Furthermore, on longer military campaigns, wives were brought along to cook, to carry, and to take care of the camp.

The best-documented example is the French Army, which operated much like a Sudanese army. Recruited largely from slaves, poorly funded, and undermanned, the French colonial forces also depended heavily on booty, particularly on the taking of slaves. These slaves were distributed both to auxiliaries and to tirailleurs. Furthermore, it was women who were important. Generally, the military men did not talk openly about the practice, since that could have jeopardized their enterprise, but there are numerous letters in the archives:

I am going to distribute the slaves in order to have fewer mouths to feed. Of course, I will keep a certain number for your men, who will be available to them after your campaign; you can tell them that from me in order to stimulate them a little. (A.N.S., 1891)

It is probable that these slave wives fed their husband-masters.

Let us move one step further down the social ladder. I have always been skeptical of statements that some slaves became wealthier than their masters. It was possible, but assuming it did occur, it was probably very rare, given the slaves' obligations. I have also been skeptical of frequent statements that male slaves could take more than one wife. They could, but did they? When I interviewed, one of my first questions was whether a slave could take a second wife. The answer came back with virtual unanimity from both freeborn and servile informants: the master was obligated to provide this male slave with one wife, but the slave could and often did take a second.

Patrick Manning suggests that the surplus of women was a late-nineteenth-century development (Manning 1981). If his argument is correct, the western Sudan should be divided into two zones for the period before the mid-nineteenth century. In the coastal zone, most of the exports were men, and there was a surplus of female slaves available for distribution. Polygyny was thus widespread. In the interior, a large part of the savanna exported mostly female slaves north. Here, Manning argues, male slaves predominated, and thus did not marry. This changed only after 1870. If Manning is correct, the validity of my assumptions about slave polygyny is limited in both time and place. I am inclined to think that the death rate among men meant that women were always more numerous among the slaves, but differences in ratios undoubtedly influenced the availability of female slaves for distribution as spouses and concubines. Where there was a significant surplus of slave women, spouses could obviously be provided for male slaves. This was important in the last years of the nineteenth century, because increasingly large accumulations of the newly enslaved posed a real threat to the social order.

It is clear that the importance of slave marriage was not simply the desirability of servile offspring. Marriage permitted both male and female slaves to have some form of normal social existence. It made life more satisfying and gave the slave a stake. Marriage, even in the attenuated form known by slaves, played a crucial role in integrating the slave into the dominant society, and children cemented that integration. But that does not explain the second wife. Richard Roberts's research on the Maraka provides an explanation for that. Roberts discovered that slaves were rarely interested in buying their freedom. Instead, slaves often preferred to buy their own slaves (Roberts 1978:314–16). The reason was simple. The male slave did not control his offspring.[23] His offspring belonged to his wife's

23. Meillassoux has written (1979) that "slaves are different from other members of the community in that they are rightfully deprived of offspring." Slave society was thus more atomized because slaves referred not to their kin, but to their respective masters. Meillas-

master (who was usually also his master). Often, though not always, the master claimed the child's services at circumcision or when his or her adult teeth came in, that is, at adolescence. This meant that the slave had no security. If he became old or sick and could no longer feed himself, he could not count on his children. A good master took care of his indigent slaves, but there were few sanctions to guarantee that the master did this.[24] This led to many slaves buying slaves. But let us note that the same argument is valid for wives. A wife paid her own way, and could be relied on in need. Furthermore, the possibility of a second wife motivated the male slave to work and seek his fulfillment within the system and within his subaltern role. It is probable that relatively few ever took a second wife, but the possibility was important. The female slave seems not to have had a parallel option; but then, her ability to spin cotton meant that she was always of some value.

One other aspect of slave demography is worth exploring. As we have seen, a major limitation on slave reproduction was that it was cheaper to buy a slave than to raise one. This would provide a disincentive to natural reproduction only if we assume that the master paid the costs. He did not. The slave child lived with his parents until he was old enough to work full time, at which time he could be claimed by the master. This meant that the costs of reproduction were borne by the slave ménage. The master had passed on the costs, though he kept control of the product. The chief barrier to slave reproduction thus lay in the economics of the slave ménage, which Meillassoux has explored elsewhere (see appendix). The slave owed approximately the amount needed to feed an adult for a year (Monteil 1923:192). Given the conditions of the hoe agriculture, there were limits to what a slave ménage could produce. A strong healthy male could not produce much over a ton of millet, and a woman not much over half of that. This meant that it was difficult for the slave ménage to accumulate enough to buy a slave or a second wife, or to save up a reserve. During famines and after natural disasters, many a slave ménage was dependent on the master's reserve. If the master was improvident, it was the slave who starved. If the master was hard, the slave couple could easily lose the right to farm for itself. The slave ménage thus could not afford many unproductive members. A small child, an aged parent, or even a sick adult threatened the well-being of the family. Though children went to work

---

soux objects to calling the relationship between male and female slaves marriage. I do not know what else to call it. Slaves lived in nuclear family units and formed the attachments we normally associate with such units. When slaves began freeing themselves after 1905, the masters often tried to seize the children, but the French supported the rights of the slaves to their own children. (Klein and Roberts 1980:390.)

24. The absence of sanctions capable of protecting the slave was stressed by J. C. Brevié, the administrator of Bamako, in his report on slavery there (A.N.S., K 19).

young, they had to be fed until old enough to go into the fields. In spite of these barriers to reproduction, slaves did have children and they did constitute families. Having passed on the costs, the master profited. Reproductive capacity must have played some small role in the price of female slaves.[25] The slave family had no juridical existence. The slave, after all, had no lineage. Nevertheless, runaway and freed slaves often tried to free parents and children. And when slavery was deprived of judicial recognition after 1903, the transformation of slave ménages into autonomous households was one of the first results.

Frederick Cooper has suggested that within any slave system there was a balance between acquiescence and resistance, between coercion and acceptance (Cooper 1977, ch. 1). It follows from this line of analysis that slaves must be integrated into the system and motivated, either by fear or rewards, to perform their role within it. Slavery was widespread because it was effective in meeting certain needs. Sudanic slave systems lacked the coercive potential of American slave systems, though they could be harsh and certainly were exploitative. The predominance of women among the enslaved meant that there were enough women to provide concubines for the rich and powerful and agricultural labor for the army, with enough left over to provide a domestic life for the ordinary male slave. Furthermore, in the very act of accumulating, either to buy a slave or marry a second wife, the male slave was seeking fulfillment within the system and reinforcing it. It is striking that Sudanic states and slave owners trusted their slaves to bear arms. (Meillassoux 1975b:230; Roberts 1978:319 and 1981:189; Gallais 1967, 1:129–30; Pollet and Winter 1971:244.)

Women's Work

Many archival sources insist that the female's labor obligation was the same as that of the male (A.N.S., K 14, Kayes, Kankan, Djenné). This varied somewhat from society to society, but the norm was about five days a week from sunrise to early afternoon prayer (2:00 P.M.), with the slave's obligations greater and more strictly enforced within the slave mode. On closer observation, there was a division of responsibilities. Most Sudanic

---

25. According to David Tambo (1976), young girls were slightly (a quarter to a third) more expensive than boys in the Sokoto Caliphate, but nubile females tended to be two to three times as expensive. Once women passed childbearing age, this differential disappeared. Tambo argues that this pattern can only be explained by a "sexually-oriented demand for young females as concubines and child-bearers." It is quite probable that very high prices were paid for a small number of attractive females, but I doubt whether the quest for sexual gratification can explain the widespread price differential.

societies have a rather precise definition of what is men's work and what is women's. Women generally had child care responsibilities, and they gathered firewood and water and did the cooking. When slaves worked on the household's lands, they had to be fed—and within the slave mode, noble women did not cook. The men did the heavy work of clearing the fields, but certain crops were women's crops. For example, women cultivated indigo and did the dyeing among the Maraka. In general, there was an understanding about who weeded and who harvested each of the crops. Though this may have broken down from time to time, one slave rising was stimulated by an effort to mix male and female work crews (Klein and Roberts 1980:386).

Women also freely participated in industrial activities such as mining, salt making, and textile production. Whether gold was mined or salt manufactured by slave or free labor seems to have varied from area to area (Curtin 1975:198–260). In textile production, the major industry in most areas of heavy slave concentration, there was a precise distinction between men and women. Men planted and women harvested cotton. The women spun and the men wove. While much of the cloth produced was white, the most valuable cloth was indigo-dyed blue cloth. Women grew the indigo, made the dye, and dyed the cloth. The entrepreneurs of the Maraka dyeing industry were women, and most of the labor was done by their slaves (Roberts 1978, ch. 7).

Spinning was a particular problem because it took about eight hours of spinning to produce enough thread to keep a weaver busy for one hour. This meant that spinners were more in demand than weavers. Male slaves were thus free to work at other tasks. During the dry season, many worked as porters on caravans. Others packed goods, built houses, or did other kinds of craft work. Nevertheless, with cloth production crucial to household income, it was important for a Maraka or Juula household to have enough spinners to keep the weavers occupied. The use of women in spinning and dyeing thus became an additional factor pushing up the price of female slaves (Meillassoux 1975b:249–50). It meant that even women too old to do sustained field labor had a price.

Masters generally preferred that female slaves marry within the household, and sometimes insisted that they do so. When a woman married a man owned by another master, she was often purchased or exchanged. If not, she remained the property of her master and continued to work for him. Alternatively, she worked with her husband and they paid her master a fixed sum every year. Women probably produced less wealth than men but worked harder because they combined productive labor with their domestic tasks. Women's work in the savanna was considerable. Water had to be brought from the well, firewood collected, and the millet ground—

all before anyone could think of cooking.[26] Whether slaves ate at home or were fed as part of a work gang, the preparation of food involved a substantial investment of labor. Women worked a longer day than men, and probably a harder day. During the rainy season, they brought the men their food, kept the compound clean, and worked their own fields. If life was difficult at home, it was harsher on the trail. Caillié has a description of the organization of domestic life on a caravan to Djenné. The women carried loads when the caravan was on the move. When it stopped, the men rested while the women gathered firewood, cooked, and prepared hot water for the men's baths. They also spun cotton in their spare time, which they sold for their own profit in Djenné (Caillié 1830:366–68).

The woman's path to manumission was also different from the man's. Within the household mode of production, the offspring of slaves were often absorbed within several generations, but where the slave mode prevailed, slave status was hereditary and the only distinction was between those taken in their lifetime and those "born in the house." There were several ways a person could be manumitted. A slave could buy his or her freedom, generally for the price of two slaves—but women seldom had access to such wealth. Much of their labor did not produce income. Islam also encouraged manumission. It was considered a pious act. Deathbed manumissions of trusted retainers have been reported in many Sudanic societies. These probably affected older men who had served their masters well for many years. It is probable that the most frequent kind of manumission and the only one affecting women was the manumission of concubines and slave spouses. Under Islamic law, the child of a free man was born free regardless of the mother's status, and the mother was free if she bore her master a child.[27] There were, however, several limitations on this. According to Richard Roberts, Maraka slave owners often did not acknowledge their offspring and thus avoided freeing their concubines (Roberts 1978, ch. 6). Such a woman could find herself back in the slave village as she aged. Furthermore, even if freed, she remained within her husband's household as a junior wife and with no kin to turn to for support in a conflict situation. Nevertheless, we can assume that this form of manumission was widespread and involved a constant absorption of slave women into the freeborn population.

26. The relation of domestic labor to production was most vividly illustrated in interviews dealing with forced labor. One of the most consistent complaints was that the French provided workers with unground millet. Since they did not have wives with them, they had to circulate every night in neighboring villages to find women to pound it for them, presumably in exchange for part of their ration.

27. A.N.S., K 18, Thiès, Kaolack; K 14, Kankan, Kerouane, Djenné. In Gumbu, Meillassoux (1975b:240–41) was able to find few cases of manumission of male slaves.

Sexual Rights

One of the defining characteristics of the male slave's position was the absence of paternal rights. He could neither bequeath to nor control his offspring, who belonged to his wife's master. The master could claim all or part of the child's services. If the slave child was female, the master chose her spouse, or at least had to give his approval in order for her to marry. The same questions are not relevant for women. A woman would not have had these rights even if free. In fact, the question often raised by feminists is whether there was a difference between the wife and the slave. There was, but it was primarily that the freeborn wife was a member of a lineage. She had a family (see Olivier de Sardan, below, p. 137). She could call on her family if mistreated, and could return to that family to visit. The slave had no kin. She had nowhere to go if mistreated. She had little choice, because the sanctions that could be brought to bear were severe. She could be flogged or put in irons. If a concubine, she could be sent back to the slave settlement and her place taken by another more eager to please. If she were a first-generation slave, or if unpopular with other slaves, she could be sold. There are many cases of women being traded numerous times and marched long distances. There was, for example, a Malian slave who claimed to have been traded a number of times and to have been moved from her home in the northern Ivory Coast to Gao, to Ségou to Kano and then back to Gao, much of it on foot, much of it with a load on her head.[28]

A more important defining characteristic of the female slave was her lack of control over her body. One freed slave, in response to a trader's claim that she was his wife, explained to an administrator: "You know that any Juula can take for himself any slave in his troop" (A.N.S., K 13 1893). For the newly captured and the slave in transit, the matter was clear. The Malian slave cited above talked of being placed in a hut by Samori's *sofa* and visited nightly (Keita 1958–59). While being moved, the slave was a thing. She had been taken by force and had no social identity. Her only protection was the obvious interest of the slave trader in keeping his human merchandise alive. Even after being integrated into a household, the female slave had little control over her sex life. Soleillet talks of the master having the "droit de seigneur" over all of his slave women.[29] He could choose those he desired and give the others to whom-

28. Keita 1958–59. This memoir is based in part on the reminiscences of an old slave retainer in the author's family. First taken prisoner by Samori's sofa, she remained with the family when slaves were freed.

29. Soleillet 1887:141, 285. When an earlier version of this paper was presented, several scholars who had done research in West Africa thought I was being cautious about saying

ever he wished to reward. Female slaves could be given to visitors, in which case the slave was responsible for a full range of domestic chores. According to Soleillet, two slave women were given to Mage and Quinton to keep them from chasing the freeborn (Soleillet 1887:450). Both women were pregnant when the explorers departed, and one was later visited by Soleillet.[30] Meillassoux goes further:

> The master or his dependents can maintain sexual relations with her [the female slave]. The young noble, who is entrusted to a slave to learn to work, has at the same time a sexual apprenticeship with the daughters or wives of his host, who if he inadvertently surprises the young noble with one of his women, has only the right to give him a symbolic blow with his fist. (Meillassoux 1975:228)

The point of view of one slave was plaintively put to a Gambian court: "It was against my wish that the prisoner came to me at night. Being a slave I was afraid" (P.R.O., 1893).

Conclusion

All of these variables affected the difference between the prices paid for female and male slaves. One irony of the situation is that the gap between male and female prices was declining in the late nineteenth century at the very time when the number of males on the market was increasing. Clearly, a crucial variable was that reproduction was more important within the household mode of production, while slaves were purchased within the slave mode primarily for the production of commodities. Hence, within the slave mode of production the differences between male and female decreased. This is exactly what was happening in the late nineteenth century. Commodity production using slave labor was expanding, bringing in its train increased work loads, more intensive exploitation, and lower birth rates.[31]

A slave woman differed from a free woman less than a male slave differed from his free counterpart. She had little control over her children, could not accumulate, and was not sure of being taken care of in her old age; but even free women in most societies had relatively few rights and only limited control over their offspring. All but the elite were doomed to

---

what they took for granted, that a female slave was sexually available. I am, however, wary about generalizations made by an observer about another society's sexual mores. See also A.N.S., K 14, Djenné and Kayes.

30. Soleillet 1887:463. Apparently, Mage wanted the child only if it were a boy. There is no indication of what Quinton wanted. One child was born dead. The other died within several months.

31. I am grateful to Joseph Miller for suggesting this line of argument.

a harsh struggle for survival. The major difference was that the free woman was part of a lineage, to which she could turn for protection or support. She was less vulnerable. The female slave was sought, first and foremost, as a worker, and valued for her ability to produce surplus value, but it was other characteristics that made her more valued than the male. Even within the slave mode, she was valued because she was more easily assimilated, she was less likely to escape, and she helped integrate male slaves. The predominance of women helped Sudanic societies strike that balance between coercion and consensus essential to the functioning of any slave system. If less important, the role of reproducer was not insignificant. Those slaves absorbed as concubines were valued for their ability to produce offspring. For the rest, the production of more slaves was a bonus. Having passed the costs of reproduction on to the slave, the master profited from increase. This was clearly not irrelevant to the price of female slaves.

APPENDIX: THE ECONOMICS OF THE SLAVE MENAGE

There have been two efforts to calculate the production of a slave household, both for the Soninke areas. Meillassoux's calculations for Gumbu are as follows:

Production of an adult male:	1,030 kg of millet per year
Production of an adult female:	500 kg
Production of an active child:	500 kg
Consumption of an active adult:	1 kg per day
Consumption of an active female or child:	0.5 kg per day
Consumption of an inactive person:	0.25 kg per day

Meillassoux calculates the production of a unit with three producers (man, wife, and active child) at 2,030 kg per year (Meillassoux 1975b:249). Pollet and Winter calculate more modestly:

300 mudd average annual productivity
120 mudd for consumption
 80 mudd diverse other subsistence expenses.
(Pollet and Winter 1971:239)

Many of these calculations depend on how one measures the mudd. Meillassoux evaluates it at 2.24 kilos (1975a:249), Curtin at 1.75 (1975:239).

Valuable as this exercise is, we must qualify it in a number of ways. On the one hand, children are generally put to work very young in agrarian societies. Conversely, there were the ever-present dangers of drought, locusts, disease, and war. Presumably, when disaster struck, the master either reduced or forgave the slave's dues. This is common in peasant societies. It is clear, however, that any kind of accumulation was very difficult under Sudanic conditions, whether to pay for a second wife or simply to accumulate a reserve. It is also unlikely that many slaves consumed a kilo of grain per day except during the months right after a good harvest. But what is important in these calculations is that children were expensive, brought little security, and exposed the slave ménage to economic hardship.

References

Oral Sources

Interviews conducted by the author in a Wolof area in the southern Saalum. On file in the Archives Culturelles in Dakar and the Archives of Traditional Music at Indiana University, Bloomington.

Al Hajj Moussa Ba, interview on January 23, 1975, Keur Moussa Ba.
Al Hajj Abdu Cissé, interview on January 29, 1975, Sonkorang.
Mbus Fadi Cissé, interview on February 6, 1975, Thyssé-Kaymer.
Al Hajj Baba Niang, interview on January 27, 1975, Sonkorang.
Biraan Ture, interview *ca.* January 21, 1975, Samb.

Unpublished Sources

A.N.G.: Archives Nationales du Guinee, Conakry.
    Cmdt. Kouroussa to Lt. Gov. Guinée, July 31, 1904. 2 D 185.
A.N.S.O.M.: Archives Nationales de France, section Outre-Mer, Paris.
    Gov. Grodet to Minister, July 18, 1894, Soudan XIV.
A.N.M.: Archives nationales du Mali, Bamako.
    Beledugu census, n.d. 5 D 20.
    Cmdt. Bafoulabe to Cmdt. des Cercles, August 2, 1887, and September 1, 1889. 1 E 168.
A.N.S.: Archives nationales du Sénégal, Dakar.
    Reports on slavery, 1894. K 14.
    Reports on Slavery, 1904. K 18 (Sénégal) and K 19 (Haut Sénégal-Niger).
Cmdt. 2d Terr. Militaire to Gov. Gen., August 24, 1901, 2G 1/19.
    Cmdt. Kita to Cmdt. Sup., January 19, 1891. 15 G 132.
    Misc. reports, Guinea. 7 G 84/1.
Keita, Cheikna. 1958–59. "Les Survivances d l'esclavage et du servage en Afrique noire." Memoire. Ecole Nationale de la France d'Outre-Mer.
Fonds Veillard, Institut fondamentale d'Afrique noire. Papers of Gilbert Veillard.
Meillassoux, C. 1976. "The Role of Slavery in the Economic History of the Central Savannah of West Africa." Paper presented to the Seminar on the Economic History of the Central Savannah of West Africa, Kano, Nigeria.
P.R.O.: Public Record Office, London.
    Case of Regina *v.* James Edwin, 1893. CO 87/144, no. 57.
P.R.O.B.: Public Record Office, Banjul, Gambia.
    Report of Travelling Commissioner, North Bank Province, June 30, 1899.
Roberts, R. 1978. "The Maraka and the Economy of the Middle Niger Valley: 1790–1908." Ph.D. thesis, University of Toronto.

Published Sources

Austen, R. 1979. "The Trans-Saharan Slave Trade: A Tentative Census." In *The Uncommon Market*, ed. H. Gemery and J. Hogendorn. New York.

Baillaud, E. 1902. *Sur les routes du Soudan*. Toulouse.

Baldé, M. S. 1975. "L'esclavage et la guerre au Fuuta-Jalon." In *L'esclavage en Afrique précoloniale*, ed. C. Meillassoux. Paris.

Bazin, J. 1975. "Guerre et servitude à Ségou." In *L'esclavage en Afrique précoloniale*, ed. C. Meillassoux. Paris.

Bernus, E. 1960. "Kong et sa région." *Etudes eburnéennes* 8:239–324.

Bouche, D. 1968. *Les villages de liberté en Afrique noire française, 1887–1910*. Paris.

Boutillier, J. L. 1969. "La ville de Bouna de l'époque précoloniale à aujourd'hui." *Cahiers ORSTOM* 6:3–21.

Caillié, R. 1830. *Journal d'un voyage à Tombouctou et à Jenné*. 2 vols. Paris.

Cooper, F. 1977. *Plantation Slavery on the East Coast of Africa*. New Haven.

Curtin, P. D. 1969. *The Atlantic Slave Trade: A Census*. Madison.

Curtin, P. D. 1975. *Economic Change in Precolonial Africa: Senegambia in the Era of the Slave Trade*. 2 vols. Madison.

Davis, D. B. 1966. *The Problem of Slavery in Western Culture*. Ithaca.

Fox, B., ed. 1980. *Hidden in the Household*. Toronto.

Gallais, J. 1967. *Le delta intérieur du Niger*. 2 vols. Dakar.

Gallieni, J. 1885. *Mission d'exploration du Haut Niger: Voyage au Soudan Français: Haut Niger et Pays de Ségou*. Paris.

Gray, J. M. 1940. *History of the Gambia*. Cambridge.

Hopkins, A. G. 1973. *An Economic History of West Africa*. London.

Klein, H. S. 1978. *The Middle Passage: Comparative Studies in the Atlantic Slave Trade*. Princeton.

Klein, M. A. 1968. *Islam and Imperialism in Senegal. Sine-Saloum 1847–1914*. Stanford.

Klein, M. A. 1970. "Slavery, the Slave Trade and Legitimate Commerce." *Etudes d'histoire africaines* 2:5–28.

Klein, M. A. 1972. "Social and Economic Factors in the Muslim Revolution in Senegambia." *Journal of African History* 13:419–41.

Klein, M. A., and P. Lovejoy. 1979. "Slavery in West Africa." In *The Uncommon Market*, ed. J. S. Hogendorn and H. A. Gemery. New York.

Klein, M. A., and R. Roberts. 1980. "The Banamba Slave Exodus of 1905 and the Decline of Slavery in the Western Sudan." *Journal of African History* 21:375–94.

Levtzion, Nehemia. 1973. *Ancient Ghana and Mali*. London.

Lovejoy, P. 1979. "Indigenous African Slavery." *Historical Reflections* 6:19–61.

Lovejoy, P., ed. 1981. *The Ideology of Slavery in Africa*. Beverly Hills.

Lovejoy, P. Forthcoming. *Transformations in Slavery: A History of Slavery in Africa*. Cambridge.

Manning, P. 1981. "The Enslavement of Africans: A Demographic Model." *Canadian Journal of African Studies* 15:499–526.

Maugham, R. 1961. *Slaves of Timbuctou*. London.

Meillassoux, C., ed. 1975a. *L'esclavage en Afrique précoloniale*. Paris.
Meillassoux, C. 1975b. État et conditions des esclaves à Gumbu (Mali) au XIXe siècle." In *L'esclavage en Afrique précoloniale*, ed. C. Meillassoux. Paris.
Meillassoux, C. 1978. "Role de l'esclavage dans l'histoire de l'Afrique occidentale." *Anthropologie et Société* 2:117–48.
Meillassoux, C. 1979. "Historical Modalities of the Exploitation and Over-Exploitation of Labour." *Critique of Anthropology* 13:7–16.
Miers, S., and I. Kopytoff, eds. 1977. *Slavery in Africa: Historical and Anthropological Perspectives*. Madison.
Mollien, G. T. 1820. *Travels in the Interior of Africa to the Sources of the Senegal and Gambia*. Edited by T. E. Bowditch. Translated from the French. London.
Monteil, C. 1923. *Les Bambara du Ségou et Kaarta*. Paris.
Moore, F. 1738. *Travels into the Inland Parts of Africa*. London.
Park, M. 1807. *Travels into the Interior Districts of Africa*. London.
Park, M. 1815. *Journal of a Mission into the Interior of Africa*. London.
Person, Y. 1968–75. *Samori. Une revolution dyula*. 3 vols. Dakar.
Pietri, C. 1885. *Les français au Niger*. Paris.
Pollet, E., and G. Winter. 1971. *La société Soninké (Dyahunu, Mali)*. Brussels.
Renault, François. 1971. "L'abolition de l'esclavage au Sénégal: l'attitude de l'administration française (1848–1905)." *Revue française de l'histoire d'outre-mer* 59:5–81.
Rey-Hulman, D. 1975. "Les dépendants des maîtres tyokossi pendant la période précoloniale." In *L'esclavage en Afrique précoloniale*, ed. C. Meillassoux. Paris.
Roberts, R. 1981. "Ideology, Slavery and Social Formation: The Evolution of Maraka Slavery in the Middle Niger Valley." In *The Ideology of Slavery in Africa*, ed. P. Lovejoy. Beverly Hills.
Solleillet, P. 1887. *Voyage à Ségou, redigé après les notes et journaux par Gabriel Gravier*. Paris.
Tambo, D. 1976. "The Sokoto Caliphate Slave Trade in the Nineteenth Century." *International Journal of African Historical Studies* 9:187–217.
Tauxier, L. 1917. *Le Noir du Yatenga*. Paris.
Villeneuve, R. G. 1814. *L'Afrique, ou histoire, moeurs, usages et coutumes africains*. Paris.

II. PRODUCTION AND REPRODUCTION

6 *Robert Harms*

Sustaining the System: Trading Towns along the Middle Zaire

Commerce was booming along the middle Zaire in the second half of the nineteenth century: ivory prices doubled, then doubled again; the canoe fleets of the Bobangi traders ventured regularly into new regions, and trading towns such as Bolobo, Lukolela, and Irebu received huge influxes of slave laborers. The key to wealth, in those turbulent years that preceded the Belgian conquest, was trade, and the key to trade lay in the creation of elaborate organizations that mobilized the services of men and women, slave and free.

The most noticeable division of labor in the trading towns was along sexual lines. Long-distance commerce was the work of men, both slave and free. The paddlers in the trading canoes were usually slaves, and the captains were often free, but one could also find poor freemen working as paddlers while trusted slaves of wealthy merchants commanded expeditions. Women provided the support system, primarily by growing the food that sustained the men at home and on trips.[1] In this role there was little difference between slave and free. Women in both groups had great autonomy in agricultural production and reaped the benefits of any surplus they produced. Slavery was more a way of recruiting food producers than of organizing food production.

The inferior status of slave women was revealed more clearly in the second major female role: bearing children who would ensure the long-term continuity of the social group. The importance of this function lay

---

1. The common distinction between production and reproduction is here blurred because agriculture, which is normally thought of as production, was carried on largely for the purpose of sustaining the commercial system. Production was, in a sense, a part of reproduction.

less in the need for future laborers (they could always be purchased as slaves) than in the complex kin-group politics that resulted from the conflict between the new commercial firms, which were organized as tightly knit, patrilocal communities, and the inherited kinship system, organized in terms of dispersed matrilineages. In order to ensure the long-term continuity of their firms, rich traders wanted offspring who were totally under the control of the firm and who had no obligations to maternal uncles or other outsiders. To this end, the slave owners blatantly manipulated the marital arrangements of their female slaves. The women responded by maintaining an extremely low birthrate.

This slave system developed as a result of the growth of the Atlantic slave trade along the upper Zaire River in the eighteenth and nineteenth centuries. Although the people of the upper river had sent small numbers of slaves toward the Kongo and Angola coasts during the sixteenth and seventeenth centuries, they did not become major suppliers to the Atlantic slave trade until the eighteenth century, when rapidly rising prices and increased demand along the nearby Loango coast induced many groups of fishing people along the upper Zaire to become specialized long-distance traders. In the early nineteenth century, the focus of European demand for slaves shifted southward from Loango to the area near the mouth of the Zaire River, leading to the rise of Malebo Pool (formerly Stanley Pool) as the major market for traders from the upper river. During this period many upriver trading groups moved downstream to establish trading towns closer to the Pool. The traders diverted many of the slaves that had been destined for the Atlantic trade in order to populate the growing trading centers. They needed male slaves to paddle the large trading canoes, which required up to sixty paddlers, and they needed female slaves to grow food and bear children.

A shift in the international economy during the middle years of the nineteenth century provided new opportunities for the river traders to amass slaves. As the Atlantic slave trade was drawing to a close in the 1840s and 1850s, the decreasing demand at the coast caused slave prices in the interior to drop sharply. But slave production did not diminish proportionately; the political and social processes that produced slaves—warfare, judicial condemnation, debt foreclosure, and kidnapping—could not easily be halted. As a result, a steady stream of bargain-priced slaves entered the interior markets.

At the same time, the traders in the new trading centers were gaining increased purchasing power because the price of ivory on the international market increased over 400 percent between 1825 and 1875. Since ivory had been only a minor export item prior to the second quarter of the nineteenth century, most of the people living in the inland forests had no idea of its value. This gave the river traders a perfect opportunity to buy ivory

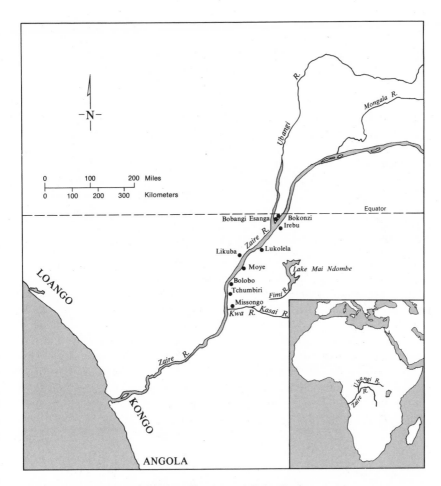

Map 6.1. The Central Zaire Basin

cheap and sell it dear, making enormous profits which they reinvested in cheap slaves. As the ivory hunters began to understand the value of ivory and raise their prices, the traders moved farther up the Zaire and its tributaries in a mad scramble for cheap ivory. Since success in this venture depended on having a fleet of canoes, the demand for male slaves as canoe paddlers rose steadily. The influx of male slaves into the trading towns created a demand for female slaves to grow food and to be wives to the traders and their crews (Harms 1981:24–47).

When Europeans first arrived along the upper Zaire River in the late nineteenth century, they found the trading centers populated largely by slaves. At Mswata, Captain Hanssens counted 290 slaves and only eight free people (Masui 1897:81). John Whitehead, a missionary working at Lukolela, noted that free people—people who could trace their ancestry back for several generations through blood ties instead of master-slave ties—could be "counted on the fingers" (Whitehead 1899:v). The most conservative estimate of the percentage of slaves in a trading town came from the town of Bonga, where Pradier estimated that slaves formed two-thirds of the population (Coquery-Vidrovitch 1969:467).

Such heavy concentrations of slaves created severe problems of control because the river societies, which were largely stateless, had no political apparatus which could uphold the privileges of the masters. While repressive measures such as sacrificing uncooperative slaves at the funerals of wealthy men or literally selling uncooperative slaves down the river were effective in keeping individuals in line, they were incapable of preventing resistance by slaves as a group. The most effective way of defusing resistance was to create positive incentives for hard work and cooperation by rewarding ambitious and talented slaves. Accordingly, masters often gave their slave canoe paddlers a portion of the profits at the end of each trading voyage. Some male slaves made enough money to buy their own slaves and canoes, and they began trading on their own, though they always took some goods to trade on their masters' behalf whenever they went on a trip. Such enterprising slaves sometimes took over the trading firm of the master upon his death. By the late nineteenth century the majority of the firms were headed by people who had begun their careers as slave paddlers. Although women had far fewer opportunities for financial gain than men, some slave women carved out successful careers in the production and trade of foodstuffs. They also purchased slaves of their own.

Masters and slaves, therefore, did not form distinct classes, because an individual could be both a master and a slave at the same time. As a result of this situation, trading firms, which were the basic social units in the trading towns, developed a segmented structure: the head of the firm owned a group of slaves, some of whom in turn had slaves of their own. Relationships among members of the firm were regulated by analogy to a patrilineage. The slave called his master "father," and he called the master of his master "grandfather." The head of the firm conducted himself much as the head of a patrilineage, except that his authority was much more absolute because he owned, either directly or indirectly, most of the members of his firm.

The key cleavage among males was between those who had amassed wealth through trade and those who had not. There were slave and free people in both categories. In the 1860s, for example, Chief Ibaka had a son, Lingenze, who was constantly getting into debt and requesting loans from his father's head slave. When Ibaka died, the head slave took over the firm, boasting to Lingenze, "You are almost my slave because I have paid your debts" (interview: Bonkanya, February 12, 1976). Similarly, one informant recalled that when his father died in the early part of this century, the slaves took all the wealth, leaving nothing to the sons (interview: Mambula, May 5, 1976).

It is uncertain whether slave buyers, in building up these firms, displayed a general preference for one sex over another. Informants claimed that men and women slaves were equally important. One recounted a well-known Bobangi folktale about a man who was sent on a slave-buying mission with the following orders: "Don't buy men, don't buy women, just buy people" (interview: Mambula, May 6, 1976). Nor do slave prices from the 1880s provide conclusive evidence. At Bolobo the council of chiefs, which fixed slave prices, made a price distinction between upriver and downriver slaves, but made no price distinction between men and women (*Missionary Herald* 1889:50). In the trading towns near the confluence of the Alima and the Zaire, however, male slaves were more expensive than females (Coquery-Vidrovitch 1969:315). The only population statistics come from a census taken at Tchumbiri in 1889 which revealed 1.4 women for every man (A.B.F.M.S., Banks 1899). The reason for the inconsistency in the data is that both men and women played important roles in the commercial economy. Men paddled canoes and fished in their spare time, whereas women produced agricultural products that sustained the paddlers. The optimum combination of male and female slaves varied according to the needs of the firm.

The most visible role played by women slaves in the trading towns was as producers of food. The growing populations of the trading centers consumed enormous quantities of cassava, and traders always carried cassava with them on trips. E. J. Glave (1893:128) left the following description of the departure of a trading fleet for Tchumbiri: "For several days the women had been busily engaged in preparing provisions for the trip, not only for the journey downstream, but for the stay there and also for the return journey, for the Tchumbiri people would take advantage of their hungry condition to charge them ridiculous prices for any food they might need." Nzolo, an informant who made a trip to the Pool to sell ivory around the turn of the century, confirmed the importance of cassava by remembering that the canoe captain had told him, "When the women have finished preparing the cassava, then we will go" (interview: Nzolo, July 28, 1976).

Cassava growing was a major industry among women in the trading villages south of the forest. Women were responsible for all stages of production: clearing the bush, planting the cassava, harvesting it, and preparing it. The preparation of cassava for a trading voyage was an elaborate process. A woman took the freshly harvested cassava to the riverbank, cut it into pieces, and then put it in the water to soak for three days. When

the soaking was completed, she slipped the skins off and returned the roots
to the water for another day. Then she removed the filaments and rubbed
the cassava across a grate to produce flour which she placed in a leaf-lined
basket that was three feet in diameter and stood up to five feet high. Large
trading canoes carried up to four of these baskets, which rode in the canoe
during the day and soaked in the river at night. Cassava prepared in this
way could last for several months. When traders wanted a meal, they took
out some flour, kneaded it into small loaves, steamed it, rekneaded it,
steamed it again, and ate it.

Women living in trading centers located in forest areas grew only small
amounts of cassava because of the shortage of cleared land. Clearing the
dense forest was normally the work of men. But since the dry season,
which was the only appropriate time for clearing the fields, coincided with
the low water season, which was the best time for fishing, men concentrated on fishing instead of clearing fields. As a result, most women had
only small fields to cultivate, so they concentrated on crafts such as salt
making, which took advantage of the salt-bearing river grasses, and pottery making, which utilized the black clay found along the riverbanks.
They traded these items to their inland neighbors in return for cassava and
other agricultural products (A.A., Political Report 1904).

A third variant in the agricultural work of women was found along the
Alima River The trading villages along the lower Alima were built on
swampy ground that was painstakingly built up in places to provide plots
for small gardens which could in no way support the population. During
the dry season, the women migrated in large numbers to camps along the
upper Alima, where they bought raw cassava and prepared it for expedition to the trading villages. Froment estimated that forty tons of cassava
per day went down the Alima from April to September, 1885 (Froment
1887:461).

Although most of the cassava eaten in the trading towns was supplied
by slave women, slavery was more a way of recruiting women to work in
the fields than a way of organizing production. The organization of work
and the division of surplus were almost the same among slave women as
among free women. The process by which slave girls first labored as part
of a working group and later gained their own plots upon marriage was
nearly identical to that for free girls. Age and marital status, not slavery
or freedom, were the key determinants of a woman's place in the production process.

A typical female slave was still a child when she began her life as a
slave in a trading town. Her owner put her in the care of one of his senior
wives, whom she called *nkolo mwene,* her mistress. A slave girl worked
in the fields as part of a working group supervised by her mistress much
as free girls worked under the supervision of their mothers. In return for

her work, the slave girl received food, clothing, and shelter. The produce of her labor went to her female master (interview: Mambula, May 6, 1976).

It is not surprising, then, that the people who profited most directly from the labor of slave girls were not the male masters, but their senior wives. While it would take a senior wife years to bear and raise enough children to form a working group from which she could extract a surplus, she could quickly create a large working group if her husband bought slave girls. The key difference between free and slave girls lay in the relative ease with which the latter could be recruited. Slave recruitment allowed senior wives at Bonga, for example, to leave the agricultural work to the slave girls while they concentrated on local commerce and social functions (Coquery-Vidrovitch 1969:467).

When a slave girl married, her status changed. She received her own house and her own garden plot. If she was given in marriage by her master to one of his male slaves, she no longer owed the master any of the produce of her fields, though a prudent woman brought him gifts from time to time. She provided daily food for her husband and prepared a large quantity of cassava for him when he went on a trading trip. If she made money by selling surplus cassava, the rules for dividing it varied according to the division of labor.[2] In savanna towns, where women did all the agricultural work, they kept all the surplus for themselves after the needs of the household had been met. In the forest villages, where men worked very hard to clear the fields, the surplus was divided equally among husband and wife (Wood 1923:191; M.R.A.C.-E., Stonelake 1931).

If the slave girl married her master, she worked just like any other wife. She was responsible for providing her share of the food for the household and for the unmarried slaves attached to it. When the master went on a trip, she supplied a share of the cassava. Any surplus, however, was hers to sell at the local market in order to buy the baskets, hoes, pots, sleeping mats, and other items she needed for keeping house. She kept any money that was left over. Sometimes a slave wife deposited her savings with her master. When she had amassed a considerable sum, the master bought her a slave girl of her own. He would call her and say "Here is your person. You are now the master of your own household. You are like a free person" (interview: Nzolo, July 29, 1976). As time passed, the master would place other slave girls in her care, and thus she would develop a working group of her own.

Although slave women had far fewer opportunities for gaining wealth and power than slave men, some women slaves became important traders

2. Here again the distinction between production and reproduction gets blurred. The agricultural produce that went to feed the husband helped to sustain (or reproduce) the commercial firms, but the surplus that the woman sold was production for her own profit.

and even ward chiefs. Bobongo, the founder of the ward called Bobongo in the village of Litimba, was a woman, perhaps of slave origin (the informants disagreed with each other on this latter point). In the early twentieth century a slave woman named Ekoko, who had become wealthy in the cassava trade and purchased several slaves, became the head of the ward of Bondembele. Both of these women gained power in exceptional times. Bobongo came to power at a time when the river trade was expanding rapidly and there was a shortage of men to head the newly formed wards. Ekoko came to power in a time of warfare and epidemic, when most of the men in line for the job had been killed. Yet their careers illustrate the possibilities that existed for a wealthy woman if circumstances were in her favor (interview: Yangawa, April 5 and April 13, 1976).

By letting slave women enjoy the fruits of their labor, the masters greatly simplified the task of control. Married women had positive incentives to maximize their production. Only new slaves and young slaves could feel that their labor was being exploited, and thus the number of potentially rebellious slaves at any given time was small. At the same time, the masters assured themselves of a regular supply of free food for their paddlers. The women had to feed their slave husbands, and they had to feed any young slaves placed in their care before selling the surplus. Because these obligations paralleled those of free women, they met with little resistance. There is every indication that slave women were efficient and productive growers of food.

While the masters did not seek to manipulate slave women as producers of food, they blatantly manipulated them in their roles as wives and mothers. It was in the realm of control over marriage arrangements that the subordinate position of slave women became manifest, and the result was an extremely low rate of natural reproduction.

Conflict between men and women over rights in children was not uncommon in the central Zaire basin. In societies with unilineal kinship systems, there was always tension between the parent whose lineage could claim the child and the parent whose lineage could not. Modern studies have found that Zairian women in patrilineal societies resent the fact that their lineages have only limited rights in their own children (Romaniuk 1967:288–89), and similar feelings probably existed in the nineteenth century as well. Conversely, men in matrilineal societies have articulated bitterness over their loss of rights in their children. The Bobangi, for example, have a proverb, "The hunter gets only the bones" (the others, who did no work, eat the meat). The meaning is that the father raises the child and cares for him, but when the child grows up the mother's kinsmen arrive to claim him, leaving the father with nothing to show for his labor.

The conflict between men and women in the trading towns was carried on within the framework of a matrilineal ideology. Free men and women, the only people who possessed real families, followed matrilineal descent. One crucial feature of this system was that a maternal uncle (called *nyango e bwele*, the male mother) enjoyed more authority over his nieces and nephews than did their fathers. He had the power to harm them through witchcraft or even to sell them into slavery.

Men sought slave wives for two reasons. First, there were relatively few free women in proportion to the demand by rich male traders of both slave and free origin. Second, many rich men who could have married free wives chose not to do so because they felt that the system of free marriages worked against them. By purchasing slave wives they could manipulate the system to their advantage.

A man could marry a free woman by either a low-priced marriage or a high-priced marriage. The low-priced marriage put a man at a considerable disadvantage. In the first place, the children from the marriage belonged to his wife's family, not his. In the second place, he had a special responsibility (called *etemu* by the Bobangi) for the woman since he was in a sense keeping her on behalf of her family. If she died while she was yet young, her family could force the husband to pay compensation which could go as high as ten slaves. A man who wanted to gain control over his offspring and get rid of his etemu responsibility could opt for a high-priced marriage, which cost between eight and fifteen times as much as the cheap marriage. Any children born of the union belonged to the husband's family. If the wife died, her family was obligated to furnish the husband with another wife. If the husband wanted to get rid of the wife, he could act as her father in arranging her marriage to another man and still claim any children she bore with her new husband. But despite the legal rights the husband enjoyed over his children, his wife's brothers could still work witchcraft on them in case of a dispute among in-laws.

Rich men could avoid both the concessions required by the low-priced marriage and the exorbitant prices demanded by the high-priced marriage by purchasing and marrying slave women. Since slaves were by definition kinless people, marriage to a slave wife gave a man total control over his offspring. He became, in effect, both the father's side and the mother's side of his child's family. Because children born to such a union had no divided loyalties, rich traders often favored them over children born to their free wives. This explains the Bobangi saying that "the children of slave wives are the masters of the village" (interview: Mambula, May 7, 1976). Marrying a slave wife had other advantages as well. The price of a slave was much cheaper than that of a high-priced marriage. Prices of both slaves and free marriages varied widely, so this point is difficult to document in a precise way. But in the trading village of Monsembe, four slaves were often given to seal a free marriage (Weeks 1913:123). A marriage to a slave woman required little ceremony; the master simply invited some of his friends over to drink palm wine and announced that he was taking the woman as his wife.

Before the rise of the river trade in the eighteenth and nineteenth centuries, marriage to a slave woman had had a very serious drawback. A key purpose of marriage had been to create a network of affinal ties with neighboring lineages and villages, and a slave marriage created no ties. In the trading towns, however, the trading firms were in fierce competition with each other. Affinal ties, therefore, became emcumbrances which compromised the autonomy and competitive position of the firm. Slave marriages provided an ideal means of avoiding such ties. By the late nineteenth century, marriage of rich traders to slave women had become the norm, while marriages to free women were rare (A.A. Grenfell n.d.).

The master himself generally married only a small proportion of his female slaves. He gave the rest of them in marriage to his male slaves. This practice gave the master a great deal of control over his male slaves because he could bestow wives as rewards or withhold them as punishment. Yet he lost nothing, because he still maintained control over both the slave woman and her offspring. His continuing control over the woman is best illustrated by the fact that a slave woman, even if married to a man other than her master, was liable to be buried with her master at his funeral. Informants stressed that a man who accepted a slave wife from his master had no guarantee that she would not suddenly be taken away and killed (interview: Mambula, May 6, 1976).

The master's continuing control over the woman's children was manifest in a contradictory way that reflected his dual role as head of an artificial patrilineage and owner of the members of his group. On the one hand, he claimed rights in the children because he was the head of their "lineage." If he requested that a child of his slave woman come to live in his household, the request was immediately granted (interview: Nzolo, July 29, 1976). On the other hand, he claimed the right to marry daughters of his slave women because they were not blood relatives (Liebrechts 1909: 66–67).

Second- and third-generation slaves moved toward full legal membership in trading town society. A second-generation slave was called *mombotela*, a designation applied to children born to a union of two slaves as well as to a union between a slave woman and her master. She had more security than a first generation slave, because she could not be sacrificed at the funeral of a rich trader, and she could be resold only in exceptional circumstances. Third-generation slaves were known as people "becoming free." If a third-generation slave married a free person, the fourth generation could have free status.

In practice, however, a person's position on the slave–free continuum was not as important as the issue of whether or not she had kin in another firm. As long as all marriages were within the firm, the master maintained complete control over the offspring, whether they had been fathered by himself or by his male slaves. All such offspring increased the manpower of the firm while maintaining its autonomy. But when a slave married someone outside the firm, the offspring had a second set of kin on whom they could count for protection against the excesses of the first. Such marriages were rare, however, and the trading firms remained overwhelmingly endogamous.

The manipulation of slave marriages formed a clear contrast to the rights held by free women in marital arrangements. As a general rule, free girls had the right to refuse suitors. If a suitor paid earnest money while the girl was still young and she refused him when she reached the age of marriage, the father paid back the earnest money. If the father had spent it, the suitor waited until the girl found a man of her choice and then acted as her father in arranging the marriage and receiving the bride price. The matrilineage of a woman married by the low-priced marriage, the most common arrangement, retained rights in her children, and she received special consideration from her husband because he had an etemu responsibility for her well-being. A free woman who was unhappy with her husband could leave him and return to her parents (M.R.A.C.-E., Stonelake 1931; A.A., Grenfell n.d.).

Slave women, on the other hand, had no say in the choice of a husband and no control over their offspring. While we have no record of what these women actually felt, we know what they did: they largely refrained from bearing children.

Visitors were astonished by the lack of children in the trading towns along the upper Zaire in the late nineteenth century. Bentley (1900, 2:229) claimed that there were a hundred children in a fishing village for every child to be seen in a trading village of the same size. A survey made by missionaries at Tchumbiri in 1889 revealed 384 adults and only 50 children (A.B.F.M.S., Banks 1889). Another missionary wrote that the traders had turned from reproduction to slave buying as a means of perpetuating themselves (Wood 1923:20).

The search for an explanation of this phenomenon must begin by considering natural factors. The problem was not dietary, because the people in fishing villages had diets nearly identical to those of people in trading villages. The problem was not genetic, because the inhabitants of the trading towns had been born in various places throughout the central Zaire basin. Venereal diseases probably played a role. Both syphilis and gonorrhea were known along the upper Zaire in the late nineteenth century (Whitehead 1899:313; Coquery-Vidrovitch 1969:461, 468); but syphilis may have been introduced to the area only in the 1880s. Some medical studies during the colonial period claimed that there was a correlation between low birthrates and high incidences of venereal diseases (Retel-Laurentin 1974:47–55), but other specialists have disputed this conclusion (Romaniuk 1967:310–14). The disease factor could also help to account for differential birthrates between fishing and trading villages. The fishing villages followed stricter codes of sexual conduct, providing fewer opportunities for venereal diseases to spread. Yet disease cannot provide a total explanation. Some venereal diseases, such as syphilis, take years to develop and would not affect women during their most fertile years.

The other factor to be considered is voluntary population control. This explanation was favored by missionaries and colonial officers who, unfortunately, left little concrete evidence. The population control argument must therefore be constructed indirectly by examining whether the women had the means and the motives.

Although contraception techniques are not mentioned in the accounts of nineteenth-century explorers and missionaries, such techniques were probably well known. Modern fertility studies have revealed a wide variety of contraception techniques known in the central Zaire basin, and it is unlikely that they were introduced by the Europeans. The two most popular methods were douching with a chemical mixture after intercourse, and muscular movements after intercourse to make the sperm flow out the vagina. Blockage of the uterus by a cloth tampon was known, but rarely used (Romaniuk 1967:292–96).

Abortion techniques were also well known along the river in the nineteenth century. The most common method was to douche with a liquid prepared from the bark of the *mondengu* tree (Whitehead 1899:185). Another method used a preparation made from the roots of the *ingongo* vine (Windels n.d.:99). Both of these methods were thought to be effective only during the first three months of pregnancy. Since the trading towns brought in slaves from all parts of the central Zaire basin, a number of other techniques were probably known as well. Modern fertility studies have revealed a large number of abortion methods in the central Zaire basin. There were also techniques for sterilization. A missionary cited a case in which a young woman dug in the clay of the riverbank to make a shallow pool, filled it with a liquid preparation, and sat in it for several hours. After that she was sterile (Wood 1923:72–73). Unfortunately, none of these preparations has been chemically tested. Yet Romaniuk (1967:291–92), in his study of fertility problems in Zaire, concludes that at least some of them were probably effective.

Late nineteenth- and early twentieth-century observers argued that abortion, rather than contraception, was the major means of population control (Wood 1923:72–73; Weeks 1913:129–33; A.N.S.O.M., Darré 1925). Although this seems strange to modern Americans, the preference for abortion has been documented in a number of nonindustrial societies. Three reasons have been given for the primacy of abortion. First, abortion techniques are often simpler than contraception techniques. Second, abortion is easier to hide from the husband. Third, because most sexual contact does not result in pregnancy, contraception methods seem like a waste of time, whereas pregnancy presents a concrete situation which can be eliminated with a single act (Romaniuk 1967:294).

The final method of population control was infanticide. While there is no indication that this was common, there is one case on record in which a mother drowned her newborn baby while she was bathing it. The mother claimed that it was an accident, but the neighbors suspected that she had done it deliberately (Liebrechts 1909:83).

The analysis of motives behind population control follows two complementary lines. One line of reasoning stresses the psychological effects of forced partnerships, lack of parental rights, and unstable relationships in discouraging women from having children. Studies in modern Zaire (Romaniuk 1967:288–89) have shown that women who are married against their will have higher rates of abortion than those who marry voluntarily, and this factor would help to account for abortions among nineteenth-century slave women as well. Moreover, most slave women came from societies in which their own matrilineages enjoyed extensive rights in their offspring. In the artificial partilineages that structured the trading societies, the masters enjoyed exclusive rights in the offspring of the slave women and could deprive a woman of her children at any time. Modern studies in the area (Romaniuk 1967:288–89) have shown that abortion is more frequent in patrilineal societies than in matrilineal ones because women have less incentive to bear children who will be controlled by another lineage. The same principle would have operated in a more intense way in the nineteenth-century slave societies. Finally, the instability of partnerships may have discouraged childbearing. One source of instability was the masters, who sometimes shifted women from partner to partner. An explorer noted that in one month Ndombi, a rich trader, replaced twenty-five of his slave wives with new ones (Coquery-Vidrovitch 1969:330). Another source of instability was that women often took lovers while their imposed partners were away on trading trips. Since pregnancies from such unions had serious consequences, women practiced population control.

The other line of analysis weighs the costs of childbearing against the benefits. The most obvious cost was that of feeding a child until he or she began to contribute to the household economy. Because slave women owned their agricultural produce, the cost of feeding children was borne by the women, not their masters. The cost of raising boys was much higher than that of raising girls. Although boys sometimes fished with hooks or set snares to catch small animals, they made no substantial economic contribution until they were old enough to paddle canoes. Girls, on the other hand, began helping with household and agricultural tasks soon after they could walk (Wood 1923:36). Another cost came from lost productivity due to pregnancy and childcare. Because agricultural production was the only way a woman could improve her condition, frequent childbearing could hinder a woman from getting ahead.

Against these costs, the tangible benefits were limited. In most African societies, children formed a sort of old-age insurance, but slave children in the trading towns owed primary loyalty to their masters, not their biological mothers. At the same time, it was the master, not the biological children, who had primary responsibility for supporting elderly slave women. The other potential benefit was help from girls in the fields, but this had to be weighed against the cost of raising boys and the time lost in childcare. On balance, therefore, the costs were probably equal to or greater than the benefits.

Slave masters, on the other hand, analyzed the costs and benefits of slave reproduction in a different way, distinguishing between short- and long-term benefits. Because it took at least sixteen years before a boy became an effective paddler, the birth of a boy provided no short-term benefits to a trading firm. In an era when life expectancy was probably around forty years and the commercial economy was subject to wild fluctuations, the wait was too long to be part of the master's commercial strategy. As one informant noted, "If you wait for children, you won't get rich" (interview: Eyala, May 15, 1976). In the long term, however, children were considered a good thing. It cost the masters nothing to raise them, and children promoted the long-term continuity of the firm.

Because short-term success required the purchase of slaves, not natural reproduction, the masters had an ambivalent attitude toward the low birthrate. Although in individual cases men expressed anger at their wives for failing to bear children (Week 1913:130), they accepted the low birthrate as an inevitable consequence of the system, and they rationalized it in terms of a theoretical explanation that fit comfortably within the local cosmology and was consistent with the explanations they gave for other types of misfortune.

The theoretical explanation was based on the assumption, common in the area, that wealth and health were interrelated in such a way that any man who wanted more than his share of wealth had to pay for it by sacrificing the health of members of his family. It was said that a man who wanted wealth bought a charm which gave him control over an invisible magical agent which stole money from rival traders in order to make its master wealthy. Later, the agent demanded that its master give up the life of a member of his family in payment for the services rendered. The trader then designated a family member, who would eventually get sick and die.

Informants said that at one time there had been many children born in the trading villages, but the traders got so greedy that they gave them all up in return for wealth. Once all the children were gone, the greedy traders began to promise the spirits of children yet unborn to the magical agents. Most men became deeply in debt to their magical agents, so as soon as a child was conceived, the agent came and stole it away. Thus many children were conceived, but few were born (Harms 1981:197–215).

Conclusion

Europeans who visited the upper Zaire passed contradictory judgments on the merchants in the trading centers. Some observers praised the industry and enterprise of the trading peoples; others noted that the trading centers were dying out because of their low birthrates. These two phenomena were, in fact, related, and the link between them could be found in the exploitation of female slaves in their roles as wives and mothers. By manipulating marriage arrangements of female slaves, rich traders built up close-knit and competitive corporate trading groups which successfully expanded trade in the central Zaire basin. But the trade-off was a low birthrate. Thus the traders were forced to buy new slaves continually in order to keep up the populations of their villages. This system worked fine as long as profits from the ivory trade were high and slaves were readily available, but with the coming of the colonial period, many of the slave populations of the trading centers simply died out and disappeared. Consider the following segment of an interview I conducted in the former Bobangi trading center of Bolobo (Yangawa, April 7, 1976).

QUESTION: When Ekoko died, who succeeded her?
ANSWER: When Ekoko died, nobody was left to be chief of [the ward of] Bondembele. It simply became the family of Bondembele. There were only two or three people left.
QUESTION: Where did the other people go?
ANSWER: The other people died. The Bobangi didn't bear many children. They just bought people. If a man bought somebody and that person died, it was finished. You had to have a lot of money to buy people. If you had no more money, the people were finished for good. The Bobangi diminished in that way.

References

Oral Sources

Tapes of the interviews are deposited at the Archives of Traditional Music, Folklore Institute, Indiana University, Bloomington.

Bonkanya (native village: Bolobo), interview on February 12, 1976.
Eyala (native village: Bokonzi), interview on May 15, 1976.
Mambula (native village: Tchumbiri), interviews on May 5, 6, and 7, 1976.
Nzolo (native village: Tchumbiri), interviews on July 28 and 29, 1976.
Yangawa (native village: Bolobo), interviews on April 5, 7, and 13, 1976.

Unpublished Sources

A.A.: Archives Africaines, Brussels, Belgium.
    Grenfell, G., n.d. Response to questionnaire, A.I. (1370), IX/A/2.
    Political Report, Irebu, September 11, 1904. AE (346) 9.
A.B.F.M.S.: American Baptist Foreign Missionary Society Archives, Valley Forge,
    Pennsylvania.
    Banks to Billington, October 15, 1889.
A.N.S.O.M.: Archives nationales, Aix-en-Provence, France.
    Darré. 1925. "Projet d'évacuation des Bangalas." AE 5 D 60.
M.R.A.C.-E.: Musée Royal de l'Afrique Centrale, Section d'Ethnographie, Ter-
    vuren, Belgium.
Stonelake, A. R. 1931. "Response au questionnaire sur le droit indigène," Terr.
    Muskie, 3.
Windels, A. n.d. "Chefferie des Pama-Bakutu." Typescript in the possession of
    the author.
Wood, L. 1923. "Bobangi Life and Christian Education" Ph.d. dissertation, Uni-
    versity of Chicago.

Published Sources

Bentley, C. 1900. *Pioneering on the Congo*. 2 vols. London.
Coquery-Vidrovitch, C. 1969. *Brazza et la prise de possession du Congo*. Paris.
Froment, E. 1887. "Trois affluents français du Congo." *Bulletin de la Société de
    Géographie de Lille* 7:458–74.
Glave, E. 1893. *Six Years of Adventure in Congo-Land*. London.
Harms, R. 1981. *River of Wealth, River of Sorrow: The Central Zaire Basin in
    the Era of the Slave and Ivory Trade, 1500–1891*. New Haven.
Liebrechts, C. 1909. *Souvenirs d'Afrique*. Brussels.
Masui, T. 1897. *Guide de la section de l'État Indépendant du Congo à l'exposi-
    tion de Bruxelles-Tervuren en 1897*. Brussels.
Missionary Herald. 1889. London.
Retel-Laurentin, A. 1974. *Infécondité en Afrique noire*. Paris.
Romaniuk, A. 1967. *La fécondité des populations congolaises*. Paris.
Weeks, J. 1913. *Among Congo Cannibals*. London.
Whitehead, J. 1899. *Grammar and Dictionary of the Bobangi Language*. Lon-
    don.

7 *Margaret Strobel*

Slavery and Reproductive Labor in Mombasa[1]

The idea that women are closely linked to reproduction would appear to be self-evident, if not a platitude. Yet the implications of that linkage are underestimated if one conceives of reproduction only in the sense of biological production. A brief discussion of women's reproductive labor in industrial societies will illustrate the usefulness of a broader conception of reproductive labor.

Recent feminist scholarship has attempted to explore the significance of the association of women with reproductive labor in a broad sense: the reproduction of new human beings, the daily restoration of human beings, and the reproduction of ideology or culture. Some scholars argue that the subordinate position of women in capitalist societies is tied to this association of women with reproductive labor, because under capitalism value is accorded not through reproduction but through the production of commodities with exchange values. The domestic work performed by women, they say, buttresses the assumption that women work for pin money and thus can receive lower wages or need not work at all. The association of women with restorative services within the family translates in the labor force into an overrepresentation in the service sector. Moreover, the role of women as nurturers, which derives from the division of labor within the family, leads some women into public life as "social housekeepers," as reformers who patch up people ravaged by capitalism. Feminist schol-

1. The research for this paper was conducted with the help of two grants: a Fulbright-Hays Doctoral Research Abroad Fellowship and a Woodrow Wilson Doctoral Dissertation Fellowship in Women's Studies.

I thank William Barclay, Frederick Cooper, Martin Klein, and Claire Robertson for their helpful comments on earlier drafts of this paper. A version of this article appeared as "Slave and Free in Mombasa," *Kenya Historical Review* 6, nos. 1 and 2 (1978).

arship focuses on the interplay between the family and extrafamilial institutions. The family or household is seen as the place where individuals
are enculturated, where they learn behaviors appropriate to their gender
and class (Edholm et al. 1977; Eisenstein 1979; Kelly 1979).

From this perspective, the importance of women's reproductive role
goes beyond their bearing children. Scholars studying African slavery,
however, have tended to see the significance of women's role in reproduction in the limited sense of their providing additional slaves or dependents
(Miers and Kopytoff 1977; Meillassoux 1972; articles in this volume). In
this essay I attempt to examine the kinds of reproductive work that women
did at the time of slavery in Mombasa and the implications of the association of female slaves with reproductive work. The conclusions are tentative only, deriving from a single household in Mombasa, a seaport on the
Swahili coast, at the turn of the century. First I describe the society and
economy of Mombasa and the household in particular, both its slave and
freeborn members. Next I analyze in detail the work of each of the members, specifically with regard to the reproductive aspects of such work.
Third, I suggest the hypothesis that those slaves whose work was primarily reproductive, that is, women slaves, were most likely to be integrated
into the kin group and by this means into the culture of the slave owners.
Finally, I examine slaves' experiences after abolition in 1907: how the
degree of acculturation or integration affected the slaves' responses and
what form of work was frequently taken up by female ex-slaves.

Mombasa

By 1900 Mombasa was already a cosmopolitan, culturally diverse East
African port with a population of 25,000, most of whom were Muslims.
The population included British administrators, Indian traders, and Baluchi soldiers. However, the core of the town consisted of African slaves
and freeborn people and Arabs from the Hadramawt and Oman. Wealthy
land- and slave-owning families comprised the upper stratum of this core.
This group evolved out of intermarriage between indigenous, long-time
African residents—the Twelve Tribes—and Arab, primarily male, immigrants. The middle layers included some slave owners among the traders,
sailors, artisans, and laborers drawn from the poorer ranks of Twelve Tribes
and Arab society. In addition, some freed slaves rose to this level. On the
bottom rung were slaves brought from Central and East Africa, particularly after the 1840s. Constituting perhaps 10 percent of the population,
they provided agricultural, maritime, and domestic labor. Ethnicity and
social status were not congruent, although Omani Arabs tended to be on
the top and in the middle, Twelve Tribes people scattered among the ranks
of the freeborn, and African slaves on the bottom. Over the centuries these

various ethnic groups adopted, to a greater or lesser degree, characteristics of Swahili culture, namely Islam, the Swahili language, and various Swahili practices and customs (Cooper 1977; Strobel 1979).

At the turn of the century Mombasa's economy focused on trade and agriculture. The town was growing in commercial importance, a process that accelerated in the colonial period as the railroad and colonial policy established Mombasa's role as the primary conduit between East Africa and the international capitalist economy. Hence for Mombasa the period under discussion was a transition from a subsidiary role in the nineteenth century to one as a highly developed seaport (Janmohamed 1978).

As Mombasa grew in commercial importance, its agricultural sector declined. This decline was linked to a general dislocation in agriculture following the abolition of slavery in 1907, when the transition to agricultural wage labor was uneven (Cooper 1980). Colonial attempts to establish cotton and sisal plantations near Mombasa diminished by World War One, and subsequent agricultural policy shifted to promoting white settler agriculture upcountry. Mombasa had not experienced intensive exploitation of slave labor in the production of millet, sesame, and coconuts, as had Malindi to the north. In the late nineteenth century, small farms that raised coconuts, vegetables, and grain were most common in the area surrounding Mombasa. Some farms were cultivated by poorer farmers, either by themselves or working with a few slaves; other areas utilized slave labor or a system similar to tenant farming, with slaves turning over a portion of their produce to their owner or performing some collective labor for him or her (Cooper 1977).

Thus, in the period under discussion Mombasa was an area loosely integrated into the world capitalist economy through commerce. In addition to agricultural produce, Mombasa exported ivory, gum copal, and skins. These items were obtained through caravans financed by Mombasa's wealthier Twelve Tribes people and Arabs or in trade with Kamba and Mijikenda intermediaries (Cooper 1977).

The Household

The data come from extensive interviews with a woman who grew up in the household discussed here as the daughter of a freeborn man and his concubine. Bi Mariamu's[2] remarks on slavery and slaves emerged initially in discussions of her life history rather than of slavery itself. It is possible that additional slaves were owned by the free members of the household, agricultural workers with whom Bi Mariamu would have had little contact, but there is no reason to believe that her knowledge is incomplete.

2. This and other names (except Hidaya) are pseudonyms.

The freeborn members of this household were essentially from the Twelve Tribes, the indigenous African population of Mombasa, although occasionally Arabs or people from the neighboring islands of Zanzibar and Pemba married into the lineage. The head of this household was a woman, Bi Aisha, whose kin ranked in the middle layer of Mombasa society. Because her parents were not wealthy, Bi Aisha inherited nothing, but each of two marriages netted her a farm and some slaves. She purchased other slaves with her own money. Thus, exercising her right under Muslim law to own property in her own name, Bi Aisha gathered around her slaves and farms, which in turn produced enough money to support her. In addition, she received maintenance money from her husband while she was married. Bi Aisha had no children herself, a phenomenon which was not uncommon in Swahili society.[3] Following coastal practice, she fostered and raised children of near and distant kin. These children eventually were given her slaves and later inherited her farms at the time of her death around 1900.

Bi Aisha was able to influence and control people around her because she owned property. Though not extensive compared with the holdings of Mombasa's wealthiest individuals, her property made it possible to attract dependent kinfolk to her household (Cooper 1977:103). Bi Aisha, not her husbands,[4] directed the economic enterprises of her farms and slaves; she, not they, directed the activities of her kinfolk.

Two other freeborn members of the household were Bi Hadija and Mbaraka. Bi Hadija was Bi Aisha's niece. She lived in the household

3. Demographic data are lacking to quantify the low fertility of coastal people at the turn of the century. However, fragmentary evidence indicates that the Arab and Afro-Arab population of the coast had lower fertility than the African Mijikenda population. The Provincial Commissioner of the Coast Province indicated in a letter to the Chief Native Commissioner on March 31, 1919, that Mijikenda women were popular as wives because a "large proportion" of "Swahili" women were sterile (K.N.A., Coast 1/24/243). In Malindi District to the north of Mombasa, the District Commissioner H. R. Tate referred to the "childless households" of "Swahilis" and "Arabs" (K.N.A., Seyidie Province 1/37:2). The Takaungu Sub-District Annual Report of 1912–13 offered population statistics according to which children constituted 25 percent of the population with the comment that "the proportion of Swahili children to mature men and women is significant of the Swahili aversion to the responsibility of parenthood" (K.N.A., Seyidie Province 8/157:18). More recently, the 1962 Kenya census indicated that Muslim African women had a lower fertility than African Christian women (*Kenya Population Census* 1962:68). Finally, a late-1950s demographic study of Pangani, on the northeastern coast of Tanzania, indicated a fertility rate lower than that of the lowest European countries, and determined that infertility was a long-standing and common problem (Tanner 1959–60:66, 79).

4. Unfortunately, because I was interested only in Bi Mariamu's family and her female relatives during the interviews, I did not inquire about Bi Aisha's husbands. Bi Mariamu portrayed them as peripheral to Bi Aisha's economic and social life.

during the periods when she was not married. She died after Bi Aisha did, some time between 1900 and 1907. She had several slaves and two farms, one which she inherited from Bi Aisha and one given to her by her husband. Mbaraka was the grandson of an *mzalia*, a slave born in the household. His mother was born of a freeborn father, and thus was free herself. She was given the name of Bi Aisha's own sister. Bi Aisha adopted Mbaraka into her household and gave him two slaves. He and his Mijikenda wife lived with Bi Aisha until she died, at which time he, along with the father of Bi Mariamu, inherited one-third of a farm.

Bi Aisha, Bi Hadija, and Mbaraka lived together in a house in what is now the Old Town of Mombasa. Living there also were Bi Mariamu as a child, her parents and siblings, and various slaves and their descendants. This house was the main house, called *jumbe* in Swahili. Not all the slaves attached to Bi Aisha lived here, but they all interacted with her as head of the household and with other freeborn people resident in the house. The composition of the household changed over time, with deaths, births, and marriages, but the household continued to function as an economic and social unit until deaths, marriages, and the abolition of slavery scattered many of its members.

At least thirty-two slaves were attached to the household. Bi Aisha owned twenty-eight, Bwana Hamisi (Bi Mariamu's father, a distant relative of Bi Aisha) bought one himself, and Bi Hadija bought or was given three. Information is available about thirty of these thirty-two slaves. Nearly two-thirds, nineteen were female; eleven were male. Whether this imbalance had something to do with the sex of their owner is unclear. More likely, the predominance of females was related to the urban setting, for there is some evidence that female slaves outnumbered male slaves resident in Mombasa at the turn of the century (Cooper 1977:229).[5] Perhaps male slaves were away from town more often as sailors and porters or were more concentrated in agricultural areas outside of town.

The work performed by members of Bi Aisha's household reflects a broad portion of economic activities in Mombasa at the turn of the century. Characteristic of freeborn women of her means, Bi Aisha herself did not directly participate in the economy as a producer or trader (Strobel 1979:62–73). Instead, she delegated a male relative who was raised by her to attend to her financial affairs. Bwana Hamisi, Bi Mariamu's father, was the overseer for one of Bi Aisha's farms. Because she did not think this work was sufficiently productive, she told him to go trade in communities north of Mombasa. He sewed Swahili caps and clothing for sale. He traded cloth for food grown on the coast north of Mombasa, hired porters to carry the

5. In Zanzibar Town, however, males outnumbered females (Cooper 1977:222).

foodstuffs to Mombasa, and sold the food to Indian merchants. Then he brought the money to Bi Aisha, who presumably used it for subsistence for the household and for further investment.

Possibly some of the women in the household made handicrafts for sale. Later in her life, when the death of one husband and divorce by another made Bi Mariamu economically vulnerable, she plaited mats and sold them for her upkeep. But she did not mention such activity being part of the household economy while she was growing up.

The work of the slaves attached to the household is outlined in table 7.1. Not surprisingly, women rather than men were employed within the household as cook, nanny, or food buyer. However, nearly equal numbers of men and women worked for wages and returned at the end of each month to give Bi Aisha half. The most common wage work for women was to cook for Indian families, who were forbidden by law to own slaves. Men had a greater variety of jobs—porter, boat or ferry conductor, casual laborer, food seller, and carpenter (see Wright 1975:805, 818).

Productive and Reproductive Labor

Within the household, slaves were engaged in what Marxists would term both productive and reproductive labor.[6] Although analytically distinct, these categories were sometimes both represented in a single slave's work. Moreover, other slaves produced use values for Bi Aisha but were not productive in the Marxist sense of the term.

Productive Labor

Marx distinguished productive labor from other forms of labor under capitalism in that productive labor produces surplus value which the capitalist can invest, thereby creating more capital. Briefly, surplus value is the value produced by a worker beyond that needed to reproduce himself or herself, that is, value over and above the culturally defined cost of subsistence. Productive labor is not defined by the creation of a tangible item. Rather, productive labor results from the appropriation of a worker's labor by a capitalist and from the use to which the surplus is put.[7]

6. My use of the term productive labor differs from the definitions used by Harms, this volume, p. 95; and Broadhead, this volume, p. 162.

7. Debates have raged about whether or not unpaid housework is productive labor and generates surplus value. Such discussions emerged as the feminist movement challenged Marxism to integrate women's experience more fully into its theory. Often the debates reflected a rather mechanical assumption. As Zillah Eisenstein explained the early argument, if "domestic labor is [seen as] directly exploited labor creating surplus value . . . then women can be considered the proletariat and hence potentially revolutionary because of their direct relation to capital" (Eisenstein 1979:169–70). Thus some feminists argued

Table 7.1
Slave Occupations

Occupation	Female	Male
Farm labor	3	3
Within household		
Nanny	1	0
Cook	1	0
Food buyer	1	0
Concubine	2	0
Miscellaneous	1	0
Subtotal	6	0
Wage labor or self-employed		
Porter, carter	0	2
Boat conductor	0	2
Food seller	0	1
Cook	5	0
Carpenter	0	1
Casual laborer or own business	2	2
Subtotal	7	8
Unknown	3	0
TOTAL	19	11

Caution must be employed in transferring concepts derived from the analysis of capitalism to precapitalist societies, or in the case of Mombasa, to a community in the early stages of integration into a world capitalist economy. A key difference between an advanced capitalist society and one such as Mombasa lies in the importance given to reproductive work. Under capitalism the dominance of production is reflected in the low value

---

that unpaid housework does indeed produce surplus value; some Marxists disputed this proposition or accounted for domestic labor in other ways; some feminists objected that the concepts of surplus value and productive labor as Marx outlined them dismiss women's work by placing it in a subsidiary category. I believe that to distinguish between productive and reproductive labor is not to dismiss the latter as unimportant. It clearly is necessary work. In addition, reproductive labor done without wages in the home, for example food production and processing, relieves the family of the need to purchase commodities to fulfill household needs. Moreover, "the question of whether women are oppressed as proletarians does not hinge on whether domestic labor can be squeezed into the preexisting categories of wage labor, surplus value, and 'productive' work. Rather, woman's revolutionary potential emanates from the very nature and organization of the work as *domestic* work—both in its patriarchal and in its capitalist elements" (Eisenstein 1979:170). My point is that the analytic distinction between productive and reproductive labor can be useful: I hypothesize that those slaves engaged in reproductive labor for their owner were most likely to be integrated into the household. Furthermore, the distinction between doing housework for wages and not for wages is an important one to the worker, for whom wages offer a degree of independence.

given to reproductive labor, which is most often performed by women. As mentioned earlier, such work and the people who do it are seen as worth less and are paid less or nothing. In Mombasa, however, reproductive work was valued and, I will argue later, had significant ramifications for integration into freeborn society and culture.

These cautions aside, in the case of Bi Aisha's household, the concept of productive labor is appropriate in that a portion of the surplus product generated by slave labor from agricultural products or wage labor was invested in the commercial activity of Bwana Hamisi. In the households headed by such capitalists as dhow owners, traders who financed ivory caravans to the interior, or large-scale plantation owners, this analysis of productive labor would also be appropriate. The fact that Mombasa was still a slave society in the initial stages of becoming a major seaport in a capitalist world economy at the turn of the century complicates the analysis but does not invalidate it.

By this analysis, of the twenty-seven slaves whose occupations we know, those engaged in productive work would include the six farm laborers, the food seller, the porter, the carter, the boat conductor, the casual laborers, the carpenter, and the employed cooks.[8] We would have to have more

8. Several of the occupations in table 7.1 concretely illustrate productive labor. First, slaves employed by persons other than their owners—the porter, carter, and boat conductor—did not produce a tangible item; they provided a service for some individual or company involved in trade. Still, the task of loading or transporting is essential to the process of production, hence these men produced surplus value for their employer(s) and were engaged in productive labor by the definition provided earlier (Barclay and Stenger 1975:50). To the extent that Bi Aisha used for subsistence the half of their wages that they returned to her, they were producing surplus, not surplus value for her. To the extent that she used their wages for investment in Bwana Hamisi's trading activities or to purchase additional slaves, they were producing surplus value for her as well as for their employers.

Next, although they were also employed for wages outside the household, the five female cooks were in a different position from the porter who produced surplus value for his employers but not necessarily for his owner. The cooks performed reproductive labor for their employers, the daily maintenance of family and workers. But to the extent that Bi Aisha used their wages to invest in her nephew's trade or to purchase additional slaves, they were productive workers vis-à-vis her. That is, to the degree that she acted like a present-day maid agency, which hires out maids and reinvests the surplus value they create, she was the capitalist and they the productive workers.

The third example involves the six slaves who lived and raised food crops on the farms owned by the freeborn members of the household. The freeborn members of the household lived off their surplus labor, that is, what was extracted from the slaves above their own subsistence. But they could be considered productive workers only if the food was not directly consumed by the household (this would be creating use values for the household) but was sold or traded, and if the resulting money or goods were reinvested. In the case of Bi Aisha's farms, the female slave living there with her son brought both the proceeds from the sale of food and the unsold food itself to the household; hence she generated both use values and commodities for her owner.

specific knowledge of the conditions under which their work was done and what Bi Aisha did with the surplus to make certain judgment. Furthermore, the latter six categories may have been productive in terms of the slaves' employers but not vis-à-vis Bi Aisha, or vice versa.

Reproductive Labor

Turning to reproductive work, we can distinguish three categories: biological reproduction, daily reproduction, and reproduction of the relations of production. The first includes bearing and rearing children to increase the number of slaves or freeborn members of the patrilineage. The second category includes various domestic tasks necessary to sustain the household on a daily or periodic basis—subsistence food production, cooking, washing, collecting food, carrying water, and so on. The final category, the reproduction of the relations of production, has two components: the generation and transmission of the ideology that supported the slave/free, female/male hierarchies, and the provision of services that attested to the high social status of the freeborn members of the household. The sexual division of labor was such that these three forms of reproductive labor were allocated largely, though not exclusively, to women.

Because of the intermingling of precapitalist and capitalist elements in Mombasa society, the biological reproduction of both additional patrilineage members and additional slaves was important for building a large following. These people were valued as markers of social status as well as producers of wealth. As Cooper has shown, power and position resulted from having a large following of dependents—be they slave or free, clients or relatives (Cooper 1977:213–14, passim). Hence the reproduction of individuals by slave and freeborn women, whatever the child's legal status, was of consequence. When, in the case of farm or wage slaves, they contributed directly to creating surpluses for their owner, they were additionally valuable.

A male head of a household or of a grouping of relatives, clients, and slaves controlled access to both the freeborn and slave females under him. A letter from Mbarak bin Rashid Mazrui, a leader of anti-British resistance on the coast, both illustrates this authority and suggests that women may have been challenging it. Mbarak bin Rashid Mazrui admonished the new British administrator to enforce the Islamic principle of *kafa'a,* under

---

Among the freeborn members of the household, Bwana Hamisi was a productive worker as well. Given his dependent relationship to Bi Aisha, his tasks of sewing and trading would appear to be productive labor. He was not just an independent petty entrepreneur, but a dependent relation who turned the results of his efforts over to Bi Aisha. In addition, a portion of his work as overseer of his farm was productive labor: according to Marx, that part of supervision that involves the necessary coordination of tasks is productive, that part which involves maintaining slave order is not (Barclay and Stenger 1975:50–51).

which women are supposed to marry someone of their own rank or better: "If any Mazrui woman either free or slave comes to you to tell that she is going to get married to a man other than her own caste[,] you will please not allow this. . . ." (K.N.A., Coast 1/67/14).

Among the freeborn, biological reproduction was regulated by Islamic patrilineal principles with regard to marriage and descent. Virginity was highly prized, and proof of virginity was required upon marriage. Children in a freeborn marriage belonged to the husband's patrilineage, though they might be raised by the mother herself, by her mother, by the father's mother, or by other friends or relatives.

Relations between freeborn men and slave women were complex legally. A slave concubine who bore a child to her master could not be sold and was freed upon the master's death. The child of a slave concubine and freeborn master, for example Bi Mariamu, was a freeborn, though not always socially equal, lineage member. A slave woman could not be married to her own master without being freed first; but she might be married to a man other than her owner without being freed (Strobel 1979:49–50).

Slave marriage was supervised by the slaves' owner(s). Indeed, the ex-owner's right to assent or not to a former slave's marriage was disputed into the 1920s, a dying vestige of slave owners' hegemony (Strobel 1979:51–54). The offspring of two slaves owned by the same person belonged to that person; that of slaves of different owners belonged to the female's owner, as was the case with Songhay-Zarma slaves (Olivier de Sardan, below, p. 139). That female slaves cost more than male slaves suggests the importance of the biological reproductive function (Cooper 1977:195–96). In this regard, the slaves of Bi Aisha's household must have proved a disappointment. Of the twenty-seven adult slaves, eleven (seven women, four men) had children by a master, another slave, or a freeborn man. Five (four women, one man) married but had no reported children. A substantial number, eleven (seven women, four men), did not marry or have children.[9] Of the sixteen children (slave and free) known to have been born to slaves, eleven were reported as surviving at least into early adulthood. Demographic information on fertility of both slaves and freeborn is lacking, but contemporary observers believed the slave birth rate to be low (Cooper 1977:132–33, 220–21; Meillassoux, above, p. 51).

Biological reproduction in itself did not place a slave in any special

9. It is unclear why such a large number of female slaves did not marry, given the norm in both Swahili society and their natal or ancestral societies. Demographic imbalance is not a likely explanation. Though demographic data are lacking, Cooper finds a relatively even sexual balance at least for Zanzibar and Pemba (Cooper 1977:222–23). Whatever the reason, remaining single and childless increased the dependence of these slave women on the household, particularly in their old age. Those who did not marry may have cohabited and thus been less dependent on their owners.

Table 7.2
Slave Marriages and Fertility[a]

Marital Status	Had no children	Had children	Total number of children
Females married	4	5	7[c]
Concubines	0	2	5
Males married[b]	1	4	7[c]
Females not married or concubines	7	0	0
Males not married[b]	4	0	0

[a]Females: N = 18 adults (1 female died as a grown child). Males: N = 9 adults (1 male died young, 1 male's marital and fertility status is unknown).

[b]Assumed not to have children if none were mentioned.

[c]Includes one child of free status in each category. Due to overlap from slaves being married to each other, there are a total of eleven individual children born to slaves married to other slaves or to free men. These eleven, combined with five children born to concubines, total sixteen births.

relationship to the owner. There is no evidence that slaves who had children were favored over those who did not. However, slaves who had already achieved a special relationship—concubines—were favored as a result of biologial reproduction. At the death of her master, the concubine who had given birth to his child was freed.

Most of the female slaves in Bi Aisha's household were engaged in daily reproductive tasks: child care, cooking, marketing, and other such work. In addition, the growing of food by farm slaves for use in the household constituted such daily reproduction. In the latter case the work itself did not necessarily result in social intimacy between owner and slave. But the other tasks, which took place in and about the main house, did result in intimacy. This intimacy had ramifications for acculturation and integration, as I will discuss later.

Work of slaves or dependents in this second category, daily reproduction, often served to benefit freeborn women more directly than freeborn men, since daily reproduction was the sphere of women to a greater extent than men (cf., from this volume, Robertson and Klein, p. 16; Harms, p. 101; Keim, p. 148). Given the lack of mechanization to assist in processing food, making clothing, and cleaning, the use of slaves for such work would be no small relief for freeborn women.

The final category, the reproduction of the relations of production, involves the reproduction of the values and behavior patterns necessary to maintain the system of hierarchy in its various aspects of gender, class, and race or ethnicity. The ideology of slave inferiority was expressed both in proverbs and deferential behavior (see also Olivier de Sardan, below, p. 141). Associating slaves with nature, disorder, and impurity, the dominant ideology of the freeborn asserted, for example, that "the slave is a brute beast, an enemy of God and the Prophet" (Taylor 1891:78). The slave's greeting, "Shikamoo" (I clasp your feet), was a way of humbling oneself. Similarly, slaves were forbidden to wear shoes in the presence of their owners. As part of the gender hierarchy, freeborn women were thought to require a male mediator with the outside world, due to their "weakness in body and weakness in thought." A freeborn woman was to be obedient to her husband. The ideology of wifely obedience appears not to have been applied to slave women married to male slaves (Strobel 1979:55–56, 85, 91).

Women, as well as men, were crucial to the transmission of this ideology of hierarchy. Of course, male religious teachers and officials purveyed these values, but freeborn women also articulated this ideology and maintained its hegemony. Freeborn women were noted for composing and reciting poetry, an important component of Swahili high culture. In *The Advice of Mwana Kupona upon the Wifely Duty*, composed in the 1850s by the wife of the Sheik of Siyu to the north, Mwana Kupona outlined the obedience, charm, beauty, and good manners expected in a proper freeborn wife. In addition, she instructed the young woman to maintain social distance with slaves (Werner and Hichens 1934). (People were still reciting this poem in the 1930s, a testimony to the endurance of the ideology.)

In this category of reproduction we might also include the aspects of child care that entail transmission of culture generally to the young freeborn or slave child. At a young girl's puberty, for example, the act of initiating her into womanhood in the manner imitative of the freeborn—individually, privately, without collective ritual—reinforced the hierarchy of class. And, conversely, the act of initiating a slave child into puberty according to rites brought to Mombasa by slaves was an act asserting slaves' cultural integrity and autonomy (Strobel 1979, ch. 8).

Another aspect of reproducing the relations of production would be the luxury services provided for a freeborn mistress (or master) that made life more pleasant and/or served as a token of their social superiority. For example, slave women collectively carried the *ramba* or *shiraa*, the tent-like apparatus under which freeborn women walked, singly or in groups, to protect their modesty. This manifestation of purdah gave way by 1910 to the individually worn *buibui*, presumably in part because of the abolition of slavery, not just a change of fashion (Strobel 1979:74). Similarly, in wedding rituals of the freeborn, slave women performed tasks that combined work with ritual. They rubbed the skin of the freeborn bride with ground sandalwood to make it soft and light; they painted henna on her hands and feet; they served the bride and groom on their "honeymoon" (Strobel 1979:11). To perform such tasks as these reinforced the system of hierarchical social relations. To have refused to do them would have called into question the right to demand they be done.

In their daily life both male and female slaves participated in the reproduction of the relations of production. However, biological and daily reproductive tasks were done by the female slaves of the household. The concentration of women in reproductive work had significant implications for the integration of the women into freeborn society and culture.

Reproductive Labor, Assimilation, and Integration

Aside from the category of direct biological reproduction, the extent to which a slave participated in daily reproduction and the reproduction of the relations of production for his or her owner correlated closely with the extent to which he or she was integrated culturally into the freeborn strain of Swahili culture and socially into the household itself. Biological reproduction by slaves who might engage in farm labor or other productive work did not necessarily result in closer social and cultural ties or spatial proximity to their owner. Similarly, the slaves who did productive work as wage laborers might lead lives of relative autonomy, while still being attached to the main household economically and as followers. But for slaves who were involved in the daily events of the household, both the pressure in favor of and the advantage of adopting the dominant freeborn culture were stronger than for slaves living on Mombasa's mainland outskirts. A woman who adopted "civilized" manners and behavior (from a freeborn perspective) might be taken as a concubine and, having given birth to a freeborn child, be given her own freedom at her master's death. To participate in the freeborn lifestyle, even in a subordinate position, might make one feel above other slaves who maintained more of their ancestral culture (see also Olivier de Sardan, below, p. 141).

Women's puberty rites represented one element or measure of cultural assimilation. At the turn of the century, rites associated with slaves carried, in the view of the dominant culture, the stigma of low status. Participation in such rites might, conversely, be seen as a rejection of assimilation. Collective puberty rites are common among the peoples living in central and eastern Africa in the areas from which slaves were captured. However, for Mombasa's orthodox Muslims menstruation was a private affair, to be discussed between the young girl and an adult woman, but not to be shared with others. For these and other reasons, Mombasa's freeborn population eschewed participation in the slave's puberty rites, which developed as a slave subculture over the years (Strobel 1979, ch. 8). Bi Mariamu's account stressed the freeborn people's disdain for these rites, which are led by women called *makungwi*. As she explained, "The dance of people who were not free was the makungwi's dance. . . . A child who was known to be freeborn did not go to the makungwi. The Nyasa, Nginde, and Yao, whoever wished it herself, [did it] among themselves. Some slaves here in town did not send their daughters [to the makungwi]. . . . Many don't like it themselves. You hear that they will be 'washed' in the freeborn manner."

Within Bi Aisha's household there were three makungwi. None had been born into the household; all were purchased. Takosani, Bwana Hamisi's first concubine, taught the rites to Faida, who was one of the farm slaves and herself became a kungwi. Indicative of the cultural blending of the rites, Takosani came from east-central Tanzania, Faida from Malawi. A third woman who joined the makungwi was a Nyamwezi from central Tanzania. Bi Mariamu suggested that the slaves were pressured not to join: "Bi Aisha did not like her slaves to be sent to the makungwi to be beaten and to dance naked, except for Takosani, who wanted it herself, and Faida, to whom Takosani acted as a mother. . . . The others refused to go to the makungwi, even those from tribes where many makungwi practiced. When they came here and were purchased, they could not go to the makungwi." Bi Mariamu is unclear as to whether the female slaves were not permitted to join the makungwi or chose not to. No doubt both occurred. For some slaves, continuing ancestral rites in a modified way maintained their own cultural identity. For others, celebrating puberty privately, in the freeborn manner, was a step up the status ladder. Bi Mariamu's own nanny was a Yao woman, from a society in which female rites were prominent, yet respect for these rites was not communicated to Bi Mariamu.

Bi Mariamu's statement that slaves in town were less likely to perform makungwi's rituals is ambiguous. It might indicate that the urban milieu was central to the transmission of the slave owners' component of Swahili culture, as James de Vere Allen has argued (Allen 1974). Or it might reflect the effect of proximity that would operate most strongly with slaves involved in daily reproduction within the household. Since makungwi performed their rituals inside town limits until 1934 (when they were outlawed there), urban living by itself appears to have been insufficient to determine whether or not one took on the dominant class's culture.

Evidence from the household is not conclusive on this question, but it supports the hypothesis that a slave's involvement in tasks of daily reproduction and service discouraged participation in activities of the makungwi. Proximity to the residence of her owner in and of itself was less closely correlated with whether or not a woman chose to be a kungwi than was involvement in daily reproduction. Of the three makungwi in the household, only one had close ties to the main household. She was a concubine who in fact moved out of the central house when her child died.

Table 7.3
Relationship of Residence and Work to Status as a Kungwi (N = 17)

Active as kungwi	Residence			Work		
	Near	Far	Unknown	Daily reproduction	Not in daily reproduction	Unknown
Yes	1	2	0	0	3	0
No	4	7	3	4	9	1

None of the three did daily reproductive tasks in the main household. The remaining fourteen women who were not makungwi included those who lived near and far, both on the mainland farms and in the household, and those who were and were not engaged in daily reproductive work. Thus, living far away and being engaged in productive rather than reproductive work did not assure that one would become a kungwi; but living in or near the main household and doing daily reproductive work would influence one away from becoming a kungwi.

Reproductive work had implications for one's life following abolition as well. As table 7.4 indicates, about half of the slaves or former slaves who were still alive in 1907 were freed by the colonial government. Most of the others had been manumitted. It is significant that the manumitted slaves were women involved in reproductive labor. Bi Mariamu's mother, a concubine, was freed upon the birth of her first child. The other concubine, Takosani, was not officially freed, but neither was she treated as a slave. A third woman was freed when she was given the job of raising Bi Mariamu and her siblings. A fourth, who cooked for the household, was manumitted because of old age, and a fifth for unspecified reasons.

The case of one of these women, recalled by Bi Mariamu, suggests that doing daily reproductive work strengthened one's chances of manumission:

Table 7.4
Methods of Altering Slave Legal Status

Method	Female	Male
Died prior to 1907	8	7
Freed by government	6	2
Manumitted[a]	5	0
Redeemed	0	1
Ran away	0	1
TOTAL	19	11

[a]Includes the ambiguous case of Takosani. See text.

Baadadhiki [meaning *baada ya dhiki, faraji,* "after hardship comes relief"],
her work was to cook in the kitchen. She didn't marry. She was married where
she came from [Yao territory]; when she came here she didn't marry again.
She was granted her freedom by Mwana Hadija. She freed her in writing: "She
is not my slave. I have used her many days. It's over. Now she is a *huru* [freed
slave]." Still Baadadhiki accompanied her to places. For example, if there were
somewhere to spend the day, a wedding, Mwana Hadija said, "Let's both go."
They both spent the day. If there were food and she wanted to take some, she
would do so. [When Mwana Hadija died,] she stayed with a slave from the
same household (my father's concubine who had been married off to another
man and lived in her own quarters).

Significantly, Bi Mariamu was confused about the status of slaves after
abolition. Her confusion indicates that abolition in many cases meant little
change in people's lives and that many of the relationships built through
years of paternalistic slavery continued after abolition, or manumission,
as in Baadadhiki's case (see also Keim, below, p. 155).

The continued close ties after abolition between freeborn members of
the household and slaves who performed reproductive tasks are seen further in Bi Mariamu's recounting of the life of Hanammoja.

Bi Aisha bought Hanammoja [meaning "God has no favorites"]. She gave her
to my father, but he did not make her a concubine. Hanammoja just lived
around here, that's all. She worked as she wished, for example at trading. At
the end of the month she brought money to the house. My father didn't insist
on slavery and hard work. A person stayed and worked as she liked. If she
came to the house and there was no water, she would draw some and fill the
jug. . . . Then, "I'm going home." "OK, you may go."
    When I lived at Bibi wa Shafi, servitude had been eliminated, except for the
case of a person who wanted to work herself, like Hanammoja. She was like
my mother, so in the morning she would come and sweep for me. She lived in
her own rented house. In the morning she came to sweep for me, she drew
water for me, she cooked food for me. That's it, children have been born there
and she has raised them and made them like her own. You can't come and tell
her, "Do this." No, she will do as she wishes. And if you have a chance to buy
some clothes, you give them to her. It's only friendship—done not out of slavery, but as your friend. Once the English had come you didn't dare call a person
a slave. Mama, that's all. You send her on errands, she is useful to you if she
wants to herself out of her kindness. If she is kind, she will feel, "I wasn't
treated badly there, I had no troubles. I don't want to stop greeting people from
our home. And I raised those children." So, she will come by and greet you,
and if you have a problem she will look after you. If she has gotten something
of special value, [she thinks,] "I will bring it to my child, there." And if you
have nothing, but you have money, "Mama, buy sugar so that you can drink
tea." During our time we didn't have slaves; they were our mothers and friends,
that's all.

Bi Mariamu's romanticization of slavery, should not be taken at face value. Dependence limited slaves from making free choices. Still, in this case and others in Bi Mariamu's family, the relationship between owner and ex-slave continued after abolition.

Hanammoja's post-abolition work career illustrates a common option open to female slaves—reproductive work for wages. The economic development of Mombasa favored occupations of men more than women: porterage, longshore work, and other work associated with the port. Women took paid domestic work, became prostitutes or casual wives for the migrant workers from upcountry, or engaged in petty business provisioning the workers. All of these options represented reproductive work in the sphere of wage labor or petty trade.

The career of another female slave, Hidaya, is indicative of the business activity of women of the lower stratum of society. Before abolition Hidaya was a wage earner. After 1907 she sold palm wine, a common occupation for women until the colonial administration restricted it in the second decade of the century (Strobel 1979:136–38). According to Bi Mariamu, after Hidaya learned that palm wine was forbidden by Islam, she quit that profession and entered real estate. She used the palm wine profit to buy a few houses, which she rented out. Finally she sold all of her houses and built the Hidaya mosque, the only one in Mombasa financed by a woman (Berg and Walter 1968:74–75).

Interestingly, the option of domestic wage work underwent changes after World War One. Males began to replace female workers in domestic service occupations except that of child care. The causes of this change are not clear. It is possible that colonial taxation policies, which demanded that males but not females pay taxes in cash, encouraged men to find domestic work, given the relatively few options for male wage labor. Mombasa oral sources suggest that female ex-slaves chose petty trade over domestic wage work. As one freeborn woman said, the former slaves got "big heads." However biased this view, it is quite conceivable that ex-slaves would choose, if possible, work that was not associated with former servile status.

Conclusion

Several implications follow from the observation that in this household, and on the Swahili coast generally, there existed sexual division of labor in which reproductive work fell largely to women. Most obviously, for concubines, biological reproduction represented a route to manumission that was unavailable to men. More important, daily reproductive work brought female domestic slaves in close contact with their mistresses, whose task it was to supervise the household economy and work. Such contact could become intimacy and could foster the assimilation of slave women into the dominant culture of the freeborn. Certain forms of domestic work in fact required the learning, if not internalizing, of freeborn values and culture (Gillis 1979:152). For example, nannies, cooks, seamstresses, and those who physically served their owners had to recreate the material culture of the freeborn or behave according to freeborn standards. They spent their day among the freeborn members of the household and under their eye. In the case of nannies, they played an important role in socializing the young freeborn children. Thus, female slaves who performed reproductive work for their owners appear to have had greater opportunity and impetus to be absorbed socially and culturally into the world of their freeborn owners.

Finally, female slaves performed essential reproductive tasks, even within a stratified society in which most slaves' role was to produce surplus value more than to increase the number of lineage members. The use of the term "reproduction" in the limited sense of biological reproduction has obscured the other important functions of daily reproduction and the reproduction of the relations of production that were performed by these women.

References

Oral Sources

Interviews conducted by Margaret Strobel in Mombasa, 1972–73, 1975.

Unpublished Sources

K.N.A.: Kenya National Archives, Nairobi.
  Coast 1/24/243.
  Seyidie Province 1/37, Malindi District Quarterly Report 17/1/12, p. 2.
  Seyidie Province 8/157, Takaungu Sub-District Annual Report 1912/13, p. 18.
Janmohamed, K. 1978. "A History of Mombasa, c. 1895–1939: Some Aspects of Economic and Social Life in an East African Port Town during Colonial Rule." Ph.D. dissertation, Northwestern University.

Published Sources

Allen, J. 1974. "Town and Country in Swahili Culture." In *Perspectives des Études Africaines Contemporaines*. Cologne.
Barclay, W., and M. Stenger. 1975. "Surplus and Surplus Value." *The Review of Radical Political Economy* 7:48–64.
Berg, F., and B. Walter. 1968. "Mosques, Population and Urban Development in Mombasa." *Hadith* 1:47–100.
Cooper, F. 1977. *Plantation Slavery on the East Coast of Africa*. New Haven.

Cooper, F. 1980. *From Slaves to Squatters: Plantation Labor and Agriculture in Zanzibar and Coastal Kenya, 1890–1925*. New Haven.

Edholm, F., O. Harris, and K. Young. 1977. "Conceptualising Women." *Critique of Anthropology* 3:101–30.

Eisenstein, Z. 1979. "Developing a Theory of Capitalist Patriarchy and Socialist Feminism." In *Capitalist Patriarchy and the Case for Socialist Feminism*, ed. Z. Eisenstein. New York.

Gillis, J. 1979. "Servants, Sexual Relations, and the Risks of Illegitimacy in London, 1801–1900." *Feminist Studies* 5:142–73.

Kelly, J. 1979. "The Doubled Vision of Feminist Theory: A Postscript to the 'Women and Power' Conference." *Feminist Studies* 5:216–27.

Kenya. Ministry of Economic Planning and Development, Statistical Division. 1966. *Kenya Population Census 1962*. Vol. 3, *African Population*. Nairobi.

Kopytoff, I., and S. Miers. 1977. "African 'Slavery' as an Institution of Marginality." In *Slavery in Africa*, ed. S. Miers and I. Kopytoff. Madison.

Meillassoux, C. 1972. "From Reproduction to Production." *Economy and Society* 1:100–101.

Strobel, M. 1978. "Slave and Free in Mombasa." *Kenya Historical Review* 6, nos. 1 and 2:53–62.

Strobel, M. 1979. *Muslim Women in Mombasa, 1890–1975*. New Haven.

Tanner, R. 1959–60. "A Demographic Study in an Area of Low Fertility in Northeast Tanganyika." *Population Studies* 13:61–80.

Taylor, W. 1891. *African Aphorisms*. London.

Werner, A., and W. Hichens, eds. 1934. *Utendi wa Mwana Kupona (Advice of Mwana Kupona upon the Wifely Duty)*. Medstead.

Wright, M. 1975. "Women in Peril: A Commentary on the Life Stories of Captives in Nineteenth-Century East-Central Africa." *African Social Research* 20:800–819.

8 *Jean-Pierre Olivier de Sardan*[1]

The Songhay-Zarma Female Slave: Relations of Production and Ideological Status

On the eve of colonization, about half of the Songhay-Zarma population was made up of slaves, a group that included both trade slaves and domestic slaves.[2] As women constituted a good half of the population, scarcely 25 percent of the population was neither slave nor female. The point of view of this freeborn male quarter of the population has furnished, as elsewhere, the basis for research on a people, their culture, and their history. Though the universe of women and the universe of slaves often overlap with that of the dominant local class and sometimes are even integrated with it, these universes form autonomous fields that do not always involve the same perception of things as is had by the larger society because they do not hold the same position within it. Fortunately, anthropology has belatedly discovered the existence of slaves and women. It is not, however, enough simply to describe the condition, the status, or the cul-

---

1. Translated by Martin A. Klein.
2. Strictly speaking, neither the term *trade slave* nor the term *domestic slave* is correct. Trade slaves were those enslaved during their lifetime by feuds, wars, and raids. They were not exported in any significant numbers and were used in production. Equally important, domestic slaves were not always a part of the master's household. Many lived apart in autonomous households and paid tribute to their masters. The terms *trade* and *domestic* do indicate the modes of reproduction of these two categories: the one reproduced through exchange, the other within the domestic community. These terms have also long been conventional terms, as is the French term *captif*. Though *captif* was originally used by the colonial administration to avoid using the term slave, it is now used over large areas to translate indigenous words meaning "slave."

ture of dominated groups, whom the dominant culture of the male and freeborn considered as inferiors and tended to ignore. It is also necessary to rehabilitate the language, ideology, perception, and point of view of slaves and women in order to get a more complete understanding of the societies and cultures of which they were part.

Unfortunately, the following pages will not completely fill the need, because I did not undertake a systematic inquiry among ex–female slaves about their situation both as women and as slaves.[3] So I will try to deal with the problem in the only "objective" way that seems possible—in terms of the division of labor. Who did what task? The response to that question depends neither on the way the society studied presents itself nor on the ideological patterns of the anthropologist. By contrast, if we look at the status of females, and particularly of female slaves, we find ourselves looking at the dominant ideology of the society in question, which was both masculine and freeborn, and at that of Western anthropology, which is also male-centered. Thus, it is not neutral to speak of the "exchange of women" or of the "reproductive function of women." It is necessary to reexamine the problem—and the analysis of the Songhay-Zarma female slave will help us in this—because men also can be exchanged and men have a reproductive function. Marriage and birth only exist through social roles which cannot simply be taken as "neutral" or as "objective functions." I will thus try to question the dominant ideology about the functions assigned to women, and especially to female slaves.

Such an approach, which might be surprising to historians, is not simply due to an anthropological point of view on the past, but also reflects methodological constraints. A social history or a historical anthropology of the Songhay-Zarma can be constructed only with great difficulty before the nineteenth century because local oral traditions are dissimilar and poorly structured and because knowledge with historical and sociological content rarely has more than two generations of depth. As for written sources, they deal only with the long-gone medieval Songhay empire and reflect the preoccupations and point of view of the Islamic intelligentsia of the time (Olivier de Sardan 1975).

So, in this paper the sources available on the question of female slavery (like other precolonial social structures) are limited essentially to: a) personal interviews with contemporary Songhay-Zarma peasants on precolonial institutions and customs; b) the testimony of colonial archives (administrators' reports and district monographs) as well as the descriptions

---

3. This article is based on fifteen years of research on Songhay-Zarma civilization. The reader who desires more detailed and descriptive accounts which contain information on slavery can consult Olivier de Sardan 1973b, 1976, and 1982.

of travelers and explorers (such as Barth); c) the observation of "surviv-als," largely at the ideological and symbolic level.

The pages which follow are thus an attempt to construct a "sociology of the past" limited in time to the late nineteenth century. But within this sort of "diachronic slice," different strata shine through, which testify to the tangled presence of social and ideological structures reflecting two distinct stages: an earlier "lineage" stage, in which slavery played only a minor role, and a more recent "slave" stage (either medieval or appearing in the nineteenth century), which is linked to the development of social cleavages, to the appropriation of power by an aristocratic caste, and to an increase in warfare (Olivier de Sardan 1982).

The status of women has certainly been modifed by this passage to a "class" system, particularly in the increasing social importance of slaves and the transformations of the symbolic systems which accompanied it, though numerous traces persist from the earlier lineage period.

Before considering the sexual and social division of labor and the place that female slaves had in it, and before linking this situation with the roles, the status, and the symbols associated with them, we must briefly describe the major precolonial relations of production. It is difficult to isolate one social relationship, such as the master/slave relationship, from others (el-der/younger, aristocrat/peasant, and so on), and still more difficult to iso-late one pole of a contradiction (the female slave) from its opposing poles (the freeborn male or female, the male slave, the man . . .).

Songhay-Zarma Society

The Songhay-Zarma inhabit western Niger (on both sides of the river) and eastern Mali. Their sociopolitical structures had changed between the medieval Songhay empire and the beginning of French colonization. They were divided into small chieftaincies, linked by complex and fluctuating alliances and conflicts between rural aristocrats, often dominated by Tuareg nomads. They absorbed groups of diverse origins. Though there were traces of the Islamization that took place during the era of Askia Mo-hammed, the mass of peasants converted, or reconverted to Islam only with the Fulbe revival of the nineteenth century. Slavery had a consider-able extension. More than half of today's population is of slave origin. The social stereotypes associated with the status of slave or slave descent are still alive, although the corresponding social and economic relation-ships have largely disappeared. No descendant of a freeborn person will marry a descendant of a slave, and everyone in a village can say who is "slave" and who is "free." Cheek and rudeness are considered appropriate for slaves, modesty and generosity the attributes of nobles.

Relations of Production and the Domestic Community in the Nineteenth Century

The fundamental unit for the processes both of production and of consumption was the domestic community, which grouped from twenty to fifty persons or more under the authority of an elder whom I will call the patriarch. It was not really a lineage, because political disorder and the mixture of peoples had long since destroyed any global lineage structure and prevented it from serving as a general system for the organization of society. Four relations of production can be distinguished:

1. The relationship between the patriarch and the young. In this patrilineal and patrilocal society, the patriarch controlled most of the labor of the different nuclear families (younger brothers, sons, nephews, their wives and children). The men worked together in the collective fields; the patriarch managed the stocks of millet and daily consumption, and was responsible for the basic clothing of everyone.

2. The relationship of master and domestic slave. The domestic slave (*horso*, a term of Bambara origin) was born in the household. He or she could neither be sold nor mistreated, under threat of magical punishment. Horso were feared because it was believed that they had magical power. Classed as relatives, horso were addressed by the master's children as "father" or "uncle" or "aunt," yet were treated more or less like perpetual minors.

3. The relationship of master and "exchange" slave. I am speaking of those often called "trade slaves," taken in recent raids or purchased, who had not been exported but were being used within the domestic community. Their reproduction took place through exchange, since their offspring entered the domestic slave category (see Olivier de Sardan 1973b; and above, Meillassoux.) Although the domestic slave was integrated into kinship relationships, the exchange slave (called *cire banniya*, literally *inferior slave*) was considered like the cattle. Exchange slaves could be submitted to any treatment, sold, given away, beaten, chained. They were not people but a commodity. They were not yet resocialized as domestic slaves, horso.

4. The relationship between men and women. Unlike the above, the relationship of production between men and women took place within a very elaborate division of labor. The sexual division of labor was (and still is) the basis of the agricultural production process. The cycle for the production of millet, the staple crop, is an example. The overlapping of male and female tasks within the production process made the cooperation of men and women indispensable. The relations of production described above were marked by an inequality of status and a control by the patriarch either

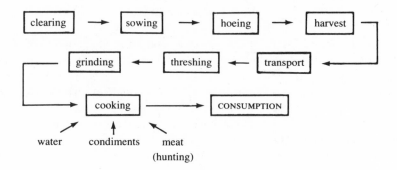

Figure 8.1. Stages of Production and Preparation of Millet.

of labor or of the product of labor. By contrast, the inequality between men and women was marked by a rigid division of labor. This hid female surplus labor and made it more difficult to measure. There were different relations of production—a woman could be a female dependent, a domestic slave, or an exchange slave—but on the level of production and of expropriation of surplus, the difference is not always clear. We must thus grasp the articulation of the relationship.

Among free but poor peasants, the domestic community may consist of only two relationships—elder/younger and male/female. This was also true of "autonomous" domestic slaves who entered into a tributary relationship with their masters. I have not spoken of tributary relationships because they were external to production and beyond the domestic community. Slaves living in separate domestic communities or distinct wards often paid dues to the aristocracy of the village. Other forms of tributary relationship were the payment of goods by simple peasants to their chiefs and by whole villages to Tuareg overlords.

The elder/younger and the male/female relationships thus constituted the basis of all domestic production. With colonization, the former disappeared, the unit of production was reduced to the domestic family, and the sexual division of labor remained as the basic relation of production within the framework of semicommercial agricultural production. Differences of class within the peasantry, founded on unequal access to land, are still rare and have relatively little importance.

In precolonial times, when the male/female relationship combined with the elder/younger one, men and women were in neither face-to-face nor complementary relations within the nuclear family. Men worked in the fields or repaired the houses. Women ground the grain, carried water from the well, or cooked, but within the framework of collective action appropriate to each sex. It was thus the eldest wife of the patriarch who controlled or coordinated female labor. The elder/younger relationship was found in a certain sense within the universe of the women as well as within that of the men. Women were exploited or dominated *on the economic level* through the person of the patriarch and as a result of the unequal sexual division of labor. The woman was thus not exploited or dominated by her own husband.

Let me underline that as elsewhere, Songhay-Zarma society was male-dominated and male-centered, at least at the level of the dominant ideology, of public discourse, and of public power. There were also gynocentric ideologies in the same way that there were ideologies specific to the horso, the domestic slaves.

Male and Female Slaves within the System of Production

Male and female slaves were thus included within relations of production which already existed, both structurally and historically, and continued a parallel existence. Slavery did not provide the basis for a social and economic revolution reorganizing production around a new class structure. Domestic slavery, in particular, developed within a preexisting matrix of male/female and elder/younger relationships. Male and female slaves were managed by the patriarch and integrated into production within the domestic community. Male slaves were given the same male tasks as dependent younger males. Female slaves received female tasks. Conversely, all dependents (male offspring, slaves, women) had the right to possess and cultivate their own personal fields (*kurga*), whose product belonged to them. Within aristocratic families, the significant number of slaves and tributaries made it possible for women and younger members of the family to be released from productive labor either because of age or military commitments. In more modest freeborn families with only one or two slaves, possession of slaves simply permitted a larger domestic community without modifying its function.

With the male trade slave things changed a little. The owner could do whatever he wished with such a lowly slave. Here there was a possible modification of the sexual division of labor. Such an inferior slave could be forced to grind grain or draw water. Only his labor force counted, and it could be used wherever it seemed most useful. The reverse was less true. An inferior female slave would not, in general, be put to work in the fields. Perhaps this was a consequence of the male-centered ideology which placed greater value on male tasks, which exalted the difficulty of male labor and the symbolism of physical strength, and which could not admit that women were capable of weeding and clearing land.

Trade slavery remained economically marginal. The simple fact that this relation of production could only reproduce itself through exchange (trade, gifts, raids) limited its extension. Although there was always a reserve supply of inferior slaves, production could not depend on them, and slavery as a relation of production could only exist within the interstices of other relations of production.

As far as female slaves were concerned, the sexual division of labor remained the dominant structure. The domestic slave and even the inferior slave performed so-called female tasks alongside female dependents.

From the economic point of view, the condition of the female slave was not particularly unusual and was determined by age and sex. It is precisely this contradiction between the absence of a relation of production specific to the female slave and the importance of connotations associated with her status which seems interesting to me and which I would now like to analyze.

Social Status of Slaves

To do this, we must explore the semantic field within which the term *slave* is found. In effect, Songhay-Zarma society structured its sociopolitical symbols on a radical opposition between *borcin,* the freeborn and noble male, and *banniya* (or *tam*), the slave. Each category had a very precise corresponding physical and psychological ethnotype. Nobles were delicate-featured, slender, and harmonious. They were generous, modest, discreet, and well-mannered. Slaves were rough and rude. They had no sense of shame (*haawi*) and therefore were crude, immodest, and impertinent.

Although the status of the domestic slave was different from that of the exchange slave, both found themselves in the same position when seen within the slave/freeborn dichotomy. There was no special term for the trade slave as a social category. In contrast, the domestic slaves could be identified as horso, but they returned to the totality of slaves (banniya) when that totality was opposed to that of the freeborn (borcin).

Banniya has a feminine equivalent, *kongo.* Any female slave was called kongo. But there was no female equivalent to horso. It is as if there was no need to specify whether she was a domestic slave. Besides, we have seen that the position of the female slave in the system of production depended little on whether or not she was a horso, which was different from the situation of the male. Conversely, we can ask if the connotations linked to the term *kongo* keep us from applying the characteristics of the trade slave to the totality of female slaves, whatever their status and that of their spouses.

On one hand, the female trade slaves benefited on the economic level from an identity of their functions with those of the female domestic slaves and, as a result, with those of the female dependents, which made their situation less difficult than that of the male trade slaves. On the other hand, on the social level the female trade slave was associated with all of the stereotypes of the kongo. Within the field of production, the female slaves were women. Within the social field, they were slaves.

We must recall here that the point of departure for slavery, its "historical truth" in a certain sense, was kidnapping. Without men and women taken in raids, sold, and traded, without trade slaves taken prisoner during wars, bought on the market, there would have been neither freeborn (defined by opposition to slave) nor horso as a specific condition. In fact, the acknowledged status of the slave, which was manifest in the slave's integration both into the domestic community and into the society, was that of horso. The banniya/borcin dichotomy existed on the semantic level without necessarily determining the real status of the female slaves (kongo). This dichotomy was a sort of return to the sources, permitting the application to the totality of slaves, male or female, horso or not, of stereotypes which did not correspond to the real conditions of their integration.

This appears more clearly for the women, especially if we take a step back to the time of the original kidnapping. The bulk of the prisoners taken in a raid or during a war were women and children. It is often stated that adult men were rarely taken, either because they defended themselves desperately or because they were put to death. With a man, there was a constant risk of escape. We are not dealing here with people systematically organized for the production and export of slaves. Furthermore, the exchange value of a female slave was higher than for a male slave. To understand this, we must turn to values other than the productive function. Clearly, the female trade slave had a "value added" greater than her place in the division of labor. We can isolate two elements here, her role as sexual property and her reproductive function.

The Female Slave as Sex Object

The conception of the inferior slave as merchandise meant that the master could do with this person whatever he wished. This offers a supplementary possibility in the case of women. They could be sexual assets which the master appropriated for his own use. There is abundant evidence that such was the case. This differentiated slave women from free women. The attitude of the society towards premarital sexual relations varied from region to region, but in the case of the freeborn girl, the choice of sexual partners before marriage was freely made. As in most African societies, rape was unknown. Marriage had a variety of meanings—the alliance of two families, the foundation of a social and eco-

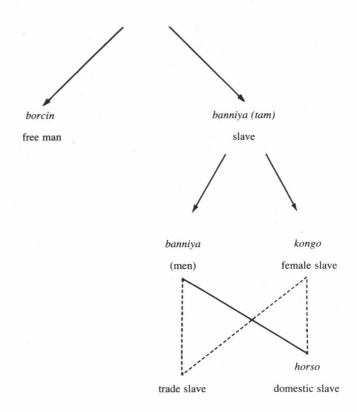

borcin   banniya (tam)

free man   slave

banniya   kongo

(men)   female slave

                                    horso

trade slave   domestic slave

———— Status defined by an indigenous Songhay-Zarma concept.

-------- Status not defined by an indigenous Songhay-Zarma concept.

Figure 8.2. Slave and Free: The Semantic Field.

nomic order, the expression of sexual inequality—but it was never the
sale of a sexual right. This is in contrast to classical Western bourgeois
society, where marriage is all of these things as well as sexual rights. In
spite of Islamization and polygamy, the autonomy of women remained
quite extensive, even in the area of sexual desire. They often took the
initiative in separation or divorce. The wife had the right to deny her
husband sexual access, and to leave her husband's house to stay for a
while with her family.

From this point of view, the existence of female slaves was an innovation and introduced into the culture the notion of the woman as object, available for the sexual interests of the master. This is certainly why immodesty and crudity are part of the slave ethnotype, particularly for the female slave. This is true both in the dominant ideology of the freeborn and the dominated ideology of the slaves. The griot (in this case, by choice of profession) and the female slaves are the archetypes of the slave, with whom the social and psychological characteristics of the slave are most vividly associated: bluntness of speech, obscenity, absence of shame.

The kongo might be a female domestic slave. When she was, she found herself in an ambiguous area where she had both a master and at the same time a husband (generally a slave of the same master). While the master could not abuse her as if she were a simple slave, he was in a position of force in relation to her. Although she was no longer objectively a sexual commodity, she still carried some of the attributes of one. The marriage of two domestic slaves was certainly modeled on that of the freeborn, but it tended to be a bargain-basement marriage which, though taken seriously by the horso, was much less seriously treated by the freeborn. It did not have the same consequences, particularly in questions of descent and inheritance.

The Female Slave as a Producer of Offspring

For the freeborn the production of offspring was done by two people through marriage, and posed the problem of descent, that is to say, the claim of one group or another on the children. For slaves, the production of offspring took place within another context: from the point of view of the freeborn, descent was secondary. What counted was to whom the child belonged. Although the Songhay-Zarma were (and are) patrilineal and patrilocal, slaves were ruled by a form of matrilinearity and matrilocality. The child of two slaves belonged to the master of the woman, just as the increase of a herd belonged to the owner of the cow. This principle was equally valid for the horso and for the simple slave. The livestock model appropriate for the trade slave was also applied to the horso. This confirms our hypothesis that the ideological matrix for slavery was based on the trade slave.

The production of children within free families operated through the complex ritual of marriage and was integrated within a network of rights and duties toward various parents and ancestors. The most important relationship, the official one, was patrilineal. It determined the name, the principal rights of inheritance, and all that was associated with virilocality. Nevertheless, unofficially and discreetly, matrilineal descent persisted. As elsewhere, the notion of "children of the same mother" (*nya-ize*) implied affection and mutual aid, while the symmetrical concept, "children of the same father" (*baabi-ize*), evoked rivalry and competition. It was not simply polygyny that forged the ties between children of the same wife in opposition to those with half-brothers and half-sisters born to the other wives. The level of divorce, which in precolonial times was matched by a high percentage of widows, was such that each man and each woman had on the average three successive spouses. Furthermore, the notion of nya-ize was related to that of "descent by milk." On another level, the opinion of the maternal grandparents was considered in the marrying of a son or daughter, and they received part of the bridewealth. This bridewealth can be considered as compensation for the concession of political and economic rights over future children by the woman's family. Its development may well have been linked to the transformation from matrilinearity to patrilinearity which seems to have accompanied Islamization. Various traces persist in memory and in custom of an earlier descent system in which matrilinearity was preeminent.[4]

If the combined effects of patrilineal structure and the male-centered ideology make it possible for anthropologists to use the notion of "exchange of women," then an earlier matrilineal descent system involved an "exchange of men." We must remember that it was not men and women who were exchanged, but rights, relations, and assets. Furthermore, these exchanges had as their basic symbolic support neither the man nor the woman, but the future children. In contrast with slavery, this exchange system disappeared or lost most of its importance. From the point of view of the master, the only person who counted in the public ideology, it made little difference whether or not the children of the kongo were bastards. This was the supreme insult among the wellborn. It also mattered little who the fathers were. The status of the slave made it possible to define the production of offspring strictly in terms of the reproductive role of the woman. The man was no longer necessary to determine who held what right over offspring with patrilineal and matrilineal groups. The biological father and mother both lost these rights, which belonged only to the woman's master. Of course, there was a contradiction between this ideological edifice and the way the horso actually lived. They sought to reproduce the forms of social organization of the freeborn, and thus adopted their forms of marriage and descent, though it was the structure put into place by the nobles that won out in cases of conflict. The nobles controlled the state and the courts. The law that a slave belonged to his mother's master was one of the few absolute and uncontested laws in effect during precolonial times.

4. For a fuller discussion of evidence of earlier matrilinearity, see Olivier de Sardan 1982.

There was one other absolute rule, though of another kind. A free woman would never have thought of marrying a male slave. But the reverse was not true. Free men could and did marry female slaves. Why?

The Concubine

The female domestic slave could sometimes be married to the freeborn male. She then became a *wahay*, a concubine in the Muslim sense. Her status changed. She was purchased and given a place in the household of her "free" spouse. Theoretically, she was free and her children were also free. They could even accede to a chieftaincy if the father was a chief. However, such offspring were always pursued by malevolent rumors which recalled their servile origin, and diverse oral traditions made much of insults suffered by various distinguished aristocrats born of wahay. *Wahay-ize*, "child of a wahay," had a pejorative connotation, and furthermore was frequently replaced by *kongo-ize*, "child of a slave."

Let us compare the advancement involved in a female slave becoming a wahay with two other forms of manumission: ransom or redemption, *fansa*, which permitted the recovery of relatives recently taken prisoner; and manumission according to Koranic law, *sawan*, which was little done in rural areas and was of little importance to the horso who were already integrated. In fact, a kongo really became a wahay only if she brought children into the world. She had to be the mother of freeborn children to become truly free herself. In marrying a freeborn person, she only went half way, being no more than a sexual object for him. If she were no longer to be a producer of slaves, then she had to provide him with free-born offspring. While ransom represented a return to the *status quo ante* (reintegration into the society of birth), manumission remained a luxury of the Muslim aristocracy, allowing their lowly slaves to go where they wished. For a female slave, the fact of being married to a freeborn involved advancement to a new status, which was both original and ambiguous. She owed it only to the good will and desire of her master-spouse, and she could fully assume it only in "giving" him children. These children, in effect, escaped the servile status of their maternal family, even forgetting and denying an origin which remained shameful, and abandoning any form of matrilineal descent. In a sense, the concubine only left her slave condition paradoxically and equivocally through two socio-ideologic traits that characterized the kongo: sexuality and the production of children. She had to be married, which entailed sexually attracting a freeborn male, in order no longer to be only a sexual object, and she had to produce children in order no longer to be only the producer of slaves.

The Wet Nurse

There was one other role assumed by female captives, which was at the heart of the distinction between horso and trade slave, and which referred to one of the remaining forms of matrilineal descent: that of wet nurse.

The role of milk as a common symbol of kinship and of alliance was central. The "children of the mother," nya-ize, defined themselves as having been nursed by the same person, or in a metaphoric sense, as descendants of the same ancestor, as "kin through the women." If the normal social production of children within the framework of marriage was done by two people at a minimum (except in the case of slaves), nursing was specifically feminine, and milk became the support of matrilinearity. From this fact, relations of political alliance were set up or were reinforced by kinship models, which were often sealed by a "milk pact." Two elders drank together the milk of a cow which on its first calving had given birth to another cow. Henceforth, an irrevocable alliance (*hasan-nda-hini*) united their descendants, and whoever violated it would be punished through the force of this pact. The milk, drunk together, created a kinship link of the maternal type, which today is often cited jokingly as a token of relationships between two distinct ethnic groups.

The relationship between a master and his horso slave of the same generation resembled this sort of "cousinhood," and was included in this type of alliance (hasan-nda-hini). It was, in fact, the best guarantee of the horso's status, because the master who mistreated or sold a coeval horso would be punished without any human intervention simply by the play of the hasan-nda-hini. In effect, both had drunk or could have drunk the same milk, because, born in the same house at the same time, they were or should have been nursed by the same wet nurse. The mother of the horso became to a certain extent the mother of the freeborn child, and he in turn became the "milk brother" of the horso child. Recourse to slave women as wet nurses thus implied, in a society where the symbolic role of milk was very strong (magic and sorcery were presumed to be transmitted through milk), an integration of slave women as "mothers," which in turn reinforced the use of kinship terms to designate specific relations between masters and horso family slaves.

With this, we come in a certain sense back to our point of departure. If, at the level of production, nothing differentiated the female domestic slave from other women, by contrast, at the level of symbols and of social status, the female domestic slave was clearly differentiated from the free woman by being included within the stereotype of the female slave. Nevertheless, she could, through the nursing function, achieve a status analogous to that of free women and through that be the support of the most specific feature of African slavery, domestic slavery.

In bringing into the world her own children, the domestic slave only expressed the slave condition. These births, essentially fatherless, inevitably reproduced the social system of captivity. By contrast, in nursing the children of her master, the female domestic slave became a relative, a member of the family. Her own children equally profited from the milk she gave to the young freeborn. In the first case, she was simply a brood mare who brought forth human stock. She was like a cow. In nursing, she became a mother.

Glossary

baabi-ize: children of the same father.
banniya: slave.
borcin: freeborn noble male.
hasan-nda-hini: special permanent alliance between individuals and between their descendants.
horso: domestic slave.
kongo: female slave.
nya-ize: children of the same mother.
wahay: concubine.
wahay-ize: child of a wahay.

Selected Published Sources

Diarra, A. 1971. *Femmes africaines en devenir, les femmes zarma du Niger.* Paris.
Gado, B. 1980. "Le Zarmatarey, contribution à l'histoire des populations d'entre Niger et Dallol Mawri." *Etudes Nigériennes.* Niamey.
Kimba, I. 1981. "Guerres et sociétés, les populations du Niger occidental au 19° siècle." *Etudes Nigériennes.* Niamey.
Olivier de Sardan, J. P. 1973a. "Personnalité et structures sociales; à propos des Songhay du Niger." In *La notion de personne en Afrique noire,* ed. G. Dieterlen. Paris.
Olivier de Sardan, J. P. 1973b. "Esclavage d'échange et captivité familiale chez les Songhay-Zarma." *Journal de la Société des Africanistes* 43:151–67.
Olivier de Sardan, J. P. 1975. "Captifs ruraux et esclaves impériaux du Songhay." In *L'esclavage en Afrique précoloniale,* ed. C. Meillassoux. Paris.
Olivier de Sardan, J. P. 1976. *Quand nos pères étaient captifs, récits paysans du Niger.* Paris.
Olivier de Sardan, J. P. 1982. *Concepts et conceptions songhay-zarma (histoire, culture, société).* Paris.
Prost, A. 1970. "Statut de la femme songhay." *Bulletin de l'IFAN* 22:2.
Rouch, J. 1953. *Contribution à l'histoire des Songhay.* Dakar.
Rouch, J. 1954. *Les Songhay.* Paris.

9 *Curtis A. Keim*

Women in Slavery among the Mangbetu c. 1800–1910[1]

Among the Mangbetu-related peoples of northeastern Zaire, slavery must be viewed primarily as an institution for improving control over the physical and social environment. The inhabitants of the region between the Uele and Nepoko Rivers, with abundant land and numerous enemies, found it advantageous to capture foreigners and to employ them in production and defense. Slaves increased the wealth and power of their owners and contributed to status and the ability to survive. It was in this context that female slaves (*amudjaandro*) became important. Females were easier to capture and control than males, and they were more quickly integrated into the owner's lineage; they were unarmed, untrained in combat, and conditioned for submission to males. Moreover, women carried on a major proportion of the productive work and were capable of reproducing the population through their children (interviews: Abesionzi; Mezeri). It is not surprising that efficiency in the use of foreign resources usually meant the enslavement of women.

Most sources on Mangbetu slavery state that female slaves outnumbered male slaves significantly. For example, Armand Hutereau, a Belgian who carefully studied aspects of Mangbetu society in the first decade of the twentieth century, described slaving operations after talking to Mangbetu and closely related Meje informants: "If the chief does not accompany the [slaving] expedition, the warriors bring back to him the hands and genitals of the enemies whom they have killed as proof of their courage and to show that they only killed men. Women and children must be imprisoned

1. Research for this paper was done under fellowships granted by the Social Science Research Council, the American Council of Learned Societies, and the Fulbright-Hays Doctoral Dissertation Abroad Program. The statements and conclusions are those of the author.

and brought back to the village as slaves" (Hutereau 1909:84). While Hutereau's report is illogical (body parts of enemies would be no proof that only men were killed), it strongly suggests that the Mangbetu preferred women and children as slaves.[2]

Female slavery, however efficient, had disadvantages. Women could fulfill only one type of economic need: "women's work." Amudjaandro contributed cultivating, cooking, housekeeping, pot making, basket weaving, and bearing children. The commodities produced in these activities were basic to livelihood but, with the exception of children, they were not highly regarded exchange items (Keim 1979:323–26). Moreover, the efforts of the amudjaandro benefited primarily the free wives of their (male) owners rather than the owners themselves. By contrast, male slaves did "men's work" and could thus relieve their owners of personal toil and complement their owners' capacities. Their products—game meat, fish, palm oil, buildings, defense, porterage, and sometimes iron—were highly valued both in themselves and (in some cases) as currency. The difference in roles between male and female slaves is illustrated in Mangbetu oral history. Whereas female slaves appear only as mothers of rulers, male slaves are celebrated as fathers, hunters, fishermen, diviners, soldiers, builders, and smiths. In one story, for example, the male slave Manziga was an excellent trapper. When Manziga's master promised guests that the first slave to appear would be killed to provide meat for a feast, he was greatly grieved to see Manziga, but then greatly relieved that this slave brought with him two wild pigs, a product of his trapping ability and a substitute for his own flesh. Manziga became the father of Nabiembali, the great Mangbetu conqueror (A.A.M.A.E., Bertrand 1932:79–80). A skilled male slave, although dangerous, could be an extension of his male master, thus meriting high regard. The female slave, although easily controlled, produced less valuable commodities.

Women and Lineage Slavery: Amudjaandro

The fact that the peoples of the Uele-Nepoko region were organized in patrilineages explains why they preferred female slaves. While the Mangbetu are renowned for kingdom building in the nineteenth century, re-

2. Today a few elders state that there were formerly as many male as female slaves (interviews: Boza; Ongoro). This apparent contradiction of other sources is most easily explained as a misinterpretation. At any moment, someone who looked at Mangbetu society from the inside might have believed the numbers of male and female slaves to be more nearly equal than was actually the case, because slave women could "disappear" into lineages through marriage while slave men remained visible. This must have been especially true after 1900, the period remembered first-hand by informants, when the supply of new and therefore visible slave women decreased as a result of the colonial experience.

gional institutions remained largely those of the less centralized subject lineages. Only the Mangbetu rulers, a small minority of the population, had the organization and resources to begin to increase the proportions of slaves to free persons and males to females. For the rest of the population the largest coherent descent group, the *nebasadjo kpwokpwo,* averaged under two thousand people and did not have the organizational means to capture, control, and integrate either large numbers of slaves or large proportions of male slaves. Slaves probably made up under 20 percent of the total population.[3]

The preference for female slaves in lineage society was not merely the result of being unable to capture and control male slaves. Also at issue was the delicate balance between older and younger males. In lineage government, elders claimed leadership and its prerogatives by virtue of their knowledge of culture and their ability to coordinate society. But younger men could assert themselves because they controlled defense and a significant proportion of production. The ownership of male slaves was a potential source of conflict between these generations. If owned by elders, male slaves could eliminate the leverage of younger males; if owned by younger men, they might furnish the number of followers necessary to break away from the elders' control. Male slaves, in performing men's tasks, struck at the heart of lineage government. Female slaves went largely to older males, and provided garden production and domestic care; they did not significantly affect the capacity of their owners to control younger males. As the elders died, their amudjaandro were passed to the younger free males (interview: Kaniki).

The threat of male slaves to the balance of lineage government is illustrated by the career of Nabiembali, the first Mangbetu *nekinyi kpwokpwo* (great ruler). As a young man Nabiembali used his slaves and followers to conquer and rule lineages which had traditionally been governed through the authority of elders. To a significant degree, Nabiembali's slaves produced the goods and fought the battles which permitted him to bypass the elders and take power. In particular, the male slave Dakpala, leader of a small slave army, became an indispensable aid to the nekinyi kpwokpwo. When Nabiembali aged, he used his male slaves against some of his own sons. He refused to recognize the sons' claims to power commensurate with their increasing contributions to Mangbetu prosperity. He could ignore their demands—which were legitimate under the lineage system of

3. An estimate of 20 percent is considerably less than the impression given by some European observers (P.R.O., Armstrong 1910:6–7; Junker 1892, 3:100). The more objective visitors to the area did not place much emphasis on slavery and agree with oral sources which show that outside of the royal Mangbetu lineage it was rare for lineages to own more than a few slaves (Casati 1891, 1:127, 282; Hutereau 1909:62–63, 81–84; interviews: Abangobo; Akangwe; Mande; Mezeri).

rule—because he had the support of his slave Dakpala and other non-Mangbetu factions. The rebellious sons finally deposed Nabiembali, but some traditions report that his dying act was to disown them and pass the Mangbetu symbols of power to Dakpala. It was Dakpala who eventually killed the offending sons and established a rival dynasty (A.A.M.A.E., Bertrand 1932:48, 79–80; Denis 1961:41–61; Hutereau [1922]: 276–91). Thus, under the control of either the young or the old, male slaves were potentially dangerous to the order of lineage society precisely because they were more valuable than female slaves.

The lineages gained nearly all of their slaves through raids or war; crime, indebtedness, and famine only occasionally led to enslavement. *Matibu taapu*, "we took him in war," was the most common designation of a newly enslaved person (Van der Kerken 1932:9; interviews: Tahapu Adruanodra; Mezeri). Whenever possible, captives were taken in pairs—as mother and daughter, father and son, or as uterine sisters or brothers—as a precaution against witchcraft, which was thought to be passed from parent to children of the same sex. With such a pair in their possession, the captors could kill and dissect one individual to see if he or she was a potential witch (indicated by the condition of the gallbladder), and the other could then be pronounced fit or unfit to become a slave. Alternatively, the captive was judged by an oracle (interviews: Abesionzi; Iode, August 21, 1976; Monganga Ndona).

The decision as to the disposition of a female slave was, like her capture, usually a corporate activity. If taken prisoner in a war involving the maximal lineage, she could be passed to the leaders to serve their needs. More commonly, a female slave belonged to the minimal lineage that captured her, and the ranking males of that lineage decided her fate. A range of social and economic priorities dictated the particular use of each female captive, but the most important aspect of her placement was that in her new society she was kinless. Thus in marriage she would provide her husband with labor, but no kinship ties. Since the ideal of manhood in Uele-Nepoko cultures was closely associated with the relationship between a man and his brothers-in-law, a kinless wife was clearly an inferior wife. A common Mangbetu phrase, "the bridewealth never finishes," signifies that the gift-giving relationship between a man and his brothers-in-law was a secure trading link and, most important, a source of pride for husband, wife, and in-laws (interviews: Iode, September 29, 1976; Mande; Ngato Manzibulata).

The kinless female slave could rarely become the first wife of a self-respecting free man. Instead, she was often married to a low-status male: a male slave, a client, or a poor relation. Thus she served to increase a lineage's stock of dependents without detracting from the position of the lineage vis-à-vis its neighbors and without giving male slaves dangerous extracommunity links. A female slave could also be married to an older member of the lineage, but in this case she typically became a secondary wife. For men who already had the high status of considerable extralineage links and duties, the kinless nature of a slave wife was a benefit. She effectively increased the productive capacity of the household without increasing obligations. Moreover, she improved the standard of living of senior wives, which, one suspects, had a favorable effect on conjugal relations (interviews: Akangwe; Boza; Iode, September 29, 1976).

The kinlessness of the female slave largely determined her status and treatment. She could not become a wife in the true Mangbetu sense, for her family had not received bridewealth, and no bonds had been formed between her lineage and her husband's. Therefore she did not deserve respect. According to one Mangbetu elder, "A free wife merited dignity and was dowered. A slave wife had no dignity. She could not respond when her husband spoke. You became father, mother, brother, sister to her. She could not leave. One preferred a free wife because she could go to her family and bring back drink [i.e., gifts]" (interview: Boza). This total lack of kin placed the female slaves in the category of property for the Mangbetu. Mangbetu elders compare slaves to chickens, livestock to be disposed of or eaten at will (literally and figuratively) (interviews: Akangwe; Kaniki; Mezeri). Hutereau (1909:82) wrote that

> Slaves . . . are the absolute property of the master. He beats them, sells them, trades them, mutilates them, executes them, subjects them to the poison ordeal whenever it pleases him, without interference from the village head.
> Slaves have no right to legal protection; they have a right to justice by the chief in only one instance: if they have undergone successfully the *noele* [poison] ordeal their master must indemnify them for having wrongly accused them.

Both male and female slaves were harshly disciplined and expected to perform laborious tasks which others did not care to do: clear fields, gather firewood, carry water, prepare food, build houses, dig iron ore, cut palm nuts, and so forth (Hutereau 1909:63; interviews: Akangwe; Manziodo). On the other hand, there is evidence that their masters sometimes treated them with respect and occasionally offered them gifts (Hutereau 1909:62–63). Slaves also had the (admittedly risky) possibility of escape to kinder lineages (Casati 1891:282; Christiaens 1896:20; Czekanowski 1919:154; Schnitzer 1889:208).

Both male and female slaves could expect to remain socially inferior throughout their lives. Yet opportunities emerged in slavery which allowed slaves to move from their original complete dependence on their captors toward greater responsibility and status. Many of the opportunities were determined by factors specific to each slave's situation: ethnic group; intelligence and speaking ability; fertility; skill at farming or handicrafts; owner's age, status, and personality; and so forth. Generally the more valuable the slave was or could become to the owner, the more likely he or she was to be integrated quickly into the new society.

Status advancement also depended on sex. Women did "women's work"— production basic to life but often not highly valued by the males who dominated the society. Consequently the amudjaandro were often considered unspecialized producers who were replaceable if not expendable. For a woman slave the best route to integration into her owner's society was through her most valuable product—her children. If she produced many children, she would be celebrated. Moreover, she could advance in status vicariously through her children and grandchildren. If married to a free man, she gave birth to free children (though they were not equal, for they had no maternal uncles to defend them). If married to a slave, she could still hope to see her children with a higher status than her own; the Mangbetu considered being "offspring of slave" less onerous than being "slave." After several generations, her descendants were likely to be grafted onto her owner's family tree, their separate roots forgotten (interviews: Abangobo; Manziodo; Sadi).

Male slaves had greater potential status mobility than female slaves, for a man's production was more highly valued than a woman's. Male slaves who were obedient, respectful, and skilled could expect to receive wives, to trade and accumulate goods, and to participate with their masters in hunting and war (Laplume 1909:461; interviews: Abangobo; Kodika Kasongo; Mezeri). They could also expect to be "freed" after several years of faithful service. Freedom in this case seems to have meant liberation from daily work for the master and a closer integration into his lineage. Freed slaves were not permitted to leave, and they still owed some service to their former masters. As with female slaves, their foreign origins and those of their children were always remembered, and it was only descendants several generations away who might have been completely assimilated (Casati 1891:282; interviews: Mande; Mezeri). It was not impossible, however, for a male slave or a former slave to become a ruler. According to oral tradition, Manziga and Dakpala, respectively Nabiembali's father and captive, were slaves who achieved the title nekinyi. Manziga is reputed to have been a slave who became the ruler of his master's lineage through his skill (A.A.M.A.E., Bertrand 1932:79–80; interview: Iode, September 29, 1976). Dakpala served Nabiembali as hunter and commander of all his slaves and later broke away from the Mangbetu to found a rival kingdom.

One further aspect of female slavery among the lineages is the role it played in the emergence of the Mangbetu kingdoms in the early nineteenth century. In the Uele-Nepoko region, with its many linguistic and cultural groupings, frequent marriages with slaves provided an avenue of exchange for technology and culture. Contractual marriage—that is, marriage between free persons—tended to promote cultural inbreeding and stability because it was usually limited to contiguous and homogeneous linguistic units. Marriage with slaves, however, facilitated culture change and technology transfer because it often transcended linguistic and geographical barriers. Female captives were taken in raids on peoples who lived at a considerable distance. The amudjaandro of lineage society must stand out as one of the most significant means of culture modification, even if there were many others. In several centuries of interaction before the Mangbetu conquest, the societies of the Uele-Nepoko region became sufficiently homogeneous to make unification based on Mangbetu principles feasible. The extent to which the rulers shared basic cultural assumptions with their subjects permitted them to organize kingdoms by modifying local lineage practices (Keim 1979:21–62).

Female Slavery in the Mangbetu Kingdoms: Ambeiandro

In the nineteenth century the Mangbetu lineage came to dominate many of the peoples between the Uele and Nepoko rivers. About 1820 the Mangbetu and their followers began to conquer the peoples in that region. One by one, groups of Mangbele, Mabisanga, Madi, Bangba, Mayogo, Meje, and others fell under Mangbetu control. By 1840, Nabiembali—the conqueror and first nekinyi kpwokpwo—succeeded in establishing the Mangbetu as a noble class of considerable wealth and power. This Mangbetu success rested largely on the personality, opportunism, and reputation of individual leaders, rather than on well-established, centralized institutions. The Mangbetu created a veneer of unity primarily by modifying lineage institutions to suit ruling a multiethnic kingdom. Consequently the nekinyi kpwokpwo could not maintain the cohesion of his original conquest and his territory began to fragment. After 1850, Nabiembali's brothers, nephews, and sons ignored the interests of their lineage and founded separate Mangbetu kingdoms (Keim 1979, chs. 1–3).

By the end of the century, the traditional form of slavery was still predominant, but at Mangbetu capitals the kingdom builders had made significant modifications of lineage slave-holding institutions. One of the most important changes in the kingdom organization was that the Mangbetu royal lineage cultivated an exclusiveness within their kin group, perhaps as a way to protect their increased wealth and power. They felt themselves to be privileged possessors of social skills, and were proud of their "elongated heads, straight noses, and light skins" (interview: Iode, August 21, 1976). Unlike common lineages, the Mangbetu did not desire to make their kin group as large as possible by integrating foreign slaves. Thus the Mangbetu rulers had to find ways to profit from the work of slaves while keeping them outside of the royal lineage.

One new method of employing slaves was for the nekinyi kpwokpwo to allow his wives to become slave owners. The ruler gave *ambeiandro* (female royal slaves) to his wives to help with work in the house and field. The ambeiandro worked with and for the wives in cultivating fields, carrying water, searching for firewood, caring for children, preparing food, and completing the numerous other tasks of Mangbetu women (interviews: Abangobo; Iode, August 21, 1976). By giving each wife one nambeiandro or more, the nekinyi kpwokpwo managed a work force of at least several hundred female slaves. Since most captives and slaves given in tribute continued to be females and children, this was a useful way to keep them at the capital without integrating them into the Mangbetu lineage. The ambeiandro contributed significantly to the production and prestige of the capital. They augmented its population and increased the nekinyi kpwokpwo's ability to furnish visitors with food—an important ingredient in the Mangbetu concept of hospitality and leadership. Moreover, the ambeiandro gave the nekinyi's numerous wives a greater stake in his rule by providing labor and prestige (Keim 1979:120–22; interviews: Abangobo; Iode, August 21, 1976; Kodika Kasongo).

Another important change was that the Mangbetu no longer feared the presence of male slaves as much as did common lineages. While female slaves remained the majority, their proportion among royal slaves decreased (interviews: Iode, August 21, 1976; Kaniki; Mezeri). One of the tactics was to settle male slaves in a few slave villages outside the capital, where they were available to serve as a small military force dependent on the nekinyi kpwokpwo. In times of peace, the village slaves provided a labor reserve for building at the capital and for porterage, and their wives' gardens contributed to feeding the capital. Other male slaves served in the capital as artisans and servants, and, like the village slaves, they could not expect integration into the royal lineage (Casati 1891, 1:127; Junker 1890, 1:100).

A further change under Mangbetu rule was that the nekinyi kpwokpwo had a much larger supply of slaves than did the common lineages. With more slaves, the rulers could increase their power through redistribution and conspicuous consumption. In regions where the Mangbetu were undertaking conquest, the gift of a slave wife was an important way of attracting soldiers and subjects. Arrangements between a conquering nekinyi kpwokpwo and his gift-receiving warriors corresponded to a lineage clientship category called *mangoumiku naandro,* referring to a person who received a wife from a lineage head in return for submission (A.A.M.A.E.,

Bertrand 1932:80–81; Van der Kerken 1932:9; interview: Iode, August 21, 1976). However, such contract relationships were not as important among the Mangbetu as they were among the neighboring Azande, where each ruler derived much of his power from his position as wife giver.[4] Well-established Mangbetu rulers gave ambeiandro less often as a part of a contract than as a reward to family and friends or as largess symbolizing Mangbetu power. Wife giving tended to highlight the role of the nekinyi kpwokpwo as a great and potentially generous leader. Informants typically praised the preabolition kings by saying, "He might even have given a man five slaves at a time," or, "If asked, he might even have given a poor man a slave wife" (interviews: Boza; Iode, August 21, 1976; Katekapa; Kodika Kasongo).

The increased supply of slaves to the Mangbetu kings also allowed them to destroy some of their captives in displays of wealth. More specifically, one can attribute most reports of cannibalism among the Mangbetu to wealthy persons who were consuming, were pretending to consume, or were rumored to consume, slaves as they might consume chickens. Dakpala's son Yangala, for instance, is said to have had an enclosure where he kept tender young captives to be fattened and eaten (interview: Gbagba; see also Junker 1892, 3:100). Where cannibalism occurred among the Mangbetu, it does not seem to have been a ritual act, but an act of conspicuous consumption (see Casati 1891, 1:175, 185; Junker 1891, 2:248, Schnitzer 1889:193, 206; Schweinfurth 1874, 2:92–93; interviews: Boza, Kaniki; Kodika Kasongo; Monganga Ndona; Mezeri).

Finally, Mangbetu rule modified lineage practices by creating additional social positions between slaves and free men. This was true figuratively, for the Mangbetu often called their subjects "slaves." It was also true in fact. For example, some of the slave wives which the nekinyi kpwokpwo gave to his followers were not truly kinless. As communication increased, due to Mangbetu centralization of government, it became more difficult to conceal the kinship ties of slave wives. This is illustrated by the slave wives of Dakpala—Idala and Lepita—who were gifts from Nabiembali and the mothers of Dakpala's sons. Knowledge of their lineages was preserved so that later, when the sons themselves became rulers, the sons had the crucial military support of their mother's brothers (Hutereau [1922]:252;

---

4. Jan Czekanowski, an ethnographer who visited the Mangbetu in 1908, wrote that the Mangbetu rulers had villages of young men who expected wives in return for military service (Czekanowski 1919:55). No other evidence supports this assertion. Mangbetu informants know of no such villages. Wilhelm Junker, who traveled in the region in 1881–82, remarked that the southern Zande ruler, Bakangai, kept a large number of women to give to followers, but he made no similar observations about the Mangbetu rulers he visited (Junker 1890–91, 1–2: passim).

interviews: Modelengwe; Monganga Ndona). In both these instances the Mangbetu seem to have created servile categories similar to slavery but without the kinlessness of lineage slavery.

These changes which the Mangbetu made in lineage slavery reflect the increasing centralization of kingdom building. Yet by the end of the nineteenth century the Mangbetu lineage had not firmly established its legitimacy or completely transformed lineage government. Thus, in the case of slavery, it was impossible for Mangbetu kings to monopolize the use of slaves for themselves. In the collection and division of booty, for example, the Mangbetu ideal was that all subject lineages were to bring all valuable goods such as weapons and slaves to the nekinyi kpwokpwo for division and redistribution. In practice, most of the spoils of war remained at the lineage level and a contribution was sent to the nekinyi kpwokpwo (interviews: Katekapa; Kodika Kasongo; Makaraka; Tungi). Lineages retained many slaves for their own use and were not dependent on the king for their supply. Similarly, the nekinyi kpwokpwo expected to collect tribute in goods and slaves from all subjects, yet most of the tribute came from his relatives and in-laws and from subjects living near the capital (interviews: Boza; Kodika Kasongo; Mande; Mezeri; Palaba). There was no system of regular and required exactions, and many people gave in an irregular or token fashion (Hutereau [1922]:79; interviews: Mande; Gbondodra). As of 1900 the Mangbetu kingdoms were still makeshift kingdoms, built on less than a century of experience in centralization. Succession feuds, rebellion, and foreign attacks repeatedly destroyed capitals, fractured territories, and forced the Mangbetu to begin anew. Under these circumstances, lineage slavery remained the dominant mode of slavery in the Uele-Nepoko region until abolition in the colonial period.

A brief reference to foreign slave traders is appropriate before continuing. From 1873 to 1885, long-distance slave traders from the Nile River held the balance of power in the northern Mangbetu kingdoms. These foreigners enslaved some Mangbetu and their subjects and exchanged them northward to Arab states. However, the effect of this trade on regional slave-holding patterns was quite limited due to its short duration, the remoteness of the Uele-Nepoko region, and the resistance of the Mangbetu and their subjects. Most slaves considered to be "Mangbetu" who reached Arab markets actually came from Mamvu lands to the east, an area frequently raided by the Mangbetu themselves (Keim 1982). Later, from 1887 to the early 1890s, Swahili slave traders reached the southern Mangbetu kingdoms from the Zaire River. They stayed until expelled by King Leopold's Free State forces, but their effect on slave holding was insignificant (Lotar 1946; Lotar 1935:675–76; interview: Iode, September 29, 1976).

Abolition and the End of Slavery

The colonial period in the Uele-Nepoko region began in late 1891 with the arrival of a Congo Free State expedition. In the decade which followed, the Free State moved rapidly to expel the Swahili, establish government posts, and dominate inhabitants. Its policy of "divide and rule" meant the liberation of many subordinate lineages and the regulation of the succession of ekinyi kpwokpwo. In order to exploit the resources of the area, the colonizers excluded private traders and required the production of ivory and rubber. Many Mangbetu rulers resisted this foreign domination and pressure to produce for export, and led their subjects to anticolonial violence. By about 1905, however, open rebellion had clearly failed, and the Mangbetu kings turned to exploiting the colonial system for their own purposes (Keim 1979:292–300, 203–8).

The foreign conquest meant an end to the warfare and the slave raids of the nineteenth century. The few extant administrative reports of the 1895–1910 period seem to indicate that as European power spread into the region, inhabitants found it increasingly difficult to procure captives, which had been the favored means of obtaining female slaves in precolonial times. In order to obtain the slaves they wanted for wives and prestige, lineages and Mangbetu alike turned increasingly to kidnapping and to trade (A.H.U., Lemaire 1898; A.A.M.A.E., Longobardo 1909). It is in this light that the somewhat exaggerated 1910 report of British Acting Consul Armstrong might be understood: "In this district slavery is rife. In no other part of the Congo nor indeed in any other part of Africa that I have visited, is slavery carried on so openly. No attempt whatever is made to hide it. Natives are bought and sold, and officials take no notice whatever of the act" (P.R.O., Armstrong 1910:6). This growing trade in slaves was largely in the form of bridewealth payments; amudjaandro were too valuable to be wasted by not procuring something even more valuable in return. According to the Mangbetu historian Mezeri, "Without a daughter you could not hope to have a slave" (interview). In this atmosphere it also became difficult to keep slaves, for when a man wanted to marry a free woman his future in-laws would often ask for and would receive the man's slaves (interview: Abangobo). Thus a growing proportion of amudjaandro came to function as a high-priced prestige currency, as well as productive and reproductive capital.

During the early colonial period the Mangbetu rulers were able to procure slaves more easily than could their subject lineages, for they controlled greater resources. It is probable, however, that the number of royal slaves also decreased at this time; there is no sign of the Mangbetu developing new uses for slaves. This situation may have resulted from the restricted supply of captives and from increasing colonial surveillance. It was also due to the fact that the Mangbetu elite found new economic opportunities elsewhere. In an effort to extract goods and labor from Uele-Nepoko populations, the colonizer gave the Mangbetu coercive powers which they had not possessed in precolonial times. Subject lineages had a growing sense of being made to work for their Mangbetu rulers without adequate compensation and without choice. In short, they had a sense of being enslaved. This was particularly true in the rubber-bearing southern forests. Thus Armstrong's report (A.A.M.A.E., 1910:6–7), cited above, understandably confuses "slave" with "subject." He wrote that in the east the Mamvu were "completely enslaved . . . by Mangbetu and Mangwele [Mangbele] chiefs" acting for the Belgians. In regions south of the Bomo-kandi River he asserted that slaves formed the "larger proportion of the population" and were resisting their Mangbetu masters. In fact, the resist-ance was from subject lineages who considered themselves free. This is shown in the May 1910 *Monthly Report* (A.A.M.A.E., Acerbi) of the Bomokandi Zone which recorded that as word spread among the Mang-betu subjects that "Bula matari alingi mokobe te!" (The state no longer permits slavery!), there was considerable confusion. The subjects thought that this meant they were free to rule themselves once again, and the Belgian officials had difficulty making it clear that the abolition decree referred only to "domestic" slaves.

In 1910 the Belgians made it an offense to call people slaves and to hold slaves in the Uele-Nepoko region. There was, however, no way to enforce the decree effectively or to bestow on freed slaves the rights and privileges associated with freedom among the Mangbetu. Most slaves, especially women, remained in their places, content with their lot or afraid of the difficulties of attempting to find their former homes and reestablish them-selves among their kin. One explanation given by the Mangbetu for this tendency stresses that the slaves feared being killed by their own peoples as Mangbetu spies (interviews: Akangwe; Palaba). This is a way of ex-pressing the fact that while remaining among the Mangbetu, former slaves could gauge their future. Were they to return to their kin—now strangers—their future would be uncertain. The Uele-Nepoko region provided few alternatives to staying with former masters. By 1910 there were still only limited extralineage opportunities in colonial administration, production, or commerce.

The important question concerning the emancipation of slaves among the Mangbetu is not where freed persons went, but whether their status changed. Did they have new rights? Were they more highly regarded? For the female slaves the answer is no. The state's decrees were administered through courts and police, controlled largely by lineage elders and Mang-betu rulers. Although the colonizers were sensitive to their subjects' con-sidering someone a slave and would punish offenses, these European outsiders could hardly distinguish between a free wife and a slave wife. The amudjaandro remained kinless, without status and without protection. For a slave woman who was the wife of a free lineage man and now "free" herself, hope still rested largely in the opportunities which would be available to her offspring. Likewise, slave men and their slave wives who were now "free" still found themselves at the bottom of the Mangbetu social hierarchy. They were no longer the legal property of their masters, yet they depended on their former owners for integration into a community. Their treatment improved only slowly, and their new status was often similar to that of clients who offered services in return for patronage. While some former slaves were integrated into local lineages, even today there are descendants of slaves among the Mangbetu who are considered *ebasai*, or foreigners (interviews: Boza; Kodika Kasongo; Manziodo; Mezeri; Sadi).

Slave status faded most slowly for royal slaves. Like the royal slaves of the nineteenth century, those of the twentieth were not easily integrated into the noble Mangbetu lineage. One elder reported that even after abolition, "slaves went in the morning to serve the nekinyi kpwokpwo and help his wives. These were old slaves because we no longer took young ones in war" (interview: Mande). Such slaves after 1910 were mostly women, because women could neither establish their own households or marry into their owners' lineages. As late as 1923 a police report charged Nekinyi Kpwokpwo Zebuandra with keeping slave women (A.H.U., Officier de Police Judiciaire). Informants most often assert that the real end to slavery was connected with the deaths of royal slaves in the 1940s and 1950s (interviews: Gbondodra; Mande; Sadi; Tungi). In 1972 the author was introduced to a former slave woman who was still serving a nekinyi kpwokpwo. Royal slavery in the colonial period was less harsh than it had been in the nineteenth century, but it was persistent.

Conclusion

Among the Mangbetu the role and importance of women in slavery can be considered a function of both economic and social organization. At the lineage level, the presence of female slaves provided labor and children for mastery of the environment without disrupting the political balance between dominant older males and ambitious younger males. Through marriage with free men, female slaves and their children could be quickly integrated into lineages. Male slaves were not as numerous as female slaves because they could have interfered seriously with the functioning of the lineage society by giving their owners leverage to use against opponents.

In the nineteenth century the Mangbetu royal lineage began to centralize Mangbetu-related lineages. The existing kinship-based societies remained basic to regional politics and economics, but the Mangbetu rulers also fashioned new institutions suitable for multiethnic, territorial government. Thus while lineage female slavery was always the predominant form of slavery, new forms appeared which corresponded to Mangbetu state-building needs. For example, the royal lineage employed female slaves as domestics and refused to contaminate their lineage by integrating slaves into noble genealogies. In addition, male slaves now served as soldiers and artisans.

With colonialism, slavery became illegal among the Mangbetu. Yet because there were few opportunities outside of lineage or royal communities, few slaves gained immediate liberation from their low social and economic status. Those least able to throw off their servile positions were royal slave women.

Glossary

nambeiandro (pl. *ambeiandro*): female royal slave.
namudjaandro (pl. *amudjaandro*): female slave.
nekinyi kpwokpwo (pl. *ekinyi kpwokpwo*): Mangbetu "great ruler."

References

Oral Sources

Tapes of the interviews are deposited at the Center for African Oral Data, Archives of Traditional Music, Indiana University, Bloomington.

Abesionzi, interview on September 21, 1976.
Abangobo son of Ndanzi, interview on January 5, 1977.
Akangwe, interview on October 5, 1976.
Boza son of Mbule, interview on January 20, 1977.
Gbagba, interview on January 30, 1977.
Gbondodra, interview on March 24, 1977.
Iode son of Mbunza interviews on August 21, 1976, and September 29, 1976.
Kaniki son of Ndula, interview on February 10, 1977.
Katekapa, interview on January 30, 1977.
Kodika Kasongo, interview on August 19, 1976.
Makaraka, interview on September 8, 1976.
Mande son of Babanoo, interview on March 29, 1977.
Manziodo, interview on September 7, 1976.
Mezeri son of Bili, interview on February 18, 1977.
Modelengwe son of Misa, interview on February 2, 1977.
Monganga Ndona, interview on January 8, 1977.
Ngato Manzibulata, interview on January 5, 1977.

Ongoro, interview on October 14, 1976.
Palaba son of Gbolongo, interview on January 20, 1977.
Sadi, interview on October 13, 1976.
Tahapu Adruanodra, interview on January 7, 1977.
Tungi son of Gita, interview on January 19, 1977.

Unpublished Sources

A.A.M.A.E.: Archives Africaines du Ministère des Affaires Etrangères, Brussels.
Acerbi. January, 1911. Rapport mensuel sur la situation générale, District de l'Uele, Zone de Bomokandi, May, 1910.
Bertrand, R. 1932. Notes pour servir à l'étude des Mangbetu.
Longobardo. July, 1909. Rapport mensuel sur la situation générale, District de l'Uele, Zone de Bomokandi, July, 1909.
A.H.U.: Archives de la Sous-Région du Haut-Uele, Isiro, Zaire.
Lemaire, A. January, 1898. Rapport sur la guerre Zeboinda.
Officier de Police Judiciaire. April 14, 1923. Relégation de Danga.
Keim, C. 1979. "Precolonial Mangbetu Rule: Political and Economic Factors in Nineteenth-Century Mangbetu History." Ph.D. dissertation, Indiana University, Bloomington.
P.R.O.: Public Record Office, Kew Gardens.
Armstrong, J. P. November 3, 1910. Report. F.O. 367, 359, X/M 00403.

Published Sources

Casati, G. 1891. *Ten Years in Equatoria and the Return with Emin Pasha*. Translated by Mrs. J. R. Clay. Vol. 1. London.
Christiaens. 1896. "Le pays des Mangbettus." *Causerie du cercle africain*. Brussels.
Czekanowski J. 1919. *Forschungen in Nil-Kongo-Zwischengebiet*. Vol. 2. Leipzig.
Denis, P. 1961. *Histoire des Mangbetu et des Matschaga jusqu'à l'arrivée des Belges*. Tervuren.
Hutereau, A. 1909. *Notes sur la vie familiale et juridique de quelques populations du Congo belge*. Tervuren.
Hutereau, A. [1922.] *Histoire des peuplades de l'Uélé et de l'Ubangui*. Brussels.
Junker, W. 1890–92. *Travels in Africa, 1879–1889*. Translated by A. H. Keane. 3 vols. London.
Keim, C. 1982. "Long-Distance Trade and the Mangbetu." *Journal of African History* 23.
Laplume. 1909. In *Les Mangbetu*, ed. C. Van Overbergh and E. De Jonghe. Brussels.
Lotar, L. 1935. "Souvenirs de l'Uele." *Congo* 16:655–84.
Lotar, L. 1946. *La grande chronique de l'Uele*. Brussels.

Schnitzer, E. 1889. *Emin Pasha in Central Africa*. Translated by Mrs. R. W. Felkin. New York.

Schweinfurth, G. 1874. *In the Heart of Africa*. Translated by E. E. Frewer. Vol. 2. New York.

Van der Kerken, G. 1932. *Notes sur les Mangbetu*. Antwerp.

10 *Susan Herlin Broadhead*

Slave Wives, Free Sisters: Bakongo Women and Slavery c. 1700–1850

The question of the role played by females in the Bakongo system of slavery, particularly in the period from the early eighteenth century to the middle of the nineteenth century, is both intriguing and elusive. Interest in the subject is heightened by the fact that in the basically agricultural, matrilineal Bakongo society, women, both slave and free, were of particular importance as both productive and reproductive resources. Further interest stems from the fact that the Bakongo were active slave traders and that the slave-trading patterns of the period led to an increase of females in local societies (Thornton 1980). Finally, the subject is an interesting one because of the major role played by slaves in Kongo in a period characterized by political decentralization, ruralization, democratization, and more generalized citizen participation in commerce.[1]

In examining the role of women in Bakongo society and their relation to slavery, the most helpful theoretical model is that developed by Karen Sacks (1979). In her recent work on the roles of women in several patrilineal African societies, Sacks divides women's roles analytically into two categories, one associated with the status of sister and the other with that of wife (Sacks 1979:110–12). In general she links sisterhood with positions of autonomy, ownership, solidarity, and power; while wifehood is linked with positions of subordination, dependence, and isolation. The bulk of her case studies involve societies practicing what she terms a "kin corporate mode of production" (Sacks 1979:115–22), an analytical model which also is useful for looking at Bakongo society in this era. The central feature of Sacks's model is that the means of production are owned collec-

1. For the political history of the Kongo kingdom in this period, see Broadhead 1979a: 615–50.

tively by groups of kin, lineages, or lineage segments, whose essential relationships are those obtaining among siblings. Women in such a system participate in the ownership of the means of production through their status as sisters. In most of the cases described by Sacks, young women in their childbearing years are confined to the wife role, producing children for their husbands' lineages and laboring in their husbands' fields and compounds. Older women, on the other hand, are often more able to assume the role of sister, helping to advise on the affairs of their lineage and commanding the services of daughters-in-law. Through these cases Sacks demonstrates that there is a major contradiction between woman's place as wife and as sister. She further shows through the use of this model that focusing on women's roles is a fruitful way to approach the analysis of whole social systems (Sacks 1979:139–92).

Although Sacks does not approach directly the question of women as slaves, the distinctions she makes between the rights, powers, and duties of women in their role as sisters and as wives can be used to illuminate the position of both free and slave women among the Bakongo. In this matrilineally oriented society a free woman's reproductive capacity was not ordinarily transferrable by marriage. Thus, in contrast to the case of women in most patrilineally organized societies, for free Bakongo women the tension between spouse and sibling roles was lessened because the role of wife was secondary. The primacy of sister status at the expense of the wife role is epitomized in the lifestyle of royal princesses in Loango in the eighteenth century. They could choose any man for a husband, even if already married, and dismiss him at will (Proyart 1776:90). For most women, however, the primacy of sister status during the reproductive years basically meant access to divorce.

Slave women, by contrast, enjoyed no legal rights as siblings. Despite the fact that, as Miers and Kopytoff (1977:30) point out, they served as "sister surrogates" in the reproductive sphere, they had no recognized birth lineage. Thus, following Sacks's model, they functioned exclusively in the role of wife or dependent within the lineage which owned them. This means that the greatest contradiction in the spouse-sibling roles in the case of Bakongo women appeared not during the different stages in a single woman's life, but rather between the roles of different categories of women. The most obvious distinction was between that of free and slave women, with the latter confined, as we have seen, to a permanent wife position. There were also class distinctions in "women's places," with noblewomen generally having greater access to positions of power based on their status as sisters in ruling families. Like their brothers, at least in some circumstances, they could aspire to head households, and this apparently was the key to power within the aristocracy.

Bakongo men could only use their reproductive capacities on behalf of their lineage through marriage to, or cohabitation with, a slave woman. The offspring of slave wives of male slaves also normally belonged to the lineage owning the woman. A freeborn woman could be reduced to de facto slavery if her lineage deserted her, defaulted in its obligations, or otherwise lost its rights in her offspring. A woman without legally recognized ties of sisterhood was a slave, often to her husband's lineage.

Although it did not affect her reproductive services, marriage did transfer a part of a free woman's productive services: specifically, it obligated her to grow and prepare food for her husband, her children by him, and sometimes his relatives as well. Marriage also served to join two lineages and create a unit of production which combined the specialized labor of males and females. The marital household was the fundamental unit of Bakongo society. To the daily needs of their households women contributed grains and vegetables; pots and baskets; and cooking of the major daily meal. Men provided the hoes with which their wives farmed, goods obtained through trade or the hunt (salt, meat, fish, imported items), and tree products (bananas, palm oil, palm wine, building materials, buildings, and the cloth woven from tree fibers). Both spouses ordinarily participated in child-rearing (Thornton 1979:81–84; Laman 1953–68, 2:41; MacGaffey 1977:240).

Almost all women in Bakongo society spent their reproductive years functioning on a daily basis mainly in the role of wife. This applied equally to slave or free women, with the exception only of aristocratic women during the seventeenth and part of the eighteenth centuries. Male slaves owed only their productive services to their owner. Although they generally participated in the male productive sphere, they were sometimes required to do normally female farming tasks. They were socialized in the role of sons (albeit perpetual ones), as were clients and other political (that is, non-lineage) subordinates. These male affiliations constituted the heart of the political world of alliance and clientage and were reflected in its language. Female links were those of lineage, ownership, and belonging.

Two recent studies have looked at the practice of slavery among the Bakongo in well-documented periods. John Thornton has reconstructed seventeenth-century social structure from the abundant missionary and diplomatic records of a period when literacy in Portuguese was common among Bakongo nobles and the foreign Catholic establishment in the kingdom was well staffed.[2] He convincingly portrays a centralized monarchy socially anchored in a dominant and even culturally distinct Mwissikongo[3] aristocracy, which was town-dwelling and supported by a

2. Thornton 1979:288–305. This includes an excellent bibliographic essay on mainly seventeenth- and early eighteenth-century source materials.
3. This is rendered *Mushicongo* by Thornton (1979). The form *Mwissikongo* originated in the work of Anne Wilson (1977).

combination of large, centrally located slave-worked plantations and an extensive tribute system for gathering the surplus production of the rural peasantry (Thornton 1979:53–54, 56–57).

Wyatt MacGaffey (1977) has used late nineteenth- and early twentieth-century missionary and merchant observations to describe the slavery of the late precolonial and early colonial eras. By this time, when European influence and control were being established, slave status appears mainly as a question of lineage politics, and there is often little to distinguish slaves either economically or socially from their "free" kinspeople or neighbors (MacGaffey 1977:243–47). The distinct noble class had disappeared, along with political hierarchization and most economic distinctions between groups. Only the hierarchical ideal and some titles remained from the older order. It is clear from the two accounts that the institution of slavery, along with society in general, changed dramatically in the interval.

The processes of social change have not been studied in detail for the period between those covered by the Thornton and MacGaffey studies because relevant historical sources are comparatively thin. Those that exist do not often deal accurately (or at all) with Bakongo daily life. Missionaries, a staple source of information in both the earlier and later eras, visited less and less frequently, and for shorter and shorter stays, so that their interest in and ability to comment upon social detail diminished.[4] Because the kingdom generally excluded foreign traders from the interior, there were few other possible outside commentators. The exceptions are those who visited the north coast (Sonyo, Cabinda) or the far south (Mossul) in the eighteenth century, and those who took up residence on the coast as factors and merchants in the nineteenth century. While most of the coastal observers had a very clear interest in the slave trade, few were interested in slavery as it was practiced locally. All were male.

Despite these handicaps, it seems worth the effort to look at this period for itself, not simply as a projection of earlier or later periods. There are some available contemporary data from which it is possible to get useful clues. This is especially important in order to provide a base from which to examine the important question of the impact of colonialism on social class and sex roles. Without this base it is dangerous to read back from the time after abolition of the slave trade and the establishment of colonial political and economic domination to even as far as the mid-nineteenth

---

4. After mid-century only the accounts of Cherubino da Savona (1759–74) and Rafael Castello de Vide (1781–87) reflect extensive travels in the countryside. Only de Vide gives day-by-day accounts of part of his stay. Two accounts of Savona have been published: in Jadin (1963:343–419) and in Toso (1974:135–214). Castello de Vide's account was published in Italian translation in Civezza (1894:314–402).

century, when Kongo polities were autonomous and economic practices related to slavery were different as well.

What follows is an attempt to use existing contemporary data, in conjunction with fuller data from earlier and later periods, to draw the broad outlines of Bakongo social change, focusing especially on the roles of women in relation to slavery. Several relevant broad social trends can be discerned in this period. Political power generally became more decentralized. The numbers claiming Mwissikongo origins increased, but they could not continue the old slave-based aristocratic lifestyle unchanged. Slave trade–based foreign commerce increased, with participation in it becoming more general through the mechanisms of caravans and tightly regulated public markets. Access to slaves as an investment became more general, with women being preferred to men.

Demographically the population was stable or slowly increasing, with most people settled in dispersed rural villages. Subsistence agricultural production occupied most Bakongo, especially women. However, at the same time, commerce grew more important in Kongo. Especially from the early nineteenth century, more and more men participated at least part-time in the Atlantic trade. In areas near the coast this directly affected women as well because of the rise in demand for agricultural products. European imports had had a very serious impact on the production of local cloth and tools by the mid-nineteenth century in those areas which participated in Atlantic commerce. Also by the mid-nineteenth century, aristocratic control over the trade in and distribution of prestige goods such as slaves, cloth, and guns had weakened considerably. Access to coastal commerce by then was increasingly in the hands of large European firms, their agents and subsidiaries. Finally, in about 1860 the Atlantic slave trade itself disappeared, thus effectively confining the market for slaves to the resources of local investors only, and drastically reducing the profitability attached to their sale or exchange.

Historical Foundations of Eighteenth-Century Slavery

Bakongo society and economy in the early eighteenth century in most respects continued patterns set during the centralized period, before 1678. Distinct class lines divided seventeenth-century Kongo society, although within each of the two classes gender and kinship ties were critical in governing individual activities. The ruling class, the linked noble lineages and households which made up the Mwissikongo aristocracy, controlled the centralized monarchy, were Christian, and were often literate in Portuguese. They lived, or aspired to live, in São Salvador, the royal capital. They dominated both the internal economy and the international trade in prestige goods and slaves. The rural peasantry lived in dispersed villages.

They maintained themselves by subsistence agriculture. However, they also managed to produce enough surplus to support a small local elite[5] and contribute a considerable amount to the ruling aristocrats as well. A major contribution of the peasantry in this regard was their production of specialized items such as cloth and salt, which provided royal revenue and facilitated regional trade (Thornton 1979:64–65). Among the peasants, females predominated in agriculture and males in production of such local trade items as cloth and salt.

The rural free peasants constituted only a part of the support of the nobility. At least an equal contribution (the difference between maintenance and luxury) was made by slaves. Commerce in slaves profited the nobility in this period, providing, as it continued to do through the eighteenth century, access to prestigious foreign goods and the means with which to purchase them. However, it was the services of slaves, mobilized locally in São Salvador and Sonyo,[6] which provided the seventeenth-century nobility with their distinctive and luxurious lifestyle. The slaves of the Mwissikongo provided more than levies in kind on their own production, as the peasants did. They also contributed direct productive and reproductive services to the state. Specifically, slave-worked plantations in the capital region produced special foodstuffs for aristocratic use. Slaves and their offspring also provided household servants, retainers, and soldiers for the court.

The slave settlements of the two larger towns of the kingdom were basically organized on the model of the settlements of the rural free peasantry. To facilitate this system, masters were expected to arrange for their slaves to marry and produce families which could in time form subordinate branches of the noble lineages. In theory, the agricultural slave households which made up the bulk of the towns' populations differed from their rural free counterparts in that they were not members of land-owning lineages. Despite this legal distinction, it seems likely that in both sectors the producers themselves, the women who did most farm work, made production decisions. However, there was a significant difference in the overall organization of production between these two sectors. In slave households, both husband and wife functioned not only in terms of the usual sex division of labor but also as servants of the state. Specifically, they were required to work in fields especially designated to grow the millet preferred for consumption in aristocratic households. The direction of this production was in noble hands. Both male and female slaves per-

5. The *nkuluntu,* or village headmen, and the *itome,* or priests of the land, were the principal local offices (Thornton 1979:54; Wilson 1977:23–25).
6. These two towns were the only real ones in the kingdom. Below them were the rural villages.

formed this farm work. Thornton has estimated that this system of concentrated, supervised, plantation labor in the town areas produced a surplus which was sufficient to support about 15–20 percent of the population in leisure. Some of those fed by this system were slaves themselves: the servants, wives, and retainers in noble households. It was from the slave populations settled in the urban areas that the king, and in the late seventeenth century his rival in Sonyo, were able to raise substantial armies (Thornton 1979:60–63).

As was the case among peasants, the household was the fundamental social unit for the aristocracy. However, noble households differed significantly from peasant ones. They did not support themselves. Also they were quite large—that of a seventeenth-century king was a city within the city. Membership consisted largely of women and children, both slave and free, organized under the supervision of a highborn principal wife or wives (Thornton 1979:118).

Slave wives were widely kept among the nobility. In the first half of the seventeenth century such wives and their royal children figured prominently in the intricacies of royal succession politics. In this period noble status, including eligibility for the throne, was not calculated matrilineally but bilaterally from the founder of the Christian dynasty, the sixteenth-century king, Affonso I (Wilson 1977:154). By either set of rules, the children of slave wives belonged to the lineage of their father, since they had no separate lineage on their mother's side under Kongo law.

Not all noble households were headed by men. Prominent noblewomen sometimes headed their own households and participated directly in political life, joining or organizing noble factions and even governing districts or provinces. Some women, such as the Queen Mother and the female members of the royal council, were granted lands of their own for a living (Wilson 1977:35–36). Others appear to have inherited land and governing positions through their position as sisters within a particular branch of the various noble lineages. Such noblewomen, like their brother household heads, had control of both household slaves and agricultural workers. Details of the marriage patterns of such women are not known, although there are reports indicating that in some cases spouses settled in different places, each maintaining his or her own household.

The Eighteenth Century

In the last quarter of the seventeenth century and the first decade or so of the eighteenth century the Kongo countryside was racked by a long series of civil wars. The capital was abandoned, and noble households dispersed to provincial bases. Slaves and other clients followed their noble masters, or decamped, attaching themselves for safety to new households, providing soldiers and retainers for the wars and agricultural labor for their new patrons. As the condition of war continued, many Bakongo retreated into the forests and hills where they built stockaded villages to avoid the perils of endemic unrest.

During the eighteenth century the international slave trade became the principal form of long-distance commerce for the area. Many of the slaves, shipped in increasing numbers and at escalating prices from the coastal states' well-organized markets, came from interior sources beyond Kongo borders. By mid-century the Zombo of the northeastern border area had become specialists dealing in "pagan" slaves from distant lands. In Kongo the king and the dispersed nobility competed for a share of this trade by setting up and controlling markets and taxing goods in transit through their domains, as well as by directly investing and dealing in slaves and the foreign goods that were purchasable only with slaves. The use of imported cloth, guns, and powder especially distinguished the elite. As late as the 1790s, special clothing distinguished men and women alike from their poorer neighbors (Brasio 1972:39).

The slaves preferred for export were young adult males. Enslaved females found a ready market within Kongo, usually as slave wives. A late-century missionary maintained that ten to twenty wives elevated a husband to the status of "great man." Only the poor had just one wife. Even slaves could have more than one. Further, his informants maintained that many more men than women were exported, leaving a surplus of women of marriageable age in the population (Brásio 1972:26–27). A recent study of the area affected by the Angolan slave trade (including parts of Kongo) suggests that the practice of exporting more males indeed led to heavy concentrations of adult females in the population of the region (Thornton 1980:422). However, it seems just as likely that a growing local demand for slave wives led instead to a surplus of males for export. Since Kongo was mainly a transit area for the eighteenth-century trade, a net population gain seems likely.

Although some raiding by nobles on rural villages continued in the first decades of the century, most new slaves in this period were obtained by purchase from inland sources, through natural increase, through judicial or quasi-judicial proceedings,[7] in payment of debt, by default of relatives, or by voluntary acceptance of clientage. After 1715 the kingdom politically entered a relatively stable period. The endemic civil wars among large noble factions came to an end, reappearing only during periodic struggles over succession to the throne. Warfare continued, but gradually became more ritualized as the now virtually autonomous noble domains

---

7. Local wars often qualified as "quasi-judicial" proceedings in the late eighteenth century (Brásio 1972:42).

sought to minimize casualties as well as establish territorial claims (Broadhead 1979b).

The use or abuse of judicial processes relative to witchcraft are implicated by one observer as a means of reducing the conspicuously wealthy and turning entire large households into slaves (Brásio 1972:36). Legally such Kongo-born slaves couldn't be exported, since there was a ban on the sale of Christian (Catholic) slaves to heretics (for example, English Protestants). There were also restrictions on the foreign sale of locally born slaves generally (Martin 1972:167). However, neither ban prevented the export of Kongo-born persons entirely. The missionary de Vide, resident in São Salvador in the 1780s, waged a vigorous, though largely futile, campaign against the export of Christian slaves (A.C.L., Ms. Vermelho 396:239, 254, 257).

Most Bakongo slaves, especially women and children, probably did stay in the kingdom. Their enslavement was a means of transferring power from one lineage or domain to another. The need of nobles for followers and rural peasants for protection led to a situation in which much of the free peasantry entered into some kind of dependency relationship with a local lord. Coupled with an end to the specially organized slave-worked plantations of the towns, the differences between various forms of peasant dependency became blurred. All rural villagers owed a percentage of their productive capacity to some combination of local and regional officials, and doubtless sometimes to more than one set. Only household slaves and slave wives of the wealthiest noblemen and noblewomen continued the distinctive lifestyle of the centralized period.

Settlements, in the fluid political climate of the times, tended to be located not only by the usual criteria of soil fertility and water supply, but also with security precautions in mind. People preferred forest locations and circuitous access pathways (A.C.L., Ms. Vermelho 396, fls. 63–64). Ordinary homes were small rectangular affairs clustered into tiny hamlets (*libata, sanzala*) or amid a few dozen or so related households, surrounded by cultivated clearings and forest resources. Larger villages or towns (*mbanza*) were made up of these hamlets in close proximity. A mbanza was also the seat of a noble lord or *infante*, descendant of one of the kings of Kongo (Brásio 1972:40–41). It was in the mbanza of the countryside that the Mwissikongo established their households, courts, and centers of government. Each mbanza attracted not only peasant clients, but also *fidalgo* (Mwissikongo) allies, relatives, and clients of the ruling lord, and their slaves, wives, and retainers. These scattered centers of noble government continued to order their affairs with reference to the old kingdom, although the basis of their wealth had shifted from access to the centralized tribute system to control over a combination of local tribute and capital for investment in foreign commerce. Aristocratic rulers still defined themselves in relation to their participation in the kingdom and in the associated Christian cult. They maintained family-based networks of allied domains, monopolized titles and the circulation of prestige goods, and were able to afford a more lavish lifestyle than was generally available, including larger households, more wives and slaves, some personal servants, retainers and wealth enough to afford a title, the use of foreign goods, and proper burial in one of the by then ruined churches, preferably in São Salvador (Broadhead 1979a:629–34). In this system noblewomen served to create and maintain aristocratic networks through marriage as well as supervise noble households, their husbands' or their own.

Despite the relative stability of the aristocratically dominated political and social life after 1715, this period saw the slow deepening of major contradictions between the ideals and pretensions of the nobility and their actual situation. The old style luxury, social dominance, and even cultural distinctiveness of the Mwissikongo had been based on the resources concentrated on the royal town of São Salvador with its magnificent court, religious establishment, army, bureaucracy, and thousands of slave laborers. This monopoly of resources could never be recreated in the decentralized structure of the succeeding period. Every noble center became in fact a competitor with its neighbors for the resources, especially the labor resources, of the population. Located as they now were in dispersed centers, surrounded by peasants, the nobility increasingly found their lives and their culture interwoven with those not only of their aristocratic, but also of their ordinary neighbors. In these circumstances more noble households, like those of peasants, relied on the services of wives for agricultural production.

Generally speaking, nobles, particularly noble males, needed to rule, to head a domain, in order to maintain status. In the period of the centralized monarchy careers were open to ambitious young nobles in the bureaucracy of the state, in São Salvador and the provinces, in the church, and through these, in commerce. In the eighteenth century, while opportunities in commerce expanded somewhat, careers in government and the church declined drastically, as the scale of the provincial establishments was relatively small and the missionary presence slight. A typical mbanza averaged around 2,000 inhabitants, and the size of the average autonomous political unit was limited to a radius of no more than 20 to 25 miles, which was as far as it was feasible to transport bulk goods for tribute from dependent peasants (Thornton 1979:59, 273). As the number of persons with claims to noble status grew, either the size of the establishment of each had to become correspondingly smaller, or some with claims to noble status had to live as dependents of others, eventually with little except their pretensions to distinguish them from those of peasant origins.

Early in the century, a nobleman tended to have one official wife, usu-

ally a noblewoman of good family. They were married in a Catholic ceremony, if a priest was available (Toso 1974:214, Cuvelier 1954:56). The
practice of Christian marriage fell out of favor with the aristocracy toward
the end of the century (Brásio 1972:26). Why this should be so is not very
clear, since even when Christian marriage was more widely practiced it
did not inhibit the nobility from taking other wives. On the contrary, the
possession of many wives, both slaves and women of high status, was a
major distinguishing characteristic of the noble class. Since descent, as
we have noted, was calculated bilaterally among the nobility, the number
of those with some claim to noble status was inflated in each generation.
In practice this meant that the status of fidalgo became more widespread
and less distinguished. Fewer and fewer of those whose descent linked
them to the old aristocracy could afford either titles or the lifestyle which
could set them off from their peasant neighbors and tributaries. The household of the ordinary Mwissikongo who headed only a small rural libata,
serving as a councilor or retainer of a more prominent lord, therefore
tended to become like those of the neighborhood. Such officials had more
in common with the village headmen of the traditional peasant society
than with the bureaucracy of the old nobility. Wives of such men could
not afford servants, but produced their own food crops. Only the presence
of several wives could ameliorate the work load for women in this situation.

Peasant producers—the women, slave or free, who cultivated the major
subsistence crops—had assured access to land, and controlled production
(Brásio 1972:36). There is no mention in this period of the kind of directed, specialized production undertaken by slaves earlier in the capital
region. The household team of husband and wife or wives was the norm.
Women did the major work of cultivation, although male slaves may have
had to do it also in some circumstances. Although free and slave women
both were organized productively as wives, free women maintained independence from their husbands by contributing agricultural produce and
children to their own lineages. These contributions connected them centrally to the important political processes of domain building and tribute
and gift exchange.

As the focus of most aristocrats' lives became more local, the localized
matrilineage emerged again as the center of affairs. At the same time the
political superstructure of the kingdom tended to become more remote
from the functioning of daily life. In this context the role of women changed
in the direction of emphasis on the wife aspect that had long been more
emphasized in rural areas. The political arena of the noble sisterhood, like
that of their brothers, was reduced. At the same time, more and more
female slaves were being integrated into the role of junior co-wives in

small or medium-sized households. Thus the social mobility of slave women continued to reside in their reproductive capacities. A successful mother, a woman who founded a slave branch of her husband's lineage, could expect to approach de facto status of sister in her husband's lineage in her old age. The successful slave wife, in a lineage whose sisters were not productive, could have her children adopted into free (full membership) status by their father's family. There is no data on how widespread this practice might have been in the eighteenth century, but certainly the decreasing scale of political organization and the consequent blurring of class distinctions would seem to have offered such opportunities to more individual slave women and their children.

If, as seems likely, there was a trend toward a predominance of females in the work force and a fairly strict division of labor by gender, some changes might be expected in levels of production in the subsistence sector. A change in the diet as a result of the availability of more field crops (produced by women) and fewer tree crops (produced by men) might be postulated. However, there is little evidence for this one way or the other. Among male-sphere food products, only salt is specifically mentioned as scarce, and there is no evidence that this was connected to a shortage of men. However, there is evidence of change in productive patterns outside the realm of food production. Such traditionally male-manufactured goods as cloth and hoes were gradually replaced in the Kongo economy by imported European and Asian versions. This particularly affected the production of cloth money in this period.[8] Production of cloth for personal use continued in the interior well into the nineteenth century. However, the wearing of imported cloth was a status symbol, which slowly spread from its restricted place among the aristocracy.

Despite the fact that by the end of the eighteenth-century most persons of Mwissikongo heritage did not live much differently from the generality of rural Bakongo, there continued to be, throughout this period of slave trade prosperity, a segment of the nobility which was able to prosper and use its prosperity to establish its rule over the loosely joined provinces that made up the Kongo kingdom. As had been the case under the centralized monarchy, some Mwissikongo noblewomen continued to head their own households and to govern in various provinces. The territories said to be under the Queen in the 1780s included districts and provinces in the heartland of the kingdom, in the São Salvador region. Another district was

---

8. Uniformly sized palm cloth squares were in widespread use both as currency and as a part of a distinctive noble dress early in the century, according to Lorenzo da Lucca (Cuvelier 1954:56). By late in the century only the shell currency of earlier times was in wide circulation.

controlled by the widow of a former king. The royal princess, whose brother was prince of Kibangu[9] and heir apparent to the throne, maintained her own household, traveling about the countryside with a retinue of bodyguards and female slaves (A.C.L., Ms. Vermelho 396, fl. 186). Slave wives also continued to figure in royal politics. The late-century king Henrique I was the son of a slave woman (Brásio 1972:42).

Very little is known about the households or marriage patterns of women rulers in the eighteenth century. What is known is that there were certain areas which were headed, for most of the century, by a succession of females (Toso 1974:208). Only in the case of the Queen is the mechanism for assigning territory to women at all apparent. The Queen's territories were explicitly assigned to her for her support, and seem to have been given over for her lifetime (A.C.L., Ms. Vermelho 396, fl. 73). Whether the territories "traditionally headed by women" had come to have female rulers through their having once been the lands assigned to queens is not clear, nor is the mechanism for maintaining these lands in female hands.

Although there were a few women political leaders in the upper levels of the aristocracy, there are few references to females exercising formal political power at the local level. The only rulers mentioned in the Queen's lands, for example, were male (A.C.L., Ms. Vermelho 396, fl. 73). However, there is some evidence to suggest that women were nonetheless influential in the affairs of the rural countryside and had been since at least the seventeenth century. There are some intriguing references in the work of Anne Wilson in this regard in her discussion of seventeenth-century rural matrilineal descent structure. With the more rural focus of life in the eighteenth century, local lineage politics assumed greater importance. It was at the level of the *kanda* (clan, lineage) that society assigned the ownership of land and the membership of persons for purposes of marriage. Each kanda defined itself in terms of common descent from a founding mother. Local tradition defined the territory owned by each. The kanda were headed by women, who enjoyed high status but no particular political power with the office. Political power resided, not in the somewhat abstract realm of the clan, but in the localized lineage segments settled in the rural hamlets and headed generally by the senior brother of the senior lineage. Lineage sisters could head the segments as well, but only in the absence of qualified males. It is clear from these practices that the sphere of practical politics was normally associated with male lineage members, but that women held regular positions of influence and were sometimes eligible to assume formal power as well (Wilson 1977:22, 29; Toso 1974:208; Cuvelier 1954:97).

9. Kibangu was a hilltop town, whose proximity to São Salvador and defensibility combined to make it a favorite royal stronghold.

Although European observers of the period saw women only in their status as wives, or occasionally rulers with female slave entourages, they nonetheless make it clear from their observations that women were actively involved in the community life of the times. Women are noted as traditional healers and diviners and as patrons of the Christian church. Women participated in the councils of the elders and in the communal festivals which were occasioned by the arrival of a missionary. Women served as the commissariat for armies and, of course, cultivated two crops a year, cooked the food, and participated in the distinctively female aspects of such community events as initiation, childbirth, marriage, and funerals. With the exception of those functions which required full membership in a lineage, such as council membership or kanda leadership, slave women apparently participated in the normal sphere of women's activities. Under this circumstance it is not hard to imagine how the question of slave origins could become subject to debate within a couple of generations as, on the one hand, success in reproduction, production, and alliance building created opportunities for slave branches to better themselves, and, on the other hand, lack of children, poor productivity, or witchcraft convictions reduced some free families to slave status.

In theory, slave identity was forever. However, for some people in rural villages the question of origins was becoming less relevant than that of current status. There was one group of slaves, however, which came into existence as result of missionary endeavors, and which, contrary to this general rule, guarded their slave identity zealously, even after the missionaries had left. These were the "slaves of the church"—the community of workers who had served the mission stations and the households of the missionaries themselves. Because their connection to the church exempted them from noble exactions, and because this connection itself also conferred status, these slave communities chose to maintain their corporate identities under the title, if not the substance, of slavery.

The slaves of the church are interesting not only as a commentary on the position of slaves within Bakongo society, but also because the descriptions of the slave-based missionary households of the period provide the only detailed accounts available of the functioning of slaves in the aristocratic households which served the missionaries as models. The slaves of the missions were divided into two groups: agricultural workers and household servants. The agricultural workers were settled in dependent villages near the mission house and grew food for the community. Missionaries saw to it that they married. Their lifestyle, except for its heavy Christian overtones, was typical of that of the countryside. Household servants, in this case, were distinctive because they consisted entirely of young men and boys. No women were allowed in the house (A.C.L., Ms. Vermelho 396:218–24). However, even this practice had a rough counterpart in the grander noble households of the time. It was customary for the sons and nephews of vassals to live in the lord's household to serve him and learn court etiquette, administration of justice, and the political skills of governing. The communities formed by the slaves of the church continued to function as a separate corporation long after the death of an effective missionary effort. Those located near the capital played a role in royal politics well into the nineteenth century (Brásio 1966, 1:25–27).

A phenomenon like the masterless "slaves of the church" serves to point up the fact that slavery was not one thing but several different things among the eighteenth-century Bakongo. The widespread use of women as slaves served to transfer involuntarily what could not be transferred voluntarily: female reproductive services. For males, slavery was a variant form of clientage, which was the major form of political mobilization for the eighteenth-century Bakongo. Slaves generally were a necessary ingredient of political power and prestige.

Quite apart from its labor resources aspects, slavery in its commercial aspect also had an important impact on Kongo. Trading in slaves, particularly exporting them, was profitable. The profits of this trade were escalating in the eighteenth century (Toso 1974:199). This profitability, in combination with the decentralized political structure of the times, fueled the spread of commercialism generally among the Bakongo. This change was more than economic. By the nineteenth century it had had a wide effect on Bakongo society, including the position of women and slaves within that society.

Early in the eighteenth century, a missionary resident in the important coastal town of Sonyo felt called upon to comment on the general disinterest of the population in anything commercial (Cuvelier 1954:76). Clearly, in this period, only the upper reaches of the elite were participating in and being affected by international trade or its local networks. In contrast, by the second half of the eighteenth century missionaries noted the effects of commerce in several sectors of society, from the well-organized porterage services between towns to the increased emphasis everywhere on wages, and the roadside food markets that provided sustenance for the increasing number of travelers in the region. A somewhat bitter observer in 1795 felt that most Bakongo would do nothing without payment, and anything for gain (Brásio 1972:32).

The Nineteenth Century

In many respects social changes in the period to the mid-nineteenth century continued the patterns set in the century before. However, the pace of change in some areas of life was notably faster. Modifications in the institutions of slavery and the status of women were both closely related to economic change, which became more rapid in about 1800. Economic change was led by changes in the slave trade and was followed by the dramatic increase in cash crop exports from about 1840.

Early in the nineteenth century the French and the British, who had dominated the overseas shipping along the north coast, left the slave trade. Angolans, as well as Brazilians and other Americans, moved into the coastal area, reorganizing the trade in their wake. They were followed in the 1840s and 1850s by large Dutch, English, and French commercial firms. Unlike their eighteenth-century predecessors, the European merchants of the nineteenth century established land-based operations. They settled in convenient enclaves along the Atlantic coast and the banks of the Zaire, where they established business ties with local authorities. The number of coastal settlements, both African- and European-run, increased dramatically in the first half of the nineteenth century.

Changes associated with coastal commerce affected the various Kongo regions differently and at variable rates. They also affected men and women differently. The most rapid and substantial changes occurred in coastal areas themselves—the regions where European merchants were established, especially along the Zaire and the northern coast between Ambriz and Sonyo where new settlements sprang up. Older coastal settlements, towns near the coast, areas crossed by major caravan routes, and areas where major regional markets were located formed the second most rapidly and deeply affected areas, while the rest of the interior, including many older power centers such as the royal capital, São Salvador, were passed by or struggled to adjust.

The profits of the clandestine slave trade centered on the Zaire River ports attracted many men to the coast and enriched older established merchants such as those from Cabinda. Coastal lords, adapting the commercial organization developed earlier in Loango and Ngoyo, established themselves and their allies as brokers in the reorganized trade. The most successful became "kings" of the new towns. The most common title adopted by this new commercial elite was *mafouk* (broker). The "kings" of the new commercial towns were also the mafouks. These merchant lords both engaged in commerce on their own behalf and carried on such public functions as charging customs to Europeans, regulating local businessmen, and providing auxiliary services to both the African and European communities. They released goods on credit in the interior and were able to obtain capital not only through their lineage and their business profits, but also directly from foreign business houses. Not only African, but foreign merchants established coastal settlements. A notable aspect of foreign factories for our purposes is that, like their missionary counterparts, they set up all-male households which served to reinforce the male-dominant aspect of coastal business.

The older coastal and near coastal or interior market towns followed more closely traditional Kongo models of commerce and government. The commercial connection was important but integrated more closely. In Ambriz, for example, in the 1840s, the king, who was elected by his council on a periodic basis, did not participate directly in coastal trade. He had gone to the coast in his youth, but once elected was prohibited from even viewing the sea. He played the more traditional role of collector of customs, regulator of markets, and official receiver of foreign visitors (Tams 1845:182). Some version of this model held for the interior generally—with the major variable being the extent of commercial opportunity available. It is notable that a "daughter" (titled female relative) was sent by the Ambriz ruler to visit with the foreign dignitaries. She was accompanied by only two (male) retainers. Small gifts were exchanged along with the small talk. The purpose of the whole thing beyond this is not clear (Tams 1845:188–91).

In the coastal areas, which were in direct contact with the proliferating foreign establishments, social mobility on the basis of business success and connections became the rule. It was possible for ambitious men to aspire to elite status through their control of large numbers of wives, clients, and slaves. Many could establish themselves as heads of small domains. Captain Tuckey (1818:160) noted that all successful men referred to their homestead as their town. In the families founded by such men, the practice of matrilineal inheritance became clouded (Martin, forthcoming). They sent their sons as well as their nephews into business, educating them and giving them money for slaves to begin on their own (Tuckey 1818:160).

In this system the position of elite women deteriorated. Descriptions from Zaire-region merchant households indicate that women functioned mainly as wives. Women's quarters were set off. Women were segregated at public events. It was reported that some merchants offered the sexual favors of their wives, daughters, or other female relatives to European men (Tuckey 1818:108, 124, 160, 181). This suggests that the position of women as sisters was weakened not only by changes in the inheritance structures, but also by changes in the political economy of marriage. Coastal merchants increasingly needed to build ties of alliance with European suppliers. In this context they probably preferred purchasing slave wives to the expense and complications of establishing marriage alliances with free women.

The coastal commercial centers were largely male worlds, segregated from the productive complementarity of the traditional household. Men in this system could purchase most of the goods they had traditionally produced, from cloth and hoes to alcoholic beverages and hardware. Even lesser opportunities associated with the changing coastal economic structure were available almost exclusively to young men. They established credit associations to enable each other to get into business without traditional family mediation (Weeks 1914:70). By serving on the coast they could learn the ropes and a smattering of French, English, Spanish, or Portuguese. Boma, a major Zairean entrepot, was characterized in the early nineteenth century as a kind of university for the teaching of English to local men (Tuckey 1818:179). With their wages, skills, and foreign connections, such men could aspire to become merchants or brokers themselves. Even those who served only as servants or porters could accumulate the means to acquire a wife, slave or free, before returning home to establish households of their own (Tuckey 1818:160; Monteiro 1875, 1:205). Once established back home, they could use their coastal connections on annual dry season business trips to the coast.

Although the changes were less profound in the interior, available evidence suggests that social mobility generally increased for men and decreased for women. The changes in commerce offered direct opportunities for advancement almost exclusively to men. As a result, more males could aspire to making themselves heads of towns. Those who were successful invested their savings in slaves, or in gifts to attract wives and clients. The wealthy could also invest in some of the trappings of the old nobility. For example, for a modest fee, one could buy entry into the Order of Christ. This aristocratic title association had accepted only high nobility and Church functionaries as members as late as the 1780s. However, titulars were a dime a dozen by the account of a mid-nineteenth-century Portuguese observer (Sarmento 1880:49). The prerogatives of the title were shared by the principal wife of the titleholder.

In the small towns and villages of the interior, change came quite gradually and in limited ways. The way that most households functioned, the way women organized agriculture, the basic staples of diet, marriage patterns, and the basically matrilineal descent structure remained about the same. Women could not participate directly in coastal commerce in the ways men did. Activities associated with international commerce in the slave trade era were largely an outgrowth of traditional male productive activities. However, women did have some expanded economic opportunities associated with their traditional sphere of food production.

During this period of clandestine slave trade, persons waiting to be exported were held in large numbers in barracoons near the coast. These facilities, along with coastal factories and towns, were supplied with foodstuffs from farms in more fertile areas inland. When the slave trade began to be effectively curbed and Europeans instead offered cash for agricultural produce such as groundnuts, women switched to these crops, causing food shortages in coastal areas by just after mid-century (Monteiro 1875, 1:129–33). With the expansion of local and regional commerce, women also expanded their participation in local markets. They ran roadside food stands for the benefit of commercial caravans. The expansion of women into certain marketing areas, however, did not necessarily afford them the same kinds of opportunities for social mobility that it did for men. Most food was sold by barter, or for local currency. Relatively few women had access to direct purchase of European goods or slaves. These were largely in the male sphere.

In a situation of expanding commercialization and competing commercial centers within a few days' walk of most of the Bakongo heartland, the old system of tribute from clients became largely anachronous. The only income possibilities left from the old order were those already associated with control over roads, markets, and fees collected for the granting of titles and certain other ritual services. The ability to own slaves became widespread. Successful coastal merchants had many, and almost anyone in the new wage-earning class of porters, housemen, sailors, and so on, could aspire to slave ownership, even those who themselves were of slave origins. However, the dispersal of the old aristocracy and the general competitiveness between domains meant that few in the interior could aspire to having many slaves. Slaves themselves acquired a better bargaining position. Even Garcia V, an early nineteenth-century monarch said to possess 300 slaves, had to pay his slaves wages in cloth and palm wine in order to retain their services (A.P.F., Congo: VI, fl. 370v; Jadin 1970:159).

The position of Garcia V vis-à-vis his town, which was 50 percent slaves, illustrates the degree to which even the most traditional aristocrats had been transformed into merchant princes. Successful princes of this type could do fairly well, as exemplified by Henrique II (1841–56), the last king of the slave trade era. He built São Salvador into a settlement of about 18,000, of which 3,000 were said to be resident in his "town" (Castro 1880:64). He collected the usual fees and market profit, but also had the strength to enforce transit taxes regionally, conduct a lively foreign policy, and defeat an attempt on his throne supported by the "slaves of the church" who were still headquartered near the capital (Brasio 1966, 1:26). It is important to note that a strong São Salvador was dependent upon the ability of the king to recruit not only armed men, but agricultural labor, that is females, as well.

For female slaves, the position of wife and ultimately mother continued to be the only avenue of entry into society. By mid-century, social leveling had proceeded in most of the country to the point that all wives, from those of the king to those of slaves, were engaged in agricultural work.

The leisure class among women had virtually disappeared. However, the wives of the wealthy did have the assistance of junior co-wives and sometimes slaves as well. Polygynous households were said to be preferred by women, who felt that they reduced the workload. The presence of co-wives also increased the amount a woman might have available to sell on her own account. Women owned their own produce. While slave wives could use expanding market opportunities to increase their contribution to and therefore their status in their husband's group, such opportunities were not sufficient to allow free women to compete with their brothers, economically or politically.

Because of the increased importance of the commercial sector of the economy in relation to the subsistence sector, and the general confinement of women within the latter, it is not surprising that fewer women were noted in political offices in this period. The Queen Mother was still important in royal politics. The chief wife of Henrique II participated in his daily audiences while his other wives served as retainers on important public occasions (Castro 1880:64; Sarmento 1880:54–55). But the women so noted are all wives, and the political importance of São Salvador itself was limited by then. In the small, autonomous domains of the countryside, women were noted in the fields and in the markets, but not as rulers or as members of ruling councils.

Conclusion

The 150 years between 1700 and 1850 encompassed the period of greatest Kongo participation in the Atlantic slave trade. During this time the incorporation of female slaves formed the single most important outgrowth of slave trade affecting the Bakongo. Women were preferred as slaves. They were the tillers of the soil and the producers of laborers for Bakongo matrilineages. Through at least half of the period, women were prominent within the Kongo political system. Their political power was based on their position as sisters in aristocratic lineages and their ability to participate in the building of political alliances from a position as household head.

However, the increasing emphasis on commerce in the nineteenth century tended to close off traditional power avenues for women and reduce most of them to a more strictly wife position, from which they could not exercise independent political power. Most women of political influence in the later period were in the position of wives to prominent men. Despite their loss of political power, women continued to be the backbone of the Kongo economy and played important roles in the local politics of matrilineage and family.

References

Unpublished Sources

A.C.L.: Academia das Cienças, Lisbon.
Ms. Vermelho 396, "Viagem do Congo do Missionario Fr. Rafael Castello de Vide, Hoje Bispo de S. Tome (1788)."
A.P.F.: Archivo da Propaganda Fide, Rome.
Scritture Referite al Congo, VI, Pietro Pablo da Bene, "Relazione dello stato in che attualmente se trova il Regno del Congo" (1820).
Thornton, J. 1979. "The Kingdom of Kongo in the Era of the Civil Wars, 1641–1718." Ph.D. dissertation, University of California, Los Angeles.
Wilson, A. 1977. "The Kongo Kingdom in the Mid-Seventeenth Century." Ph.D. dissertation, University of London.

Published Sources

Brásio, A. 1966. *Angola*. Spiritana Monumenta Historica, Series Africana. Vol. 1. Pittsburgh.
Brásio, A. 1972. "Informacão do Reino do Congo, de Frei Raimondo de Dicomano." *Studia* (Lisbon) 34:19–42.
Broadhead, S. H. 1979a. "Beyond Decline: The Kingdom of the Kongo in the 18th and 19th Centuries." *International Journal of African Historical Studies* 12:615–50.
Broadhead, S. H. 1979b. "Luso-Kongolese Armed Conflict in Northern Angola: An Historical Perspective." *Etudes d'Histoire Africaine*. Forthcoming.
Castro, A. 1880. "O Congo em 1845." *Boletim da Sociedade Geografia* (Lisbon) 2:53–67.
Civezza, M. 1894. *Storia Universale delle Missioni Francescana*. Vol. 7, pp. 314–402.
Cuvelier, J., ed. and trans. 1954. *Relations sur le Congo de P. Laurent de Lucques*. Memoirs 32, Institute royale coloniale Belge.
Jadin, L. 1963. "Aperçu de la situation du Congo et rites d'election des rois en 1775, d'après le P. Cherubino de Savona, missionaire au Congo de 1759–1774." *Bulletin de l'Institit Historique Belge de Rome* 35:343–419.
Jadin, L. 1970. "Les Survivances Chretiennes au Congo aux XIX⁰ Siècle." *Etudes d'histoire africaine* 1:137–85.
Laman, K. 1953–68. *The Kongo*. 5 vols. Stockholm.
MacGaffey, W. 1977. "Economic and Social Dimensions of Kongo Slavery (Zaire)." In *Slavery in Africa: Historical and Anthropological Perspectives*, ed. S. Miers and I. Kopytoff. Madison.
Martin, P. 1972. *The External Trade of the Loango Coast*. Oxford.
Martin, P. Forthcoming. "The Making of Cabindan Society, Seventeenth to Nineteenth Century." In *The Formation of Angolan Society*, ed. F. Heimer.
Miers, S., and I. Kopytoff, eds. 1977. *Slavery in Africa: Historical and Anthropological Perspectives*. Madison.

Miller, J. C. 1976. "The Slave Trade in Congo and Angola." In *The African Diaspora: Interpretive Essays,* ed. M. L. Kilson and R. I. Rotberg. Cambridge, Mass.

Monteiro, J. J. 1875. *Angola and the River Congo.* 2 vols. London.

Proyart, A. 1776 *Histoire de Loango, Kakongo, et autres royaumes d'Afrique.* Paris.

Sacks, K. 1979. *Sisters and Wives: The Past and Future of Sexual Equality.* Contributions in Women's Studies, No. 10. Westport, Conn.

Sarmento, A. 1880. *Os Sertões d'Africa (Apontamentos de Viagem).* Lisbon.

Tams, G. 1845/1969. *Visit to the Portuguese Possessions in South Western Africa.* London. Reprinted in New York.

Thornton, J. 1980. "The Slave Trade in Eighteenth-Century Angola: Effects on Demographic Structures." *Canadian Journal of African Studies* 14:417–27.

Toso, C. 1974. "Relazioni inedite di P. Cherubino Cassinis da Savona sul 'Regno del Congo e sue Missioni.'" *L'italia Francescana* 49:135–214.

Tuckey, J. K. 1818. *Narrative of an Expedition to Explore the River Zaire.* New York.

Weeks, J. H. 1914. *Among the Primitive Bakongo.* London.

III. THE SLAVE EXPERIENCE: CASE HISTORIES

11 *Edward A. Alpers*

The Story of Swema: Female Vulnerability in Nineteenth-Century East Africa[1]

The recent surge of interest in the slave trade and slavery has revealed a fund of previously untapped documentation that lay dormant until historians began to pose a new set of questions about these aspects of the African past. For East Africa, among the most revealing new sources have been the life histories of former or freed slaves which were published under either missionary or colonial patronage (Madan 1886; Mbotela 1934; Rashid bin Hassani 1936; Kilekwa 1937). These published African testimonies have typically come from males, although Marcia Wright (1975) and Margaret Strobel (1979) have recently begun to explore women's experiences of slavery in East and Central Africa. In the course of working on nineteenth-century eastern Tanzania, I uncovered a hitherto neglected text which records the earliest such life history, and the first one published (Bwanikwa's appears to have been the second) that concerns a female. It is her story that gives rise to this chapter.

The story of Swema does not, in fact, focus on the central questions addressed by this volume concerning female slavery in African societies, for like some others who were freed by the British naval antislave trade patrol or by one of the several European missionary societies in East Af-

1. I am especially grateful to Père Bernard Noël, *archiviste* of the Congrégation du Saint-Esprit, Paris, for permission to use the private archives of this important missionary society, where the documentation for this chapter was located, during June 1978, as well as for his permission to publish the full text of Swema's story. My research during this period was generously supported by the National Endowment for the Humanities. My thanks are also due to the editors for encouraging me to write this essay and for their valuable comments on the original draft. I am no less grateful to participants in the Seminar in African History at the University of California, Los Angeles, spring quarter 1981, for their remarks on the revised draft.

rica during the nineteenth century, Swema was enslaved but never actually worked as a slave (cf. Madan 1886, Histories Nos. 2, 6, 7). Nevertheless, her testimony is valuable for what it reveals about the production of slaves for market, while it also enables us to ask whether being female made one especially vulnerable to enslavement in the context of the East African trade.

Before turning to these questions, it is important to say something about the circumstances in which Swema's story was recorded and then published in order to appreciate potential biases in the text. Indeed, we must ask ourselves if the fact that her narrative was preserved as part of the Roman Catholic missionary propaganda effort in East Africa in any way invalidates her testimony.

The document on which this chapter is based is an unpaginated manuscript of thirty-two pages which is entitled "Histoire d'une petite esclave enterrée vivante; ou L'Amour filial" ["History of a little female slave buried alive; or filial love"; hereafter cited as "Histoire"]. The original oral text was recited by Swema in Swahili "to the little girls of the Catholic mission of Zanzibar" ("Histoire":202), where she had found refuge after having been left to die in an unmarked, shallow grave on the edge of Zanzibar Town. There is no indication as to when the text was transcribed in Swahili, and no copy of the original text appears to exist, but the French translation was completed by Père Anton Horner (1827–80), Superior of the Congrégation du Saint-Esprit mission in East Africa, at Zanzibar on July 26, 1866. We can safely assume that a number of months or perhaps even a few years had passed between the recording of the text and the events described in Swema's account of her enslavement and passage to Zanzibar, as she would have had to learn Swahili (her mother tongue being Yao) and had already been baptized by then. Although Père Horner states frankly that his purpose in bringing Swema's tale to the Christian youth of Europe was to reveal "the sorrows of this poor child, who has at your age already suffered inexpressible woes, in order to make you understand how you must be cognizant before God who has saved you from similar trials" ("Histoire":201), he does not tell us why, of all the children at the mission, Swema's story alone was worth recording. By contrast, the Anglican mission at Zanzibar brought together a dozen such narratives from all over East Africa in Madan's *Kiungani*, and the existence of an abbreviated life history by one of the Spiritans' first African clergy suggests that the same could have been done by them (A.C.S.E., Isa 1876).

Lacking any evidence other than Swema's story itself, I am inclined to think that the circumstances of her rescue from burial and her personal struggle to embrace Christianity were unique and also offered a dramatic opportunity to publicize the work of the mission. Indeed, Père Horner could not have failed to recognize in Swema's story all the elements of the

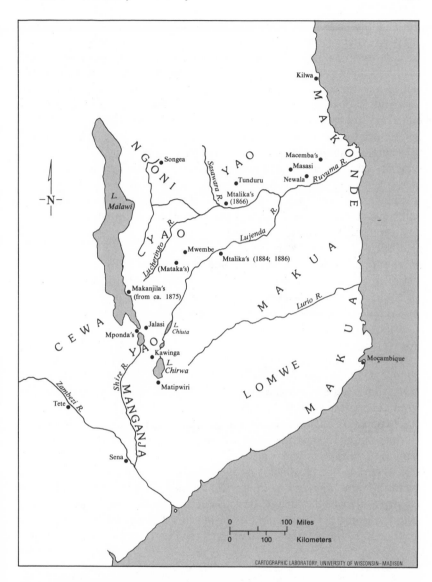

Map 11.1. East Central Africa in the Later Nineteenth Century. Adapted from E. A. Alpers, "Trade, State and Society among the Yao in the Nineteenth Century," *Journal of African History* 10:3 (1969): 408.

Christian metaphor—an innocent who undergoes great suffering, is personally reviled, is left for dead and buried, and who rises again from the grave to assume a new life through redemption and baptism—which would have had the most direct symbolic appeal to its young Christian readership. I must nevertheless emphasize that Père Horner was a careful, intelligent observer of African life who seems generally to have refrained from either falsifying or embellishing the evidence upon which he based his opinions. Moreover, we have other convincing examples of his attention to accurate ethnographic detail, evidence that though he may have been typically ethnocentric in his interpretation of African society and beliefs, he was nevertheless an honest recorder of what he witnessed.[2]

It must be clear to any reader of Swema's tale, however, that the translation which has come down to us has been shaped to conform to mid-nineteenth-century French literary conventions. Her story simply does not read like that of a ten-year-old, and in this respect may be contrasted with the structure and use of language in the passage quoted from Madan at the end of this essay. That Père Horner took some literary license with Swema's narrative seems beyond question, then, but it is my contention that his overall integrity as a reporter of what he observed in East Africa gives us reason to believe that he did not tamper with her story in any substantive way.

When Père Horner's manuscript finally was published in 1870 by Monsignor J. Gaume, Apostolic Pronotary to Paris, both the audience to which it was addressed and the purpose for which it was intended had undergone certain changes. Whereas Père Horner intended Swema's trials and salvation to serve as a cautionary and inspirational tale to all Christian youth, Monsignor Gaume specifically addressed it to Christian girls and enjoined them to contribute to "the ransom [*rachat*] of the young girls of East Africa" as part of "the charitable activity of Catholic young girls and women."[3] He furthermore directed their attention to the similarity of this charitable activity to that of the Oeuvre de la Sainte-Enfance, which was dedicated to the ransom of Chinese infants (especially female) who were sold or abandoned by their parents, and encouraged them to raise the forty or fifty

2. See, for example, Ricklin 1880:229–51, which reproduces Horner's extremely valuable observations made in 1870 on Luguru/Kami history, culture, society, and economy, which I have carefully evaluated in the context of oral data gathered in 1972–73 and more recent ethnographic literature; and A.C.S.E., Horner 1869, for Horner's remarkable description of a female spirit possession cult at Zanzibar, which I have similarly analyzed in Alpers 1981.

3. From a missiological point of view it is worth noting that the verb *racheter* implies redemption as well as repurchase or ransom. Monsignor Gaume was a notable figure in urging conservative reforms of French secondary education and a very successful author in his own right (*La Grande Encyclopédie*, 18:616).

francs necessary to ransom a young child at the slave market in Zanzibar and to send their money to the Spiritains or to himself in Paris (Gaume 1870:4, 9, 34, 220, 222). Not coincidentally, the Oeuvre de la Sainte-Enfance was also one of the principal financial supports of the Zanzibar mission, so the decision to publish Swema's story was part of a conscious effort to generate funds for the work of the Holy Ghost Congregation. As part of his appeal for funds, Monsignor Gaume took considerable liberties with Père Horner's original French text, frequently changing words and adding or deleting passages in Swema's testimony, while also adding a considerable amount of linking text between chapters that did not exist in the original manuscript in order to give the book added dramatic effect. Nevertheless, the basic text remains intact as published by Gaume, while a later variant published by Père L. A. Ricklin not only remains true to the original, but also adds some biographical details about Swema after her conversion (Ricklin 1880:130–34). The continuing dramatic appeal of Swema's story would also seem to account for a play published more than a decade later by the prolific Père Alexandre Le Roy, which concerns a Yao chief, his daughter, and the slave trade (Le Roy 1884).

Although the reasons for recording and publishing Swema's story were scarcely disinterested, then, even considering the literary license taken by Monsignor Gaume there seems to be no basis for questioning the essential reliability of her recorded testimony.

Swema's story begins with a description of Yaoland, where she was born in about 1855.[4] Although she provides no precise location for her natal village, her description of the surrounding peoples suggests that it was in the northeast quadrant of Yaoland, somewhere between the Lugenda and Ruvuma rivers. And while it is true that her recollection of Yaoland during her early childhood smacks somewhat of a "Merrie Africa" image, her depiction of the country as agriculturally abundant accords well with other contemporary sources. Her remarks that rice was cultivated expressly to exchange for beads, cotton, and salt with passing Arab caravans and that accusations of sorcery often led to severe social disruption bear witness to the ubiquitous influence of overseas trade in the early 1860s ("Histoire":202–3; Gaume 1870:85–87, 92–93). Swema tells us that her father was the foremost hunter in their village, and that because of his prowess there was always meat in their pot. When he killed an elephant, he sold the ivory to the caravans "in exchange for what was necessary to us to live well." Indeed, her account leaves no doubt that her family was quite well off: "My mother and my older sisters were covered

4. Swema is said to have been about ten years old when her story was recorded and about twenty years old in 1875, so she was probably born in about 1855 (Gaume 1870:84; Ricklin 1880:144).

with beads, and even wore clothes from overseas at home." Swema's family also always had salt, either through her father's trading or from his collection of saline grasses, which he sometimes gathered in the bush ("Histoire":203; Gaume 1870:101–4).

That the prosperity of Swema's family was heavily dependent on her father—"our protector and provider" ("Histoire":203; Gaume 1870:116)— becomes apparent in her account of the disasters that followed his death from a lion attack during a communal hunt. While Swema, her mother, and her sisters continued their agricultural tasks and tended to their few domestic livestock, before long the entire country was ravaged by an invasion of locusts. In three days' time all crops and everything green was stripped bare, and "soon the entire country was no more than an arid desert." In the ensuing famine that seized the country,[5] those who had salt were able to provide for themselves by salting the locusts, but as Swema tells us, "since the death of my father, we lacked salt completely." For a while her family was able to survive by eating the goats and chickens that they possessed, but without fodder their livestock soon perished, and in the decay of putrifying animal cadavers which no one could bother to bury, epidemic disease arose which further decimated the weakened population. In time, both of Swema's older sisters and her infant brother died. Alone with her mother, Swema left her home and struck out to seek refuge in another country ("Histoire":205–6; Gaume 1870:119, 124–27).

What we lack for this part of Swema's tale is social information on everything other than her nuclear family. Why did the family of a man who was allegedly a leading figure in his village not receive a helping hand in the period between his death and the locust invasion? Why was there no divination at his grave to establish whether or not his death had been caused by sorcery, as was normal practice among the Yao and was recorded earlier in Swema's own account of the burial customs of her people ("Histoire":202–3; Gaume 1870:91–92; cf. Abdallah 1919:19–21; Coissoró 1966:124–25)? Swema also makes no mention of the prescribed purification of her mother, but as she was still a child and apparently not yet initiated, she may have been unaware of this required widow's ritual (see Stannus 1922:240–46; Sanderson 1922:93; Coissoró 1966:152–54). Nevertheless, if her father had settled uxorilocally, which was the usual practice among the Yao, then her mother's elder brother would have taken

5. While the exact date of the beginning of this famine cannot be established, it was clearly the same famine that caused the abandonment of the fertile territory south across the Ruvuma which Livingstone traversed on his way to Mwembe in July 1866. At year's end, the repercussions of the famine were still being anticipated in terms of lower slave prices at Zanzibar, where the famine was expected to drive many people into bondage as a last means of survival (Livingstone 1874, 1:79; A.C.S.E., Horner 1866). For a similar response to famine in 1884, see Cooper 1977:126–28.

responsibility for her and her children as the guardian of his uterine sorority group (*asyene mbumba*). Indeed, this would have been true even if Swema's mother had settled virilocally, in which case another possibility would have been her inheritance by one of her late husband's brothers. The possibility exists, too, that Swema's father was an outsider in his village and had not formed any permanent bonds with the dominant matrilineage at the time of his death. Moreover, if Swema's mother was of slave origin she would have had no social identity beyond that of her husband's wife (see Alpers 1969:409–12). Such speculation notwithstanding, it seems highly unlikely that Swema's family lived in social isolation in her community, as that would be contrary to all principles of Yao social organization. Perhaps in the process of acculturation to Catholicism Swema gave greater emphasis to her nuclear family than was the norm for Yao. Given Horner's interest in ethnography, however, I believe that we can reasonably assume the omission of clarifying detail to have been Swema's and not his. Whatever the situation may have been, the point remains that after the death of Swema's father, her mother and her mother's children found themselves in an extremely vulnerable position.

Swema and her mother succeeded in finding the refuge that they sought at three days' walk from their old village. There they built a hut and began to clear a plot of land for cultivation, after borrowing from a neighbor two sacks of sorghum millet (*mtama*), one for planting and one for consumption. But the year was "generally bad," and the harvest failed completely. Pressed by his own need, their neighbor came to collect his debt. Swema's mother "threw herself at his feet and begged him to grant us a little delay," which he did ("Histoire":206; Gaume 1870:131–32). Swema's mother then turned her energy to making pots for sale, but despite her ceaseless efforts, she was unable to pay a quarter of the debt at the end of her period of grace. Reduced to this state of impoverishment and indebtedness, and completely without protection, Swema's mother found her predicament made graver by the arrival of an Arab caravan in the general vicinity. As Swema states, "Who does not know how the passage of caravans is always dangerous for the weak? Evil subjects habitually steal children and poor people, whom they sell to the Arabs for salt, cottons, and beads. Creditors profit from circumstance to extract the payment of debts. When the debtors are unable to pay, one seizes their slaves or their own children. Often it happens that they are reduced to selling themselves into slavery" ("Histoire":207; Gaume 1870:133–34).

To be sure, anyone, male or female, could be victimized in this manner during the height of the slave trade in East Africa, but it seems highly likely that an unprotected woman was particularly threatened in these circumstances. Indeed, if we are to believe Swema, her mother fully recognized the extent of her own vulnerability, for the morning after the Arab caravan had arrived near where they were living we are told that she awoke to find that her hair had turned white, as she had "foreseen the blow that was going to strike us." That very morning their Yao creditor arrived at their hut "with two elders of the tribe and an Arab." Swema continues:

> Without asking permission, he entered our hut and said with severity to my mother: "Mother of Swema, you haven't anything to pay in return for my two sacks of *mtama*: for that reason I am seizing your child.
>
> "You are my witnesses," he said to the elders. Then turning towards the Arab, he said to him: "Well, Sir, it's settled, six *coudées* [about three meters] of American cloth for this little girl."
>
> The Arab took me by the hand, made me stand up and walk; examined my teeth, and after several moments of thought responded: "It's fine; come take the six coudées of cloth." ("Histoire":207; Gaume 1870:135–36)[6]

In an action supported by the legal precedent of the society, then, Swema was taken as payment for her mother's debt and sold into slavery, a phenomenon which is also recorded by Robertson and Wright (this volume). It is also worth noting here that while the creditor was careful to observe legal custom by having two village elders witness the transaction, he was equally secure in his knowledge that Swema's mother was in every respect defenseless against his brusque entry into her hut. His disregard of accepted manners attests vividly to her complete lack of status in the community (cf. Abdallah 1919:14–16).

With the rest of her family dead and no one with whom she could seek protection, Swema's mother threw herself at the Arab's feet and asked if he would let her stay with her daughter, protesting that despite appearances she was still young and able to carry a tusk of ivory to the coast. Although she was not formally selling herself into slavery, this is what she was doing in effect. Indeed, had she remained in Yaoland, she probably would have suffered the same fate, since solitary survival was virtually impossible and her only option would have been to attach herself to a local lineage as a client with little security against being sold to the next caravan that came along. For the weak and defenseless, voluntary enslavement was the only sure form of protection in later nineteenth-century East Central Africa, as Bwanikwa also recognized when she agreed to marry Wafwilwa (see Wright, below, p. 258).

Here again we must ask to what degree being female affected a person's vulnerability in these circumstances. Certainly, the same fate could befall a man, but a single man could also try to attach himself as a warrior to a local warlord, or seek employment as a caravan porter, or finally take to

6. For comparative slave prices in the interior and the difficulty of establishing these figures accurately, see Alpers 1975:242 and Renault 1971, 1:82–90.

brigandage by joining one of the roving bands of so-called *maviti* who plagued what is now northern Mozambique and southern Tanzania in the last decades of the century. None of these options guaranteed freedom, as the slave trade generated a high degree of false security and double-dealing which often saw men being secretly sold at the coast when they thought they were free to return home (Alpers 1975:230), but they did provide channels for reestablishing one's economic and social independence which were denied to women.

Available roles for women in Yao society were quite restricted. According to Clyde Mitchell, three decades ago the ultimate position accorded to women centered on the concept of motherhood, for in becoming a mother a woman could aspire to becoming a village founder. Matrilineal solidarity was expressed by saying that "we are of one breast," and women as mothers played an essential role in the important boys' initiation ceremonies (*lupanda*) and gave vital support to their sons who managed village affairs. One aspect of their role as founders of matrilineally based villages was their generally superior knowledge of village genealogies compared to men. Finally, nothing was more feared than the threat of a mother's curse, which apparently reflected her special relationship to the ancestral spirits of the matrilineage (Mitchell 1956:134–35, 136; cf. Feierman 1974:32). At the same time, however, it is equally evident that in all daily family affairs men not only ruled supreme, but also considered women to be helpless and utterly dependent on men. Thus, the principal contradiction in Yao society was between dominant men and their mothers and sisters, without whose unified support the men could not achieve wider political influence, let alone obedience within the basic uterine sorority group (Mitchell 1956:149–52, 176).

It must be emphasized that a woman could not normally exercise political authority among the Yao (Mitchell 1951:316–19). Furthermore, the subordination of Yao women was also greatly exacerbated by the impact of international trade, which emphasized male and disparaged female roles in the social relations of production. As Yohanna Abdallah recorded more than sixty years ago, "Should anybody say, 'I am a Yao,' not having visited other countries, he is not a Yao at all, and everybody laughs at him, saying, 'This is a woman, not a man'" (Abdallah 1919:29).

There were, however, at least four important ritual roles open to Yao women. The first was to be local leader (*mtelesi*) of the girls' initiation rites (*ciputu*). The mtelesi was responsible for directing the instruction of all the eligible girls (who were usually about ten to twelve years of age) in a chiefdom. Thus, her authority was much wider than the village in which she resided. Duff Macdonald reported a century ago that the standard fee received from the guardian of each initiate (*mwali*) was about eight yards of cloth, so that the position also gave the mtelesi an important source of income. Regrettably, none of the descriptions of ciputu that we possess indicate the manner in which a woman gained access to this role (Macdonald 1882, 1:125–26; Stannus 1922:269–72; Mair 1951:60–63). The second special woman's role was also associated with the female life cycle and concerned the first quickening with child. The ceremony around this event was called *litiwo,* and according to Hugh Stannus "in every district there [was] generally some woman who arranged and conducted the ceremony." The skills required by this specialist, who was called either the *nakanga* or mtelesi, were apparently handed down from mother to daughter (Stannus 1922:274).[7] The third of these roles, and perhaps the most powerful, involved spirit possession and the manifestation of important ancestors through female mediums. Such a woman, who was called *juakuweweta,*[8] according to Macdonald was "either the principal wife of the chief" or "in some cases a woman without a husband" (Macdonald 1882, 1:61–62, 94). Finally, the fourth role was the powerful one of witch-detective (*mbisalila* or *mavumbula*), but this institution was clearly adopted by the Yao from the neighboring Mang'anja after the Yao invasion of the Shire highlands in the mid-nineteenth century, so we cannot assume that it was known in the part of Yaoland where Swema lived. (Macdonald 1882, 1:207–11; Stannus 1922:299–300. For definitions in the Mang'anja language, see Scott 1892:299, 300.)

Given what little we know about Swema's mother, it is unlikely that any of these essentially ruling-class female roles were open to her, any more than they were to most Yao women. Inasmuch as she lacked both matrilineal kinsmen and affines to call upon at her husband's death, her decision to offer her services to the Arab slaver, while it was no doubt partly owing to the bonds of affection between mother and daughter, was also at least partly a matter of simple self-preservation.

As it happens, her decision was not a fortunate one. At first, she succeeded in carrying the elephant tusk assigned to her and received a daily ration of food for her efforts. Swema also carried some things belonging to the Arab, but her market value did not depend upon her labor as a caravan porter. Their food, which was carried by other slaves, prepared by the advance guard of the caravan, and distributed on the arrival of the main body at each night's encampment, usually consisted of a porridge of millet or beans, and occasionally included roast bananas or sweet potatoes. "To prevent desertion and at the same time husband the strength of the porters of the merchandise, the leaders take care during the march to feed the slaves well who are under their command," we are told by Swema

7. Stannus's informant's mother and grandmother were both nakanga, as was she. Sanderson (1954:184) gives the alternate title for the conductor of the litiwo ceremony.

8. Sanderson (1954:285) defines the verb stem (*-weweta*) of this title as "rave, as in a nightmare or trance; prophesy (in the biblical sense)."

("Histoire":208; Gaume 1870:143–48). In time of want, it is not difficult to see the attractiveness of servitude in exchange for regular meals.[9]

After the first few days of the march to the coast, during which time Swema admits to enjoying walking and to having an increased appetite, things became more difficult for her mother, who was charged with a very heavy burden. As the caravan moved away from the well-watered country of northern Yaoland onto the dry steppe between the Ruvuma and the Kilwa coast, "the most ardent thirst became a cruel torment for everyone" ("Histoire":209; Gaume 1870:152). Swema's mother was seriously weakened, and after she fell many times her load was taken over by a slave on the orders of the caravan leader. Swema's illusion that her mother was being spared further suffering was rudely shattered when it came time to receive their rations that evening and the Arab ordered, "The mother of Swema is worthless; she will no longer have a ration!" ("Histoire":209; Gaume 1870:153). When Swema tried to share her food with her mother, she was taken to eat her meal in front of the Arab. The following day, Swema's mother sought nourishment by eating some grasshoppers, some millet leaves, and a little red earth. Unable to eat in the knowledge of her mother's need, Swema had to be force-fed by her master's servants ("Histoire":209; Gaume 1870:153–55).

The recourses to which Swema's mother was reduced by this famine were not unique. Horner also remarked the phenomenon of earth eating during the famine of 1866–67, saying that it was done to fill the stomach in the absence of food. He believed, mistakenly, that slave traders cared little for the nourishment of their slaves; in fact, the scarcity of food probably made it impossible for them to feed their slaves properly and thus to have them in prime condition for sale at the coast. He also commented that medical autopsies on dead juvenile slaves at Zanzibar often revealed a large earth ball in the stomach (A.C.S.E., Horner 1867, 1877). The economics of the slave trade worked to Swema's advantage, since it was her capacity as a future unit of production which was at stake, but cruelly discriminated against her mother, whose labor value was apparently judged to be worth no further investment, as Meillassoux notes (this volume).

The caravan then entered a plain which had been laid waste by fire, leaving nothing green, no insects, and no birds in the trees. All that remained "was an immense extent of earth charred and blackened by the fire" ("Histoire":209; Gaume 1870:155). In these conditions it was impossible for Swema's mother to sustain herself by the kinds of famine food that are known among virtually all East African peoples. The fire even

---

9. During the devastating famine of 1884 a French missionary remarked that "one has even seen free Nyamwezi men sell themselves in order to have something to eat" (A.C.S.E., Courmont 1884).

denied her the red earth "to delude her stomach." When the caravan finally stopped for its first night in this sombre desert, the Arab leader ordered that Swema's mother be chased out of the camp and threatened severe punishment for anyone who tried to give her anything to eat. She was all but dead, Swema reports him as saying, and the next day would be her last ("Histoire":209; Gaume 1870:155–57). At daybreak, when the caravan was ready to continue its journey to the coast, Swema was forcibly wrenched from the arms of her mother, who had to be severely beaten to make her surrender her daughter ("Histoire":210–11; Gaume 1870: 167–68).

Before their final separation, Swema tells us about her last night in her mother's arms. In this final encounter Swema's mother laments the fate of her daughter, asking why she, too, had not died with her sisters and brother. "'I would have at least had your tombs, a comfort of which no one would have been able to rob me.'" She also decries her inability to follow her daughter or to return to the graves of her other children, being destined to die unmourned in a strange land. Finally, she expresses her sorrow for Swema's enslavement, describing it as a fate more bitter than death, for which only the tomb provides a resting place ("Histoire":210; Gaume 1870:164–65). Given the environment in which Swema's story was recorded, it is quite possible that this passage is sentimentalized or even fabricated. But Swema's comment that her mother sang this lament "according to the custom of burials in my country" ("Histoire":210; Gaume 1870:166) lends a certain credibility to a testimony which not only moves us, but also enables us to understand something of how people viewed enslavement in nineteenth-century East Africa (cf. Johnson 1924:35, 75–76).

Swema resisted separation from her mother, being impervious to blows from sticks, and eventually had to be forcibly carried by another slave so that the caravan could get on its way. Although there is some embellishment of her story at this point by Monsignor Gaume, it is clear from the original manuscript that Swema gave up her will to live and was beaten in vain to try to move her along towards the coast. So she continued to be carried and abused. When the slave who unwillingly bore her complained to the caravan leader, "'Why carry this cadaver any longer? You can surely see that this little girl is only fit to be eaten by the crows,'" he replied, "'I can't leave her here, I bought her on behalf of my patron. If I abandon her, I will lose a *piastre* which comes to me for each slave head'" ("Histoire":211–12; Gaume 1870:173–76).[10]

Both the abandonment of Swema's mother and the unwillingness to abandon a dying Swema reveal the brutally simple economics of the slave

10. The piastre or Spanish dollar was a silver coin worth about five francs in the 1860s.

trade. The Arab caravan leader had invested his patron's capital in Swema and was clearly accountable for it. Not only did he stand to lose a piastre were she not delivered at the coast, but he would also probably have to make good his patron's loss. Thus he was determined to protect that investment and his own delivery fee, not to mention his reputation for reliability before his patron. By contrast, while Swema's mother would have represented a clear profit for both himself and his patron, except for the cost of feeding her between the interior and the coast, she was expendable precisely because she represented no capital investment.[11] Therefore her abandonment represented no accounting loss, while her presence in the caravan was a financial burden under the straitened circumstances of that year. Had the season been more favorable, it is likely that she would have received a ration in payment for her porterage and her sale at the coast would have represented a windfall profit. But it was not. Moreover, it was the very conditions of that particular agricultural season which drove Swema into slavery and carried her mother along in her wake.

At last the caravan reached Kilwa, where it remained several days while preparations were made for the sea passage to Zanzibar. For Swema it was "a respite from suffering." Left alone to recover her strength, she huddled in the darkest corner of the house where the slaves were placed. Although she had plenty of water available to slake her thirst—"the only consolation which called me back to life"—Swema remained listless and unaware of her surroundings, her senses numbed by her long period of suffering ("Histoire":212; Gaume 1870:177). One morning all the slaves from her caravan boarded a small Arab vessel and set sail for Zanzibar. Tight packing made it impossible for Swema and those with her to turn over, and even breathing was difficult. Their misery was compounded by seasickness, extreme heat, and great thirst. After a chilly night with high winds, the next morning each slave received a small amount of sweet water to drink and some dried manioc root to eat. This difficult regime lasted for six days and six nights, and Swema emphasizes the hardships that the cramped conditions, lack of sustenance, and extreme variability of temperature imposed on all the slaves. When they finally reached the port of Zanzibar Town, Swema seems to have been suffering from extreme dehydration, and her vision was impaired by "a fog which obscured the view" of the city ("Histoire":212; Gaume 1870:181–85).

In her weakened state it is not surprising that Swema recalled little of her initial hours on shore. By the time she reached their destination in

11. We have virtually no accurate data on the costs of food and other carrying costs for the East African slave trade. While there are some very useful data on these costs for the employment of free labor in the East African caravan trade during the last quarter of the nineteenth century, I do not think it advisable to attempt to interpolate these into the specific circumstances of Swema's slave caravan.

town—a large stone house—it was already nightfall. There Swema learned the real disposition of power in the slave trade: "I saw the leader of the caravan, whom I had regarded as the most powerful person in the world, stand humbly before another Arab, who seemed to reproach him in a language that I didn't understand" ("Histoire":213; Gaume 1870:189). Swema soon realized that it was she who was the problem, and though she was ordered to stand up "in a language which resembled that of my country," she was unable to rise. " 'This slave is lost,' said the new person. 'It's too bad, it's annoying. Six coudées of cloth, the cost of transport by land and sea, and the customs duty, at least five piastres [twenty-five francs] of losses. Leader, in future don't again commit such stupidities. Khamis and Marzouc, place this cadaver in a straw mat and carry it to the cemetery. It's useless to nourish it any longer because one can't save it.' " ("Histoire":213; Gaume 1870:189–90).

If we can accept this scene as being literally accurate—in which case it must have been played out in Swahili, not Arabic—then we again have vivid testimony to the crude economic reasoning which the slave trade engendered, and to which both Swema and her mother fell victim. Unfortunately, we do not know enough about the economics of the slave trade in East Africa to know if this was a typical decision or if it only reflected the market situation at the time of Swema's arrival at Zanzibar.

The remainder of Swema's narrative concerns her actual burial in a shallow grave, her fears at being left for dead, and her rescue by a young creole man from Réunion who heard her muffled cries and carried her to the Spiritains' mission in Zanzibar Town. While most of the final pages are primarily of missiological interest, the very struggle of Swema to accept Christianity also tells us something about the traumatic impact of her enslavement and her passage to Zanzibar from the interior of East Central Africa. According to Swema, she learned her catechism readily and was eager to be baptized for the great nourishment and consolation that she found in this new religion. But when she reached the fifth condition of the Lord's Prayer, "And forgive us our trespasses, as we forgive those who trespass against us," Swema was unable to pardon the Arab who had been the cause of her mother's death and her own suffering. At the urging of her confessor, she tried to pardon her tormentor and had succeeded in convincing herself that she had done so. But a dream in which she saw herself as a crow tearing away with her beak at the flesh of the bleeding Arab and beating him with her wings in the middle of a burning desert awakened her to the depth of her hatred ("Histoire":215; Gaume 1870:205–8). What more powerful image of the retribution of the weak and vulnerable could one find than this disquieting nightmare?

The circumstances of Swema's salvation are so classically Catholic that they remind us again why her story alone was recorded at such length by her new protectors. While Swema was attending the ill in the mission one day, a number of badly wounded Arabs from a slave ship that had been attacked by the British antislave trade patrol were suddenly brought in for emergency treatment. To her horror, Swema's tormentor—the Arab leader of her caravan—was among them. Overcoming her deepest feelings, Swema dressed his wounds as ordered by the Sister in charge, and through that act, she tells us, she found salvation. She was shortly thereafter baptized as Madeleine ("Histoire":216; Gaume 1870:212–17). By 1875, when she was about twenty years old, she was preparing to become a Sister of Mercy, and in April 1876 she had received her novice's habit at Réunion, having taken the name of Sister Marie Antoinette.[12] In July 1876 she took her first vows (Ricklin 1880:144). Thus, torn away from her family and her society by the slave trade, Swema found a new life and a new security in which she was no longer susceptible to the random victimization that she had once experienced. In this, her story must bear strong resemblance to the individual struggles to find security and protection among all those other African women who had come to terms with being slaves on Zanzibar itself, not to mention elsewhere in East and Central Africa, as Bwanikwa's story confirms. If in the telling of her story Swema consciously or unconsciously reflected the Christian symbolism embodied in the Catholic teaching she had just accepted, this does not invalidate the substance of her narrative.

Perhaps the most important insight to be gained from Swema's story concerns neither her former life among the Yao nor her new life among the Catholic neophytes of Zanzibar and Réunion, but instead the connecting link between them—the slave caravan. Swema's narrative of the journey to the coast is more detailed than any other we possess from the nineteenth century, and what strikes one most forcefully about it is the strong parallels to the liminal state experienced by initiates during a rite of passage from childhood to adulthood, or from commoner to chief. During the march to the coast all normal rules of behavior from the slave's original society were discarded, while those of the slave society into which the individual would soon pass were not yet understood or established. The only rules that counted were those of the caravan. But if we can legitimately speak of a caravan subculture in nineteenth-century East Africa among peoples like the Yao, Nyamwezi, and Kamba (Alpers 1969:416–17; Alpers 1975:19–20; Roberts 1970:65–67; Cummings 1975:172–85, 273–82), this must be understood as a society freely entered into, and those individuals who made but a single journey from the interior to the

---

12. For the attempt to create a congregation of African nuns in East Africa, see Kieran 1966:142.

coast to become slaves cannot be said to have participated in it. Indeed, as I suggested at the beginning of this study, Swema was neither free nor slave during her march to the coast, but only captive, her status uncertain in her own eyes and her future unknown.

Finally, without minimizing her physical deterioration and her feelings about her mother's fate, it seems possible that this suspension between fixed social states at least partly accounts for Swema's loss of will to live during this traumatic period of her life. But in this I do not think that Swema's predicament was affected by her being female. At least one of the Kiungani narratives, that of a Makua boy who was about the same age as was Swema during her march to the coast, expresses much the same sense of liminality at one point in his much longer, and possibly more typical (like Bwanikwa's succession of owners), hand-to-hand passage from interior to coast. "I kept on thinking and thinking, and fancying," he states, "'I shall never get to a quiet, settled place, where there is no more going away and being sold over and over again.' I kept on brooding over this, and I could not get my food down; yet some of those people pitied me, but I refused to eat. I used to say I had had enough, because I was very, very sad indeed; and, besides, I had no one to play with" (Madan 1886:41).

If being female was an important part of being a slave, as is illustrated elsewhere in this volume, it seems less likely that it directly affected individuals on the march to the coast. Indeed, Swema's story differs mainly in detail rather than in essential themes from the published narratives of young boys who were the victims of the slave trade. Here what counted were the captives' future productive functions, while their perceptions of the peculiar environment of the slave caravan were arguably dominated by their total absence of social identity, whatever their sex.

APPENDIX:
HISTOIRE D'UNE PETITE ESCLAVE ENTERRÉE VIVANTE,
OU
L'AMOUR FILIAL

A la jeunesse chrétienne,

Chers Enfans,

C'est à vous heureux enfans de l'Europe que je destine ce petit livre; à vous qui avez eu le bonheur de naître dans le sein du christianisme préférablement à vos pauvres petits frères d'Afrique, qui croupissent encore dans l'ignorance, les ténèbres et l'ombre de la mort.

En vous offrant ces quelques pages, je ne me propose pas de faire un ouvrage de fantaisie, mais de vous raconter la vie et les malheurs d'une pauvre petite fille esclave, qui l'infinie bonté de Dieu a fait arriver a la mission catholique de Zanzibar, par des voies bien extraordinaires.

C'est de la réalité que vous allez lire, puisque je ne fais que traduire en français ce que votre petite soeur a raconté en saouhéli qui est la langue de son pays. Vous me demanderez peut-être, mes chers enfans, pourquoi je désire vous conter une paraille histoire. Eh bien! je vous dirai franchement mon but.

Je vous mets sous les yeux les malheurs de cette pauvre enfant, qui à votre âge a déjà souffert des maux inexprimables, afin de vous faire comprendre combien vous devez être reconnaissants envers le bon Dieu qui vous a preservé de pareilles épreuves.

Introduction

La ville de Zanzibar est la capitale de l'île de ce nom et d'un vaste royaume, qui comprend toute l'étendue de l'Afrique orientale depuis le Cap Guardafui, jusqu'au Mozambique.

La Côte Orientale d'Afrique a été fréquentée par les commerçants Arabes et Indiens depuis l'antiquité la plus réculée.

Plusiers savants très distingués sont d'accord pour voir dans ces contrées l'Ophir dont parlé la Bible au sujet de navires Phéniciens envoyés par le roi Salomon pour chercher de l'or et de l'ivoire. Sous les successeurs d'Alexandre le Grand en Egypte ces parages étaient fréquentés par de nombreux navires. Il est probable qu'à cette époque il existait des colonies Arabes sur la Côte au Nord de la ligne, pendant les guerres qui ébranlèrent l'Arabie après la mort de Mahomet. Une partie des partisans d'Ali chassées de leur patrie fondèrent quelques colonies arabes dans les contrées qu'on appelle aujourd'hui Benadir.

Une colonie sortie quelques temps après du Golfe Persique fonda sur la même côte Brava et Macadschu ou Magadoxo.

Enfin vers l'an 400 de l'Hégire une Colonie sortie de Schiraz sous la conduite d'Aly fils du roi de cet endroit fonda la ville de Quiloa, qui devint ensuite la capitale d'un grand royaume.

En 1498 quand Vasco de Gama parut pour la prémière fois dans ce pays, le royaume de Quiloa s'étendait depuis Sofala jusqu'à Mombas, et les îles de Zanzibar, de Monfia et de Pemba en faisaient partie. Le royaume de Mélinde était indépendant.

Les villes de Lamo, Civy, Pata, Merka, Brava, et Magadoxo faisaient de petites républiques gouvernées par les chefs des tribus qui les habitaient. Les Portugais se rendirent maîtres de toutes ces villes, sans pourtant y mettre de garrison.

Ils se contentèrent de faire reconnaître le roi du Portugal comme Suzerain par les roitelets de ces divers pays, et ruinèrent les villes de Quiloa et de Mombas.

Ce n'est que longtemps après le voyage de Vasco de Gama qu'ils entreprisent de fonder des colonies réelles sur la Côte Orientale d'Afrique en 1569 au Mozambique et en 1594 à Mombas.

Mais les Portugais au lieu de travailler à la civilisation chrétienne de ces pays si vastes et si fertiles, s'abandonnèrent au débordement des passions les plus déréglées, et Dieu rejeta ces mauvais ouvriers.

Exaspérées par la cupidité et la cruauté de ces conquérants, les populations se levèrent comme un seul homme contre eux. L'Iman de Mascate Soultan ben Sif leur prêta secours, et les Portugais furent chassés ou massacrés, et tout le pays jusqu'au Cap Delgado tomba en 1698 sous le sceptre de l'Iman de Mascate.

Les souverains de Mascate ne changèrent rien à l'organisation politique du pays, le laissant presque indépendant et gouverné par les chefs de tribus et des princes descendants des anciens Sultans de cette contrée.

Des gouverneurs établis dans quelques localités plus importantes représentaient l'autorité de l'Imanat.

Sous des princes belliqueux et entreprenants cette autorité était tantôt reconnue, tantôt méconnue.

Sous des princes faibles et après la révolution qui détrona en 1744 l'ancienne dynastie d'Oman des Yareby, la Côte Orientale d'Afrique se détacha presque tout entière de l'Imanat de Mascate.

Plus tard un prince d'une nouvelle dynastie de Bou-Saidi Said ben Ahmed la soumit de nouveau à l'Imanat, et son petit fils Said ben Soultan père du Sultan actuel de Zanzibar, transporta en 1828 sa residence à Zanzibar après avoir soumis presque toute la Côte du Zanguebar.

Après la mort de ce prince, l'Imanat de Mascate fut divisé en deux royaumes, celui de Mascate placé sous le sceptre de Seid-Touéni qui vient d'être assassiné par son fils Salim, et celui de Zanzibar sous celui d'un prince arabe vraiment distingué Seid Medjid actuellement regnant.

Mais il est temps d'en venir à l'histoire que je vous ai promise.

Histoire de Madeleine racontée par elle-même aux petites filles de la mission catholique de Zanzibar.

Je suis née dans le pays d'Uamiao dont je ne connais ni la grandeur, ni les forces, ni la tribu, car j'étais encore bien jeune quand je l'ai quitté. Tout ce que je sais, c'est que mon pays est situé entre celui d'Allamnyndi et celui d'Uaniassa.

A l'Est d'Allamnyndi demeurent les Uaguindo qui avoisinent les peuples riverains de l'Océan, sujets du Sultan de Zanzibar. Les Uaniassa s'étendent jusqu'aux grands lacs, qui bornent leur pays au Couchant. Au Sud nous avons les Makua et au Nord Uelwanda.

Mon pays natal est de toute beauté. D'un côté vous voyez des ruisseaux à l'eau limpide, qui sillonnent de vastes plaines couvertes d'une agréable verdure, d'énormes rochers à pic, qui sont le refuge de nos villages en temps de guerre, et qui semblent perdre leurs cimes dans les nues. De l'autre côté vous voyez de vastes forêts remplies de gibier et surtout de bêtes féroces.

C'est dans ces repaires que rugissent la nuit le lion et le tigre, et que passent des troupeaux d'éléphants dont les dents nous enrichissent. C'est dans ces mêmes forêts que sont placés nos cimetières pour lesquels on choisis l'endroit le plus isolé.

Voici de quelle manière on fait les enterrements chez nous. On dépose le cadavre dans une petite cabane construite de branches d'arbres vertes. À côté du corps (si c'est celui d'un homme), on met des sagaïes, des arcs, des flèches et un bouchier. Si c'est le corps d'une femme, on mets a côté de lui des marmites, de l'upava (grande cuillère en coco), et toutes sortes de petites objets de ménage.

Les parents du défunt déposent aux pieds du cadavre un grand plateau de farine de mtama (petit maïs du pays) pour faire de la bouillie.

Le lendemain matin ils viennent visiter la case funèbre. Si la farine de mtama a disparue pendant la nuit, on en conclut que la mort était naturelle, et on invite alors tous les voisins pour faire un grand répas.

Si au contraire la farine reste intacte, le décès est attribué au sortilège. Dans ce cas la famille s'arme pour rechercher et punir le coupable.

Le défunt fait-il partie d'une famille puissante, la guerre s'allume aussitôt dans tout le pays, au point que souvent des villages entiers disparaissent par suite de cette cruelle et déplorable superstition. Voilà, chères amies, où en est mon pays, qui malheureusement ne connait pas encore le bon Dieu. Mais ce n'est pas encore tout comme vous allez le voir.

C'est dans nos forêts que demeure le Zimé.

C'est un être méchant qui mange le monde, et qui fait éprouver de cruelles maladies aux personnes qui passent auprès de sa demeure, sans lui faire quelque offrande. On dit que ce Zimé aime passionement la musique.

Lorsqu'un personne qu'il attaque a le courage de chanter ou de battre du tambour, il commence à danser. Sa tête, ses bras, ses jambes se séparent, ses yeux sortent de la tête, et chaque membre du corps danse séparément.

Lorsque le matin arrive, aux prémières clartés de l'aurore tous les membres se ramassent et disparraissent.

Quant à nos villages, les maisons ne sont pas rapprochées comme ici. Chaque case est separée de celle des voisins par une vaste étendue de champs, dont on cultive une partie, et dont l'autre est reservée aux pasturages du bétail.

On tient beaucoup à cet usage qui permet de garantir les récoltes contre les dégats que causeraient les singes, les oiseaux, ou d'autres animaux, et le bétail contre la dent vorace des bêtes sauvages. Cet usage a encore un autre avantage, en ce que l'ennemi ne peut pas en temps de guerre surprendre tout le monde à la fois, ni incendier toutes les cases.

Les champs de mon pays sont d'une fertilité remarquable. On y plante deux fois par an des haricots, des lentilles, du mtama, du miarelli, des courges, des concombres, des patates, du manioc, des brèdes, du maïs, et des ignames.

Les bananiers y poussent comme les arbres des forêts.

Dans les endroits humides, on plante du riz non pas pour le manger dans le pays, puisqu'on ne l'aime pas, mais pour l'échanger avec les caravanes arabes contre des verroteries, de la cotonnade, et du sel. Mon père était fort courageux et répute le meilleur chasseur de la contrée. Pendant toute l'année notre case était approvisionnée de viande. Comme il tuait parfois des éléphantes, ma mère et mes soeurs ainées étaient couvertes de verroteries, et portaient même à la maison des vêtements d'outre-mer, Moi-même j'étais également couverte de verroteries, mais c'était mon unique vêtement. Comme vous le voyez, mes chères amies, dans mon enfance je n'ai connu que des plaisirs. Que j'aime à me rappeler ces jours de bonheur où je ne connaissais pas encore les misères de la vie qui m'attendaient!

Le matin mon père accompagné de ses amis partait pour la chasse. Ma mère et mes soeurs allaient cultiver la terre, tandis que je gardais les moutons dans les environs de la maison.

J'étais ordinairement en compagnie de quelques petites filles de mon âge, et nous chantons ensemble comme des oiseaux du bon Dieu. Le temps nous paraissait ainsi bien court, et nous voyions arriver avec plaisir le soir qui me ramenait mon père.

Quelle joie pour moi, lorsque je voyais mon bon papa, enchanté de sa chasse plier sous le poids du butin! Mes soeurs allumaient aussitôt du feu au milieu de la case. Dans un instant le feu pétillait et des quartiers entiers de chevreuils tournaient au-dessus de la braise. On faisait cuire une énorme marmite d'ugali (espèce de bouillion épaisse de mtama). Les grandes jarres de pombé (bière du pays qu'on fait avec le mtama fermenté, en d'autres termes avec du petit maïs fermenté) préparé dès la veille se vidaient peu-à-peu. Nous avions même presque toujours du sel pour assaisonner notre nourriture, car lorsque les caravanes n'en portaient point, mon père savait s'en procurer. Comme il connaissait les forêts à une grande distance, il connaissait également les endroits où se trouvent les hautes herbes dont la cendre sert chez nous à faire du sel.

Mon père apportait souvent à la maison de grands sacs de cendre, et c'est alors qu'ils fallait voir tout le monde à l'ouvrage. L'un cherchait du bois, l'autre de l'eau, un autre lavait la cendre, passait l'eau à travers un linge; un autre faisait bouillir cette même eau toute la journée, et le soir nous avions quelques parcelles du sel. Mais aussi chez nous ne mange pas du sel qui veut.

J'étais tellement heureuse dans mon enfance que souvent lorsque j'allais a la rivière puiser de l'eau, j'entendais dire aux enfans de nos voisins: "Voilà l'heureuse Suèma, qui mange tous les jours de la viande et du sel." J'étais fière d'entendre prononcer ces paroles, puisqu'elles faisaient l'éloge de mon père. On disait aussi quelquefois: "Voila Suèma, la propre aux cheveux bien tressés." J'étais encore bien contente de ces paroles, qui étaient l'éloge de ma mère. Ah! chères amies, pourquoi ces jours de bonheur ont-ils sitôt fini? Jusqu'à présent je ne vous ai montre que le beau côté de ma vie; vous allez voir dans un instant parquel évènement terrible commence l'histoire de mes malheurs.

Mon père s'était arrangé avec un de nos voisins pour faire la chasse au menu gibier. Dans ce but, on avait préparé sur les sentiers et dans divers endroits des forêts, des fosses profondes et couverts de branches et d'herbes. Ce travail terminé, toutes les familles des chasseurs se réunirent pour faire la battue. Ce fut pour la prémière fois que je fus admise à faire cette chasse commune.

En partant je fus heureuse et contente, sans songer le moins du monde au danger. A peine arrivés dans la forêt, nous formions la chaine, de manière à être distances les uns des autres de plusieurs traits de flèche, et c'est en marchant que nous cherchions tous à resserrer le cercle. Nous criions à gorge deployée pour effrayer le gibier.

Les chasseurs armés de sagaïes et d'arcs marchaient les uns devant la battue; les autres disperses dans la forêt derrière les trappes, cherchaient à poursuivre les animaux, qui par leur adresse auraient évité les fosses.

Au bout d'un certain temps nous nous approchions du lieu destiné au principal episode de la chasse. Un bosquet très touffu nous séparait de la ligne des trappes. La troupe des traqueurs devenait à tout moment plus épaisse et les cris plus perçants. Je marchais à côté de ma mère et de mes soeurs. Devant nous à peu de distance marchait mon père, tenant la flèche toute prête sur la corde de son arc. La battue était déjà sur la lisière du fourre dont je vous ai parlé.

Tout à coup un rugissement terrible sort du bosquet environnant. Tout le monde est comme pétrifié, et les cris de la battue sont remplacés par le silence le plus profond.

Les echos de la forêt répètent le rugissement du lion, qui, les yeux enflammés, la crinière herissée, battant la terre avec sa puissant queue, paraît sur la lisière de la forêt. Il s'approche des chasseurs, que restent immobiles de terreur. Sa marche un peu oblique le même directement vers nous. Il passe à côté de mon père et s'arrète, prêt à bondir sur mes soeurs et sur moi.

Au même moment un autre cri terrible réveille les échos des forêt. Mon malheureux père se précipite sur le féroce animal. Sa flèche et ses sagaïes jadis si sures manquent leur but; le couteau à la main, mon père s'élance contre le lion, dont avec ses bras crispés, il saisit la féroce crinière.

Les cris, les rugissements, et la frayeur m'avaient tellement glacé le sang dans les veines, que je ne voyais plus alors ce qui se passait. C'est à peine si j'ai pu apercevoir un tourbillon de sang, une masse rouge roulant par terre et disparaissant dans les forêts.

Et après! Après hélàs! nous pauvres orphélines, nous nous assîmes en sanglotant sur la terre rougie du sang de notre père, de notre protecteur, de notre nourricier.

Aussitôt la battue cesse, la forêt devient sombre et solitaire, et nos sanglots seuls rompent son triste silence.

La nuit nous trouve au même endroit, et les rugissements de la hyène rappellent à la pensée de ma mère, mon petit frère qui était resté à la maison.

Ma pauvre mère désolée se lève, mais avant de partir elle construit un petit cabanon avec des branches d'arbre a l'endroit rougi par le sang de mon père. Elle y dépose la sagaïe, le carquois, et les flèches. Ensuite nous mîmes toutes nos provisions sur une feuille de banane à l'entrée de la case funèbre, et nous quittâmes cet endroit sans regarder en arrière, comme on revient d'un enterrement.

C'est de ce jour fatal que datent mes malheurs.

C'était la prémière nuit que notre pauvre case était sans feu et sans lumière, triste et silencieuse.

Toutefois le lendemain chacun se mit à son travail habituel, mais plus de chansons, plus de gaîté.

Oh! que j'étais malheureuse alors!

Je ne savais pas encore les vérités saintes que j'ai apprises ici.

J'ignorais que nous sommes sur la terre pour aimer Dieu, prier, souffrir, et gagner le Ciel. Ne sachant pas prier, mon amour pour mon père et la douleur de l'avoir perdu, me poussaient à la haine des créatures.

Je reprochais au soleil sa lumière, aux oiseaux leurs chants. Je maudissais mon existence, et les voix joyeuses de nos voisins au lieu de m'égayer m'irritaient, puisqu'elles semblaient insulter à mon malheur.

Oh! comme on souffre quand on ne connait pas Dieu et qu'on ne sais pas le prier!

Bientôt une affreuse calamité vint désoler non seulement mon famille, mais encore toute la contrée dont toutes les récoltes furent ravagées par des nuées de sauterelles.

En trois jours tout avait disparu; les plantes céréales étaient mangées jusqu'á l'écorce. Toute la contrée ne fut bientôt plus qu'un désert, nu et aride.

Ce fléau causa une famine atroce et cruelle. Les gens qui avaient du sel faisaient quelques provisions de sauterelles salées.

Hélàs! depuis la mort de notre pauvre père ce condiment si utile nous manquait complètement.

Pendant quelque temps nous vivions en mangeant les chèvres et les poules qui nous restaient; mais nos troupeaux ne trouvant plus la nourriture suffisante, la mortalité se mit parmi eux. Ce fleau fut suivi par un autre plus cruel encore.

L'air corrompu par des milliers d'insectes et de corps d'animaux morts qu'on négligeait d'enterrer, produisit une grande épidémie sur les hommes. Notre contrée naguère si gaie et si peuplée devenait de jour en jour plus vide et plus silencieuse. Chez nous, nous avons tant pleuré, qu'il se formait comme des ruisseaux de larmes dans notre demeure. Notre malheur était si grand, que nous ne plaignions plus ceux d'entre nous qui mouraient. Aussi portions-nous dans la forêt sans verser une larme mes deux soeurs que nous venions de perdre.

Ma mère ajoutait même tout bas: "Elles sont bien heureuses d'en avoir fini avec le malheur."

A la mort de mon petit frère ma mère ne pleurait plus non plus; seulement au lieu de le porter à la forêt, elle le déposa dans la case même, et me prenant par la main, elle partit avec moi le long des rivières sans regarder derrière nous.

Le changement de localité produisit un heureux changement sur ma mère. Elle reprit courage et à trois jours de marche de notre village, nous batîmes une hutte et nous commençâmes à défricher un terrain. Un voisin fut assez bon pour nous prêter deux sacs de mtama; l'un pour planter, l'autre pour manger jusqu'à la récolte. Je ne puis pas dire que la joie était de nouveau rentrée dans notre demeure; néanmoins, ma mère était plus calme, et moi j'étais heureuse de ne plus la voir pleurer. Cependant notre tranquillité ne fut pas de longue durée.

L'année a été généralement mauvaise et la récolte a manquée complètement. Notre créancier, pressé lui-même par le besoin est venu réclamer les deux sacs de mtama qu'il avait eu la bonté de nous prêter. Ma mère fort embarrassée de cette demande se jéta à ses pieds en le suppliant de nous accorder un petit délai. Mais le sursis qu'elle obtint fut tout-à-fait insignifiant.

Sans perdre courage dans son malheur, ma pauvre mère eut récours à son activité et à son adresse dans les travaux de poterie en terre. Jour et nuit elle ne cessa de travailler dans cette industrie à laquelle je coopérai selon la mésure de mes forces. Mais comme vous le savez, mes chères amies, les ouvrages ce genre rapportent fort peu de chose dans certaines contrées. Aussi malgré notre extrême activité étions-nous incapables de payer le quart de notre dette à l'expiration du délai fixé par notre créancier.

Il revint donc à la charge et trouvant notre insolvabilité plus qu'ennuyeuse, il s'en alla en proférant des ménaces qui nous furent fort pénibles.

Pour comble de malheur, une caravane arabe passa à la même époque dans les environs.

Qui ne sait combien le passage d'une caravane est toujours dangereux pour les faibles. Les mauvais sujets ont l'habitude de voler des enfans et de pauvres gens pour les vendre aux Arabes pour du sel, de la cotonnade, et des verroteries. Les créanciers profitent de la circonstance pour éxiger le paiement des dettes. Lorsque les débiteurs ne peuvent pas payer, on saisit leurs esclaves ou leurs propres enfans, et souviens il arrive qu'eux-mêmes sont réduits à l'esclavage. Il n'a du reste rien d'étonnant dans cette étrange conduite, car la cupidité n'a ni frein ni bornes dans les âmes étrangères à la charité chrétienne.

Un jour nous apprîmes que la caravane s'est arretée tout près de notre demeure. De là une inquiétude mortelle se répandit de tous côtés. La nuit les sanglots de ma mère me réveillèrent plusieurs fois. Je n'osai pas lui demander la cause de ses larmes dans la crainte d'augmenter son chagrin. Du iᴖᵗe nous étions si habituées à pleurer ensemble!

Mais le matin je ne fus pas longtemps sans m'apercevoir que ma pauvre mère avait été toute la nuit sous la pression d'une douleur extraordinaire.

Quel ne fut pas mon étonnement de voir que ses cheveux étaient devenus blancs comme du lait!

Pauvre mère! elle avait prévu dans sa sollicitude maternelle le coup qui allait nous frapper.

Dans la matinée notre créancier vint chex nous avec deux vieillards de la tribu et un Arabe. Sans demander la permission, il entra dans notre hutte et dit avec dureté à ma mère.

"Mère de Suèma, vous n'avez pas de quoi payer mes deux sacs de mtama; je saisis pour cela votre enfant. Soyez-moi témoins," dit-il, "aux vieillards." Et se tournant vers l'Arabe, il lui dit, "Eh bien! Monsieur, c'est convenu, six coudées de toile américaine pour cette petite fille." L'Arabe me prit par la main, me fit lever, marcher, examina mes bras et mes jambes, m'ouvrit la bouche, examina mes dents et après quelques instants de réflexion répondit, "C'est bien, viens prendre les six coudées de toile."

Pendant tout ce temps ma mère était restée comme anéantie. Lorsque notre cruel créancier lui dit qu'il me saisissait pour sa dette selon l'usage légal du pays, elle frappa une main contre l'autre et se couvrit le visage. Sa douleur comprimée jusque là éclata en sanglots déchirants capables de briser un coeur de pierre, au moment où l'Arabe voulut m'emmener avec lui.

Elle se jeta à ses pieds et d'une voix qu'aucune langue ne saurait exprimer, le supplia de l'emmener avec moi, "Je ne suis pas encore vieille," dit-elle, "malgré la couleur de mes cheveux blanchis par le chagrin. Je suis encore assez forte pour porter une dent d'éléphant. Ah! de grâce, ne me séparez pas de ma fille qui est mon unique consolation sur cette misérable terre sur laquelle j'ai eu tout à souffrir. Ne m'accablez pas, Seigneur, dans ma douleur," ajouta-t-elle, "ne me réfusez pas cette grâce. Du reste je suis sobre et me contente de peu de chose. Je sais faire de la poterie en terre. Je vous serai utile comme esclave. Je vous promets de toujours bien travailler. Ah! de grâce, Seigneur, emmenez-moi. Ayez pitié d'une pauvre mère qui ne veut pas se séparer de son enfant."

Ces paroles arrachées au coeur affligé d'une mère qui ne veut point se séparer pour toujours de sa fille unique touchèrent l'Arabe. Je crois cependant que cet

Arabe qui consentit à nous réunir toutes deux à sa caravane, fit plus attention aux futurs travaux de poterie qu'aux larmes de ma mere. Quoi qu'il en soit du motif determinant sa décision rendit le calme à nos âmes éprouvées.

Le lendemain de grand matin la caravane se mit en route. Ma mère reçut pour sa charge une dent d'éléphant et moi je portai quelques hardes.

Voici la manière de voyager d'une caravane;

Aussitôt après minuit quelques serviteurs de maitre prennent les devants en portant avec eux des haches et des cordes pour construire les huttes, des outres pour l'eau, quelques marmites pour faire cuire la nourriture, et un grand tambour pour réunir la caravane.

Ils sont en outre munis d'une corne d'antilope qui passe pour être le talisman contre les lions, et qu'on achète ordinairement auprès des plus fameux sorciers du pays.

Au point du jour on donne le signal de départ. Un homme marche à la tête de la caravane, et porte un petit drapeau qui passe pour être ensorcelé. C'est bien plutôt le signe distinctif de quelque puissant chef de la contrée, qui couvre de sa protection la caravane moyennant les cadeaux d'usage.

Viennent ensuite les esclaves qui portent les provisions de route, l'ivoire, la gomme copale, et les hardes de maître. Ce dernier accompagné de quelques serviteurs fidèles forme l'arrière-garde.

A midi l'Arabe fait sa prière. Pendant ce temps tout le monde se repose deux ou trois heures. On se met ensuite de nouveau en route et on marche jusqu'à l'étape de nuit.

L'avant-garde a soin de marquer son chemin en couvrant d'herbes et de branches tous les endroits qui croisent les sentiers principaux. Vers le soir elle bat du tambour pour conduire plus sûrement les pas incertaines de la caravane.

Arrivée à l'étape, cette dernière a l'avantage de trouver les huttes toutes faites. On les construit ordinairement avec des branches d'arbres et des herbes sèches. Dans la meilleure des cases on se sert de branches pour construire le lit du maître, auquel on prépare la couche avec l'herbe la plus douce. On y ajoute les nattes et des traversins. On s'occupe ensuite de la distribution de la nourriture de la troupe pour laquelle tout a été également préparé à l'avance. Le repas consiste habituellement en bouillie épaisse de farine de mtama ou de haricots. Quelquefois aussi la ration se compose de bananes rôties ou de patates douces.

Pour éviter la désertion et en même temps pour ménager les forces des porteurs de marchandises, les conducteurs des caravanes ont soin de bien nourrir pendant le trajet les esclaves qui sont à leurs ordres.

Les deux ou trois premiers jours de notre voyage se passèrent assez bien. Cette course augmentait même mon appétit qui avait plus de facilité à se satisfaire que chez nous. J'aimais naturellement beaucoup à marcher et par bonheur ma charge n'étais pas lourde.

Mais il n'en fut pas de même de ma pauvre mère. Le premier jour elle marcha à la tête de la colonne; le deuxième, elle se trouva déjà au milieu et le troisième elle eut peine à suivre la queue de la caravane. A tout moment elle déposait sa charge. Sa respiration pénible trahissait sa fatigue, et chaque pas montrait les efforts surhumains qu'elle faisait pour continuer son chemin. Toutes ces souffrances de ma pauvre mère que je ne pouvais point soulager furent autant de poignards qui me percèrent le coeur.

Les jours suivants la caravane eut le tort de s'éloigne du ruisseau qu'elle avait suivi jusque là, et la soif la plus ardente devint un tourment cruel pour tout le monde.

Ma mère épuisée par sa charge tomba plusiers fois. La voyant incapable de continuer plus longtemps à porter son lourd fardeau, le maître de la caravane ordonna à un esclave de porter à sa place la dent d'éléphant qu'elle avait trainée depuis notre départ.

Je fus un moment consolée et même étonné de voir ces sentiments d'humanité dans un arabe. Mais ô cruelle déception!

Quel ne fut pas mon chagrin lorsque le soir j'entendis retentir à mes oreilles cet ordre barbare donne a l'esclave chargé de la distribution des vivres, "La mere de Suèma ne sert à rien, elle n'aura pas de ration." Quelle nouvelle pour une fille qui aime tendrement celle qui lui a donner le jour!

A force de dissimuler je parvins cependant à partager ma nourriture avec ma pauvre mère. Malheureusement le féroce arabe s'aperçut de ma petite ruse, et me fit frapper jusqu'à faire couler le sang. L'ordre fut immédiatement donné de me servir ma ration en présence du maître, et de me surveiller le plus strictement possible. Le jour suivant ma pauvre mère eut pour toute nourriture quelques sauterelles, quelques feuilles de mtama, et un peu de terre rouge.

Quelle position pour sa pauvre fille!

Le soir je ne pouvais pas manger; j'avais honte de porter à ma bouche la bonne nourriture qu'on m'offrait.

Comment un enfant qui voit sa mère mourir de faim pourrait-il avoir le courage de manger? Comment être insensible aux souffrances d'une mère?

Ce sentiment filial fut si mal interprété par le maître dénaturé qu'il me fit battre de nouveau, et je fus forcée d'avaler ma nourriture arrosée de mes larmes, sans avoir la consolation de la partager avec ma bonne et infortunée maman.

Le lendemain, oh jour de malheur! notre caravane entra dans une plaine dans laquelle on venait de mettre le feu qui s'était étendu à perte de vue. On ne voyait plus nulle part un brin d'herbe verte. Plus d'insectes, plus d'oiseaux dans ces parages. Ce qui frappait la vue, c'était une immense étendue de terre carbonisée et noircie par le feu. Impossible a ma pauvre mère de se procurer la moindre parcelle de nourriture par même de la terre rouge pour illusionner son estomac.

Pendant cette journée je l'ai vue plusiers fois tomber épuisée de fatigue et d'inanition. Ce n'est que grâce à des efforts désespérés qu'elle reussit a arriver péniblement jusqu'à l'étape du soir.

Au moment de la distribution de la nourriture quelques paroles inhumaines me déchirerent de nouveau le coeur, "Qu'on chasse cette vieille de l'endroit du campement et surtout qu'on veille bien à ce que personne ne lui donne rien à manger. Quiconque enfreindra cet ordre sera puni sévèrement," dit le maître de la caravane à l'esclave chargé de la surveillance de la troupe. Il continue en ces termes, "Demain, s'il plaît Dieu, nous en serons débarrassés; demain elle nous laissera tranquilles, je l'espère; c'est aujourd'hui sa dernière étape, car elle n'en peut plus."

Ces paroles étaient accompagnée d'un rire féroce qui en expliquait la sinistre signification.

Comment vous dépeindre, chères amies, ce qui se passait dans mon coeur pendant que ce barbare prononçait de gaité de coeur, l'arrêt de mort de la seule personne que j'aimais passionement en ce monde, de ma bonne mère qui m'aimait toute, et qui a fait tout de sacrifices pour moi?

Les mots douleur, torture, désespoir sont bien faibles pour exprimer ce que je souffrais intérieurement, Ah! la seule pensée de ces tourments me fait frisonner à l'heure qu'il est!

La nuit nous campions à la belle étoile, l'incendie de la savane ayant consumé toutes les herbes et toutes les broussailles. C'était pour moi un heureux malheur qui me permit de rejoindre ma malheureuse mère. Lorsque je crus tout le monde endormi, je me glissai comme un serpent en dehors du camp. L'obscurité de la nuit et la couleur noire de la plaine favorisèrent ma fuite.

Je dois l'avouer, à peine éloignée du camp de quelques centaines de pas, je me sens saisie d'une grande frayeur, car je n'avais point l'habitude de marcher seule dans une nuit obscure. La peur me glace un instante le sang dans les veines, mais au même moment l'amour que j'ai pour ma mère se reveille plus fort que jamais, et je m'écrie tout haut, "Que ne ferait pas une fille pour sa mère chérie? Ne vaut-il pas mieux que je meure avec elle plutôt que de survivre à sa mort?" Ces paroles me donnèrent du courage et je poursuivis hardiment ma marche. Bientôt j'entendis de sourds gémissements qui me firent reconnaître la voix de ma mère et l'endroit où elle se trouvait. D'aussi loin que possible je lui crie, "Ma mère consolez-vous, voici votre enfant qui vient pour vous soulager."

Elle entend ces paroles qui lui font pousser des soupirs d'amour et d'attendrissement. Lorsqu'enfin j'eus le bonheur de l'approcher, elle me serra dans ses bras amaigris, posa ma tête sur ses genoux, et alors je sentis ses larmes couler sur mes cheveux. Elle me berça autant que ses forces le lui permirent comme elle berçait autrefois mon petit frère. Dans ce moment elle chant tout bas en sanglotant comme on chante chez nous aux enterrements.

"Suèma mon enfant! pourquoi n'est-tu pas morte avec ses soeurs? J'aurais en au moins vos tombeaux, à bien que personne n'aurait pu me ravir. Heureuse est la mère qui peut rendre l'âme en pleurant sur les tombeaux de ses enfans! Les tombeaux de tes frères et soeurs sont loin et tu vas te séparer de moi à jamais; et moi malheureuse je n'ai ni la force de te suivre, ni celle de retourner auprès des ossements cheris des nôtres! Oh! où vas-tu ma malheureuse enfant?

La mort n'est pas aussi amère que l'esclavage. Qui va desormais peigner et tresser tes cheveux? Qui va laver ta tête?

Ce sont la rosée froide du matin et les pluies de la mauvaise saison qui lavent la tête de l'orphéline; et les larmes lavent le visage de l'esclave. La terre humide est sa mère. Le tombeau est sa patrie, seul endroit ou elle pourra réposer son coeur endolori."

C'est ainsi que chanta ma mère en sanglotant selon l'usage des enterrements de mon pays.

Et moi comme vous pouvez facilement vous l'imaginer, j'avais le coeur bien gros. Les larmes ne coulaient plus de mes yeux, car je me sentais étouffée par le douleur. Il me semblait que j'avais le gosier rempli de charbons ardents. Un hoquet convulsif me déchirait la poitrine. Cependant la fatigue d'une longue et pénible journée de marche, le doux bercement et la voix plaintive de ma mère m'endormirent peu-à-peu. Au point du jour je me fortement serrée. Je me réveille et m'aperçois que c'est ma mère qui me serre dans ses bras.

Tout à coup j'entends résonner les pas des hommes qui me cherchent. Ils approchent de plus en plus et enfin quelques-uns nous découvrent et appèllent leurs compagnons. Ils nous cernes de toutes parts. L'Arabe roulant des yeux terribles me saisit par la main et cherche a m'entrainer par force.

Ma mère m'embrasse et me serre si fortement contre elle, que l'homme cruel ne réussit pas à nous séparer, et nous traîne pendant quelques pas toutes les deux par terre.

"Frappez cette maudite vieille, exterminez-la à coups de baton," hurla-t-il d'une voix rauque et tremblante de colère.

Aussitôt une grêle de coups s'abat sur tout le corps de ma malheureuse mère. Malgré toutes ces souffrances elle ne desserre pas les bras et me tient toujours étreinte.

"Frappez, frappez, tant qu'il vous plaira," chuchota-t-elle, "frappez pour que je meure avant de me séparer de mon dernier enfant."

Le maître entend ces paroles et son âme farouche ne veut point laisser au malheur cette dernière consolation.

"Frappez," dit-il, "frappez fortement la petite."

La douleur causée par la bastonnade m'arrache des cris plaintifs. Enfin les forces manquent à ma mère, ses bras s'ouvrent, on me saisit et on m'emporte.

Faisant un dernier effort ma mère se met à genoux, étend douloureusement les deux mains dans la direction de l'endroit vers lequel on m'entraîne. Un instant après je la vois s'affraisser sur elle-même. Elle tomba sans doute évanouie et suffoquée par la douleur.

On essaya de me faire marcher à coups de baton. Mais vains efforts! A chaque pas je cherchais à rétourner chez ma mère, et accablée de douleur je tombais par terre.

Le maître fatigué de ma résistance ordonna à un esclave de me porter et la caravane se mit en mouvement.

Bientôt nous arrivons sur le sommet d'une colline. Je regarde en arrière et au milieu de la plaine brûlée, je vois pour la dernière fois ma mère les bras étendus vers moi. J'eus alors la douleur de voir une énorme quantité de corbeaux voltiger auteur de sa tête, et attendre avec impatience le moment de sa mort pour la dévorer. Vous devinez, mes bonnes amies, ce que mon coeur dut éprouver en ce moment.

Je ne vous dirai rien, chères compagnes, de notre voyage depuis cet endroit jusqu'à Quiloa qui est une ville située au bord de la mer.

Toutefois il est bon que vous sachiez que pendant ce trajet j'ai versé tant de larmes qu'à force de pleurer mes yeux se sont gonflés à faire peur. Je croyais que j'allais devenir aveugle. On recommença à me battre pour me faire marcher. Toutes ces cruautés furent inutiles, car je ne fus pas capable de me tenir debout, tant le chagrin m'avait anéantie.

"Maître," dit le domestique au conducteur, "pourquoi porter plus longtemps ce cadavre? Vous voyez bien que cette petite fille n'est bonne qu'à être mangé par les corbeaux." "Je ne puis pas la laisser ici," repondit-il; "je l'ai achetée pour le compte de mon patron. Si je l'abandonne je perdrai une piastre (5 francs) qui me revient par tête d'esclave."

L'homme qui me portait était furieux de sa corvée. Le malheureux faisait tout ce qu'il pouvait pour se débarrasser de son fardeau. Chaque fois qu'il arrivait à l'endroit de l'étape, il me jetait de toute sa force par terre. Passant sous les arbres et par les broussailles, il ne manquait jamais de me faire écorcher le dos par les branches. Et ce qui est vraiment affreux, c'est que cette conduite inhumaine provoquait l'hilarité et l'approbation de mes malheureux compagnons de captivité.

Je passais quelques jours à Quiloa; c'était pour moi un répit dans mes souffrances. Là personne ne me maltraitait. J'étais couchée dans le coin le plus sombre de la case. L'eau se trouvait presque à ma portée, ce qui me permettait d'éteindre à volonté ma soif ardente, seul adoucissement qui me rappalait à la vie. Pour le reste tout m'était indifférent. Je comprenais à peine où j'étais, et je ne conservais qu'un vague souvenir de mes longues souffrances.

Tout le temps écoulé depuis la séparation d'avec ma mère jusqu'au moment d'alors, se presentait à moi comme un songe terrible. Il me semblait que ce rêve devait finir, que tout ce qui m'entourait devait s'évanouir, et que je m'éveillerais un jour à côté de ma pauvre mère dans la petite case où nous étions si tristes, mais si heureuses en comparaison de notre sort actuel. Voici qu'un beau matin on me porte à bord d'un boutre qui doit se rendre à Zanzibar.

Les esclaves qui se trouvent dans la même bande commencent à trembler de tous leurs membres, et à se lamenter d'une manière étrange. "Ah! disent-ils, nous sommes perdus. Nous allons à Zanzibar où il y a des hommes tout blancs qui mangent les Noirs."

Quoique je fusse généralement indifférente à tout ce qui se passait autour de moi, je ne pouvais reste longtemps dans cet état dans le boutre où mes souffrances redoublaient. Nous étions si serrés que non seulement on ne pouvait pas se tourner, mais pas même respirer. La chaleur et la soif devenaient insupportables, et un fort mal de mer augmentait encore mes souffrances.

La nuit le vent frais du large nous glaçait en nous couvrant à chaque instant de l'écume de la mer qu'il soulevait par la violence de son souffle. Le lendemain chacun de nous reçut un peu d'eau douce et un morceau de racine de manioc sec. C'est ainsi que se passèrent six longues journées et six nuits plus pénibles encore. La faim, la soif, le mal de mer, la transition subité d'une grande chaleur à un froid insupportable, l'impossibilité de réposer la tête un moment à cause du manque de place, enfin toutes ces souffrances réunies me firent regretter pour la première fois le temps de notre pénible voyage à travers le désert. Mais courage! notre existence va changer, car nous voilà devant l'île de Zanzibar.

Un bon vent continue à gonfler notre voile triangulaire, et bientôt nous nous trouvons devant la grande ville. Deux coups de canon font trembler le boutre. On amène la voile et on jette l'ancre.

J'entends mes compagnons d'infortune admirer la ville murée, la ville blanche. A tout l'instant ils passent de l'admiration à la crainte. Quant à moi j'avais devant les yeux, comme un brouillard qui m'obscurcissait la vue. Je ne me sentais plus vivre que par la seule pensée qu'une fois à terre on me donnera peut-être à boire. Oh! quelle cruelle souffrance que la soif!

Je ne me rappelle pas bien la manière dont nous avons été débarqués, ni combien de temps nous sommes restés à la Douane. La vue de cette immense foule de Noirs, qui portent des charges, les cris qu'ils poussent pour marquer le pas m'ont tellement étourdie, que je ne pouvais pas me rendre compte de mille objets que je voyais. Du reste il faisait déjà un peu sombre et lorsque nous arrivions au lieu du dépôt des esclaves qui est une grande maison en pierre, il faisait complètement nuit. Là j'ai vu le conducteur de la caravane, que j'avais regardé comme le personnage le plus puissant du monde, se tenir humblement devant un autre Arabe, qui paraissait lui faire des reproches dans une langue que je ne comprenais pas.

Je pense qu'il le grondait à cause de moi, car plusieurs fois il me montrait au doigt.

Il m'ordonna de me lève. Je fis beaucoup d'efforts pour lui obéir mais sans pouvoir réussir.

"Cet esclave est perdu," dit le nouveau personnage. "C'est dommage, c'est contrariant. Six coudées de toile, le transport par terre et par mer et le droit de la douane, au moins cinq piastres (25 francs) de perdues. Conducteur ne fais plus à l'avenir de pareilles bêtises. Khamis et Marzouc mettez ce cadavre dans une natte et portez-le au cimetière. C'est inutile de la nourrir plus longtemps, car on ne le sauvera pas."

Aussitôt dit, aussitôt fait. Les deux esclaves me prennent, m'enveloppent dans une vieille natte qu'ils ont soin de bien lier avec des cordes de coco.

Ils attachent cette espèce de paquet à un long baton, et m'emportent ainsi loin de la maison du maître.

J'étais si bien enveloppée dans la natte que je ne pouvais absolument rien voir. Le bruit de la foule m'avertissait qu'on me portait à travers les rues de la ville.

A ce bruit succèda bientôt le frôlement de branches qui m'avertirent que nous passions par des broussailles.

Enfin on s'arrête; on me jette par terre; je sens le sable et je comprends qu'on m'enterre vivante.

La couche de sable qui me couvrit fut si légère que j'entendis les pas des porteurs qui s'en rétournèrent à la hâte. Je fus comme ensevelie dans un profond silence et une peur atroce s'empara de tout mon être. J'avais, il est vrai, beaucoup souffert jusqu'à ce jour; ma vie avait été plus féconde en souffrances qu'en joies, et cependant la seule pensée de la mort me causait une terreur inexprimable. Je fis donc des efforts extraordinaires pour me dégager de la natte, mais vains efforts! Ce fut même avec beaucoup de peine que je pus dégager le haut de mon corps pour ne pas être suffoquée par le sable.

Au même moment je me mets à crier de toutes mes forces. Ma voix se perd dans le silence de la nuit. Deux ou trois fois il me semble entendre les pas de personnes, qui passent tout près de moi. Je crie alors plus fort, mais ma voix au lieu de me procurer du sécours, effraie ces promeneurs nocturnes que j'entends s'éloigner à la course. Le silence se fait de nouveau autour de moi.

Tout-à-coup les broussailles s'agitent tout près de l'endroit où je me trouve. J'ai un moment d'espoir. Soudain un troupeau de chacals m'entoutent en hurlant. Mon sang se glace de frayeur. Mes cris et les mouvements désespérés que je fais, les tiennent quelque temps éloignés. Peu-à-peu ils s'encouragent et j'entends de plus en plus près leurs aboiements.

Enfin ils detèrrent le bas de mon corps et je me sens mordue aux pieds. Je pousse un cri et je perds connaissance.

Lorsque l'usage de mes sens revint, je me trouvais dans une chambre aux parois blanches comme je n'en avais jamais vu. J'étais couchée dans un bon lit et couverte d'un drap blanc. Deux personnes aux figures blanches comme je n'en avais jamais vu de ma vie se tenaient au chevet de mot lit, et surveillaient attentivement chaque mouvement que je faisais. Elles étaient vêtues de blanc et de noir. C'étaient nos bonnes Soeurs, ces dévouées Filles de Marie, qui sert de si tendres mères pour nous qui me soignaient.

Voyant leurs robes noires je croyais un instant que j'étais morte, et que je me trouvais dans le pays des esprits "Peponi." Ma première pensée était pour ma mère.

"Où est ma mère?" démandais-je plusiers fois aux Soeurs que je prenais pour des esprits.

"Sois tranquille," me repondit l'une d'entre elles, "ta mere va venir tout à l'heure."

On me présenta alors une boisson d'un gout délicieux. J'en bus à longs traits et puis je m'endormis.

Vous désirez sans doute savoir ce qui s'est passé lorsque j'ai perdu connaissance au milieu d'une bande de chacals. Je vais vous le dire et vous allez voir, chères compagnes, par quelle voie admirable la divine Providence me sauva la vie.

M.N. jeune Creole de l'île de la Réunion ne pouvant pas dormir cette nuit là, eut l'heureuse fantaisie de faire la chasse aux chacals. Armé de son fusil de chasse il vint au cimétière et se dirigea vers l'endroit d'où partaient les aboiements des bêtes. Au lieu de s'enfuir comme les autres passants, il poursuivit les chacals qui me mordaient les pieds.

Voyant devant lui un paquet qui remuait un peu, le jeune homme voulu savoir ce que c'était. Il s'arrête, délie les cordes, déroule la natte et apercevant un corps humain dont le coeur battait encore, me charge sur ses épaules, et me porte à la mission catholique où nos bonnes Soeurs me reçoivent avec un heureux empressement. Le jeune homme reçoit en même temps les plus chaleureuses félicitations des Soeurs pour la belle oeuvre de charité qu'il venait d'accomplir.

A partir de ce moment je fus heureuse.

Je pourrais donc terminer mon histoire là où finissait mes malheurs. Mais je crois utile de vous faire le récit d'un fait d'une grande gravité pour moi, et qui est intimement lié à la chaîne de mes malheurs.

Nous avons toutes appris ici avec bonheur les divines et consolantes vérités du christianisme.

Chaque parole de Notre Seigneur a été pour nous une lumière nouvelle qui nous a remplies de consolation.

Orphélines, nous avons trouvé de bonnes mères dans les Soeurs qui nous ont fait connaître notre père par excellence, le Père Céleste. Nous avons été méprisées, persécutées, maltraitées.

Eh bien! on a su nous rendre chers ce mépris, ces persécutions, et ces mauvais traitements. On a fini par nous persuader que nos larmes du passé nous ont attiré les bénédictions de notre bon Jésus, qui nous comblera un jour d'une grande gloire, si nous sommes de bonnes chrétiennes. Sans patrie, sans famille, nous avons tout rétrouvé dans cette bonne mission, qui nous remplace si bien notre famille et qui nous monte le chemin de la véritable patrie où il n'y a plus de souffrances. Toutes les vérités que la Soeur catéchiste nous a enseignées m'ont procuré une ineffable consolation. Mon âme les savourait comme je savourais autrefois un verre d'eau fraîche dans la soif qui me brûlait à travers le désert.

Mais lorsque la bonne Soeur expliquait l'Oraison Dominicale et qu'à la cinquième demande elle citait ces paroles, "Et pardonnez nous nos offenses comme nous pardonnons à ceux qui nous ont offensés," je sentais mon coeur se révolter intérieurement. Tout le reste est bien, me disais-je, mais cela est insupportable. Je ne pouvais pas contenir plus longtemps ma révolte intérieure melée de douleur.

"Comment," m'écriais-je, "ma Soeur, comment je dois à pardonner à l'Arabe qui a frappé ma mère mourante? Oh! non jamais. Comment je dois pardonner à l'assassin de ma mère?"

"Oui, mon enfant," repartit la Soeur, "Notre Seigneur tout Dieu qu'il était, a souffert les derniers outrages. Il a tout pardonné et à même prié pour ses bourreaux." "Mais ma Soeur," répliquais-je, "une chose pareille m'est impossible. Je crois que si je disais, oui je pardonne, mon coeur me répondrait que mon pardon n'est pas sincère." "J'ai pitié de toi, ma bonne et pauvre Madeleine, à cause des longues et cruelles souffrances par lesquelles tu as passée, et à cause de l'obstacle que tu mets toi-même à ton Baptême qui aurait comblé tous tes désirs."

"C'est bien dommage, mon enfant, tu as appris avec tant de zèle ton catéchisme, et voici que tu ne veux pas rénoncer sincèrement à cette vilaine haine, comme tu renoncerais volontiers à Satan, à ses pompes, et à ses oeuvres. Avec cette haine pas de baptême possible. Mais prie, ma fille, je prierai aussi pour toi et avec l'aide de Dieu ton coeur changera de disposition."

Je me mis donc à prier et au milieu de la prière je me sentis tantôt changée et soulagée, et tantôt malheureuse. Dans la journée je croyais plusiers fois pouvoir dire sincèrement: Oui, je pardonne de tout mon coeur à cet homme cruel, mais je rêvais ensuite la nuit que j'assistais de nouveau à cette scene atroce qui s'est passé dans la vallée brûlée. Je rêvais que j'étais changée en corbeau, que cet arabe gisait sanglant au milieu du désert, que battant fièrement des ailes, je le déchirais avec mon bec.

Je racontai à la Soeur ce rêve qui lui fit venir les larmes aux yeux. Elle me dit avec douceur, "Prie, mon enfant, le bon Dieu aura pitié de toi."

En attendant on fixa le jour de mon baptême, et ce jour arrivé on se vit obligé de me différer le sacrement de la régénération à cause de mes dispositions qui m'étaient guère modifiées.

Un matin on vint dire à la Mère Supérieure qu'on venait de porter à la salle à pansements qui est contigue à l'hôpital, plusieurs Arabes blessés dans un combat qu'ils ont soutenu contre les Croiseurs Anglais. C'était mon tour d'aider aux Soeurs dans leurs charitables travaux. Je m'empressais de préparer tous les objets qui régardaient mon service. Bouilloire d'eau tiède, cuvette, éponge, bandes à pansements, tout fut prêt dans quelques instants. Portant plusieurs de ces objets, j'entre dans la salle à la suite des Soeurs.

Oh! surprise étonnante!

La prémière personne qui s'offre à mes regards c'est notre ancien conducteur de caravane qui a frappé ma mère mourante.

Je le voir dans un état horrible et difficile à décrire. Sa tête fendue d'un coup de sabre, sa poitrine sanglante, tuméfiée, profondement labourée par plusieurs coups de baïonnette, m'ont fait une telle impression que j'ai failli laisser tomber par terre les objets que je tenais dans mes mains. Je n'ai pu m'empêcher de m'écrier, "Mon Dieu, c'est l'Arabe!" La Mère Supérieure se tourna vers moi et me dit d'une voix pleine de bonté, "Madeleine, ma fille, tes malheurs méritèrent une récompense. Et voici que dans sa miséricorde Notre Seigneur t'envoie l'occasion de faire un acte bien méritoire. Nous devons tous aimer nos ennemis et prier pour eux. Heureux ceux qui ont assez de générosité pour rendre le bien pour le mal! Dieu leur en tiendra compte un jour. Un peu de courage, mon enfant, et la victoire sera à toi. C'est toi, ma chère fille, qui vas panser cet homme."

J'obéis en tremblant à l'ordre de la mère; je saisis le linge et je commence à laver les plaies. Le premier essai me coûte beaucoup. Outre le dégoût que j'éprouvais mes lèvres sont prêtes à maudire mon ennemi. Je me rejouissais intérieurement de ses souffrances. Peu-à-peu je me surmontai, et à ces mauvais sentiments succéda une pitié profonde. Je fus moi-même étonnée du changement qu'il s'était opéré en moi, et je compris alors toute la douceur de la charité chrétienne.

Après le pansement de ces malheureux je me rendis en cachette à l'oratoire des Soeurs, et là agenouillée devant l'autel de la sainte Vièrge, je m'écriai un peu haut en sanglotant. "O Marie, ma Mère, ayez pitié de ce malheureux auquel vous m'avez inspiré le courage de pardonner de tout mon coeur. Oui, je lui pardonne maintenant avec sincérité." A ces mots je sentis comme des gouttes d'eau tomber sur ma tête. Je me retourne et je vois la bonne Soeur catéchiste qui m'avait entendu prononcer les paroles de pardon.

Elle versa des larmes d'attendrissement en benissant le bon Dieu et la sainte Vièrge pour la grâce de ma conversion. Elle fut si heureuse qu'elle me serra sur son coeur, comme fit jadis ma pauvre mère lorsque je la vis pour la dernière fois.

Ce jour était un Dimanche.

Le soir on me donna un belle robe blanche et une démie heure avant la bénédiction, le troupeau du bon Pasteur s'accrut d'une brébis, la société des fidèles d'un enfant de plus. La sainte Eglise en me conférant le Baptême ajouta à mon nom de Suèma celui de Madeleine, qui m'est mille fois plus cher que mon prémier nom.

Je passai le reste de la journée à remercier Dieu, qui par des voies bien cachées mais bien admirables m'a fait arriver aux bienfaits du christianisme.

Je me disais à tout moment intérieurement, "Qu'ai-je fait pour avoir été préférée a tant de millions d'infidèles qui n'arriveront jamais au même bonheur?"

Pénétrée de cette pensée je voulais témoigner ma reconnaissance à notre divin Maître, et j'étais un peu embarrassée pour savoir ce que je pourrais faire de plus agréable à son divin Coeur.

J'entendis alors comme une voix qui me dit intérieurement, "Madeleine, vis chrétiennement et puis cherche à faire tous les efforts pour travailler à le conversion de tes pauvres compatriotes."

"Oui, oui, mon Dieu," m'écriai-je, "j'en prends la résolution devant vous. Toute ma vie je travaillerai dans ce but. Je vous prierai tous les jours, afin que dans votre infinie miséricorde, vous ayiez pitié des infidèles de l'Afrique Orientale, et que vous leur envoyiez des missionnaires qui leur montreront le chemin du Ciel!"

Zanzibar le 26 Juillet 1866

Horner missionnaire apostolique
de la congrégation du St. Esprit
et de l'immaculé coeur de Marie,
Supérieure de la mission catholique
de Zanzibar

A Notre Vénéré Père!

Du haut des splendeurs de la gloire dont vous a revêtu le divin Jésus que vous avez tant glorifié par vos pensées, vos paroles, vos actions, et vos écrits, daignez ô Vénéré Père, agréer l'hommage filial de ma reconnaissance et de mon amour.

Soyez béni d'avoir écoute l'inspiration divine, qui malgré les oppositions humaines vous a porté à fonder une Congrégation de prêtres missionnaires spécielement dévoués aux âmes les plus pauvres et les plus abandonnées. D'avoir sauvé par là et rendu sauveurs d'âmes tant de jeunes gens, qui sans vous n'auraient jamais connu le chemin de la perfection, et qui se seraient peut-être perdus dans le monde.

D'avoir inspiré à tous ceux qui ont eu le bonheur de vous approcher le pur amour de Jésus, que vous aimiez tant à leur faire considérer comme le vrai et unique modèle du missionnaire.

Soyez béni, ô Vénéré Père, de m'avoir détourné du danger de manquer ma vocation;

De cette inépuisable charité que vous m'avez témoignée dans mes maladies, et surtout dans ces heureux et doux moments que j'ai eu le bonheur de passer seul à seul avec vous;

De m'avoir rappelé par toutes vos actions le *transiit benefaciendo* du divin Sauveur.

Demandez au coeur de Jésus pour moi, une partie de cette éminente sainteté dont le vôtre fut si rempli, afin que je devienne votre vrai disciple, comme vous le fûtes vous-même de Jésus.

Obtenez du coeur immaculé de Marie si rempli d'amour pour tout ce qui souffre, la foi à tant de millions d'infidèles de l'Afrique, qui croupissent dans l'ignorance, les ténèbres, et l'ombre de la mort. Souvenez-vous ô Père bien-aimé, que de votre lit de mort autour duquel la piété filiale avait rassemblé vos enfans, vous donniez une bénédiction spéciale à l'Afrique et par conséquent aussi à la mission alors future de Zanzibar.

Obtenez-moi le vrai zèle du missionnaire fondé sur l'intime conviction que c'est Dieu seul qui donne l'accroissement.

La véritable abnégation, l'humilité, la charité, et l'esprit de sacrifice que vous nous recommandiez si instamment un moment avait de paraître devant Dieu.

Daignez bénir ces quelques lignes que je dépose respecteusement sur ce tombeau chéri où vos restes vénérés reposent au milieu de vos enfans auxquels ils crient du sein de la terre.

Sacrifiez-vous pour Jésus, et vous trouverez le chemin de la vraie gloire et du veritable bonheur! Amen.

Horner

References

Unpublished Sources

Alpers, E. A. 1981. "Female Subculture in Nineteenth Century Zanzibar: The *Kitimiri* Spirit Possession Cult." Paper presented to the Symposium on African Women: Historical Dimensions, University of Santa Clara, May 15–16, 1981.

A.C.S.E.: Archives de la Congrégation du Saint-Esprit, Paris.

Courmont to Director, l'Oeuvre de la Sainte-Enfance, Zanzibar, October 20, 1884. 196-A/XIII.

Horner, "Histoire d'une petite esclave enterrée vivante; ou L'Amour filial," Zanzibar, July 26, 1866. 194/V.

Horner, "Compte-rendu de la mission du Zanguebar pour l'Oeuvre de la Ste. Enfance pour 1866," Zanzibar, December 31, 1866. 196-A/XII.

Horner to Director, l'Oeuvre de la Sainte-Enfance, Zanzibar, October 20, 1867. 196-A/XII.

Horner to Gaume, Zanzibar, July 1, 1869. 196-A/XII.

Horner to Director, l'Oeuvre de la Sainte-Enfance, Zanzibar, December 31, 1877. 196-A/XII.

Henry Isa to Grandes Scholastiques de N.D. de Langonoet, Zanzibar, January 3, 1876. 196-A/IV.

Cummings, R. J. 1975. "Aspects of Human Porterage with Special Reference to the Akamba of Kenya: Towards an Economic History, 1820–1920." Ph.D. dissertation, University of California, Los Angeles.

Kieran, J. A. P. 1966. "The Holy Ghost Fathers in East Africa, 1863 to 1914." Ph.D. dissertation, University of London.

Published Sources

Abdallah, Y. B. 1919. *The Yaos*. Arranged, edited, and translated by M. Sanderson. Zomba.

Alpers, E. A. 1969. "Trade, State, and Society among the Yao in the Nineteenth Century." *Journal of African History* 10:405–20.

Alpers, E. A. 1975. *Ivory and Slaves in East Central Africa: Changing Patterns of International Trade to the Later Nineteenth Century*. London, Berkeley, and Los Angeles.

Coissoró, N. 1966. *The Customary Laws of Succession in Central Africa*. Lisbon.

Cooper, F. 1977. *Plantation Slavery on the East Coast of Africa*. New Haven.

Feierman, S. 1974. *The Shambaa Kingdom: A History*. Madison.

Gaume, J. 1870. *Suéma, ou La Petite Esclave Africaine enterée vivante: Histoire contemporaine dediée aux jeunes chrétiennes de l'ancien et du nouveau monde*. Paris.

Johnson, W. P. 1924. *My African Reminiscences, 1875–1895*. London.

Kilekwa, P. 1937. *Slave Boy to Priest: The Autobiography of Padre Petro Kilekwa*. London.

La Grande Encyclopédie. 1886–1902. 31 vols. Paris.

Le Roy, A. 1884. "'Andalouma,' Scenes Africaines; drame en cinq actes." *Annales de l'Oeuvre de la Sainte-Enfance* 35:74–144.

Livingstone, D. 1874. *Last Journals*. Edited by H. Waller. 2 vols. London.

Macdonald, D. 1882. *Africana, or The Heart of Heathen Africa*. 2 vols. London.

Madan, A. C. 1886. *Kiungani, or Story and History from Central Africa*. Zanzibar.

Mair, L. 1951. "A Yao Girls' Initiation." *Man* 51, art. 98:60–63.

Mbotela, J. J. 1934. *Uhuru wa Watumwa*. London.

Mitchell, J. C. 1951. "The Yao of Southern Nyasaland." In *Seven Tribes of British Central Africa*, ed. E. Colson and M. Gluckman. Manchester.

Mitchell, J. C. 1956. *The Yao Village: A Study in the Social Structure of a Nyasaland Tribe*. Manchester.

Rashid bin Hassani. 1936. "The Story of Rashid bin Hassani of the Bisa Tribe, Northern Rhodesia." Recorded by W. F. Baldock in *Ten Africans*, ed. M. Perham. London.

Renault, F. 1971. *Lavigerie, l'esclavage africaine et l'Europe*. 2 vols. Paris.

Ricklin, L. A. 1880. *La mission catholique du Zanguebar: Travaux et voyages du R. P. Horner*. Paris.

Roberts, A. D. 1970. "Nyamwezi Trade." In *Pre-Colonial African Trade*, ed. R. Gray and D. Birmingham, London.

Sanderson, G. M. 1922. "A Note on Ceremonial Purification among the WaYao, Nyasaland." *Man* 22, art. 55:91–93.

Sanderson, G. M. 1954. *A Dictionary of the Yao Language*. Zomba.

Scott, D. C. 1892. *A Cyclopaedic Dictionary of the Mang'anja Language Spoken in British Central Africa*. Edinburgh.

Stannus, H. S. 1922. "The Wayao of Nyasaland." Harvard African Studies, *Varia Africana* 3:229–372.

Strobel, M. 1979. *Muslim Women in Mombasa, 1890–1975*. New Haven.

Wright, M. 1975. "Women in Peril: A Commentary on the Life Stories of Captives in Nineteenth-Century East-Central Africa." *African Social Research* 20:800–819.

12 *Claire C. Robertson*

Post-Proclamation Slavery in Accra: A Female Affair?[1]

On November 5, 1874, the British government of the Gold Coast Colony issued a proclamation which outlawed slavery and the slave trade, and so emancipated the slave population of Accra, which was to become the capital of the colony in 1877.[2] This was one of the later events in the long history of British efforts to abolish slavery and the slave trade. The proclamation did not succeed in its aims.[3] One of the reasons for this failure can be found in the dominance of females in slavery and the slave trade in Accra. The female role in the economy both helps to account for the persistence of slavery as an institution and illuminates the consequences of the imposition of a capitalist mode of production on a corporate kin one.[4] In this essay I will first seek explanations for the persistence of slavery in the unbalanced change in the sexual division of labor within the Gold Coast economy, and then give an extended example in the form of a life history of an ex-slave woman who belonged to a Ga family. By comparing her life with those of her peers we can develop a better appreciation of the impact of slavery and abolition at an individual level.

The Ga are a people practicing patrilineal descent who have inhabited the West African coastal area around Accra for as far back as archaeolog-

1. The research for this essay was supported by National Defense Foreign Language and Social Science Research Council/American Council of Learned Societies grants. I am particularly indebted to Mr. A. A. Amartey for his help with not only giving information, but also translating tapes and tracking down fugitive pieces of information after I left Accra.

2. The antislavery and slave dealing ordinances were the first to be passed upon the establishment of colonial rule in the Gold Coast Colony.

3. For a superlative review of the literature on Gold Coast abolition and an alternative explanation of its failure, see McSheffrey 1977.

4. Further development of this theme is in Robertson (forthcoming).

ical and written historical records go. Until after World War Two they composed the majority of the population of Accra. They had close contact and intermarriage with neighboring matrilineal Akan peoples, in particular. Until the second half of the nineteenth century they were predominantly involved in fishing and farming, with the women trading the produce from both. The wealthier element in the population—mostly male chiefs and elders—were heavily involved in the European export slave trade. Despite this factor, large-scale ownership of slaves was rare among them. Perhaps this was because of the rather small scale of the political system, which was decentralized and could not organize labor in the manner of the Asante, for instance. The largest influx of slaves who stayed in the area, in fact, came after abolition, when groups fleeing the Akan moved south to form villages on the Accra plains.

Slaves appear mainly to have been held individually or in pairs by families which assimilated them to varying extents. Classificatory kin relationships facilitated assimilation, so that a slave woman was often treated as a junior female and called her mistress and the mistress's sisters "mother." Slave women helped their mistresses in productive activities like trading, farming, and home processing of foods for sale. The residential system in which men lived with their male patrilateral relatives and women with their female matrilateral relatives in separate compounds facilitated gender-based production groups (Robertson forthcoming, ch. 4). This is the background for the following story.

An Analysis of the Failure of the 1874 Proclamation[5]

The proclamation was successful neither in emancipating the slaves nor stopping the slave trade in Accra. With regard to emancipation, it initially had some impact, judging from the court records. Word got around that if a slave went to the District Commissioner and got a piece of paper declaring her free, all of her troubles would be over. A small industry grew up whereby certain men took bribes from slaves in exchange for getting the coveted appointments with the District Commissioner (G.N.A., SCT 17/ 4/2:263–64, case 1876). The appeal must have been strong, particularly for those who were maltreated and had obtained few rights in their owners' families. Some women from outside the Colony fled to Accra to get

5. The data base for this portion of this essay consists mainly of 131 court cases taken from the Accra District Commissioner's Criminal and Civil Court Records for 1874 to 1918 (no records of slave cases were found after 1918). These were supplemented by interviews with A. A. Amartey, Alhaji Mohammed Makwei Laryea, and E. A. Ammah in 1978. I am indebted to Daoud Yemoh for his help in compiling the court records. Cases are prefixed by SCT and SNA in references to them by the Ghana National Archives, and I have followed suit.

their freedom, and were protected by the governor from being repatriated (G.N.A., SNA 11/1770, case August 31, 1877). Some owners invoked fetish to keep their slaves with them (G.N.A., SCT 17/4/2:276–77, case 1876). Slave concubines sometimes left their masters and (for the first time) were able to claim legal possession of their children (G.N.A., DC Court 164/2, 585:264, case December 1, 1876). However, there were only fifty-two cases concerning slave dealing or holding someone in bondage in the court records from 1874 to 1880, nineteen of which involved a slave or her relatives seeking her freedom. Some cases were undoubtedly not recorded. Cruickshank (1853/1966, 2:229), who served as a magistrate at Cape Coast in the 1840s, reported giving some thousand slave redemption tickets over several years, and said that slaves could redeem themselves for £8, their going price at that time. However, there is no evidence of a similar flood of manumission requests at Accra. Of the seventy-nine cases from 1881 to 1918, only six involved efforts to attain freedom. Most cases had rather to do with slave dealing. Slave dealing continued, then (the last recorded case I found was from 1939), and most slaves probably stayed where they were in Accra, as noted by the missionaries.[6] Why? Aside from the distinct lack of British enthusiasm for social revolution (Mc-Sheffrey 1977), there are indigenous reasons for the failure of abolition.

Effective abolition only occurred through the change from labor-intensive activities to more capital-intensive ones. This change came at different times for the two sexes. Before the third quarter of the nineteenth century, Ga men and women in Accra had a roughly equivalent economic organization which was facilitated by their residential pattern. To perpetuate the system of men and women living in separate compounds, husbands requested their wives to visit them at night and boys were sent to live with their fathers at around age six.[7] This residential pattern may have been perpetuated to facilitate the organization of informal education and labor in which boys and girls served their apprenticeships under their parents of the same sex, and then became partners in the business as they matured. The boys until the third quarter of the nineteenth century became mostly farmers and fisherman, activities in which income would increase with the available labor force. But in 1857 the Basel Missionary Society opened a workshop in Osu (now part of Accra) to teach men skills such as carpentry, masonry, and shoemaking. This had a strong impact on the Ga men, who quickly incorporated the teaching of these skills into their own ap-

6. The wife of the late Ga Mantse (probably Nii Tackie Yaboah) and another woman were acquitted of a slave dealing charge in 1939. *Gold Coast Independent*, January 7, 1939:13; McSheffrey 1977:8.

7. This is still the predominant residential arrangement for Central Accra Ga, but more for women than for men, again reflecting differential rates of absorption into capital-intensive production or service jobs.

prenticeship system. By the 1870s Accra was the principal source of skilled labor on the West African coast (Szereszewski 1965:8–9).

Meanwhile, formal education of a European type, introduced permanently in Accra by 1839, was producing boys with clerical skills (G.N.A., Debrunner n.d.:2, 6). The market for their skills improved drastically with the shift of the administrative capital of the Gold Coast Colony from Cape Coast to Accra in 1877. With both artisanal and clerical work becoming the main modes of employment for Ga men, their need for male slaves diminished greatly, since a larger supply of men in such services would simply reduce wages, as in fact happened with the clerical workers. By 1889 there was an oversupply of the clerically trained, who could not all find jobs, and wages went down (G.N.A., ADM 5/3/7:153–54).

Such education and opportunities were not open to women. Female slaves were still needed by women to help with their labor-intensive tasks, but male slaves were rapidly becoming superfluous. Thus, among the fifty-nine slaves whose sex could be determined referred to in cases arising from 1874 to 1885, 40.5 percent were male, compared to only 11.1 percent of the seventy-two slaves whose cases arose from 1886 to 1918. Most of the slaves were children aged from about five to ten when they were bought. Altogether, 78.8 percent of the 131 slaves were female. The higher desirability of girls was also indicated in the prices paid for them. Among thirty-seven cases for which data were available (thirty girls and seven boys), the mean price paid for a girl was £6.11 compared to £5.3 for a boy. Omitting the two cases of purchase at Salaga in the north, the average price for a girl was £6.18, giving a price ratio of 100:75 for females: males sold in the south.[8]

Of the forty-six cases where the location of the sale was evident, 39.1 percent were at Accra. The usual location for such sales was the slave market in Ussher Town called Gua Dzrano by the Ga.[9] Some took place more privately at people's houses. That so many sales were public in the capital of the Gold Coast (most of the Accra sales were from after 1877) certainly indicates indifference on the part of the colonial authorities, or

---

8. The prices were taken from cases during the period from 1874 to 1898; however, some of the transactions had taken place some years prior to the cases in which they were recorded. It was thus not feasible to make a time series for the data. Also, there were a disproportionate number of cases in 1890, which thus unduly affected the figures. There may have been a particularly conscientious district commissioner in 1889–90, since 41 of the 131 cases came from those years; these, along with the 49 from 1874 to 1877, accounted for the great majority of cases. The Salaga prices were less than half of the average coastal price.

9. Interview: Alhaji Mohammed Makwei Laryea, February 18, 1978. *Gua* refers to the god of blacksmithing; the market was next to his shrine. See also Reindorf *ca.* 1890/1966:144. Ussher Town is the oldest part of Accra.

perhaps their incapacity to stop the trade. Another 15.2 percent of sales took place in the south within about eighty miles of the coast, 21.7 percent at Salaga, and the remaining 24 percent at intermediate locations, such as Asante.

In more cases, the gender and ethnicity or geographical origin of the buyers, sellers, and slaves were evident. Most of the sellers (sixty-two) were men (72.7 percent) and northerners (45.2 percent). Twenty-one percent were Ga, 29 percent Akan, and 4.8 percent Ewe. The buyers or owners, who will concern us more here, were less predominantly men (59.8 percent), and mostly Ga (64.8 percent), as might be expected (N = 71). The origins of the slaves or pawns involved (N = 84) often resembled those of their sellers: 28.6 percent were northerners, often Grunshi, 29.8 percent Akan, 22.6 percent Ewe, and 19 percent Ga.[10] The early cases from 1874 to 1877 had more Ewe, resulting from the Asante invasion,[11] while the later ones (1887–90) involved more northerners and were presumably offshoots of Samory's raids.[12]

The earlier buyers or owners were more predominantly male than the later ones (of thirty-nine in the period 1874–85, 71.8 percent were male; of fifty-three from 1886 to 1918, 51 percent). It is obvious, then, that the demand for girls remained or increased, while that for boys declined, and there was a corresponding increase in the proportion of women buyers or owners. The girls were bought primarily to help women with their tasks, which were apportioned according to the relatively strict Ga sexual division of labor. Men did the fishing, some farming tasks like clearing the land, and most craft and literate work, while women did much of the farm labor, made pottery and soap, did all of the domestic work and raising of small children, and above all, traded. Women carried on trade in all sorts of goods, as well as the necessary home processing of commodities like beads, prepared foods for local trade, and smoked, salted, and dried fish for long-distance trade. The use of female slave labor allowed them to devote more of their time to marketing and leave the less profitable processing to the slaves and female relatives at home. Two Ga male authori-

10. The numbers concerned in all of these instances were those where the information was given. I did not distinguish between slaves and pawns because there was little distinction in practice between the two statuses; conversion between the two was constant. Most of the pawnship cases concerned Ga.

11. Reindorf (*ca*. 1890/1966:303) described another Asante invasion of Krepi in the 1830s and the many Krepi slaves who were sold as a result of the Krepi-Ga defeat.

12. Terray (1975:394) described Samory's *sofas* (soldiers) selling their captives at £2 a head at Bonduku in 1892; the going price at Salaga for a girl in about 1885 was £2 or £3. He also notes that women were worth more than men. Kuczynski (1948, 1:428) claimed that the raids of Samory and Babatu, the former of which ended in 1897, took so many women that there was still a sexual imbalance (more men than women) in the Northern Territories in 1948.

ties stated quite simply, when asked why slaves were bought, "Labor." One mentioned the desirability of slave wives as a side issue, but the productive value of slaves clearly took precedence over their biological reproductive value (interviews: Alhaji Mohammed Makwei Laryea, February 18, 1978; E. A. Ammah, January 31, 1978).

In the court cases this labor value of slaves was downplayed, of course, and more extenuating reasons were given by the accused slave buyers or owners. Several women pleaded childlessness. "I had no child of my own, so I bought her" was a typical (sometimes demonstrably untrue) statement (G.N.A., SCT 17/5/9:490, case April 14, 1890). Another woman said that she bought a girl out of "compassion" for her own childlessness after her child died (G.N.A., SCT 17/5/9:655, case July 26, 1890). Childlessness is, and probably was, considered to be one of the worst fates which could befall a woman; slave girls bought to remedy this lack were often adopted as daughters and not maltreated. One blind woman bought a girl to lead her and her blind son around Accra (G.N.A., SCT 17/5/9:509, case April 17, 1878).

Such girls as they got older often became the sexual partners of male members of the household. If a man so desired, he could take the woman to the chief (*mantse*) of the appropriate quarter of Accra and have her freed in a ceremony involving the symbolic gesture of smearing her with white clay. Only in that case would their children be free of stigma. Indeed, the children would be especially favored as products of an intrafamily marriage; "their parents belong to the same family"[13] A concubine who bore a child to her master would also usually be free, though still stigmatized. Even without this ceremony done for the mother, a slave's children would be outdoored, or named, by the owner's lineage and become junior members with inferior inheritance rights.[14] Because of the paucity of male slaves, it was very unusual for a slave woman to "marry" one, and even rarer for a free woman to do so, given the stigma attached to the children.

13. Interview: Alhaji Mohammed Makwei Laryea, February 18, 1978. The Ga practice preferential cross-cousin marriage.

14. Slaves, ex-slaves, and domestics were supposed to be excluded from inheriting property from freeborn people, but they were entitled to get support and a share of the income from the estate of the deceased. They were not supposed to participate in decisions governing the disposal of lineage (usually patrilineage) property, although sometimes they evidently did inherit it. In one case, an ex-slave not only inherited property but had control over the lineage until his death. The "legitimate" heirs, however, made an agreement secretly before his death that his offspring would not inherit, which is what eventually happened. Another example is the female ex-slave who in 1953 successfully claimed a house as her share of her deceased mistress's property. (Pogucki 1954/1968:30; interviews: Alhaji Mohammed Makwei Laryea, February 18, 1978, and A. A. Amartey, March 2, 1978; G.N.A., SCT 2/6/29:143–50, case February 28, 1953.) Ga women often inherit property from female relatives and form what might be called "informal lineages." See also Robertson 1974.

In principle, the children of any type of slave-slave or slave-free marriage were free, since only those who themselves had been sold could be slaves (interview: Mohammed Makwei Laryea, February 18, 1978). But because such "marriages" were not legally valid full marriages, the children belonged to the female slave's owner. One could not make a full marriage payment for a slave women because she had no kin to accept it for her. To be respectable in the late nineteenth century, a woman was supposed to have a full marriage arranged by her parents. But women slaves had, if anything, a small fee paid to their owners by men wishing to establish a long-term sexual liaison, an arrangement similar in its informality to the "marriage" of low-status women. For some men, especially those who were poor, slaves, or ex-slaves, buying a slave "wife" was preferable to a full marriage because it was cheaper. They could at least get rights to the children that way. A slave woman's marital status, then, was perforce like that of a lower-class woman, but with the significant difference that she had no kin either to insist on eventual regularization of the liaison or to protect her from ill treatment by her husband.[15] Her assimilation by "marriage" was incomplete, and the likelihood of her fertility suffering because of a series of irregular liaisons must have been high. Her productive rather than her reproductive functions were the main concern of her owner.

But could a slave women achieve manumission and full assimilation through raising her economic, rather than her social, status? Not easily. Male slaves were more likely to be able to accumulate cash which they could use to redeem themselves and/or to buy slaves themselves. In this respect a male slave was better off than a pawn, who had been given by his or her family to a creditor so that his or her labor could pay the interest on the debt.[16] Payment of the debt for the pawn's redemption could not be made by the pawn, but only by his or her family. In any case, men slaves sometimes managed to become heads of lineages by a fortuitous combination of economic success, pleasing their former masters, and becoming the sole owners of certain vital information imparted by former lineage heads (interview: Alhaji Mohammed Makwei Laryea, February 11, 1978). There was even a woman slave who managed to gain great influence, though not headship, by knowing the location of the family's buried trea-

15. In a 1922 slander case, one woman accused another of having a slave mother, with the implication that she had no relatives to protect her or arrange a good marriage for her. *Ga Mantse's Civil Court Record* 1922–24:62.

16. The relationship between pawnship and slavery is complex and too time–consuming to go into here at length. In the records, slavery and pawnship are often confused, one example being G.N.A., SCT 17/4/2:266, case 1876. I could find no particular word for *pawn* in Ga, but the plural of *slave, nyodzii,* is very similar to the plural of *debt, nyodzi,* indicating a possible relationship.

sure (interview: A. A. Amartey, March 30, 1978). She was, however, an exception.

Women slaves were supposed to turn over all of their earnings to their mistresses, just as junior females did. In a society where trading was so pervasive for women, these earnings must have helped their mistresses to expand the scale of their businesses. Given the free women's disabilities with respect to controlling male labor and lineage property, however,[17] men were probably in a better financial position to buy slaves. Some Ga men owned over 100 slaves which they used on bush plantations.[18] Such large-scale enterprises might have been more difficult to maintain after the proclamation; McSheffrey (1977) tells us that there were large-scale defections of slaves in the interior after the proclamation, if not on the coast. But female slaves in Accra were used mainly to help women, whatever the sex of their legal owners. A slave woman's economic status, then, was to a slave man's as a free woman's was to a free man's. Slave women were near the bottom of the status heap, but slave girls must have been in the very lowest position, debarred by legal status, age, and sex from any freedom of action. Free girls were not much better off, but they at least could look forward to assuming more rights and authority as they got older. However, the ceiling for these was inevitably lower for slave than free women.

We can find part of the reason for the failure of abolition in the nature of post-proclamation slavery, then. It was not clear that becoming free would significantly improve the status of a slave woman in Accra. She would still be a woman. But in addition, women taken from their homes as children were in a vulnerable position. Even if they remembered their place of origin, there was the problem of returning there without being reenslaved. Freeing a slave in the Colony did not remedy her legal status elsewhere. Undoubtedly many slaves preferred the devil they knew to an unknown one. Also, we cannot always assume that a woman's relatives were blameless in the matter of her initial sale,[19] wealthier than her Accra owners, or nicer to her than her Accra owners. Thus, in some of the court cases the slaves presumably lied about their relationship to the plaintiffs in order to stay in Accra. (G.N.A., SCT 17/5/9:418–20, case March 24,

17. Male lineage elders manipulated most property, whose ownership was rapidly becoming privatized in the late nineteenth century.

18. In 1868 Horton (1868/1969:133) noted that many prominent Ga merchants had coffee plantations in the bush.

19. Most of the women sellers of slaves pawned their daughters, some in situations reminiscent of Swema's (Alpers's case, above). G.N.A., SCT 17/4/3:410–11, case September 28, 1876; G.N.A., SCT 17/5/2:328, case January 26, 1883. In the former case, the girl wished to stay in Accra. Reindorf (*ca.* 1890/1966:148) noted that women were usually sold in times of famine.

1890; G.N.A., SCT 17/5/12:314, case April 13, 1892; G.N.A., SCT 17/ 4/2:204, case October 6, 1875; G.N.A., SCT 17/4/3:390–92, 410–11, cases September 18, 28, 1876.) In one case a woman from Lagos came to Accra and recognized her daughter as the slave of a Ga woman. Although recognition was mutual, the girl lied on the stand, denying her mother, because she wanted to stay in Accra. There was no other proof that she was from Lagos. Her owner, of course, denied owning a slave, so her mother went home without her.[20] In other cases where a girl sought her own freedom, the court sometimes returned her to her mistress as an apprentice; apprentices were not paid in Accra as a rule. This recourse was once made by the governor, who was obviously at a loss as to what to do with a confiscated girl slave (one wonders if he was willing to pay the customary apprenticeship fees).[21] In another case the constable simply returned a slave to her master, without any pretense of changing her status.[22]

Aside from these factors there was also the duress exerted by owners to keep slaves from fleeing or claiming their freedom. Many slaves, and even some owners, never heard of the proclamation. (G.N.A., SCT 17/5/6:450– 52, case January 19, 1888; G.N.A., SCT 17/4/2:266, case 1875; G.N.A., SCT 17/4/2:276–77, case 1875.) Slaves were sometimes forced to swear oaths, whose violation meant death, not to flee. Physical coercion was freely used, not only on slaves, but also on free young people.[23] The British magistrate, coming from a society where women were legal minors and their physical coercion by male relatives legally sanctioned, was not likely to lend a sympathetic ear to complaints of ill treatment. The general impression given by a review of the cases is that a girl who fled perpetual beatings was more likely to be returned to her owner (who sometimes claimed to be her husband, mother, brother, sister, aunt, or father) than was one who claimed freedom on principle (G.N.A., SCT 17/5/2:138, case October 3, 1881; G.N.A., SCT 17/5/2:328, case January 26, 1883). Also, unless antagonizing or impressing an upcountry chief by an assertion of British authority was a goal, owners who came to Accra to reclaim runaways were quite likely to have those slaves returned to them (G.N.A.,

20. It may be that the mother was trying to have her cake and eat it too—accept payment for her daughter and then reclaim her. G.N.A., SCT 17/5/9:603, case June 20, 1890.

21. G.N.A., SCT 17/5/10:43, case September 4, 1890. Reindorf (ca. 1890/1966:152) remarked perceptively, "the curse [of slavery] was removed by the English Government, but the country was left without a substitute."

22. G.N.A., SCT 17/5/9:430, case March 25, 1890. Many police were themselves ex-slaves, having fled to the Gold Coast Constabulary.

23. The worst treatment of slaves in Accra in the court cases involved beating with a stick and putting red pepper on a girl's private parts. G.N.A., SCT 17/5/2:328, case January 26, 1883.

SNA 11/1770, case August 31, 1877; G.N.A., SCT 17/5/10:165–66, case October 15, 1890).

Another concern for some slaves, which would militate against seeking emancipation, would have been the threat to whatever assimilation they had managed to achieve. A slave who went to the district officer to be declared free in response to the 1874 proclamation betrayed her loyalty to her owner's family and therefore lost whatever rights in that family she had managed to acquire. She might also lose her children to their father's family. For slaves who had been legally adopted by being outdoored and named according to Ga custom (Manteko 1967), seeking freedom would have been unthinkable. In theory, anyway, slaves were supposed to be fed and clothed like free people, and not maltreated. The murderer of a slave would have been drowned, like the murderer of a free person.[24] The goal in many cases was sufficient assimilation to keep the slave permanently in Accra, which meant that ill treatment was frowned upon. However, those slave owners who disregarded their slaves' welfare were more likely to be faced with desertion for another owner than claiming of freedom. In the overall scheme of things, I would not rank successful full assimilation as one of the chief reasons for the failure of emancipation.

A last reason for this failure needs to be discussed, and that is the decentralized nature of Ga slavery. In Accra there do not seem to have been large concentrations of slaves in one household; three was the most recorded in a court case (G.N.A., SCT 17/5/12:4, case September 23, 1891). This dispersion may have facilitated assimilation and mild treatment, but it also probably discouraged flight. Large groups of slaves could help each other to escape, and did so upcountry, according to McSheffrey. But the slave villages on the Accra plains seem mainly to have been composed of runaways from Akan country further north (McSheffrey 1977:9). I could not verify the fragmentary evidence I found concerning one ex-slave village five miles from Accra populated by northerners.

There were, then, a number of reasons for the failure of the abolition of slavery and the slave trade in Accra. Ranked in approximate order of importance, they were:

1. The change in the mode of production according to sex, which perpetuated the need for unskilled female, but not male, labor, and retained female labor-intensive production.

---

24. Interview: Alhaji Mohammed Makwei Laryea, February 18, 1978. Ga criminals were not enslaved. Pawnship seems to have been the chief indigenous source of slavery; most slaves were captives or prisoners of war purchased elsewhere, according to Ga ideology.

2. The youth, ignorance, and vulnerability of the female slave population, and their fear of dealing with foreigners.
3. The difficulties attached to remaining free and getting home, i.e., lack of other alternatives.[25]
4. The disadvantages attendant on being female, whether free or slave, which impeded economic success.
5. The decentralized nature of Ga slavery.
6. The possible loss of assimilative benefits and children by claiming freedom.
7. The indifferent efforts, or incapacity, of British authorities to enforce abolition, combined with their lack of concern about emancipating women, whether free or slave, and unwillingness to undermine male authority.
8. Duress exerted by slave owners.

The changing relations of production take precedence because they were what finally brought about the abolition of slavery and the slave trade in Accra.

Adukwe, a Former Slave

Adukwe (Ah-dú-kwā) was a slight, spry woman aged about ninety in 1971. She was lively with a good sense of humor and, considering her years, a fairly good memory. I encountered her first in the course of a routine house-to-house survey, and she then became a subject in a smaller survey of seventy-two women. It was not clear immediately that Adukwe had been a slave; because of the stigma attached to slavery, she did not volunteer the fact. I only found out through some irregularities in her brief life history which we initially collected, and then through another informant. Once I realized that she had been a slave, and because she was a cooperative informant, I returned to her and asked her to tell me the story of her life. By the time of these latter visits she trusted me more and was willing to talk about her experience as a slave. Because she was taken as a child, however, she had no clear recollection of her place of origin. Our last interview in 1978 failed to clarify some of the problems, because her memory had deteriorated somewhat along with her body (she was no longer able to walk). Her life history is given below with many of the ambiguities it contained, presented partly in the hope that others will be able to iden-

25. Poku (1979:36) describes the case of an ex-slave of Mossi origin in Asante, who was bought as a small girl, "married" her master, and stayed with him her whole life, even when offered her freedom. She stayed because a master was the only security such a woman possessed in the early years of the century.

tify her origins and route of descent to the coast more specifically. Afterwards I will describe how her life history differed from those of her peers and attempt an analysis of the effects of her slave status on her marital and career history.

Adukwe's Story (ca. 1890–1978)[26]

Adukwe did not know who her parents were. Her name before she came to Accra was Zama Damasoni [probably a Dagarti name meaning "goodness of the enemy" (*Damasoni*) and "hard-headedness" (*Zama*)]. When she was a young girl, before reaching puberty, Adukwe was taken by a Hausa man to help with harvesting onions from a boat.[27] He was a blacksmith. She was told by a woman there, the Fulani wife of the man, that she should leave because Hausa people were always fighting among themselves and would flog her. Zama knew that these people were Hausa like herself because they had the same scars; while she was there the man was cutting his baby to make the scars [see sketch].[28] Then she was taken by a Hausa woman for a long journey to "the source of creation, the ancient place of the Ga people." The trip was very long and arduous. She had been helping the woman with gathering, evidently, and paying no attention to where they went. One day they did not return home, but stopped at a strange house where she was given rice to eat. They continued their journey after the meal and slept in the open, much bothered by mosquitoes and afraid of wild animals. One large animal passed quite near them. They went in company with five or six other women, including a woman named Fanta whose husband Kojo was with them. He was from James Town [Central Accra], and they later settled at a village called Manhean.[29] (Later, when they arrived at Accra he sent his wife to his family house, where she subsequently bore only one child.)

After several days they arrived at a house with a statue of a soldier

26. This information, taken from tapes of interviews with Adukwe, has been translated by research assistants and edited by the author into a more coherent format to eliminate repetitious and irrelevant matter.

27. Adukwe said that Hausa was her first language, but that she had forgotten how to speak and understand it except for the command "Kawo" (Bring it). However, *Hausa* is also a generic term for northerners on the coast. The Dagarti inhabit northwestern Ghana. Riverain cultivation of shallots was known in eastern and northern Gold Coast.

28. In Accra extensive scarring was a mark of slave status, and considered characteristic of northerners.

29. *Kojo* (or *Cudzoe*) is an Akan name frequently used by Gas. Manhean could be one of several Ga villages. Adukwe's recollection of her company on the trip may have been confused—these people may have been with her at a later stage.

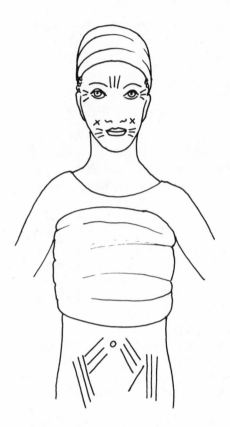

Figure 12.1. Adukwe's Scar Patterns. In 1978 Adukwe showed me that she also
had three vertical scars at the base of her neck in back. She told me that only the
ones on her stomach and mouth were done at her hometown; the rest were done
in Accra at her own request because they were fashionable at that time.

holding a short gun before it.[30] The woman went in, but Zama was afraid
to; the woman came back and they continued in the same manner until
they reached the sea, where they proceeded along a lagoon. She was taken
to a house where there were six men only, although there were women's
things and implements around. She stayed there for a long time and was
free to go outside and enjoy the sea breezes. The day she was taken away
from there she was asked who her mother was and told with some mockery that she had someone else's name, not her own.

From there a big fat Hausa man took Zama on a large motorized boat

30. Adukwe said that she later made a trip to this same place, so it was probably further
toward Accra than toward her place of origin.

across the sea. She was lifted from a smaller boat onto the larger one with a basket. They slept on the ship in the middle of the sea. A strange man gave her food to eat at every meal when he himself ate. The ship made several stops. Then a small boat took them and they were at Accra. The man who put her on the boat [probably the fat man] met her at Accra; his friend had seen to her on the boat. The former told her that they had to have permission from the police station to enter Accra, and that if it was granted he would accompany her and if not, he would not. He told her to say that she was his wife's daughter.[31] At the police station there was some discussion which she did not understand, and the man who brought her there left. She stayed the night there and asked for water. In the morning she was taken to Accra and told to wait at the beach because her cloth was not presentable. She was given a new dress sewn for her and then taken to a market where there were Hausas. Her hair, which was unkempt, was cut with scissors, and she looked beautiful.

A man named Afute [a Ga name] bought her and took her home to his family house. He named her Adukwe. His home was that of the father of the late Dr. Bruce, a prominent Ga Gold Coast physician [probably Dr. Nanka Bruce]. Afute's wife did not like her and beat her. Then Adukwe was sent to stay at Bruce's father's house at Osugbeten, an area of Osu [also called Christiansborg, now incorporated into Accra]. Afute was sick, which was the reason for the move; the whole household went. The house was at the top of the hill by the beach. Afute had uncles who lived there. From there he went traveling with his wife, taking Adukwe to stay with an uncle named Allotey Wayoo at his house at Asere [a section of Ussher Town, Central Accra]. While she was there she became very sick with a bad attack of malaria. Her "guardian" [presumably Allotey Wayoo at that point] asked the old woman who lived in the house where Adukwe would be living in 1972 in Asere to come fetch her and take her home to cure her, which the old woman did. After that Adukwe only visited Allotey Wayoo's house; she never lived there again.

When she was cured, Adukwe became the old woman's helper. The old woman, an aunt of Afute, was a trader in imported goods and defaulted on her payments to her chief creditor, a white man, at one point. The white man threatened them with slavery, but one of the old woman's male paternal relatives went to the white man and told him that he could not do that. Eventually all of the people there contributed so that the old woman could pay her debts [and possibly avoid placing someone as pawn]. Adukwe helped the old woman by accompanying her on trading trips to the villages around Accra, especially centering on a place called Olefi. Olefi was near the Odaw lagoon, and they sometimes had to use a canoe when it was

---

31. This particular lie came up in several court cases.

flooded. She would carry a headload to the place where they traded and wait for the old woman to finish selling. At this point Adukwe still had not reached puberty. She also did menial work for the white man, like hauling sand in buckets from the beach. She turned over her wages to the old woman, who had no children. Sometimes she illicitly withheld some of the trading profits from her mistress. She tried to anticipate people's wishes rather than have them call her each time for something, getting drinks for the old woman, for instance. She also helped the old woman with the making of kenkey [the staple food of the Ga, made of fermented and steamed corn dough]. This was before the advent of machines for grinding corn, so they ground it by hand.[32] Adukwe continued to help the old woman until she died, even after Adukwe had "married" her nephew. Periodically she would be in Accra working for her, although as Adukwe matured she gained more independence in trading and kept some of the profits for herself. In their trading they used as their village base a place called Oshuman, where the old woman and her nephews had strong family connections.

At one point while Adukwe was staying with the old woman she was told to pound *kokonte* [a form of *fufu*, the Akan staple food, prepared from dried cassava flour] and refused, saying that she would eat it, not pound it. On another occasion a quarrel arose over a spoon involving one of the children in the compound, a connection of the old woman's. The old woman's nephew slapped the boy because he had called him names. Adukwe intervened to defend the boy, saying that the nephew was murdering him. The nephew's older brother came and asked why Adukwe said that the child should leave the house. She said that the boy should join his brother at their father's house. At this point another person in the house came and started beating the boy. The upshot of the whole affair was that the child refused to stay there and he, Adukwe, and the old woman left that house and came to the one she was living in in 1972.

Once while Adukwe was at Oshuman they heard of a great fire at Accra [1894]. Her uncle sent someone to find out what had happened; their house had been completely destroyed, so they built a new one out of zinc sheets and moved there. Not too long after that the plague came [1908] and they were given traps to catch the rats, but they were ineffective. The rats still ran loose. During the earthquake [1939] they all slept outside because the houses were falling down; she was living in her 1972 residence then.

After she had stayed with the old woman for some time she ran away to stay at Akuse with Afute's brother and his wife, whom she helped. While Adukwe was there she had her first menstrual period and began

---

32. She also said that when the machines came, people at first refused to eat kenkey made from machine-ground corn.

sleeping regularly with Afute's brother after he quarreled with his wife and moved to a separate room.[33] The quarrel was over his paying attention to Adukwe and giving her money, which the wife was afraid Adukwe would take to Accra. The man actually was not giving money to Adukwe, but rather had lost his job as a carpenter working for the white man and was not getting the money he had before. His wife was so quarrelsome that he finally rented a room for her elsewhere while he stayed with Adukwe. Subsequently the man traveled around in his work and Adukwe went with him. From the beginning of their liaison Adukwe considered him to be her "husband," although he paid no bride price for her. They went to Ada, to Somanya, and to a village called Bodzuase [near Odupongkpehe]. They stayed at Oshuman sometimes.

While they were at Ada, Adukwe decided to send some coconuts to her husband's wife to sell. She went to get them from an Ada woman, only to be threatened with beheading upon arrival at the woman's house. Evidently she had walked on a forbidden path in going there, for which the penalty was death. But the two men there, an old one with guinea worm and a young one whom he was at first urging to kill her, spared her because she was pregnant. When she got home after this experience she had a miscarriage. She later had another miscarriage; but then she got some medicine from a woman herbalist which helped the pregnancy to stay. Her pregnancy caused more hostility from her husband's wife, as did her caring for one of the wife's children at the husband's request.

While living at the village with her husband, Adukwe got very sick with guinea worm, so much so that she was disabled completely. Consequently, her husband had to do the washing and the cooking, grinding the corn and making *banku* [a form of kenkey]. Adukwe and a female relation who also had guinea worm would lie in bed and comment that his banku and soup were not as good as their own. Sometimes he would incise her worm to give her relief, or take her to the white man to do it. They returned to Accra for the man to get work, and he would go each day to earn money, and give her some, which she would use to buy food at the market. Adukwe traded also to get money, but only earned maybe six pence to four shillings a day.

Adukwe had one child by Afute's brother. She ruptured her membrane walking, but had no labor pains for three hours afterward. She went to the market and bought fresh boiled maize and some groundnuts. Later the contractions came on, and the baby was born at about ten at night. This was before the 1906 earthquake; this daughter was still living in 1972.

Adukwe and her "husband" lived most often in a village, and stayed

33. Husbands and wives did not usually live conjugally in Accra, but this pattern changed generally in the villages, where they often shared rooms.

together for about five or ten years, before the husband left to go to Accra. He never returned. Adukwe encountered a farmer from Kojo Ashong village at the market and had a casual affair with him. He ran away when she got pregnant again, and she went back to her husband in Accra. Her husband left to work overseas, and she gave birth to the child three days after his departure. She wrote to him about it and asked him to send the "marriage things" so that she could use them to look after the child. He sent £2, which she used to repay trading debts. He was very angry about this, and beat her upon his return to Accra. He would not claim the child, refusing either to name or outdoor it.[34] He left again after resuming conjugal relations with both his wife and Adukwe. The infant died one day of unknown causes. Adukwe went out, leaving the baby on the bed between two relatives [classificatory]. When she returned it was dead. She had named the child after her husband. The child was born with a caul, indicating that it would be rich. But when Adukwe's husband had returned to Accra and seen the child he had made this prediction: "When I die I shall go with it." And soon after that prediction he died, just before the child did. He was much older than Adukwe, perhaps forty years, having had grandchildren before taking her as a concubine. She was sorry that he died, but would not have missed him if her lover who had gotten her pregnant had not run away.

Adukwe's next lover was one of her husband's fellow workers. She stayed with him only a short time, and they had no children. He gave her no support money and made no marriage payment, so she left him.[35] The same thing happened with her fourth lover, whom she met while trading. With her fifth lover, also encountered while trading, she had a child, another daughter, and he outdoored it. He also paid for the coffin for her second child. He did not support her, however, so she did not stay with him. They were not together very long when they both got sick. They were living in a village; he returned to Accra when he got well and took other lovers. She later came back to Accra and took another lover. Again this one did not support her so she left him. She probably took other lovers subsequently, but could not remember very well. Mainly she never stayed with anyone for very long after her "husband" because no one ever gave her any support money or performed any sort of marriage formalities for her.

Adukwe traded most of her life, an activity interrupted by long periods of sickness. Her two daughters who survived childhood helped her when they got older, sending her fish to sell and cloth to wear when she was at

34. A man gives a child legitimacy by naming it at the child's outdooring ceremony, which he pays for, on the eighth day after its birth. He may or may not be officially married to the child's mother (see below).

35. In this context this may mean that he tired of her and did not call her to come to him anymore.

Oshuman. She also sold corn, kenkey, and firewood at different times in her life. She used to go to Bubuashie [a village near Accra and now part of it] every morning to gather firewood to sell in Accra in the afternoon. One daughter helped her, but this trade was ruined because the railroads and the lorries started bringing firewood to Accra [in the 1920s or '30s]. She retailed corn and kenkey in small quantities in Accra. More recently, when she could no longer see, she gave up mobile trading and began making an ointment out of palm kernels. In 1972 she no longer could afford to buy the palm kernels, so used old ones given to her by people who had made stew from them. This trade was not profitable enough to support her; she only sold maybe one bottle a week for about three pence [two and one half pesewas in present Ghanaian currency]. She had to crack and cook at least one whole kerosene tin of kernels to make a bottle of ointment, so production was slow. She just did it to keep busy.

Adukwe's sources of support in 1972 were two male grandchildren and one daughter, and others in the house where she lived. They would share meals with her and give her ten shillings [one cedi] occasionally for food. She had at least seven grandchildren, and had lost track of the number of great-grandchildren. Her more prosperous younger daughter had helped greatly with her expenses until she died after the 1939 earthquake. This daughter bore two children and then died of abdominal troubles at over age forty. Adukwe's older daughter was living with her in the house at Asere and also helping her, although the daughter herself was over seventy years old. Mainly, the relatives of the old woman were helping them.

Adukwe said she did not mind being a slave, on the whole. The old woman sometimes beat her, as did Afute's wife, but she did not care. "Even if she did not treat me well, I had nowhere else to go." She felt that she had been treated as if she were the old woman's child because "whenever she ate she gave [me] some to eat, isn't that enough [to prove it]? But if you ran away due to ill treatment how could you know the sort of treatment lying in wait for you at the next place you would stay? For myself, I would stay no matter what treatment I was given." The fact that the old woman was miserly about giving her clothing and her "husband(s)" only provided her (occasionally) with food did not bother her. In fact, although she had been a slave, she did not feel that she had had such a bad life, having experienced only the same sorrows as everyone else. When people in the house where she lived [in 1972] sometimes insulted her by calling her "slave," she just insulted them back. She did not know that it was possible to go to the district commissioner to get her freedom. The only contact with officialdom that she had had was being arrested three times by sanitary inspectors for having standing water or filth in the compound. On the subject of the district commissioner she said, "What did he have to do with me?" indicating that even if she had known, she probably would not have sought her freedom, because she assumed that the commissioner was too important to be concerned with her affairs. She concluded, "I have no regrets about my life. I am prepared for what God has in store for me. If He asks me to leave this life today I will welcome it; and if He allows me to continue to bear life's burden, I will not bemoan it. I will continue with life."

Adukwe's Story: Analysis

To sum up Adukwe's place in the post-proclamation slave trade in Accra, the external aspects of her history seem typical of those who surfaced in the court cases. She was taken as a child from her home, which was probably in northwestern Ghana. The mockery incident may indicate that matrilineal people were involved in the later stages of her journey, perhaps Fante. The Central Accra people in the late nineteenth century generally traded to the West of Accra and had many contacts with the Fante, so that a northwestern place of origin for Adukwe would make sense. We do not know, however, how typical the internal, more subjective aspects of her story are, which are analyzed below.

Adukwe had a strong fatalistic streak, frequently saying things like, "It was beyond my control, what could I do?" This evidently helped her to accept tragedies in her life with resignation. For example, of the death of her child, she said, "What could I do? All life is mortal; we come into the world to die, and the child died, what more? If life were immortal they would not have died. Death can come even to me at any time and then I will be gone. . . . " But her fatalism was not necessarily pessimistic; she continued to say, "if the child dies you live to bring forth yet another. . . ."

She had earned the respect of the women in the compound. She could hold up her side in an argument, as she said, and did not hesitate to do so; she sometimes refused to obey her mistress's orders. Meanwhile, she accepted beatings philosophically and continued to serve unresentfully. This absence of resentment seemed remarkable to me until I considered her attitude toward her Ga "family."

A mechanism which would help a slave to regain or retain self-respect would be belief in complete absorption into the family. In Adukwe's case this belief was facilitated by her having been enslaved at a young age. She retained only fuzzy memories of that trip down to the coast, and she spoke no language fluently besides Ga. She may have been happy even at the beginning to find a stable situation after being shunted around here and there to several owners. She made no distinctions when talking about her owner's family to indicate that it was not her own; the frequent use of kin terms for classificatory kin in Ga facilitated this. She referred to them in terms as if she had been Afute's sister. She gave me their genealogy as her own. I got just as much information from her about Ga customs as from other women her age.

Furthermore, Adukwe's activities in Accra were similar to those of other girl children her age, as were her punishments. She did not seem to have any sense of having been discriminated against just because she was a slave. For her, her bearing of a child to a member of her owner's family must have sealed her final integration; her children were free members of the lineage. Because of Ga patrilineal descent, the father is more important than the mother in establishing lineage rights. To improve her status Adukwe may have actually sought further assimilation by entering into a liaison with Afute's brother; however, she may have had little choice in the matter. The point is that she came to consider herself a full-fledged member of the lineage, whatever others said of her, and thus achieved a modicum of self-respect.

However, judging by the externals of her situation, she was only imperfectly assimilated and her socioeconomic status was affected negatively in several ways by her slave status, which comes through clearly in the comparison of the events of her life with those in the lives of her free peers, the other twenty-nine women aged seventy through nineties. Her marital pattern shows the most striking difference. She was the only one in the group who had no form of marriage performed for her. The Ga have a whole set of marriage procedures, ranging from simply giving a little drink (*afayinodaa*) to a complex ceremonial proceeding involving great expense and three or four steps (this used to be called a "six cloth" marriage because six cloths were among the groom's gifts to the bride) (Robertson forthcoming, ch. 6). The latter form of marriage predominated among women in their eighties and nineties. Even women of low economic status usually had afayinodaa done for them, as that made it easier for the man to claim the child. Many of the women were pregnant when it was performed. So, because Adukwe was a slave of the Bruce family, she in due course became the concubine of one of its older members (who already had a wife) and bore him a child. If she had been free her first marriage would probably have been to a young man who had no other wives, and it would have been formalized with some sort of ceremony. As it was, she had no parents to demand that he pay afayinodaa. Probably her purchase price was considered to be a form of bride payment and nothing further was deemed necessary. She felt this lack strongly, and sought constantly in her various liaisons a man who would make an official bride payment to her "family" and so raise her status. For different reasons, Adzo, the Ewe slave described by Nukunya below, also had no permanent liaison or marriage.

Adukwe's slave status also affected her relations with Afute's brother's wife, her eventual "co-wife," although not as strongly as it affected her relationships with men. The wife obviously viewed young Adukwe as an active threat, which implies an equality of sorts. Her arguing with the husband over his giving money to Adukwe was typical of most Ga conjugal quarrels in Central Accra. That Adukwe helped the wife with trading, however, was a factor of her slave status, since most women traded with their female matrilateral relatives, who also provided them with capital. Adukwe's economic status was undoubtedly impaired by lack of a source of capital; unlike most women at that time she would have been most dependent on her husband for capital, since apparently the old woman did not see fit to provide her with any. Adukwe consequently pilfered small sums from her mistress on occasion, and used the money her "husband" sent from abroad for the child for trading purposes instead. Her attitude about her "husband's" death thus becomes understandable; she only regretted the loss of support. Even though her peers also mainly viewed husbands as potential sources of support, Adukwe's attitude was more matter-of-fact than that of most women.

Another consequence of Adukwe's status was her childbearing pattern. She had only three children, of whom two survived to adulthood. Her peers in their seventies, eighties, and nineties had an average of 6.4 children per woman surviving to adulthood. But then, they generally had at least one long stable marriage, or two only, which would contribute toward their bearing more children. Fertility is usually lower for women who have a number of marriages or liaisons.[36] The subfecundity of women like Adukwe also corresponds with that of other female slave populations, and reflects unconcern by the owners about the women's biological reproductive functions. Adukwe's Ga contemporaries considered her unlucky, since the desired number of children was often ten. However, Adukwe was lucky in that she did not suffer the usual fate of subfecund women in old age of having no one to provide her with support; one daughter and many descendants survived her, some of whom cared for her.

Adukwe's slave status may also help to explain why her second lover, who got her pregnant, ran away and thereby refused to claim the child. Bearing an illegitimate child rarely happened in late nineteenth- and early twentieth-century Ga society and was considered to be one of the worst disgraces which could befall a woman. Even if a man did not legally marry a woman, he would usually name the child. Sometimes the scandal could be avoided by the woman's male maternal relatives claiming and naming the child for their lineage, but of course Adukwe did not have that option. The scandal might have been doubled by her husband's refusal to

36. Because more time is spent without regular sexual intercourse between liaisons and the incidence of venereal disease may be higher.

outdoor the child. However, since she was a concubine with no pretensions to respectability in other people's eyes, the scandal may not have
been significant. For, even though she was a part of her master's family,
because of her slave status she probably was not expected to conform
entirely to their moral standards. Slavery, in a sense, might bring the freedom of society's indifference.

When Adukwe was young her slave status did not affect her working
career to an appreciable extent. Most young girls who traded at that time,
especially those serving apprenticeships, turned over their profits to their
mothers or mistresses. However, after Adukwe "married" she traded in
conjunction with her husband's wife, which deviates from the usual pattern, as noted above. Even when she later traded independently, her initial
lack of capital undoubtedly affected her profits negatively. She never developed a large-scale business, which, coming from an apprenticeship with
a successful trader from a wealthy family, she might have been expected
to do. Adukwe's description of the Osu house and the goods her mistress
traded, as well as the reputation of the Nanka-Bruce family, indicate the
family's prosperity. However, her later partnership in trade with her daughters
followed the pattern typical of free women, as did her frequent mobility
in changing residence and pursuing trading activities.[37] It is also quite
probable, however, that in her mature years no one questioned her assimilation; slavery was definitely becoming a relic of the past, so that her
slave status had progressively fewer effects.

Full assimilation was certainly indicated in the position of Adukwe's
children. They were brought up like other free children. In the usual Ga
women's compounds in Central Accra there are always many children
around, who are all treated roughly equally. Adukwe's attitudes toward
raising and punishing them were identical to those of her peers. They did
not go to school, but they were of a generation (born *ca.* 1900–1915) in
which girls generally did not go to school. School fees were the only area
where the parents' ability to pay would have made a big difference. Like
their peers, Adukwe's daughters became market traders, and one of them
was fairly successful.

Another feature of Adukwe's life which was also typical of her peers
was her increasing independence after she "married" and bore a child.
This was the usual time for women to begin trading on their own and
making their own decisions, and Adukwe was no exception, although her
connection with her "husband's" wife may have continued longer than
some apprenticeships. The stories she told of coercion and beatings mostly
dated from her days as a helper for others, not from the time when she

---

37. People of both sexes made frequent moves in taking up on various residential rights,
often to pursue economic purposes.

essentially had her own household. She frequently was with her "husband" without the wife being there. She obviously had as much independence as a free person in many ways. One might attribute this to changing times bringing better treatment for ex-slaves, but her years with her husband must have been from about 1900 to 1915 when the slave trade was still continuing, albeit on a reduced scale. Things had not changed that much. More likely, her status as woman dominated in some ways her status as slave, and did so increasingly as slavery receded in importance. The change in the dominant mode of production redefined the terms of exploitation, making it more linked to gender. Women who were successfully excluded from learning new skills filled marginal economic positions. When they did attain new skills, they eventually formed a reserve labor force employed in sex-stereotyped low-paid positions.[38]

We may fairly ask ourselves, then, which was better in Adukwe's time and place, to be a slave or a woman? The answer is surely to be a male slave, because that state could be abolished or overcome, while the disadvantages of being a woman could not be legally abolished, it seems, and seldom can be overcome, even now. As Marcia Wright observes in reference to Central Africa (below, p. 249), the statuses of free and slave women were so close that the distinction often was insignificant. The abolition of slavery did not therefore significantly improve the socioeconomic status of the Gold Coast women who were most of the slaves, because they were still women. Reindorf, expressing a Ga male view, claimed that the two British laws disliked the most by the Ga were first the one "against the cruel treatment of wives [who] had now the option of leaving their husbands," and second, the abolition law (Reindorf *ca.* 1890/1966:323).

> You were bought as a slave, you were sold as a slave.
> Give the slave water to drink;
> You were bought as a slave, you were sold as a slave.
> You were born on Thursday, and you were sold on Saturday;
> You were bought as a slave, you were sold as a slave.
> You were put on a crossroad;
> You were bought as a slave, you were sold as a slave.
> Koole, give her water to drink;
> Oshwila, give her water to drink;
> Sakumo surrounds her.
>   Ga *kple* song[39]

38. Robertson (forthcoming, ch. 5); after World War Two primary school enrollment of Accra girls increased dramatically, and by 1970 had reached parity with that of boys.

39. Kilson 1971:244–45. Kilson's exegesis for this song goes as follows: "A slave has no identity; his name may be changed at his master's whim, but a slave should be well treated. . . . [T]he central theme of this song is the subjugation of a slave to his master's

APPENDIX: A NOTE ON ANLO (EWE) SLAVERY AND THE HISTORY OF A SLAVE, BY G. K. NUKUNYA

Slavery was quite common in traditional Anlo Gold Coast society, especially in the nineteenth century, which we can deduce from the large number of people who claim slave descent. The present writer knows some of the people who originally were slaves. Most of them were brought from northern Ghana and northern Eweland, and were acquired by purchase. A few, like the woman mentioned below, were captured in wars or raids on neighboring peoples.

Anlo Ewe society had several mechanisms for the incorporation of strangers. Groups of settlers who came voluntarily to Anloga usually formed separate clans ordained by the local chiefs, and did not lose their free status. Slaves were easily absorbed into the descent groups of their masters [see Nukunya 1969]. A male slave was often adopted as a son, and received an equal share of his "father's" property which was passed on *inter vivos*. However, he probably would not have been able to succeed to his "father's" titles. Also, if the property inheritance was disputed, those of slave descent might have been passed over in favor of the true descendants.

The procedure of incorporation and liberation was a bit different for female slaves. Marriage or the bearing of a child usually signalized a woman's freedom, and her child, if the father was free, was also freeborn. A woman usually "married" a man of her owner's lineage. If another man wanted her he could seek the owner's permission and give the owner something to establish the legitimacy of the union. However, it was usually not a full-scale customary marriage. In this respect the history of Adzo below was typical. Slaves, then, did not usually suffer any serious disabilities.

Adzo (Ah-jō), a young Krobo girl, was captured while harvesting vegetables in a garden by Anlo raiders and taken directly to Woe, an Ewe coastal town. She was perhaps about ten to twelve years of age at the time of her capture, because she had not yet had the *dipo* puberty rite done for her, but she could remember a lot about her origins. Given that her first child was born in about 1905, she was probably born in approximately 1885 and captured in the mid-1890s, well after the abolition of slavery on the Gold Coast in 1874.

The fact that Adzo had not gone through the *dipo* rite had a profound influence on her life. Among the Krobo a girl may not marry unless this rite is performed. Any breach of this custom will incur serious supernatural sanctions. Adzo believed that, despite her physical separation from her people, she was still Krobo. This conviction was probably enforced by the fact that she came from a royal lineage, which inhabited a large palace with a big rock and a metal bowl in its center (probably in the courtyard) where *dipo* rites were performed. After Adzo passed puberty her owner wanted her to become one of his wives. She refused, saying, "How can I marry one who said that he would be like a father to me?"

---

will. The despised social status of a slave is conveyed through allusions to a crossroads where waste may be dumped and to changes in a slave's day name (line 4)." Kilson translated the pronoun as *him* in the song; I have taken the liberty of changing it to *her,* as there is no distinction in Ga, in any case. Koole, Oshwila, and Sakumo are gods.

She was therefore "married" to a younger cousin of the owner and had a child. The formalities that usually accompany marriage were not performed for her, so that it was not really a marriage by customary law. She decided, in any case, that she might escape the supernatural sanctions by not having a legal marriage with full formalities. Thus, she had five children in all, each with a different man.

On many occasions Adzo's children pressured her to be more forthcoming about the details of her background. This she adamantly refused to do, even though she knew her place of origin, probably because of Anlo attitudes regarding the origins of slaves. Because there was always the danger of slaves or their descendants trying to run away back to their own people, Anlo people used supernatural means to tie the slaves to their new homes. Medicines and threats were employed for this purpose. In Adzo's case the distance involved was not that great and she might have been able to make her way back, but she was convinced that any attempt to go home would cause her death. Even at her death, some ten years ago, no one knew her exact origins. She had come to be respected and loved in her new home, however.

References

Oral Sources

Interviews were conducted at Adukwe's home in Asere, Ussher Town, Central Accra. Tapes of the interviews with Adukwe are in the Archives of Traditional Music, Indiana University, Bloomington.

Adukwe, interviews from 1971 to 1978.
A. A. Amartey, interviews on March 2 and 30, 1978.
E. A. Ammah, interview on January 31, 1978.
Alhaji Mohammed Makwei Laryea, interviews on February 11 and 18, 1978.

Unpublished Sources

Ga National Archives. In possession of Nii Amugi II, Ga Mantse.
G.N.A.: Ghana National Archives, Accra.
    Administrative Papers (ADM Series).
    Debrunner, H. N.d. "The Church of Christ at Accra before 1917." Basel Mission Papers (EC Series 7/19).
    District Court Records (SCT Series).
    High Court Records.
    Secretary for Native Affairs Papers (SNA Series).
McSheffrey, G. M. 1977. "Slavery, Indentured Servitude and the Impact of Abolition in the Gold Coast: 1874–1901. A Reappraisal." Paper presented at Canadian Historical Association Conference, Fredericton, New Brunswick.
Robertson. C. C. 1974. "Social and Economic Change in Twentieth Century Accra: Ga Women." Ph.D. dissertation, University of Wisconsin, Madison.

Published Sources

Cruickshank, B. 1853/1966. *Eighteen Years on the Gold Coast of Africa.* New York.

Horton, J. A. 1868/1969. *West African Countries and Peoples.* Edinburgh.

Kilson, M. 1971. *Kpele Lala.* Cambridge.

Kuczynski, R. R. 1948. *Demographic Survey of the British Colonial Empire.* Vol. 1: *West Africa.* London.

Manteko, Y. 1967. *Out-dooring in Accra.* Accra.

Nukunya, G. K. 1969. *Kinship and Marriage among the Anlo Ewe.* London School of Economics Monograph on Social Anthropology No. 37.

Pogucki, R. J. H. 1954/1968. *Report on Land Tenure in Customary Law of the Non-Akan Areas of the Gold Coast Colony, Part II: Ga.* Accra.

Poku, K. 1979. "Traditional Roles and People of Slave Origin in Modern Ashanti— A Few Impressions." *Ghana Journal of Sociology* 5:35–38.

Pope-Hennessy, Gov. J. 1873. "On the British Settlements in Western Africa." *Journal of the* [Royal] *Society of Arts* 21:436–49.

Reindorf, C. C. Ca. 1890/1966. *The History of the Gold Coast and Asante.* Accra.

Rey, P.-P. 1975. "L'esclavage lignagère chez les tsangui, les punu et les kuni du Congo-Brazzaville." In *L'esclavage en Afrique précoloniale,* ed. C. Meillassoux. Paris.

Robertson, C. C. Forthcoming. *Sharing the Same Bowl, A Socioeconomic History of Women and Class in Accra, Ghana.* Bloomington.

Szereszewski, R. 1965 *Structural Changes in the Economy of Ghana 1891–1911.* London.

Terray, Emmanuel. 1975. "La captivité dans le royaume abron du Gyaman." In *L'esclavage en Afrique précoloniale,* ed. C. Meillassoux. Paris.

13 *Marcia Wright*

Bwanikwa:
Consciousness and Protest
among Slave Women in Central Africa,
1886–1911

This paper is the third in a series of "experiments" designed to discover and interpret the historical experience of women and of women slaves in particular.[1] Additions to this line of investigation drawn from cases in other parts of Africa are most valuable. E. A. Alpers's chapter in this volume, for example, opens the way for comparison and generalization of coastal and interior experiences. It is an interior affected but not entirely dominated by external commerce and power that is at issue for present purposes. Though this paper necessarily begins with a survey of missionary, administrative, and African male interactions and ideologies, its premise is that we can reconstruct the experience of slave women only by seeking out the most direct and immediate evidence possible for the actions and words of women themselves. Only in that way can we hope to get nearer to the consciousness of African women, and to their perception of "slave" and "free" status. Hence this paper draws heavily on the autobiography of one particular woman, Bwanikwa, and also upon the testimony given by women in early colonial court cases. These statements by women make it clear that whatever white and black men may have thought about the leniency of female "domestic" servitude, women felt themselves to be slaves in a full sense and did everything they could to emancipate themselves.

Clarification of two theoretical assumptions is in order. The first concerns lineage as a focus of history. The second has to do with the classification of the social environment and the merits of recognizing precolonial

1. The first publication in this series was "Women in Peril" (Wright 1975). Then, in "Family, Community and Women" (Wright 1977), I remedied the earlier neglect of content and paid attention to "free" Safwa women as an essential reference group for any interpretation of the life of a former slave.

quasi urbanism. Elsewhere I have argued that in East Central Africa it was colonialism which raised lineage to dominance as a staple of local politics. The commercial conditions of the latter nineteenth century gave power to chiefs and merchants whose wealth allowed them to control unrelated people.[2] Slave women usually belonged as property to a man, although they were occasionally assigned to serve and were sometimes effectively owned by other women. Kinship was an important part of the repertoire of male strategies, but women, given vigorous trade in which slaves were valuable commodities, were assets of a new order and were no longer exchanged merely in marriage. The women who became pawns or slaves had no recourse to kin and were not lineage-controlled. From the point of view of production and exchange relations, the difference is that between a sphere of influence achieved by merchant capital on the one hand and colonial merchant/industrial capital on the other. The latter restructured the lineage and ethnic community which the former destructured. The commercial milieu of the latter nineteenth century in Central Africa spawned quasi-urban conditions at places where large fluctuating populations were fed, housed, and otherwise serviced. The society of such communities may be called polyethnic and heterogeneous. In some ways they antici-pated modern towns, not least in requiring individual agility in forming and reforming relationships.[3] Slavery in such circumstances, then, was a feature of a relatively "open" society.

Western Images of Female Status

"Add slavery to polygamy, and reduce a woman to the status of a slave, then you have the sum of human degradation, the lowest creature on God's earth—a slave woman" (Campbell 1916:12). With these aggressive words in a missionary pamphlet published in 1916, Dugald Campbell appealed to British women to join in the work of Christianizing Central Africa. He counted upon the circle of mission subscribers for support, diminished though humanitarian and anti-slavery sentiment was in colonial and met-ropolitan circles in general. Furthermore, he reflected a genuine alliance with Christian women of the Luapula-Katanga region of northern Rhode-sia and Zaire which had placed him well to put forward their case. The figure around whom he built his appeal, Bwanikwa, is also the focus of

2. P.-P. Rey (1975:74) urges closer historical examination. Mary Douglas (1964) made an important statement about the social reflexes that encouraged pawnship, but attempted to isolate pawnship from slavery. Norms dominate historical processes even more in Igor Kopytoff's (1979) idealization of benevolent kinship-incorporation. See Cooper (1979) for a host of theoretical and historical objections to Kopytoff's position.

3. Historians of modern copper-mining towns consistently ignore precolonial urbanism and set up highly misleading dualism. See, for example, Bruce Fetter 1976:9.

the present paper, which inquires into the changing historical circumstances of unfree women in the period 1880 to 1911. The time was one of
commercial transformation interrupted by colonial intervention with its
institution of courts and specific mandates to abolish slavery on the one
hand and its concurrent measures of economic reorientation on the other.
Myriad crosscurrents of ideology, economic reconstruction, and social
control complicate the critical exercise of extracting material about women's
slavery and consciousness, but only by such an effort can we enlarge the
compass of social history in treating this important transitional period.

For Western observers and activists in matrilineal Central Africa in the
early colonial period, there were important social conditions and institutions seemingly more deeply rooted than slavery that required correction.
Missionaries and officials represented different interests, however, and
consequently diverged in their visions of a desirable social order. The
officials by 1911 had struck alliances with male chiefs and elders. H. C.
Marshall, the magistrate of the Tanganyika District, concluded that the
colonial courts had been too favorable to women and that the "excessive
liberties" of Bemba women should be curbed. He reported further:

> Quite recently Chief Mporokoso, after touring his villages, told me that the
> women of the country were growing out of hand, and that the results were
> becoming apparent in a decrease in the birth-rate.
> The character of the Wemba Woman must be borne in mind. . . . Always
> notably independent—always more or less of a shrew—prone to unfaithful-
> ness—she is now taking advantage of two central facts; firstly that the laws of
> the country are in her favour, and secondly that, with the present unprecedented
> influx of wealth, the taking of a lover is an easy and a profitable pastime.
> (Marshall 1910)

Junior wives in matrilineal societies, Marshall saw, had few structural
sanctions preventing their marital separation, for ritual obligations were
performed by the senior wife, and the bridewealth at stake for the junior
wives was very slight. Through a delegation of judicial authority to local
African authorities, Marshall hoped to stabilize polygamous families and
diminish anxiety on the part of husbands and elders. Local courts indeed
became the instrument for imposing norms and customs in the interests of
senior males, and with their effective monopoly of law at the family level,
complaints about female slavery and exploitation ceased to be a matter of
judicial record.[4]

Central to the missionary ideal of social order was the monogamous,
patriarchal family. An editorial in the Plymouth Brethren's journal under-

---

4. The work of Martin Chanock (1982) documents the regularization of local courts and
the attendant consequences.

scored the distance between such a notion of family and the prevailing matrilineal conditions:

> In Central Africa, socialism, polygamy, and the law of "mother right" deprives the father of all authority over his own children, and places them under the control of their mother's oldest brother, living probably in some other part of the country. All this makes it difficult . . . to apply New Testament injunctions to "fathers," "mothers," "husbands," "wives," "parents," and "children" in the family. Until there is some semblance of family life produced as a result of gospel teaching, it is out of the question to rush in to the third or church circle.[5]

African society, too, had its ideals. The first missionary in Garenganze, F. S. Arnot, reported the popular conviction that slavery was impermanent, dissolving by the third or fourth generation as full kinship rights were resumed (Arnot 1889:242). Indeed, women could be more quickly absorbed because of a persistent ambiguity as to their status and functions. Performing typical female roles alongside free but nevertheless dependent women of a household, their servitude was less explicitly coerced than that of male slaves. The contemporary Dutch scholar of slavery, H. J. Nieboer, made a universal statement about the origins of slavery that carried considerable truth in the Central African situation. When there are no laborers in the modern sense of proletarians, he wrote, and "a man wants others to perform the necessary drudgery for him, and cannot impose it upon his wife, or wives, or other female dependents . . . he must compel other men to serve him; and this compulsion will often assume the form of slavery" (Nieboer 1910:419). A slave, by this definition, was a male forced to do the labor that women would otherwise do. The practical distinction between the rights of slaves and of free women was so comparatively small that almost all definitions have presumed that slaves were male.[6]

To the official mind of the times, as represented by H. C. Marshall, "actual slavery"—hard, menial labor and the lack of inheritance rights— was a condition of men, on the whole, while domestic slavery of "people of the harem," mostly women, was not onerous.[7] By 1911, the older mode

5. *Echoes of Service* (1897:282–83). This missionary journal contains many detailed reports from the Plymouth Brethren as well as editorials on social policy. Peter H. Lary has generously shared his research notes from this source concerning the Luapula District.

6. The excellent short definition by M. I. Finley (1968) and the recent article by Orlando Patterson (1979) both imply that the slave is male.

7. Marshall 1910. J. E. Stephenson, Marshall's contemporary, made a distinction between "he" slaves, who were apt to be inveterate wrong-doers, and "she-slaves," who were pawns or hostages (Stephenson 1937:65). See also *Chirupula's Quarterly Review* (N.A.Z., HM ST 1/3, NA 2). (1950:2).

of control by chiefs over bevies of women was disintegrating and everyone knew that purchase of slaves had been effectively terminated; the antislavery chapter of colonial intervention was officially closed. Domestic slaves and servile women became less visible in all parts of the colonial record as World War One neared. Even though women were prominent parishioners, specific references to them as persons faded in the narratives and ethnographies produced by missionaries in the interwar period, and earlier material reprocessed at this time became more and more static.[8]

While norms and ideologies must be appraised continually, it is not promises of emancipation or reincorporation that are at issue, but rather the actuality of conditions obtaining for the first- and second-generation slaves—female slaves for the purpose of this discussion—within a particular time frame. For the generation in the decades before 1911, it can be shown that women were slaves in a genuine sense, and conscious of their status. Furthermore, they acted wittingly to emancipate themselves.

Bwanikwa's Life

Bwanikwa lived between the early 1870s and the late 1920s in the present-day Shaba of Zaire and Luapula Province of Zambia. Her autobiography was narrated in a Luba dialect and translated into English by Campbell, who arrived in Katanga in 1892 as a missionary of the Plymouth Brethren and met Bwanikwa for the first time in about 1895. After 1898, as an adherent, temporary employee, and self-supporting church and community activist, she was an intimate of the Campbell family. The text of the autobiography, published as an appendix to Campbell's book, *Blazing Trails in Bantuland,* covers only the time of her enslavement, about two-thirds of Bwanikwa's life. To retrieve something of her later years, it is necessary to draw upon statements mediated by the missionary.

For present purposes, the autobiography has been segmented in order to allow for a commentary upon the several phases of time, place, and circumstance that mark it.[9] The initial phase occurred in Garenganze, an African state ruled by Msiri (Msidi in some accounts) until his death in December 1891. An intermediate phase, of the greatest insecurity for Bwanikwa, coincided with the establishment of control by the Congo Free State in the 1890s. During the last phase, after the turn of the century, she moved across the Luapula River with the missionaries to Northeastern Rhodesia. In the course of these three phases, Bwanikwa underwent a

8. Some analogous problems of official, missionary, and African consensus history are treated by T. Q. Reefe (1977:192).

9. The autobiography is appended to Campbell 1934. Campbell makes a statement about its composition and translation (1934:202).

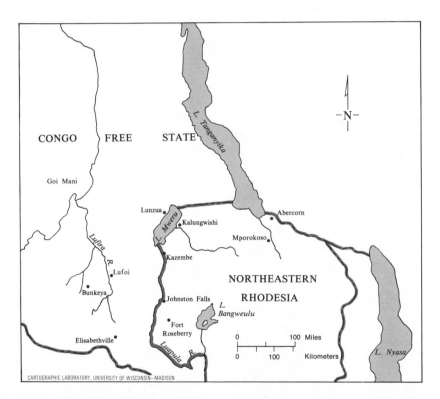

Map 13.1. Bwanikwa's Homeland. Political boundaries shown are those of the early twentieth century.

process of absorption into a household as a slave concubine; then became an uprooted person being subject to sale, making escapes and seeking protection at heavy cost; and finally succeeded in establishing for herself a strong position within a Christian community. Successive political environments shaped her options, as did changing socioeconomic conditions, but in interpreting her story we must take special care also to consider age-specific aspects of status within the female life cycle of preadolescence, fertility, and post-fertility.

Garenganze

The story has often been told of how Msiri came as a Nyamwezi trader to Katanga, established relations with the Sanga chiefs, dominated the salt and copper source areas, and superseded the Kazembes as the overlord of an area from the Lualaba in the west to the Luapula in the east.[10] In 1886, he was at the peak of his career, having made Garenganze in general and Bunkeya in particular a hub of commerce. The Nyamwezi element in the ruling group were known as Yeke. While Msiri attracted to him a number of Yeke who served various functions in the state, he also had to contend with unincorporated Nyamwezi-Swahili settlements on his domain's periphery, which had the capacity to obstruct the flow of traffic. Similarly, disturbances by the Luvale or Lunda to the west could block caravans. The Bihean group among the Ovimbundu were reliable commercial allies at the time of Arnot's journeys, and he and other missionaries reported in detail on their approaches from the Angolan coast.[11] The most active frontier of Garenganze lay in the north, where the Luba were continuously raided, tested, and made into a source area for slaves.

Administratively, Garenganze was a tribute-gathering state with personal representatives of the ruler residing in various districts. These representatives were male and female relatives or wives, women who had usually been married as a result of diplomatic exchange with a lesser ruler. The Yeke and Swahili were patrilineal in most respects, although some strata of the Nyamwezi practiced modified matrilineal succession. In superimposing his rule over the matrilineal groups in Garenganze, Msiri drew legitimacy by taking noble wives. To a certain extent, these women were hostages who could become powerful functionaries if they proved their loyalty and effectiveness. Msiri enlarged his circle of power by using not only kinship and marriage, but also investiture. Chiefs of indigenous communities sought and paid well for gradual promotions as officers of the state (Arnot 1889:234; Crawford 1912:191).

Economically, the state rested upon tribute in food gathered after the harvest, monopolies of ivory, copper, and salt, and private enterprise in slave trading (Verdick 1952:43). Warriors sent to the frontiers on punitive expeditions were allowed to retain their captives and to sell them at will. By extension, all slave owners in Garenganze had the right to buy and sell slaves without regulation. Ivory, on the other hand, was subject to the most rigorous control through a system of surveillance over its movements, from the departure of a hunting party through every step of deliv-

10. The received dynastic tradition is contained in the work of a retired administrator (Verbeken 1956). Campbell also treats it, in a summary way (1922, ch. 25).

11. Arnot 1889. Arnot also published selected letters and diaries of colleagues (1893).

ery and marketing (Arnot 1889:234). Msiri monopolized all ivory, in contrast to the one-tusk royalty generally expected by Central African rulers.

The capital of Garenganze, Bunkeya, lay in a large basin plain over which were spread many discrete settlements. According to estimates by an early Belgian administrator, there were forty-two villages with a total population of some 25,000 people (Verdick 1952:32). Msiri's principal wives presided over large communities composed in part of female slaves whom the ruler distributed to them while retaining ultimate ownership. These women formed the backbone of the agricultural labor force. During the critical periods of the agricultural cycle, the labor force was augmented by teams of men whom Msiri and his principal lieutenants supervised personally (Arnot 1889:170, 174). Bunkeya's overriding function was to generate and store surpluses of food to see its fluctuating population through the long dry season and to provision caravans.

Demographically, Bunkeya was like a port town with its own farms forming a peri-urban complex. The stable resident population was overwhelmingly female. Arnot complained both about the extent of polygamy and about the ease of divorce (1889:194). The frequent comings and goings of caravans and military expeditions offered opportunities to rearrange sexual partnerships. Amidst this freewheeling social environment, Msiri held an open court in which anyone could state his or her case. Arnot observed that large numbers of women attended the court and constituted most of the throng on major public occasions. He also drew attention to the unusual tenor of the judicial system: "The rights and privileges given to women . . . form one of the remarkable features of Msidi's government. Women are allowed to attend the courts, and to have a voice equally with the men, and Msidi succeeds pretty well in dispensing equal justice" (Arnot 1889:241).

Because slaves were not a focus of state appropriation, they could be treated with a degree of dispassionate justice and paternalism by Msiri. The case of a young slave girl who ran away from her mistress after a severe beating then traveled more than six miles by night in order to throw herself on the mercy of the ruler may be exceptional, yet it demonstrates how Msiri could accept a refugee and arrange to place her under more benevolent custody, simultaneously reinforcing his relationship with a client, the girl's new guardian, who in this instance proved to be Arnot himself (1898:245).

The heyday of Garenganze encompassed both Bwanikwa's enslavement as a small girl and her life as a young woman in the Yeke community. Her narrative is as follows:

I, Bwanikwa, was born on the banks of the Dindie, a small river in Lubaland. Our part of the country was thickly populated, and our principal chief was Goi-Mani. My father's name was Kankolwe.

My mother was called Mikomba. I was one of a family of five. Our only brother had died; four girls remained, of whom I was the second oldest. My father had a dozen wives. His head-wife was the daughter of chief Katumba. She was an important woman.

At the time I refer to, the head-wife had just died. According to Luban custom [my father] was mulcted for death dues. He was ordered to pay three slaves, as compensation for his wife's death, and to ensure inheritance by the dead wife's sister. They did not produce a sister to take the dead woman's place till the death has been paid for to the relatives. Three slaves were demanded, and my father could only raise two.

One of his four daughters had to be handed over to make a third, and I was chosen. I was the second oldest, as I said, and my father loved me. When he handed me over to my master, he said to him as we parted: "Be kind to my little daughter; do not sell her to anyone else, and I will come and redeem her." As my father was unable to redeem me, I was left in slavery.

My father did not come to redeem me, and my master sold me to some of Msidi's people who were out man-hunting. I was sold for a packet of gunpowder, worth two shillings and sixpence, and was taken to Chifuntwe's village in the Balomotwa country. At that time I was small, unable to walk.

It appears that my master had, at this time, offended the principal chief, and was ordered to pay up several slaves. Amongst those slaves given to pay for my master's crimes, I was handed over. Thus I was sold again. The chief to whom I was given in payment of a fine, handed me to one of his warriors as wife, saying, "Take her as your wife, she's young." After a while he said "She's only a young girl, and I don't want her." He sold me to a man named Mukoka for a gun. Mukoka bought me, with another woman and child, intending to sell us later to the Biheans. He took me as his wife. I bore him a child which only lived three days. His other wives were kind to me. Though he sold many other slaves to Biheans, he never sold me, nor did he threaten to do so. (Campbell 1934:210–11)

Congo Free State, 1890–99

Msiri was killed on December 28, 1891, by an officer of the Congo Free State forces. Bunkeya was immediately abandoned by virtually all its inhabitants, including Bwanikwa, and became a place of military encampment. The depredations of the Congo Free State soldiery together with the sudden removal of the dominant political figure and protector, Msiri, called into question the durability of Garenganze and social relations as they had prevailed. The moment of "conquest" must be seen in perspective, however, for the period of deterioration did not begin in December 1891. Over the preceding two years there had been a crisis in

Bunkeya, the milieu being affected by Msiri's illnesses, irregularities in supply of arms and powder, visits by rival agents of the British South Africa Company and the Congo Free State, and rebellion by tributary Sanga leaders whose alliance had been a cornerstone of the Garenganze "empire."

An increasingly irascible Msiri suspected his principal Sanga wife of disloyalty as early as 1888 (Arnot 1889:225). Charges against her and her son were then dropped as an act of grace, but in 1889 she was executed for complicity in the death of Msiri's important governor who had controlled the western approaches to the state. The Sanga took this act as a cause of war. They began to harass Msiri with guerilla tactics, burning granaries and houses in night attacks. An atmosphere of insecurity prevailed throughout Bunkeya, but Msiri endured the incursions quietly, until fresh supplies of powder could be secured (Arnot 1893:68).

Many other factors damaged the integrity of Garenganze at this time. The single word that best describes Bunkeya in 1890, 1891, and 1892 is hunger. Food production, distribution, and storage failed for a variety of reasons. Msiri was no longer healthy or secure enough to lead his men into the fields, reserves were destroyed by Sanga actions, and post-harvest tribute was hardly forthcoming. Insecurity and withdrawal of labor from cultivation in the Bunkeya valley were paralleled by a shortage of rain. During the long dry seasons of 1890 and 1891, the situation was desperate, and the foulness of the little water available drove away the missionaries as well as numbers of the inhabitants. New settlements were made in more mountainous, defensible areas and in well-watered river valleys. Msiri himself contemplated moving, but delayed in order to show that he would not "run away" under Sanga pressure (Arnot 1893:68).

The Congo Free State representatives had established an outpost on the Lufoi River, to the east of Bunkeya, in 1890. The missionaries chose a station site nearby in order to enjoy the umbrella of civilization it supposedly extended. Then, after the death of Msiri and the final dispersal from Bunkeya, many people sought refuge with the missionaries. The Free State presence meanwhile did not ease matters. Famine affected the colonial forces as it did other people. A new tributary system was difficult to install with such depleted reserves and political anarchy as existed. In 1893, locusts further damaged the crops and prospects for a speedy reconstruction. The missionaries began to distance themselves from the Congo Free State authorities and were physically estranged from 1894 to 1896, during which time they abandoned Lufoi and moved eastward to set up a new network of stations (Campbell 1934:70–71). They gathered large followings of people dislocated from the shattered Bunkeya complex. Perhaps the most extreme example of this phenomenon was Luanza. Luanza (known at first as Chipongo), on the west side of Lake Mweru, was in a zone that had been peripheral to Msiri's state. As Campbell described it,

> Luanza . . . developed into a hiding place for the riff-raff of Katanga. The flotsam and jetsam of Msidi's old, and now extinct, kingdom drifted in, and a new start was made. Murderers, too, made it a city of refuge; Arabs, fleeing for their lives from the avenging Belgians, halted, or hid in Luanza's rabbit warrens; and slavers, escaping from State prisons where they were undergoing terms of imprisonment for their misdeeds, headed for Luanza. (Campbell 1934:82)

As Campbell's account suggests, the Congo Free State engaged in campaigns against the old trading elements, both Swahili and Ovimbundu. They had also to contend with ongoing Sanga resistance and a major rebellion by their own soldiery.

After a two-year absence, the missionaries returned to the Lufira Valley in central Garenganze where Msiri's successor was beginning to reestablish a capital. They were given a large public reception by the Yeke and a warm welcome by the Belgians (Campbell 1934:95). The fertile Lufira Valley was under extensive cultivation, and the stage was being set for a restoration of the Yeke dynasty as rulers of a dependent African state. Political rewards for supplying auxiliaries were reaped after a number of actions, but never so fully as when the Sanga offered overt resistance and were finally defeated by a combined Congo Free State–Yeke force in 1899 (Verdick 1952; Verbeken 1956; Campbell 1934:101). So it was that the Garenganze oligarchy retrieved a position of importance and became administratively integrated into the unfolding colonial regime in Katanga. The missionaries, soon after the restoration was complete, developed a nostalgia for the old days: the past slavings and excesses of the Muslims and Biheans, who had been the major armed aliens in the region, paled in comparison to the Congo Free State's cruel exercise of its monopolies of rubber and ivory as well as its military license (Campbell 1934:191).

That a settled civil administration in the Congo Free State did not exist in Katanga at the turn of the century is confirmed by the memoires of Verdick, the principal official. Anti-slavery quickly vanished from the rhetoric and practice of the regime once its commercial rivals had been defeated. Much exchanging of slaves went on in Katanga without official concern except when the peace was disturbed, as for example by quarrels over the price of a slave woman, which could prompt the administrator to lock up a whole party of Biheans.[12] The colonial courts to the east of the Luapula River and Lake Mweru, in Northeastern Rhodesia, by contrast,

---

12. Campbell 1934:76. For Bihean countermeasures see *Echoes* 1896:252.

did slowly become places of appeal by slaves. But before 1899, when Kazembe capitulated, the Kalungwishi-Luapula area was one also of minimal colonial control. Much escaped the attention of officials at all times, and certainly the Collector at Kalungwishi, newly appointed in 1893, was not able to concern himself with every skirmish in the commercial and social sphere, especially when transient "Congo natives" were concerned.[13] His messengers and police might exploit the threat of his intervention in order to obtain a bribe, but a woman without a male advocate or economic resources would have found it virtually impossible to be noticed judicially.

Bwanikwa's life from 1892 to 1898 reflected the many uncertainties and efforts at reconstruction that marked the initial colonial years both to the west and east of the Luapula River and Lake Mweru:

> I lived with Mukoka till Msidi's death and the break up of his power by the Europeans. At this some of us slaves saw our chance, and fled. We scattered. Men, tired of Msidi's despotic rule, would take some or other woman slave, and both would head north, south, east, or west, in search of freedom and a new start in life. When possible, each headed for the old homestead.
>
> A well-known elephant hunter and fellow slave in the same village, whose name was Kabongo, took me, and we ran off east. Our old master set out in search of a new home and village site. We crossed the Luapula river to Kazembe's to try and begin life anew. Chief Kazembe cast his eyes upon me, and asked Kabongo to give me to him for a wife. Kabongo refused. We left Kazembe's capital, came back west, and settled in Sakungami village. We lived and cultivated there for two years. Some slaves heard of our old master having built at the Luisi river, and suggested our returning together. My husband refused at first, but afterwards agreed to join the party.
>
> When chief Mukoka saw me come back, he said, "my wife's come back." On hearing this, Kabongo was angry, and said, "No, I won't let you take her from me; she's my wife." Thus the altercation grew, and they almost came to blows.
>
> Kabongo had killed a bull elephant, and intended to give the tusks to the chief. However, owing to Mukoka taking me from him he hid his ivory in the forest, and threatened to kill some of Mukoka's people in revenge. Mukoka was afraid of Kabongo's threats, and sold me to a band of West Coast slavers who had just turned up. Said he, "If I'm not going to have her, neither shall he." He sold me to the Biheans, and I started, a slave bound for the West Coast. Immediately I left, Mukoka caught Kabongo and killed him.
>
> On the road west I took refuge with Inansala, Msidi's sister, who hid me in

13. Dan Crawford came from the Congo Free State to Northeastern Rhodesia in 1893 and met the officer in charge at Kalungwishi, an isolated youth quite baffled by Africa, "a miniature edition of Great Britain in breeches, the death sentence in his power." "There he is, day by day, looking into our wild unknown Interior, two big business-looking revolvers ever lying on his table, and full of forebodings" (1912:406). See also Tapson 1955:89–90.

one of her houses. Shortly after, she was caught and eaten by a lion. On account of her death I was afraid, came out of hiding, and travelled to the mission station. At this time I had never heard the Gospel, and was very ignorant.

I met a man named Wafwilwa, who, seeing me alone, asked me to be his wife. I refused at first, but he persisted, and would not leave me. I had need of a protector, so finally gave in, and became his wife. We lived near to the mission at Lufoi. Wafwilwa, with two others, was sent to build a mission house on Lake Mweru. We women accompanied them there. On arrival he was sent to the Government Post Office with mission letters, and Wafwilwa insisted on my going with him. His reason for my going soon appeared.

On arrival at Kalunguisi, in British territory, he sold me secretly to some Arabs for calico. I overheard whispered conversation among the Arab traders. Said one of them, "She's very pretty" (*Mzuri sana*). I became suspicious, and said to them "Who is pretty?" "Oh" they said, "we're just talking." Then I heard someone say, "She's the slave they're buying." I became afraid and began to cry. Shortly afterwards the Arabs came to me and said: "You're our slave now. Go into the house and sleep; it's night." Then I knew I had been sold again. I refused to enter the house, but my refusals were met by force.

I was pushed inside the house, and a woman kept guard over me. Wooden bars were put across the doors to prevent my escape. The woman was soon fast asleep, while I kept awake. I got up in the middle of the night, removed the bars, and getting out, ran to the soldiers' head-quarters in the Government location. I hid there. In the morning the Arabs, finding their slave escaped, went to Wafwilwa and made him disgorge his ill-gotten gains.

The soldiers threatened to report the matter to the magistrate, but Wafwilwa paid them up, and begged them to say nothing. They then handed me back to him; we recrossed the Lake and rejoined our friends. Mishi-Mishi was then a Christian, and on hearing my story was angry with Wafwilwa. I refused to live longer with him.

Mr. Campbell then came from the west coast, via Lufoi. A man in his caravan named Kawimbe, nephew of the chief Mwemmena, asked me to be his wife. I married him. Wafwilwa, seeing this, sent in his account for my keep while I was with him, and Kawimbe paid him a gun. Thus I was enslaved for the tenth and last time. (Campbell 1934:211–13).

Luapula, Northeastern Rhodesia, 1899–1911

Johnston Falls, where Campbell and his entourage moved in 1899, was a typical colonial outpost with its own dependent community of police, messengers, and traders. The spot had a natural advantage, being one of the main ferrying points on the Luapula and a center of fishing and fish trading. People from the plateau came with hoes, axes, beads, cloth, and food to exchange (Campbell 1934:114). Johnston Falls did not continue to develop as a major center, however, for it was malarial. The administration regrouped on the plateau at Fort Rosebery (Mansa) and launched a campaign against sleeping sickness in 1908 which forced most people to move from the tsetse fly–infested valley. The circulation of population between the Belgian and British territories took on new dimensions, however, reflecting different modes and levels of tax collection, the lack of forced resettlement on the Belgian banks of the river, and the opening of the Katanga copper mines for which labor recruits were sought in Northeastern Rhodesia. The flow of labor expanded especially because the local economy of resettled people was weak and officials left no question about the alternatives. Those who did not enter the wage labor market, preferably working in Rhodesia, were threatened with three months on a chain gang.[14] The inducements of high wages offered artisans in Elisabethville, the mushrooming capital of Katanga, very nearly stripped the Mbereshi Mission of its industrial personnel.[15]

The high point of the Johnston Falls mission station may have been the spontaneous movement of conversion that took place in 1905. For the Plymouth Brethren, the "end of sterile years" came at the same time at Luanza, Johnston Falls, and Koni (Crawford 1912:473). Campbell had called on the chiefs and headmen shortly before the wave hit Johnston Falls to complain that their people were unreceptive. The first break then came when an important *nganga* (medicine man) rose in church to declare his conversion. A group of seven came forward the next Sunday: and "a few Sundays after there were eleven more, and I got frightened and stopped them. I was afraid that the thing would become popular and they did not understand the step they were taking" (Campbell 1934:180). The backbone of the new movement, it emerged, was not chiefs and headmen but older women. In the homely terms of the Scots, it was "grannies," the advisors to young girls and women, who became the foremost evangelists. Their female converts often resettled in the mission community at Johnston Falls (Campbell 1934:183). There are hints that revival also occurred in the secret societies that provided an alternative way of defining affiliation in the first decade of the twentieth century. Missionaries of course regarded secret societies as seats of spiritual opposition, and they alleged that families broke up because of the increasing militancy of societies demanding that their members all be initiated (Campbell 1934:160; Crawford 1912:234–35). For a variety of reasons which deserve more research, widows and isolated women became the preponderant element in the early Christian church.

A narrative of Bwanikwa's life as a Christian at Johnston Falls must be compiled from Campbell's writings. It will be recalled that when she returned to Luanza from Kalungwishi, Bwanikwa had turned for protection

14. C.W.M., R. S. Wright to LMS Secretary, December 8, 1908, Central Africa Correspondence Box 15.
15. C.W.M., B. R. Turner to Hawkins, August 30, 1912, Correspondence Box 15.

to one of Msiri's former functionaries, a convert in mission employment.
Campbell recalled her at this time as "still a slave to her ninth master, and
wearing the sad expression so often seen in Bantu women of middle age,"
but regularly attending services (Campbell 1934:83). She probably came
into the possession of Kawimbe, Campbell's servant, shortly before they
moved back to the Lufira Valley to be near Msiri II. Part of the celebration
of the missionary's return had been the presentation of girls by the leading
Yeke; four from Msiri II and two from each of his principal officials. Other
people were deposited in the "freed slave home" after the Belgian Captain
Verdick defeated the "Arabs" and dispersed the Swahili commercial settlements. Still more were ransomed from traders by the missionary himself.
To all of these, Bwanikwa was an exception—she had joined voluntarily
(Campbell 1934:45).

The relationship of Bwanikwa with her husband was good, except that
"at times he would taunt her with the gun he had paid for her" (Campbell
1916:20). Her conversion following a serious illness was publicly celebrated by baptism before she left Katanga for Johnston Falls. It is uncertain, however, how long she worked for wages in the missionary household. She became especially close to Campbell's wife: "She is my wife's
right hand and true helper, yea, more, a real companion and sister"
(Campbell 1916:28). At Johnston Falls, she embarked on more independent activities:

> She did not so much as hint that she would like our help. She set to work. She
> was a potter, and in her spare time she dug clay, and moulded and baked cook-
> ing pots and water jars. These she sold or bartered for something else, which
> she sold again, taking care of the profits. She cultivated and planted, and dis-
> posed of the produce. She kept fowls, and sold eggs and chickens. She bought
> breeding goats, and tended them, and traded the surplus, with the result that in
> course of time she had gathered together sufficient money to buy an elephant
> gun. She bought it at Nkomba's village, on the Luapula, and adding an expen-
> sive shawl which she had bought as interest, she went to her husband, paid her
> debt, and redeemed herself.

Kawimbe "received her on the new footing of a free woman and his wife"
(Campbell 1916:24). "The neighbours knew, and in the villages along the
Luapula river, near Johnston Falls, the people found out."

> We, too, saw the difference in their relationship. As a free woman, side by
> side, he and she went off to their fields together. They ate together at home, an
> unusual thing among Africans. They sat and chatted together on the veranda of
> their house, and speaking of each other to outsiders there was the tone of def-
> erence and respect formerly lacking. About this time her husband made a
> profession of conversion . . . (Campbell 1916:25–26)

Bwanikwa satisfied missionary standards as a model for other women, being "diligent in business" and providing "a godly example" of domestic duty (Campbell 1916:28–29). She became known as a doctor, treating women in particular, and in 1905 she led other women evangelists on extended visits to villages, "at her own expense" (Campbell 1916:28). During the last years of her life, she returned to Luba country where she once again lived within a Christian community (Campbell 1934:183).

Slave Women and Colonial Courts

Cases concerning alleged slavery of women far outnumbered cases of male slaves in the courts of Northeastern Rhodesia. A full analysis of these court records requires a consideration of all the cases and detailed knowledge of the history of the boma community and its administrative hinterland. I have endeavored elsewhere to study Mbala (formerly Abercorn) in this way (Wright 1982). Here the cases have been drawn almost exclusively from the Kalungwishi (Mweru-Luapula) District Office, a choice that was made because Kalungwishi appears in Bwanikwa's narrative and was one of the two bomas which dealt with cases in the Luapula area at the turn of the century. Had she gone to a colonial court, it would have been either to Kalungwishi or to Fort Rosebery. Although this paper concentrates on Kalungwishi, a reading of court records from Abercorn, Kasama, Luwingu, Fort Rosebery, and other neighboring administrative centers confirms that the disputes heard at Kalungwishi were not unusual.[16]

Kalungwishi had become a rather quieter, less pugnacious place by the turn of the century than it was when Bwanikwa first encountered it in the early 1890s. Kazembe had capitulated, and the more settled early colonial situation redefined official functions. These included tax collection, enforcement of sleeping sickness regulations, enumerating labor, keeping an eye on the Congo border, and presiding over a small commercial and salaried nucleus in Kalungwishi itself. Court was held as cases arose.

Consciousness and Protest

The very existence of missionary patrons with antislavery convictions and the capacity to grant refuge affected women's consciousness. Bwanikwa's success not only in ransoming herself and becoming a free woman but also in approximating equality with her husband and her patron's wife was doubtless unusual. When did her ambition to be free and equal be-

16. There are several dozen pertinent cases in the Kalungwishi Native Court Record Book (N.A.Z., KTL). Case books for the surrounding districts contain more than 120 such cases, concentrated mainly in the years 1898–1906.

come fully crystallized? Campbell remarked that "a new hope seemed to arise . . . when she had reached a haven and found among the missionaries friends in whom she could trust and to whom slavery was abhorrent" (Campbell 1916:24). The opportunity that the colonial courts offered for the conduct of disputes contributed, too, to a more focused consciousness and gave new scope for manipulation.

Before turning to the conditions protested by slave women, let us consider how the ambiguities shrouding female status could be stripped away. As Arnot and other sources attest, absorption phrased in familial terms was well understood as a means of social control preferable to active coercion of slaves. The real status of a dependent women remained murky, and women resisted adverse clarification. Reluctance to give way psychologically to slave status is evident from the testimony of a certain woman called Mwawa:

> On my mother's death I lived in Lubwebwe's village and for some reason or other (I was too young then to know) he [Lubwebwe] gave a doctor some things in connection with a milando [dispute]. When my sister Chishala gave birth to a child and this child grew up Lubwebwe married her. I thought this was funny. He says he is an uncle of mine and yet he marries his grand-niece. After a long time he eventually told us we were his slaves. This child who had married Lubwebwe had a child and it was burnt one night when lying asleep. Lubwebwe was not at home at the time but when he returned, he found the child very sick: the wounds were not healed and the child eventually died. Lubwebwe then accused us, his slaves, of killing the child and told us not to bury the child till we had given him goods. We had nothing to give him but gave him a string of beads. Then he allowed us to bury the child. . . . I began to think about it and came to the conclusion that Lubwebwe was not my uncle at all, that I and my sisters were slaves only. So we looked for some of our male relatives to set us free. Then my son came to visit us and I told him about it. That day Lubwebwe beat me and told me next day he was going to take me to Mushoba to sell me as a slave. (N.A.Z., KTL Civil 11, 1908)

The legal distinction between free and slave was very often driven home when damages requiring compensation were assessed. In Garenganze, the life of a free person was compensated by the payment of slaves, the life of a slave by payment of goods (Arnot 1889:242). Slaves conscious of their status knew what had been paid for them, and Bwanikwa is representative in giving precise detail about her initial sale "for a packet of gunpowder." The usual payment for slaves was a mixture of petty commodities reflecting the near-currencies prevailing in their localities.[17] Overt sale

17. Examples of payments in the latter nineteenth century are: eight hoes and two rolls of tobacco; fifteen pieces of calico and one load of salt; three hoes and two locally woven cloths; and eight hoes, one load of salt, and four yards of calico (N.A.Z., KTL).

and the handing over of trade goods set a seal on slave status that could be legally broken on the slaves' part only by ransom.

The strategies of a female caught in slavery included many extralegal measures. As a recapitulation of Bwanikwa's actions will show, these strategies ran a gamut from accommodation, to strategic alliances, to escape. The first time she broke with a master, during the dispersal from Bunkeya, she allied herself with a fellow slave who was nevertheless an important man. Reentry into an organized community was difficult in the disturbed conditions, and Kazembe wanted a high price (Bwanikwa herself) for taking in the refugees. Refusing that option, they were obliged to retreat to Mukoka, the very ex-husband, master, village head from whom they had separated. Bwanikwa was more isolated in the subsequent sequence; she ran away from the Biheans, invoked the protection of Msiri's sister, a remnant leader of the Garenganze state, and finally returned independently to the center of Garenganze, to Lufoi and the missionaries. There she could not sustain a non-slave status. At Kalungwishi she again ran away from alien traders. Once back at Luanza, she appealed to a convert with authority in the African community, who was a former lieutenant of Msiri. It was only after she became attached to a very powerful patron, Campbell, that the social base for her final self-ransom was established.

The quest for legal emancipation through the payment of ransom outside the colonial courts sometimes met with frustration and led to appeal there, as Nasila's 1907 testimony before the Mweru-Luapula court indicates:

> I was the wife of Kazembe Kanyumbo and he said I was a slave. I took beads, value £1 and gave them to Kazembe, who released me. Kazembe Kanyumbo died and Kazembe Kambwali took over his wives and sent me back to my mother. He then took me and I lived with Kazembe Kambwali. I agreed to this and lived in his huts. Now he has taken me and given me to his capitao Sakaliata. I refused as I was not a slave and I took some beads and calico and gave them to Sakaliata. Sakaliata refused to release me. (N.A.Z., KSL AAA, 1908)

Colonial men also failed to understand the intense desire of women to perform a formal act of self-emancipation. An insistent woman caused embarrassment to J. E. Stephenson after he left the service of the British South Africa Company and became a settler. The complainant was a former nursemaid whom a chief had given to one of Stephenson's wives and who later married his cook. After the cook's death, she demanded the right to ransom herself, and when Stephenson refused, saying she was not a slave, she appealed to the District Officer. As Stephenson wrote:

Technically in her own eyes she was still Chisimongana's "slave" though she had had no job and had been doing exactly as she liked for several years previously, ever since she had married the cook. However not a bit of it—she was, she insisted, a slave, as Shaiwira had presented her as such to Chisimongana . . . and she insisted she must pay her mistress £2 in order properly to purchase her freedom.[18]

In popular perception, there was an additional definition of freedom. Women wanted to be reunited with their kinsmen or close friends, often in a cultural homeland. The missionaries were chagrined that their ideas of freedom were not acceptable to the women who lived with them as liberated slaves; they ruefully admitted that such women felt themselves slaves still, so long as they had not returned home to their relatives (Crawford 1912:219). Such reunions did eventually flourish, especially after colonial pacification curtailed slave trade and promoted lineage calculations. But once again, caution is advised in balancing the ideal against the real exercise of options. Six freed girls had once been delivered by Congo Free State officials to Campbell for fostering. By World War One, three were "Christian mothers," that is, absorbed into a new community; one had returned to long lost relatives; one had been lost track of; and one was a prostitute at Elisabethville (Campbell 1916:21).

In resolving the status of slave wives, the courts often took the step beyond facilitating ransom of calling for bridewealth payments in order to legitimize the marriage and secure the rights of husbands against resurgent lineage claims (N.A.Z., KTL Civil 63, 1906). Husbands had however to give up rights of ownership. One witness before the Mweru Luapula court, Mumba, stated: "I was taken from my village and made a slave long ago. . . . I was taken to CFS. There Simba's men caught me and took me to Kilwa Island (in Lake Mweru). Simba gave me in marriage to another slave of his Muziowandevu who is still living with me" (N.A.Z., KTL Civil 14, 1904). Muziowandevu claimed that she was not a slave and agreed to pay bridewealth to Mumba's rediscovered relatives to retain her as a wife.

Consciousness of slave status did not necessarily lead to actions aimed at ending it. A dependent enjoying relatively favorable conditions and without a relative to bring a case remained quiet. Those who arrived in court, on the other hand, sought relief from one of two sorts of situations: being subject to two masters, or being threatened with sale and/or physical abuse.

Aggravation in a slave woman's life often arose from having multiple masters. This condition sometimes surfaced belatedly. A chief or headman

18. Stephenson 1937:246. Lewanika in 1906 had accepted a fixed rate of £2 for compensation/ransom in the Barotseland Protectorate, and it prevailed in Northwestern Rhodesia. No equivalent regulation was made in Northeastern Rhodesia.

giving a woman to a client as a wife often retained certain property rights in her, as the woman well knew. Chondwa complained: "I am a slave of Musesya. Long ago I was given to Musesya by Chiwanampembe of Belgian Territory. Musesya gave me as a wife to Chiembere, a . . . native of his village, and I bore him one child. I am still Musesya's slave and want my release" (N.A.Z., KTL Civil 27, 1904). The cases already cited show that a particularly dangerous moment for a slave woman came when her owner died and his property was claimed by his heirs. Rights of owners prevailed, on the whole, over rights of husbands. Another common variant of competitive demands by two masters was persisting demands upon the labor power of women even though they had been allowed to marry. The owners in these cases were often older women who could not cope with agricultural and domestic work previously performed by the slave. Men with other domestic resources tended to give slaves away as they would a daughter, and the women's hesitancy in finalizing the transfer caused resentment. Kandegi pointed up this situation by claiming that her owner had been paid bridewealth, but then hung on: "I am Lukwesa's slave. She refuses to allow me to marry and threatens to kill me" (N.A.Z., KTL Civil 6, 1900).

Physical abuse and threat of sale were both means of intimidating slaves. Bwanikwa looked back nostalgically to the days of her life in Garenganze when Mukoka "never sold me nor did he threaten to do so." As the early colonial period became characterized by contrasting civil conditions in the Congo Free State and northeastern Rhodesia, the threat of being taken to the Congo Free State was perceived to be a threat of sale and served to propel women into court. The behavior of Kawimbe in becoming impatient and fearing for his investment in Bwanikwa bespeaks a rather different situation, however. Given her strong position within the Christian community, his harassment served rather as a goad to accelerate her self-ransom than as a plausible threat of sale.

The rapidly changing economic conditions and terms of trade in the Luapula districts after the turn of the century encouraged new modes of litigation as kin reclaimed their lost relatives, wives sought to have their marriages legitimized, and heirs tried to realize something from their legacies by demanding full compensation and quibbling over the exact sum involved. Although the colonial courts were mandated to effect emancipation, they consistently ordered compensation, and thus encouraged owners to give a full account of the price paid for the slave. Ransom thus became a way of liquidating assets in slaves even though slave trade had been abolished. The permutations of interests served by the colonial courts are too many to allow for any simple statement about their biases in such cases. Suffice it to say that they both conveyed a formal freedom that women sought and upheld the rights of owners of property.

Conclusions

Bwanikwa and others in her generation of slave women were demonstrably persons of ambition and courage, of willingness to assume normal family responsibilities and to fulfill conventional female roles. In plantation economies, emancipation was often followed by vagrancy laws and other regulations aiming to reattach "free" men to their former workplaces. In Central Africa, where slavery fitted into expanded domestic community relations of production, the reflex of the colonial authorities was to promote social control through marriage, preferably with strong principles of male dominance.

The social and economic conditions which had framed enslavement were marked by manipulation of indebtedness and calls for compensation. Women who were assets paid to meet such demands never questioned this transfer; even those who achieved freedom insisted upon sealing it by liquidating the debt. Women did protest against coercion, intimidation, and exploitation, especially when such problems arose from the necessity to work for two masters. Variables of women's life cycle and pervasive social institutions such as matrilinearity require careful attention if the dynamics of slavery are to be fully rendered. The research agenda is complex, and includes determining how general were the upward mobility and lessened sense of exploitation that were the happy lot of some slave women in Central Africa. Other women chose alternative avenues of emancipation. Attention must be given to their choices and the reasons for them, that is, to downward mobility, intensified disposability, and actions of women to moderate the ensuing conditions of slavery and exploitation.

References

Unpublished Sources

C.W.M.: Council for World Mission Archives, School of Oriental and African Studies, London.
Marshall Papers, National Museum, Livingstone, Zambia.
N.A.Z.: National Archives of Zambia, Lusaka.
    KTL, Kalungwishi Court.
    KSL, Mweru-Luapula Court.
    HM ST 1/3, Stephenson Papers.

Published Sources

Arnot, F. S. 1889. *Garenganze: Or, Seven Years' Pioneer Mission Work in Central Africa*. London.

Arnot, F. S. 1893. *Bihe and Garenganze: A Record of Four Years' Work and Journeying in Africa.* London.

Campbell, D. 1916. *Ten Times a Slave but Freed at Last: The Thrilling Story of Bwanikwa, A Central African Heroine.* Glasgow.

Campbell, D. 1922. *In the Heart of Bantuland: A Record of Twenty-Nine Years' Pioneering in Central Africa among the Bantu Peoples . . .* London.

Campbell, D. 1934. *Blazing Trails in Bantuland.* London.

Chanock, M. 1982. "Making Customary Law: Men, Women and Courts in Colonial Northern Rhodesia." In *African Women and the Law,* ed. M. J. Hay and M. Wright. Boston.

Cooper, F. 1979. "Indigenous Slavery, Commentary Two." *Historical Reflections* 6.

Crawford, D. 1912. *Thinking Black: 22 Years without a Break in the Long Grass of Central Africa.* New York.

Douglas, M. 1964. "Matriliny and Pawnship in Central Africa." *Africa* 34:301–13.

Echoes of Service (Missionary periodical of the Plymouth Brethren) 1897. "Family Relationships in Central Africa."

Fetter, B. 1976. *The Creation of Elisabethville.* Stanford.

Finley, M. I. 1968. "Slavery." In the *Encyclopedia of the Social Sciences* (New York: Macmillan), vol. 14, 307–13.

Kopytoff, I. 1979. "Indigenous African Slavery, Commentary One." *Historical Reflections* 6:62–77.

Nieboer, H. J. 1910. *Slavery as an Industrial System: Ethnological Researches.* The Hague.

Patterson, O. 1979. "On Slavery and Slave Formations." *New Left Review* 117:31–67.

Reefe, T. Q. 1977. "Traditions of Genesis and the Luba Diaspora." *History of Africa* 4:183–206.

Rey, P.-P. 1975. "The Lineage Mode of Production." *Critique of Anthropology* 3.

Stephenson, J. E. 1937. *Chirupula's Tale; A Bye-Way in African History.* London.

Tapson, W. 1954. Note in *Northern Rhodesia Journal,* vol. 2, no. 5, pp. 89–90.

Verbeken, A. 1956. *Msiri, Roi du Garenganze; l'Homme rouge du Katanga.* Brussels.

Verdick, E. 1952. *Les premiers jours au Katanga (1890–1903).* Brussels.

Wright, M. 1975. "Women in Peril: A Commentary on the Life Stories of Captives in Nineteenth-Century East-Central Africa." *African Social Research* 20:800–819.

Wright, M. 1977. "Family, Community and Women as reflected in *Die Safwa* by Elise Kootz Kretschmer." In *Vision and Service,* ed. B. Sundkler and P. A. Wahlstrom. Uppsala.

Wright, M. 1982. "Justice, Women and the Social Order in Abercorn, Northeastern Rhodesia, 1898–1903." In *African Women and the Law,* ed. M. J. Hay and M. Wright. Boston.

IV. WOMEN AS SLAVE OWNERS, USERS, AND TRADERS

14 *Carol P. MacCormack*

Slaves, Slave Owners, and Slave Dealers: Sherbro Coast and Hinterland

Introduction

Following Goody (1971), we might make a distinction between societies where land was the scarce factor of production and those where labor was the scarce factor (see also Hopkins 1973:23). The Sherbro country today has a population density of less than 100 people per square mile, and the population was less dense in the past. Today the area still has hundreds of acres of potential padi rice land. This is clearly the type of society in which labor not land is the scarce factor of production. Goody suggested that serfdom would be a feature of land-scarce agriculture societies, but slavery would bind labor to the land in labor-scarce societies (for case studies see Meillassoux 1975; Miers and Kopytoff 1977; Watson 1980). This latter prediction is quite correct for the Sherbro country.

In a more recent publication, Goody (1980) used Murdock's *Ethnographic Atlas* to make a rough calculation that slavery was a feature in 73 percent of pastoral societies and 43 percent of societies with advanced agriculture, but only 17 percent of "incipient agricultural" societies. The Sherbro country, with shifting hoe cultivation, an "incipient agricultural" economy with slavery, was in the eighteenth and nineteenth centuries therefore somewhat anomalous. However, any tendency engendered by the economic base is, in this case, overridden by geographical location. The Sherbro coast had been exposed since the fifteenth century to the demands of European trade, including the slave trade. "Legitimate" products desired by Europeans were labor-intensive, and their production further encouraged domestic slavery. I have speculated earlier (1977:184) that although patron-client relationships are probably exceedingly ancient in this area of migration and political fluidity, slavery arose in response to the stimulus of European trade (see also Rodney 1970:108, 290ff.).

271

Because the land is swampy and difficult to travel through, and population is sparse, kingdoms of the type associated with trade and horse-mounted slave raiding in savanna areas did not develop in this coastal area (see Goody 1971; Meillassoux 1975). Population remained sparse. Today chiefdoms may have no more capitalist-type commercial activity than a few small traders' shops, and some paramount chiefs' towns have less than 500 residents.

The Sherbro country deviates in other ways from statistical probabilities and theoretical models of slavery. Hindess and Hirst (1975), in their discussion of the slave mode of production, conclude with the "logical fact that no labour process specific to slavery can be constituted on any other basis than private property in the means of the production" (p. 141). Hindess and Hirst can only place slaves in a stratum of class structure if slaves are separated from the means of production; particularly from farm land (p. 127). Indeed in the Sherbro country domestic slaves were a kind of heritable property (*lok*), but the ethnographic reality in the historical past and today is that land is not a commodity. It remains the corporate estate of descent groups, and even aristocrats only have usufructuary rights to it. Slaves, incorporated into their master's or mistress's household as fictive kin, used the land much as any true descendant of the descent group used it. Land has not been a scarce factor of production to be privatized, and what precisely was wanted was slave *labor* attached to the land. Trade wars and slave raids are painful memories in the Sherbro country today, but domestic slavery as productive labor is not remembered as harsh or abusive, relative to labor expected from clients, affines, and junior kin today.

Most slaves lived in satellite villages, farming as any non-slave would farm, for domestic consumption. They produced a surplus of salt, palm oil, or other products, but today clients and junior kin—indeed the joint residential compound—does the same. The difference between slaves and others was that slaves could not change their master, but clients might change their patron, wives might leave their husband's kin group for a new husband or return to their own kin, and junior kin might shift their residential affiliation to another cognatic group or seek wage labor. This was true for the eighteenth and nineteenth centuries, and is true today.

Slaves married and managed their own domestic production. They were never used in plantation-type production in the Sherbro area. Male and female slaves farmed for their own subsistence and produced surpluses for their master or mistress, but today clients and junior kin also produce surpluses for their patrons and elders. Using gender as a variable, I have looked for evidence of domestic exploitation of women today, and have concluded that Sherbro wives are quite successful in resisting attempts by their husbands to appropriate the product of their labor. Women market much of what they produce, retaining their profits (MacCormack 1982b).

Most production was and still is for use rather than exchange. The significant difference in the eighteenth and nineteenth centuries was the presence of European or mulatto traders who delivered manufactured goods on credit directly to the area, drawing people into surplus production for the export market. Market production was perhaps better organized and on a higher level than today, when production for export is organized through the national marketing board. (The highly capitalized foreign-owned mines in the Sherbro country today are an exception.)

The essence of Sherbro slavery was not economic exploitation so much as "ownership" of persons in a social and political sense. Slaves were separated from their own descent group, were not free to enter into their own clientage relationships or marriage alliances, could not claim their own children as descendants, and were therefore made completely dependent upon the descent group of their master or mistress. Using the distinction made by Miers and Kopytoff (1977:10), they belonged *to* the corporate group as part of its wealth, as indeed kin, affines, and clients did, but they belonged *in* it only marginally. They were full dependents, but with only some rights and privileges. They could not build their own political faction from clients and descendants, nor claim ancestral legitimacy for seeking high office (MacCormack 1977).

In attempting to define marriage, Edmund Leach, following Sir Henry Maine, concluded that it is not defined by any one characteristic but constitutes a bundle of rights in a person, and all universal definitions of marriage are vain (1961:107–8). Miers and Kopytoff take a similar point of view in defining slavery in Africa (1977, ch. 1). In the further task of defining women's status in a society we must also deal with a bundle of variables.

Sherbro women have relatively high status because none are separated from rights to use farm land, the fundamental means of production. They play a major role in the production process of hoe cultivation. They control the surpluses they produce—they may market produce directly, and use the surplus for consumption, exchange, or investment. Because of a historical combination of migration and cognatic descent, aristocratic women become significant ancestors. They are therefore significant elders with rights in people who are their junior kin or (in the past) slaves. Finally, all women's status is enhanced by their being well organized in the Sande society, with religious sanctioning power. It is Sande, not men, who control the biological reproductive power of women (MacCormack 1980, 1982a).

In the Sherbro area slavery was not simply an institution facilitating

Map 14.1. The Sherbro Area.

men's greater control of the productive and reproductive capacities of
women, but was used by women for economic and political enhancement
as well.

History and Structure of Sherbro Society

This analysis is of slavery in the Sherbro coast and hinterland of Sierra
Leone, an area extending southward from the Freetown peninsula nearly
to the Liberian border. The principal ethnic group along the coast is the
Sherbro people, known in pre-seventeenth century accounts as the Bul-
lom. Mende people are most prominent in the hinterland, having moved
into that area during the period of European trade. Since the mid-seventeenth
century, Temne people have marked the northern boundary of the Sherbro
coast and hinterland.

Sherbro society is organized in ancestor-focused corporate cognatic descent groups—in groups of people descended from named ancestors or

ancestresses. The groups are corporate in the sense that land and other resources are held jointly by the descent group and managed by its elders. From the point of view of an individual, he or she has a birthright to use the corporate resources of either the mother's or the father's descent group. When adult, a person declares primary affiliation with one group by residing in its area and farming its land.

Those descent groups that originated with a person who first settled or conquered an area I shall designate as "aristocratic," although I do not wish the term to connote the rigid class structure of European aristocracy. Vast numbers of descendants are "aristocrats" in the sense that they will become respected elders, some of whom will control usufructuary rights to corporate farm land, high office, and other scarce resources. Both men and women become ranking elders who control these resources (Mac-Cormack 1982b). Other descent groups are "commoners," the descendants of migrants who entered the area later, without having made a successful bid for political power. In the past, slaves constituted a third social estate.

Political leadership has been fluid, with descent groups waxing and waning in influence. Ambitious people used slaves and clients in the past, and use clients today to clear new land and produce surpluses that can be used for political ends. In this way individuals gained political hegemony over areas, entitling their descendants to be *sem tha che*, "principal people," and holders of political office (see for example P.P., Rowe, January 28, 1876).

Ram is the Sherbro word for corporate cognatic descent group, and people who derive their social identity in descent groups by birthright are *ram de*. Slaves were not ram de, having been separated from their natal descent groups and attached, without full rights, to the groups of their master or mistress. In subsequent generations some might transcend this status (see MacCormack 1977:195ff.).

Descent groups have varying genealogical depth. Some originated in the seventeenth century, and others predate them, probably by centuries. For example, the Caulker descent group began after an English trader named Thomas Corker came from London to the Sherbro country in the service of the Royal African Company. He married a prominent Sherbro woman of the very old, aristocratic Ya Kumba descent group. Mulatto descendants became coastal traders, then chiefs in the area (Fyfe 1962:10; MacCormack [Hoffer] 1971:86ff.). Descendants claimed political legitimacy through that aristocratic woman, augmenting their claim through the use of weapons, wealth, and diplomatic skill in negotiating in the English language with colonial administrators.

These descent groups are clans in the sense that today's living descendants cannot name all genealogical links to the founder. They are also segmented, with groups of shallower genealogical depths constituting named subgroups that have competed with each other for political office and control of trade spheres (MacCormack [Hoffer] 1971:64ff.). The present-day head of a descent group bears a title which is the name of the founding ancestor or ancestress. As a term of address, the title includes the gender of the founding member and a possessive. The latter connotes respect, meaning "my elder whom I respect as my parent." It also connotes descent in the sense that a descent group possesses rights in its members. Reciprocally, the members have rights to good leadership, protection, and blessings from elders and ancestors/ancestresses.

In the Sherbro language, *mano* means people who participate by birthright in their ancestral cognatic descent groups. *Wono* were those persons separated from their ancestral group by capture or by having been pawned; they were attached, without full rights of membership, to a master's or mistress's descent group. *Wono* approximates the meaning of the English word slave. Individual freedom is not spoken of as a right or an ideal. In the past, as today, no one who was a "free" individual felt secure if detached from his or her corporate group.

Wono were a kind of property, and the Sherbro language has two words for property. *Kuu* means corporate property which is shared by all in the household or the descent group. For example, farm land, which is not a scarce resource, is kuu, and members of a descent group have a birthright to use it. *Lok* is heritable property belonging to an individual which may be sold, given away, or passed on to an heir.

These property terms apply to things and persons. Wono (slaves), involuntarily transferred to a master, were lok: property which might be bought, sold, and inherited. Slaves were not fully absorbed into their master's or mistress's descent group, never becoming part of its corporateness. They did not become kuu, but remained lok. (See MacCormack 1977:187ff.). Descendants of slave women and ram de men were more likely to be absorbed than descendants of slave men and ram de women, indicating some patrilineal bias within the institution of slavery that was absent from ordinary Sherbro descent ideology.

Marriage

In parts of East Africa, the social position of a wife "bought" with bridewealth may be similar to that of a slave (Gray 1960). However, this emphatically was not the case in the Sherbro country. Firstly, a slave (lok) was involuntarily transferred to a social group, but wives were seldom sent into marriage and virilocal residence without their consent.

Secondly, wives were the alliance link between descent groups, and an abused wife would be protected by her concerned kin. Slaves were separated from their descent group and were not an alliance link, nor did they have a group of kin who were concerned for their welfare and would mediate on their behalf. If a wife had been lazy she would be sent back to her kin, but a slave could be punished and made to conform to expectations, up to certain limits. When a marriage had failed, and differences between the two kin groups could not be successfully arbitrated, a wife could obtain a divorce, whereas slaves could not leave their master or mistress.

Thirdly, payment of bridewealth functioned to guarantee the rights of a child in its mother's and its father's cognatic descent groups. Children born into slavery, especially if they had a slave father, had no rights through their biological parents, who could only be members with limited rights in their master's descent group.

Fourthly, some wives became holders of political office, quite impossible for a slave without genealogical legitimacy or a group of his or her own kin as political supporters. Wives controlled agricultural surpluses and other wealth, sometimes using them to political ends, while slaves could not own any property, either in goods or in persons (MacCormack 1977, 1982b).

Finally, if a husband and his kin had wronged a wife, she could call upon support from her local chapter of Sande, the women's sodality (MacCormack 1979). If the husband and his kin had contravened Sande ancestral laws by being disrespectful to his wife, he could be fined by local officials of Sande. Slaves were initiated into Sande and Poro, the men's sodality, but they never rose to hold office and political power in those secret societies, and were probably only protected in very flagrant cases.

European Traders and Sherbro Descent Groups

European trade, including the slave trade, began in the 1460s when Portuguese ships began to call along the coast. Trading opportunities attracted Mende, Temne, Susu, and Fula, as well as Europeans, to this coastal area. Traders could only operate under the patronage of Sherbro notables. European traders certainly did not go into the hinterland of Sierra Leone to capture slaves, but entered into multistranded relationships with Sierra Leonean middlemen and middlewomen. Indeed, whether they realized it or not, they fitted into the classic Sherbro role of client to their black patron. They gave their Sherbro patron gifts, extended credit, and often upgraded their status from client to affine by taking a woman of the middleman's descent group as wife. (MacCormack [Hoffer] 1971:119ff.;

MacCormack 1982b; S.L.A., Lawson, December 15, 1877; February 13, 1879. See also Brooks, below, p. 296.)[1]

The aristocratic women who were wives of European traders became prime mediators between the trader and his middlemen, in a very strong position, publicly identified with trade (Martin and Spurrell 1962:x–xi; Caulker Manuscript 1908, part 2:27). Some children or more distant descendants of those unions successfully bid for political prominence, citing descent from the aristocratic "mother" (ancestress) to legitimize their claim (Lewis 1954:103; Caulker Manuscript 1908). Cognatic descent groups thus functioned to rapidly absorb male migrants. In the first generation, male traders might progress from clients to affines, and in the next generation their children became ram de (members of the aristocratic descent group) through their mothers.

The process of European traders entering clientage and then affinal relationships with an indigenous ruling group is illustrated by the family history of John Ormond, also known along the Sherbro coast as Mungo John, or Mulatto Trader. He was the son of a European who married an aristocratic African woman. While a boy, he was educated in England, returning to the coast in about 1758. He worked as an apprentice at the trading station on Bunce Island in the Sierra Leone River, but then went to join his mother, who has been described as a paramount chief at Rio Pongas in what is now Guinea. He took over his father's trading station there and built up the slave trade through raids that depopulated the area between Rio Pongas and Grand Bassam. He is said to have founded a secret society similar to Poro, the ubiquitous men's sodality in Sierra Leone, using it for his own and his agents' protection. Presumably he used young initiates as a force of warriors (see Little 1965–66). He loaned European goods to his mother's sub-chiefs, and if they did not repay the debt in slaves or forest products he raided their villages (Butt-Thompson 1926: 58–59.).

Wives as Mediators between Groups

Canray Ba Caulker, a Sherbro chief in the mid-1800s, initiated raids and wars for control of trade spheres along the Sherbro coast. In one account, bodies were piled in a great heap following a battle. Survivors

1. Mouser (below, p. 334) describes the familiar process of European traders becoming "strangers" (clients) to local "landlords" (patrons). In Guinea, as in coastal Sierra Leone, these traders commonly received a wife or wives from their patron. Mouser speculates that these wives were slave wives and therefore any daughters of these unions—who may have been prominent traders themselves—had weak matrilateral ties to indigenous kin. Ethnographic and historical evidence from the Sherbro coast of Sierra Leone clearly indicates that wives given to resident European traders were daughters, sisters, or other high-ranking

pleaded for mercy. One who was spared effected an alliance for peace between his own people and the Caulker chief. "To show their loyalty they brought about a connection between them and the monarch by giving him a wife [who was] a daughter of one of their chiefs, and when she was accepted they were sure that they were safe from any invader" (Caulker Manuscript 1908, part 1:42–43).

Another Caulker chief, Thomas Stephen Caulker, who died in 1871, acted as patron and middleman for traders and missionaries alike. Merchants made "customary ceremonies" to him, then turned imported goods over to him. He summoned his sub-chiefs and headmen, passed goods on to them, and collected primary products in return. "This was the means of making him financially strong, and presents in money and kind, together with new wives, were brought to him from all parts of the country" (Caulker Manuscript 1908, part 2:1ff.). Presumably the wives were not slave wives, who could merely produce and biologically reproduce, but were wives still attached to their descent groups, the mediators in marriages of political alliance.

Women were mediators and facilitators in other ways as well. Sherbro and Mende warriors were usually young men recently initiated in Poro, the men's sodality. The Temne and other northern ethnic groups did not have Poro in past centuries. When Sherbro and Mende warriors raided Temne towns, the Poro spirit would "speak," or roar out with a terrible voice, and the frightened men would run away, leaving women and children to be taken as slaves. The Temne wanted Poro as a social device for achieving age grades of young warriors, and to draw strength from its secret powers. Sherbro chiefs were on the ruling council of local chapters of Poro, but were not the highest-ranking officials. Delegations of Temne, traveling southward, approached chiefs and ranking Poro elders in a succession of Sherbro chiefdoms: Ribi, Bumpe, Kagboro, and finally Timdel Chiefdom. A bargain was struck with Poro elders in Timdel Chiefdom in which the Temne gave five of their women to Sherbro men. The male children of those unions were taken to Yoni, a "deep" Poro place on Sherbro Island. At puberty the boys were initiated into Poro and learned its secrets. These young men then left their mothers in Timdel Chiefdom, returning to Temne country with the secrets of Poro. The first Temne chief these young men initiated took the title Bai Sherbro, and his town was renamed Yoni Bana to commemorate Yoni, the seat of Poro power on Sherbro Island where the youths were initiated. Today that Temne area is still designated as Yoni Chiefdom, the place which gave its women to Sherbro men so their sons might bring the secret knowledge and ritual of

---

female kin of the patron, and all future claims to political legitimacy by mulatto descendants were derived through these aristocratic "mothers."

Poro to all the Temne country and beyond (MacCormack field notes, June 27, 1970).

Slaves as a Resource for Aristocratic Women

In 1976, doing fieldwork on rural economics in the coastal Sherbro area, I attempted to understand landholding patterns by asking the elders in a selection of towns to tell me the history of their towns. Land is the corporate estate of cognatic descent of groups, and these historical accounts always began with the first settler, from whom contemporary land-controlling aristocrats were descended. The land-controlling groups are designated by the name of their first settler. The title also designates the gender of the founder. *Ya* is the Sherbro word for mother or respected older woman, and *Ba* is the word for father or respected older man. One knows instantly, therefore, which areas were first settled by a woman and her kin, clients, and slaves. The following case is typical, and illustrates the way aristocratic women used slaves as the nucleus of a settlement, attracting more supporters with surpluses produced by slaves until these women became considerable political figures in their own right. (Mac-Cormack field notes, November 8, 1976. See also MacCormack [Hoffer] 1972 and 1974.)

In the latter part of the nineteenth century a young man named Charles Caulker, a member of the ruling descent group in the lower Kagboro and Bumpe rivers area, made sexual advances to a young wife of his elder kinsman, the paramount chief. As punishment, the chief sold him into slavery. Charles's sister traveled to the "North Rivers" where he had been taken. She paid the redemption price for him and brought him back to live with another aristocratic elder in the town of Mambo, on the Kagboro River (Caulker Manuscript 1908, part 2:26). Charles became a prosperous trader, acquiring wealth in people. One of his wives was a woman now known as Ya Ndama. She also was from a politically prominent descent group in Dema Chiefdom, Sherbro Island.

Ya Ndama is described as having been "a very important woman," and therefore when she came to reside virilocally with her husband at Mambo she was accompanied by many of her own slaves. Probing for more details, I was told that the slaves were probably settled upon her by her kin at the time of her marriage. It is also possible that she inherited them from her kin or her deceased previous husband. (See also Brooks, this volume.)

In polygynous households co-wives are ranked, with the first wife having unquestioned authority over all subsequent "little" wives. Indeed, at puberty, girls spend months or years in the initiation grove of the Sande society, where the class of initiates is ranked. The first girl to enter the initiation grove is analogous to the first wife in a set of co-wives. Subsequent initiates learn to cooperate under the authority of the head girl, learning the ranked roles of wives in a polygynous society.

Ya Ndama was not Charles Caulker's first, or head, wife. Because she was an aristocrat, with her own slaves, she could not easily fit into the subservient role of "little" wife. The common solution was to allow such a woman to become head woman over one of her husband's satellite villages or, as in this case, found her own village.

Charles Caulker brought Ya Ndama to his town of Mambo to "greet" his kin and wives. In one version of the story, she slept there two nights, then suggested to her husband that they settle a new town. In a complementary version, she did not want her slaves to mingle with those of her husband, and wanted a new place to settle them. She suggested they explore a tributary of the Kagboro River which she had observed on the trip by longboat to Mambo.

On the voyage of discovery, as the boat nosed through miles of mangrove swamp, Ya Ndama spotted oil palm trees rising on high ground, above the mangrove. The party cleared a way through trees that had fallen across the watercourse and finally reached a site suitable for the establishment of a town. It is a ridge of land between the vast saline tidal swamps of the Kagboro river system and a 2,000-acre freshwater swamp. Ya Ndama named the place Marthyn, meaning in Sherbro "the place to hide." Some explained it was a place where Ya Ndama could come if she had a dispute with her co-wives, or where she could secure her own slaves. However, this was also a time of constant warfare between rival coastal trading families, with large-scale looting and slave raiding. A place to hide may have been an attractive prospect indeed. It was also the time after the British government outlawed the overseas slave trade. Ships continued to collect slaves along the Sherbro coast, but would hide up rivers, such as the Kagboro River, when patrol boats came along the coast.

Because there was little dry land in Marthyn suitable for cultivation of upland rice, the staple crop, Ya Ndama directed her slaves to clear swamp for cultivation. Rice yields are up to ten times greater in the rich organic mud of swamps than they are in upland farms. This may have been one of the earliest sites of padi rice cultivation in southern Sierra Leone, and the town prospered. Immigrants came and attached themselves as clients to Ya Ndama. They traded in rice and salt, or farmed. Some were sent as children to Ya Ndama to be her wards. She was undoubtedly a ranking elder in Sande, the women's sodality, as well.

Today, members of the land-controlling descent group, ram Ya Ndama, insist that they are the descendants of Ya Ndama, not her husband Charles Caulker. The elders of Marthyn insist that the Caulkers have no right to the land because Ya Ndama was such a "big" woman, with her own slaves. It was she who first settled the place. She bore no children by Charles

Caulker, but only by other men who came to visit her. When I asked if Charles Caulker gave bridewealth when he married Ya Ndama, the reply was, "Yes, he would pay bridewealth to marry such an important woman." I then asked if he was not therefore pater to her children, even though he was not genitor. This caused the elders to "hang heads." They replied, with a shade of irritation, "We do not know how they did things in those days." They then reiterated that Ya Ndama was the founder of the town, they were *her* descendants, and the Caulkers, who are chiefs of the chiefdom, have no right to be sem tha che (principal people) in Marthyn. The present-day social reality results from an ideology of cognatic descent and local-level political pragmatism.

This is not an atypical case. Thomas Alldridge, the first British Travelling District Commissioner following declaration of the Sierra Leone Protectorate in 1896, carefully explained the generalized principle that aristocratic junior wives became village headwomen or chiefs: "It must be remembered that many of these women [chiefs' wives] did not reside with the chief, but are set over villages which are affiliated to the chief's town, and they are important people, and render much assistance to the chief. There is no sort of jealousy existing among the numerous wives, everyone knows her position." (1901:114. See also Bay, ch. 17.)

Chiefs' wives who became widows could either remain where they were as village heads or local chiefs, or initiate marriages with other chiefs in the hope of setting up their own political faction (Alldridge 1901:120). The latter would have been a better tactical move for young widows than for older established widows.

After domestic slavery became illegal in 1927, former slaves tended to remain where they were, as clients to a patron rather than slaves to a master. The patron no longer controlled their direct labor but received tribute, or *mata*. Today, mata amounts to a bushel or two of rice each harvest, given by the client family to its patron. In Marthyn, the town controlled by the Ya Ndama descent group, the incumbent head of the descent group is an elderly woman. (Heads in the past have been either men or women, though all bear the feminine title Ya Ndama.) She is a widow who had once married and left the area to reside virilocally with her husband. But as Sherbro women often do, she returned to her ancestral area in late middle age, taking her place as ranking elder. One of her sons, his wives, and various wards and clients live in her large compound. Immigrant settlers and former slaves give her tribute following the rice harvest. She uses that wealth to offer hospitality to her own relatives and to immigrants, with the hope that they will settle in her compound or her town.

Speaking in general terms, Ya Ndama expressed a clear preference that wives should use wealth from client labor to attract their own kin to reside with them. Because most women reside virilocally following marriage, they are alone and relatively powerless among their husband's kin. Membership in the local chapter of Sande gives them a base of solidarity that somewhat compensates for their powerlessness. However, beyond the political potential of the Sande society, a wife residing virilocally might also build her own faction of political supporters. In the past, that faction might have been assembled from slaves, clients, and kin. Ya Ndama described slaves as lazy and untrustworthy, clients as more reliable, but kin as the people one can always rely upon for political support (MacCormack field notes, November 14, 1976).[2]

Madam Yoko, who became one of the most powerful paramount chiefs in Sierra Leone history, provides a further case study of an aristocratic woman using clients, affines, consanguineous kin, and slaves as part of her strategy for gaining political ascendancy in the latter nineteenth century (MacCormack [Hoffer] 1974). In her role of paramount chief she assisted traders, then became a considerable trader in her own right (S.L.A., Pinkett, September 15, 1884; Sierra Leone 1899:62).

Significant numbers of women have built a localized power base into a paramount chieftaincy. In the southern and eastern provinces of Sierra Leone, 12 percent of paramount chiefs were women in 1914, and 12 percent were women in 1970 (MacCormack [Hoffer] 1972:151–52).

Women as Slave Dealers

In his journal, the eighteenth-century British slave trader and evangelist John Newton described how he was virtually enslaved by the Sherbro wife of a resident British slave dealer on Plantain Island. The resident dealer was an Englishman named Clow, who was part owner of the ship in which Newton served. He lived on one of the Plantain Islands, about a mile offshore from the Sherbro coast of Sierra Leone, at the mouth of the Kagboro River. His Sherbro wife is referred to in Newton's journal as P.I. because her name sounded like those letters to him. Newton tells us she came on board European ships with her husband on social and business calls, and ran the trading establishments on Plantain Island in her husband's absence. I do not know exactly who P.I. was, but she may have been Yampai, a name—or more correctly a title—that occurs in Sherbro

2. Ya Ndama regarded slaves as being least reliable as rural laborers. Her perspective is rather different from that at the Dahomean palace Bay describes (ch. 17). In Dahomey, succession intrigues made descendants of the royal line least trustworthy, commoners more trustworthy, and slaves the most reliable of all.

historical accounts (see Caulker Manuscript 1908, part 2:1). Yampai is correctly spelled Ya m'Pai. *Ya* means "mother or respected older women," *m'* is the contracted possessive, and *Pai* is the proper name.

During a period of a few months in 1750, while Clow was away from the Plantain Islands buying slaves, Newton fell ill with fever. According to Newton, P.I. gave him little water or suitable food, and encouraged her slaves to torment him. When her European husband returned, P.I. prevailed upon him to use Newton as a slave. He worked with other slaves in a lime grove. He was not paid, and considered himself to be inadequately clothed and fed. After about a year, another British slave dealer came to the Plantain Islands. Clow was ashamed to be seen treating a fellow countryman as though he were an African, and released Newton to work in the service of the newcomer (Martin and Spurrell 1962:x–xi).

Many of the coastal traders had close trade ties with Jamaica, especially in exchange of slaves for rum. A woman named Cambeh Jangalloh had, at different times, been wife to two African traders on the Sherbro coast with ties to Jamaica: George Stephen Caulker and S.B.A. Macfoy. On at least one occasion Macfoy sent her to Jamaica, presumably to trade (Caulker Manuscript 1908, part 2:22).

Slavery and Commoner Women

Commoner women had very little to gain from enslavement, nor did they have much to lose. Their life of farming and bearing children was about the same in either status.[3] Those who became slaves were often caught in raids. Thomas Alldridge, the first British Travelling District Commissioner, described the way villages in the Mende hinterland had accommodated to centuries of trade wars and raids. Some towns were encircled by from two to four war fences, made from living trees planted close together, with their lower branches lopped off. The living trunks were densely interlaced with vines and canes that also sprouted growth. The gates in these concentric fences were closed with doors made from slabs of hard wood (Alldridge 1901:54 and 1910:281).

When raiding groups did breach these fences or enter unfortified villages, they were likely to find mostly women and children in the villages,

3. Bay (below, p. 354) cites a 1904 survey of slaves freed in the Allada region of Dahomey. Most men returned to their home area but most of the women remained in their slave households and villages. In a patrilineal society, if women returned home, they would have to abandon their children to the husband's lineage, an especially unattractive prospect for older women. Some freed Sherbro slaves returned home, but I do not know if they had to leave their children in this nonunilineal descent system.

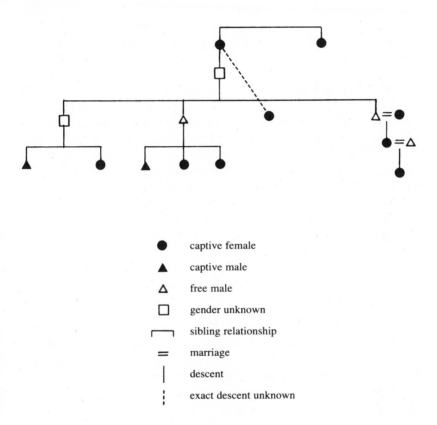

- ● captive female
- ▲ captive male
- △ free male
- □ gender unknown
- ⌐⌐ sibling relationship
- = marriage
- | descent
- ┊ exact descent unknown

Figure 14.1. Age, Sex, and Kin Status of Captives. Constructed from list in P.P., Davis, July 24, 1875.

the men either being out fighting or hiding in the forest (P.R.O., Randall, September 2, 1826; P.P., Pinkett, April 19, 1883; Gomer in Flickinger 1885:203; Wilberforce 1886:10; Hallowell 1930:6). In a list of people taken captive in 1875, most were mature women or children, kin from a single village or compound.

If commoner women avoided slavery, they might still suffer the misfortune of having to give up children, pawned as slaves. Commonly, if a man or woman could not pay back trade goods they had taken in barter, or became engaged in litigation for some other reason in the chief's court, they might be fined. If they could not raise the money, they would have to pawn someone they "owned"; that is, a junior member of their own descent group. With great stoicism, a mother would part with her own child, incurring the risk of growing old without children to care for her. Men would often make a claim upon a sister's child. In this cognatic descent system, a sister's children as well as a man's own children might inherit from him, and therefore it was the children's duty to work for him if they resided near him. Pawning was an extension of this claim upon the labor of children of the descent group. Extrapolating from contemporary ethnography according to which women are considerable traders in their own right, women may have incurred their own debts and had to pawn their own children, although I could not find records of this happening. The social tragedy would theoretically have been less for men, since they might acquire a young wife to care for them in old age, but women relied primarily on their children.

Labor of Slaves

Captives who went into the trans-Atlantic trade were either captured in raids or had been pawned. In the latter case they were part of a barter system for trade goods such as rum, gin, tobacco, guns, powder, and cotton cloth (P.P., Kortright, March 1, 1875; Alldridge 1910:280; Mac-Cormack field notes, July 14, 1970). Those who remained in the Sherbro area I shall designate as domestic slaves (wono). Domestic slaves clearly had utility in the production of palm oil and other products for export trade. They also produced surpluses of rice for the Crown Colony at Freetown.

Salt was an important product in internal African trade, providing further stimulus for domestic slavery. People in the Kagboro River area speak of notable historical figures who had large numbers of domestic slaves. One was Ban Bondo Bondopio, who lived in the upper Kagboro River area in the eighteenth century. He is reported to have acquired considerable numbers of slaves from the Kono ethnic area to the north. Some passed into the trans-Atlantic trade, but he settled many in inland farming villages, or in coastal salt-making villages (P.P., Kortright, March 1, 1875; MacCormack field notes, March 30, 1970, June 27, 1970). Yondu, the name of one of the coastal towns he founded and populated with slaves, is still a village where women farm and make salt by laborious methods from briny tidal mud. *Yondu* is the Kono word for slave.

Early in this century, the slave town of Yondu was ruled by a woman who bore the title Ya Mane. She was a high official in Sande and in Yasse, an important healing sodality which initiates both men and women

(MacCormack 1979; MacCormack field notes, July 14, 1970). Her title, designating her position as head of a descent group named after its founder, may well go back to the Mane invasion of the Sherbro coast in about 1545, an invasion led by a woman (Rodney 1970:46; Fyfe 1962:2; Kup 1962:130).

Salt, which slaves in towns such as Yondu made, was bartered in the Sierra Leone hinterland to acquire more slaves and settle new towns along the coast. In this way, persons making a bid for political leadership built up populations politically subservient to them, in an attempt to confirm a claim to chieftaincy for themselves and their descendants (Alldridge 1910:281; MacCormack field notes, May 4, 1970).

With the demand for palm oil that arose during the early industrial revolution in Britain, some slave products began to be exported. Ironically, British attempts to reorient Sierra Leone's export trade from slaves to "legitimate" trade made a market for very labor-intensive products, increasing the demand for domestic slaves. Export products such as palm oil are produced by "cooking," and are therefore within the conceptual domain of women's work (MacCormack 1982b). Indeed, the demand for these products exceeded women's capacity to produce them. From a trader's point of view, one of the "good" features of slavery was that under it men could be persuaded to do women's work, something that would be too damaging to men's self-respect for them to do voluntarily. To this day, when palm oil is made on a large scale, in concrete-lined pits, it is low-status client men who tread the oil out of the pericarp of palm fruits.

The vast majority of households in the Sherbro country today, as in the past, are characterized by a domestic mode of production and generalized reciprocities. Women do part of virtually all productive processes within the sexual division of labor. Men and women are interdependent for essential domestic subsistence. This rather balanced gender reciprocity enhances marital stability in ordinary domestic life, and underlies a relatively high social status for women (MacCormack 1982b). On the dimension of biological reproduction, women have organized control of fertility and birth through the Sande society, further enhancing women's status (MacCormack 1982a).

With a shift from domestic production to commercial production, beginning with "legitimate" trade and domestic slavery and continuing today with "modern" market export production using the labor of clients and junior kin, men may be substituted for women in the sexual division of labor. The relative ease with which low-status men were induced to do tasks normally confined to women is undoubtedly one reason why the value of women domestic slaves appears not to have been greater than that of men.

Value of Slaves

Shortly before domestic slavery became illegal in Sierra Leone in 1927, adult male and female slaves might buy, or have bought for them, manumission for a sum "not exceeding £4.00." The cost of manumission for a child "did not exceed £2.00" (Luke 1953:10; S.L.A., Department of Native Affairs, October 21, 1896). Although these figures suggest that the value of adult men and women was about equal, they must not be taken too literally. Today in Sierra Leone few things have a set price, and items such as local fines and bridewealth are matters for negotiation. Similarly, historical accounts of trade along the coast describe barter and bargaining. The age and physical condition of males and females, as well as the negotiating skill of the traders, influenced price. I have found no evidence of a set price for females vis-à-vis males on the Sherbro coast.

Describing the situation between 1870 and 1900, Alldridge gives a range of values for slaves: "I have known a man slave offered for a bushel of husk rice. . . . At normal times one head of money representing three pounds of merchandise, perhaps consisting of sixteen bushels of palm kernels or fourteen gin cases full of salt, or sixteen bushels of husk rice was the recognized price of a slave" (Alldridge 1910:281). In an earlier account, from 1830, some slaves destined for the trans-Atlantic trade were purchased for ten to twenty "bars," others for as much as eighty. The one valued at eighty bars was a young woman in good health. The following indicates the value of goods for a woman purchased by a dealer for sixty-six bars (P.R.O., Pratt, November 19, 1830).

1 gun	10 bars
4 fathoms blue baft[4]	4 "
3 fathoms white baft	3 "
4 fathoms checked baft	4 "
Tobacco	13 "
5 fathoms shallons[5]	5 "
7 fathoms pring[6]	7 "
Madrass handkerchiefs	3 "
3 fathoms satin strips	3 "
Powder	9 "
Rum	4 "
Knife	1 "
	66 bars

4. *Baft:* a coarse cheap cotton fabric.

5. *Shallons:* (sometimes spelled *shalloon*): a closely woven woolen material chiefly used for linings.

6. *Pring* (sometimes spelled *prink*): trimmings.

John Newton, the slave dealer on Plantain Island, described choosing three men and one woman from among seven individuals offered to him on November 12, 1750. Later he described obtaining two small girls, one of three feet, the other of three feet, four inches in height. He lent trade goods to the suppliers, which they were to repay when he came up the coast again. He concluded his account with some satisfaction at having "beat their price down again to 60 bars" for the two girls (quoted in Martin and Spurrell 1962:17, 24).

One might presume from Newton's account that these young girls were destined for the trans-Atlantic trade, since there is no evidence of dealers or a marketplace for domestic slaves (Luke 1953, 3:11). However, children, including girls, were often taken into domestic slavery. The girls probably would not do a full range of farming work until they were about age thirteen (MacCormack 1982b). Nevertheless, slave children were cared for until their full productive and biological reproductive potential might be realized, much as wards are taken today.

One might also extrapolate from contemporary ethnography that domestic girl slaves, when mature and marriageable, may have brought some wealth in bridewealth to their master or mistress. Today, if a man or woman fosters a girl as a ward, the bulk of the bridewealth for that girl will go to her foster mother and/or father, the lesser part being shared out to her biological kin. Since slave girls were separated by slavery from their kin, any bridewealth collected would go to master and/or mistress.

Missions

American missionaries of the United Brethren in Christ Church began their work along the Sherbro coast in 1855.[7] Some of the mission stations were founded and entirely staffed by women missionary teachers and physicians. As was the case in several evangelical American protestant denominations in the nineteenth century, women circumvented excessive patriarchal control of the church by setting up their own Women's Missionary Association, funded with women's voluntary contributions (Hough 1958). Older Sherbro people have explained to me that the church was particularly welcoming to women converts, educating aristocrats and slaves alike, enhancing the social status of all.

The earliest converts to Christianity seem to have been 1) a few high-status women and men who fulfilled the Sherbro role of patron to the

7. The United Brethren in Christ Church was organized in the early nineteenth century, merged into the Evangelical United Brethren Church in 1946, and merged again into the United Methodist Church in 1968.

missionaries without becoming affines to them, 2) their slaves who were allowed to be trained in the church schools in order to better serve their master or mistress, and 3) individual slaves who became attached to the mission, which functioned as a corporate sodality. The clergy attempted to convince aristocrats that their slaves were also "brethren in Christ." When there were disagreements between master and slave which became public knowledge, the minister attempted to intervene and mediate (MacCormack field notes, April 3, 1970). The missions also functioned as sanctuaries for people fleeing war, slave raids, and famine (Thompson 1859:335–36).

The church, of course, looked for converts among marginal groups such as slaves. Joseph Gomer, an Afro-American clergyman who survived the tropical climate and diseases for many years, wrote in 1875: "I received six into the Church lately, and dropped one. There are many of the poor slaves that would unite but for the proud Pharisees who stand at the door" (Gomer in Flickinger 1885:192). Spokesmen for the church in Dayton, Ohio, deplored slavery, but could not operate in the Sherbro country without the patronage of Caulker chiefs who were of course heavily involved in the capture of and trade in slaves (Flickinger 1889:131; Mills 1898:79; McKee 1874:127–28; McKee 1885; Caulker Manuscript 1908). In the 1870s the United Brethren in Christ missionaries purged from membership in the church at Mano all those who held slaves, practiced polygyny, were connected with the liquor traffic, or were members of the Poro society, the universal men's sodality. One is surprised that there were as many as twelve members left (Flickinger 1885:288). They must have been either women, or very low-status men, or slaves.

Mission stations paid for some children, especially girl children, who were being pawned into slavery by parents in "straitened circumstances" (Flickinger 1885:96). Some children captured as compensation for bad debts were also turned over to mission schools by a local chief (Flickinger 1885:174; Sierra Leone 1899:236). The mission station looked after these children until they were of age, then encouraged them to enter a Christian marriage (Flickinger 1885:65–66). While they resided in the mission, children filled the role of wards, giving service in households until they married. Since Christian marriage was the object, presumably the missionaries or well-to-do parishioners who fostered these children did not act as marriage guardian to the extent of collecting bridewealth, considered a heathen practice by the church. If this was the case, then the girls were functionally like slave wives, since there was no bridewealth to mark the beginning of kin group reciprocities. However, when one of these wives was treated unjustly by her husband's kin, the mission played the role of her kin, mediating the dispute on her behalf.

Conclusion

This has been a description of slavery in a swampy, sparsely settled coastal area which did not function as a trade center before the onset of European trade, and which has lapsed back into a largely domestic mode of production today. The meager indigenous economy is based upon hoe cultivation in which women play a considerable role in production. Women in significant numbers have had overt political office for as long as can be known from written histories and oral tradition. Within the ideology of cognatic descent, women are key figures in the absorption of migrant men, including European traders, into indigenous descent groups, and are therefore significant ancestresses.

By contrast, in African societies with a strong ideology of patrilineal descent, membership in the group passes through males only. But males are not biologically able to reproduce themselves to ensure the continuity of their own descent group. They compensate by acquiring as many wives as possible to bear children for the descent group. In cognatic systems, however, the descent group is not utterly dependent upon the fertility of in-marrying wives, but also enjoys the fertility of its own women for the continuity of the group. Thus, cognatic descent groups are not so desperate to acquire wives—at almost any price—as are patrilineal groups.

The status of women along the Sherbro coast has been influenced by several variables. When the colonial government attempted to reorient the economy of the Sierra Leone colony towards "legitimate" trade in palm oil, rice, and other primary commodities, it unwittingly intensified the demand for domestic slaves to produce those labor-intensive products in an area where land was plentiful but labor was scarce. Because so much of the labor in making a product such as palm oil is within the Sherbro conceptual domain of "cooking" and therefore women's work, labor bottlenecks arose within the traditional sexual division of labor. However, women were saved from excessive overwork because slave owners had enough authority over slave men to make them carry out women's tasks.

Free wives had far more utility in Sherbro social organization than did slave wives. A slave was, by definition, separated from her descent group. She therefore could not link her husband's group with her own group in political alliance. Bridewealth did not function to initiate exchange relationships of reciprocity and political alliance. "Real" marriage to link politically prominent groups and their warriors was especially important in the eighteenth and nineteenth centuries, when this coastal area was severely disrupted as a result of European trade.

Finally, aristocratic women who owned slaves enhanced their own and their descendants' political status by using agricultural surpluses from slave

labor to attract kin and clients. They thus built up their own geographically localized political faction. In some cases their descendants are local
chiefs today. A small group of aristocratic women either traded directly in
slaves or traded in partnership with a European husband. In a few cases,
the mulatto descendants of those marriages of alliance are also recognized
chiefs today.

Glossary

ba: father; respected older man.
kuu: corporate property shared by all in a household or descent group.
lok: heritable property belonging to an individual.
mano: persons who participate by birthright in their ancestral cognatic descent
   groups.
mata: tribute rendered by a client or slave to a patron or master.
ram: persons who derive their social identity in descent groups by birthright.
sem tha che: "principal people" holding political hegemony over localities.
wono: persons separated from their ancestral cognatic descent groups by capture
   or pawning; slaves.
ya: mother; respected older woman.

References

Unpublished Sources

MacCormack, C. P. (C. P. Hoffer). 1971. "Acquisition and Exercise of Political
   Power by a Woman Paramount Chief of the Sherbro People." Ph.D. thesis,
   Bryn Mawr College.
P.P.: British Parliamentary Papers, London.
   Continuation of C.1343 of 1875, Part I, Inclosure 2 in Number 15. Governor
   Kortright to Earl of Carnarvon, Report of N. Darnell Davis, Civil Commandant
   of British Sherbro, March 1, 1875.
   Continuation of C.1343 of 1875, Part I, Inclosure 13 in Number 2, Davis'
   Report, from Lieutenant-Governor Rowe to Earl of Carnarvon, July 24, 1875.
   Continuation of C.1343 of 1875, Part I, Number 53. Lieutenant-Governor Rowe
   to Earl of Carnarvon, January 28, 1876.
   C.3765 of 1883, Number 1. Administrator F. F. Pinkett to the Earl of Darby,
   Sherbro, April 19, 1883.
P.R.O.: Public Records Office, London. Colonial Office.
   267/73, 1826 Despatches. Randall to J. Reffell, Colonial Secretary, September
   2, 1826.
   267/105, Sierra Leone. W. B. Pratt, Liberated African Department to Thomas
   Cole, Superintendant, November 19, 1830.
S.L.A.: Sierra Leone Government Archives, Freetown.

Aborigines Department Letter Book, 1882–1886. Pinkett to Yoko, September 15, 1884.

Government Interpreter's Letter Book 1876–1878. T. G. Lawson to Governor, December 15, 1877.

Government Interpreter's Letter Book 1878–1880. Government Interpreter's memo to Governor, February 13, 1879.

Native Affairs Department Letter Book 1895–1896. Department of Native Affairs to Chiefs in the Protectorate, October 21, 1896.

Published Sources

Alldridge, T. J. 1901. *The Sherbro and Its Hinterland*. London: Macmillan.

Alldridge, T. J. 1910. *A Transformed Colony*. London: Seeley and Co.

Butt-Thompson, F. W. 1926. *Sierra Leone in History and Tradition*. London. H. F. and G. Witherby.

Caulker Manuscript (author unknown). 1908. *Sierra Leone Studies,* old series, nos. 4, 6, 7. Original in Sierra Leone Archives.

Flickinger, D. K. 1885. *Thirty Years of Missionary Life in Western Africa*. Dayton: United Brethren Publishing House.

Flickinger, D. K. 1889. *Our Missionary Work from 1853 to 1889*. Dayton: United Brethren Publishing House.

Fyfe, C. 1962. *A History of Sierra Leone*. Oxford: Oxford University Press.

Goody, J. 1971. *Technology, Tradition and the State*. Oxford: Oxford University Press.

Goody, J. 1980. "Slavery in Time and Space." In *Asian and African Systems of Slavery,* ed. James L. Watson. Oxford: Basil Blackwell.

Gray, F. 1960. "Sonjo Bride-price and the Question of African 'Wife-purchase.'" *American Anthropologist* 62:34–57.

Hallowell, T. F. 1930. *Life Story of Rev. T. F. Hallowell*. Freetown, Sierra Leone: Albert Academy Press.

Hindess, B., and P. Q. Hirst. 1975. *Pre-capitalist Modes of Production*. London: Routledge and Kegan Paul.

Hopkins, A. G. 1973. *An Economic History of West Africa*. London: Longmans.

Hough, S. S. 1958. *Faith That Achieved: A History of the Women's Missionary Association of the Church of the United Brethren in Christ 1872–1946*. Dayton: United Brethren Publishing House.

Kup, A. P. 1962. *A History of Sierra Leone 1400–1787*. Cambridge: Cambridge University Press.

Leach, E. R. 1961. "Rethinking Anthropology." London School of Economics monographs on Social Anthropology No. 22. London.

Lewis, R. 1954. *Sierra Leone*. London: Her Majesty's Stationery Office.

Little, K. 1965–66. "The Political Function of the Poro" (parts 1 and 2). *Africa 35:349–65; 36:62–71.*

Little, K. 1967. *The Mende of Sierra Leone*. Rev. ed. London: Routledge and Kegan Paul.

Luke, H. 1953. *Cities and Men: An Autobiography.* Vol. 3. London: Geoffrey
Bles.

MacCormack, C. P. 1972. "Mende and Sherbro Women in High Office." *Canadian Journal of African Studies* 6:151–64.

MacCormack, C. P. 1974. "Madam Yoko: Ruler of the Kpa Mende Confederacy." In *Woman Culture and Society,* ed. M. A. Rosaldo and L. Lamphere. Stanford: Stanford University Press.

MacCormack, C. P. 1977. "Wono: Institutionalized Dependency in Sherbro Descent Groups." In *Slavery in Africa: Historical and Anthropological Perspectives,* ed. S. Miers and I. Kopytoff. Madison: University of Wisconsin Press.

MacCormack, C. P. 1979. "Sande: The Public Face of a Secret Society." In *The New Religions of Africa,* ed. B. Jules-Rosette. Norwood, N.J.: Ablex.

MacCormack, C. P. 1980. "Proto-social to Adult: A Sherbro Transformation." In *Nature, Culture and Gender,* ed. C. MacCormack and M. Strathern. Cambridge: Cambridge University Press.

MacCormack, C. P. 1982a. "Health, Fertility and Birth in Moyamba District, Sierra Leone." In *Ethnography of Fertility and Birth,* ed. C. MacCormack. London: Academic Press.

MacCormack, C. P. 1982b. "Control of Land, Labour and Capital in Rural Southern Sierra Leone." In *Women and Work in Africa,* ed. E. G. Bay. Boulder, Col.: Westview Press.

Martin, B., and M. Spurrell, eds. 1962. *The Journal of a Slave Trader (John Newton) 1750–1754.* London: Epworth Press.

McKee, W. 1874. *History of Sherbro Mission, West Africa.* Dayton: United Brethren Publishing House.

McKee, W. 1885. *Ethiopia Coming to God: The Sherbro Mission.* Dayton: United Brethren Publishing House.

Meillassoux, C., ed. 1975. *L'esclavage en Afrique précoloniale.* Paris: Maspero.

Miers, S., and I. Kopytoff, eds. 1977. *Slavery in Africa: Historical and Anthropological Perspectives.* Madison: University of Wisconsin Press.

Mills, J. S. 1898. *Mission Work in Sierra Leone, West Africa.* Dayton: United Brethren Publishing House.

Murdock, G. P. 1967. *Ethnographic Atlas.* Pittsburgh: University of Pittsburgh Press.

Rodney, W. 1970. *A History of the Upper Guinea Coast, 1545–1800.* Oxford: Oxford University Press.

Sierra Leone. 1899. *Report by Her Majesty's Commission . . . Insurrection in the Sierra Leone Protectorate 1898.* London: Her Majesty's Stationery Office.

Thompson, G. 1859. *Thompson in Africa: Or, an Account of the Missionary Labours, Sufferings, Travels and Observations of George Thompson in Western Africa at the Mendi Mission.* Dayton: Printed for the author.

Watson, J. L., ed. 1980. *Asian and African Systems of Slavery.* Oxford: Basil Blackwell.

Wilberforce, D. F. 1886. *Sherbro and the Sherbroes, or a Native African's Account of his Country and People.* Dayton: United Brethren Publishing House.

15 *George E. Brooks*

A Nhara of the Guinea-Bissau Region: Mãe Aurélia Correia[1]

Mãe Aurélia Correia was one of the most influential persons living in the Guinea-Bissau region during the first half of the nineteenth century.[2] Titled "Queen of Orango" by Portuguese and Luso-Africans, her influence among Bijago, Papel, and other African societies enabled her and her husband, Caetano José Nozolini, to dominate the commerce of the Geba and Grande rivers and the Bissagos archipelago during the 1830s and 1840s.

Mãe Aurélia is representative of many African and Eur-African women traders and commercial intermediaries in West Africa from the seventeenth to the nineteenth centuries. Termed *nharas* in the Guinea-Bissau region, *signares* in Senegal, and *senoras* along the Gambia River, the title derived from the Portuguese *senhora* and signified women of wealth and influence. The most successful of these women possessed trading craft, numerous domestic slaves including seamen and skilled artisans, European-style dwellings and storehouses, and quantities of gold and silver jewelry, splendid cloths, and other wearing apparel (Brooks 1976 and 1980a; Mahoney 1965).

The evolution of "nharaship" derives from the opportunities afforded

1. I am grateful to the editors and to Joye Bowman Hawkins and Deirdre A. Meintel Machado for valuable comments on an earlier version of this paper presented at the African Studies Association conference held at Philadelphia, October 15–18, 1980. Debra Chase, Lori Bell, and Connie Strange typed, proofed, and collated the several drafts. John Hollingsworth prepared the maps. Research on the paper and a forthcoming monograph on the history of the Guinea-Bissau region was generously supported by awards from the Social Science Research Council and the National Endowment for the Humanities, and by sabbatical leave from Indiana University.
2. The Guinea-Bissau region comprises the present-day country of Guinea-Bissau, plus the Casamance River valley and neighboring areas of Guinea-Conakry (see map 15.1).

West African women by the coming of European traders. West African societies treated Portuguese and other Europeans much as they had African traders, applying to them the "landlord-stranger" reciprocities that afforded hospitality and protection for traders and their goods, while guaranteeing that their landlords (invariably a community's political and economic elite) were afforded the first opportunity to trade with the strangers, acted as middlemen in their commerce with others, and enjoyed other perquisites. One of the most important privileges accorded strangers, Africans and Europeans alike, was that of marrying a local woman, usually a woman related to a landlord so that he might derive additional advantages from kinship reciprocities. However, if marriages with strangers were arranged by the leading men of a community principally for the benefits that would accrue to themselves, such marriages likewise provided opportunities for the women concerned.

Little is known as yet concerning female economic roles in the African societies of the Upper Guinea Coast and Senegambia in pre-European times, but it is evident that the coming of European traders provided unprecedented commercial opportunities for many women. Unlike African strangers, who were generally familiar, if not extremely well informed, concerning a society's language and social and cultural practices, European strangers possessed little or no knowledge of any of these. Hence, African wives were invaluable to Europeans as interpreters of languages and cultures and as collaborators in commerce. African women took advantage of these circumstances for their own benefit no less than for that of male relatives, with the consequence that they came to exercise a crucial role as commercial intermediaries and culture-brokers between African societies and visiting European traders, a role practiced also by their Eur-African children, female and male alike. Circumstances differed in different West African societies, but whether operating as independent traders, as intermediaries for male relatives, or as partners of European and Eur-African traders, African and Eur-African women exercised leading roles in West African commerce from the seventeenth century onwards. Nhara Mãe Aurélia is an outstanding example of such women, as were her sister, Mãe Julia, and another nhara alluded to in this paper.

The commercial roles exercised by women in stratified and acephalous societies seem to have been significantly different. Insofar as generalizations can be made on the basis of available evidence, women in stratified societies—for example, Mandinka states along the Gambia River and Wolof and Serer states of Senegambia—seem not to have become independent traders in their own right, but acted as commercial intermediaries with Europeans on behalf of male family members. By contrast, in acephalous societies such as the coastal-riverine groups of the Guinea-Bissau region, women became leading traders and exercised leadership roles in their communities; in some instances, women founded their own trading settlements.

This dichotomy may be further delineated with respect to patrilineal vis-à-vis matrilineal institutions. Anthropologists generally credit matrilineal societies with providing greater opportunities for women's initiatives, and it is noteworthy that societies in the West Atlantic language group from the Wolof in Senegal to the Gola along the Sierra Leone–Liberia frontier exhibit evidence of having been matrilineal in former times. There were significant changes during the past millenium, and many of these groups became patrilineally focused and hierarchically organized. Most notable are the northernmost of the West Atlantic–speaking societies, the Wolof, Serer, and Fula, which adopted Mande tripartite social stratification comprising elites and free persons, endogamous occupational groups, and domestic slaves, as well as other Mande-derived social and cultural attributes. They are also the West Atlantic–speaking societies influenced most early and most profoundly by the spread of Islam.

By contrast, West Atlantic–speaking societies south of the Gambia River (excluding Fula) experienced considerably less social and cultural change over time and retained more matrilineal attributes. Notwithstanding that many Mande social and cultural influences are evident, more or less depending on the society, none of these societies adopted tripartite social stratification, nor until the present century did many members of these societies convert to Islam.[3]

With respect to the societies of the Guinea-Bissau region mentioned in this paper, in the nineteenth century the Bijago, Papel, and Biafada had rulers above the level of village headmen and elders, but their influence evidently was marginal and waxed and waned according to circumstances and individuals' leadership capabilities. The Biafada had at least one woman ruler at the close of the eighteenth century, and future research in written and oral sources may identify others.[4]

For all her indubitable importance, very little information is available concerning Mãe Aurélia, and almost every documentary reference concerns her relationship with Caetano Nozolini. This is owing partly to the fact that Portuguese records were sporadically kept when they were kept at all, and partly to the circumstance that Mãe Aurélia and Nozolini were slave traders and hence sought to conceal many of their commercial activities. Insofar as is known, none of their business or family papers survive, nor those of any of their children. Likewise, no oral traditions have been

3. See Greenberg 1963:8; Baumann and Westermann 1962:367–88; and Murdock 1959:259–70. Yet to be investigated is the strong likelihood that women traders exploited membership links with titled or "secret" societies.

4. Woody Toorey was the Biafada ruler at Bolala on the upper Grande River in the 1790s (Beaver 1805:275).

recorded concerning them, although that remains an intriguing possibility for the future. Given these limitations, this paper focuses on Mãe Aurélia's historical significance and attempts to delineate some of the challenges involved in writing about her and other West African women traders.

Mãe Aurélia's Antecedents

Despite the fact that family and kinship affiliations are of surpassing importance in West African societies, nothing is known for certain concerning Mãe Aurélia's antecedents. The praise-name *raínha de Orango* ("Queen of Orango"; Orango was the largest island of the Bissagos archipelago) must have flattered her, but it was surely a misnomer. For all the considerable influence of women in Bijago society, our best evidence suggests that they did not exercise rulership (but see the qualifications that follow); in any case, Mãe Aurélia lived at Bissau or on Bolama Island, not on Orango.

Mãe Aurélia's "Portuguese" names also provide few clues. *Correia*, or *Corrêa*, was a common Luso-African name on the Upper Guinea Coast, but no source links her to a Luso-African family. António Carreira, an authority on the history of the Guinea-Bissau region, surmises that Mãe Aurélia was a Papel captured as a child in a Bijago raid, and was raised on Orango (pers. comm.; Carreira 1981:32). That nothing is recorded concerning her parents and relatives, other than her sister Mãe Julia, supports this interpretation—though scholars collecting oral traditions may yet obtain such information. *Mãe* ("mother" in Portuguese), like *nhara*, was a term of respect. *Aurélia* is an archaic Portuguese word derived from the Latin *aurum*, "gold," "that shines" (Academia das Ciências de Lisboa, *Dicionário da Lingua Portuguesa* 1976, 1:645). An American is tempted to translate Mãe Aurélia as "Golden Mama," with all its connotations in American slang testifying to wealth and influence.

Only a few references are found in Portuguese documents concerning Mãe Aurélia's sister, Mãe Julia, also a wealthy nhara. Mãe Julia was likewise reputed to have great influence among Bijago due to her "noble" lineage (Barcellos 1910, 4:160). In 1837, she was one of four leading traders at Bissau who possessed dwellings along the strip of land between the Geba River and the walls of the *praça*, or fort. Besides Mãe Julia's residence, there were the houses of Mãe Aurélia and Nozolini, Joaquim António de Mattos, and Bernardino dos Santos (A.H.U., Marinho 1837). Although an important trader in her own right, it seems likely that Mãe Julia obtained imported merchandise from Mãe Aurélia and Nozolini; when gunpowder exploded and destroyed her residence in October 1840, the powder and *aguardente* lost reportedly belonged to Nozolini. The quantity of gunpowder must have been considerable: besides killing several domestic slaves and Bijago customers, the explosion damaged many other dwellings (Barcellos 1910, 4:273). Mãe Julia's reputation as a leading member of the community was commemorated by a public square, *Largo Mãe Julia*, apparently referring to the space in front of her residence. The square was noted by visitors in 1844 and 1852; the latter depicted it on a map of Bissau published in 1864 (map 15.2, number 17) (Monteiro 1853:366; Valdez 1864: vol. 1, facing 316).

Bijago history, society, and culture prior to the twentieth century have yet to be systematically investigated by scholars. Portuguese records attest that from the sixteenth to the nineteenth centuries Bijago were far-ranging and greatly feared raiders who supplied numerous captives to European slavers. There are reports of considerable inter- and intra-island conflict in the Bissagos archipelago, at least during some periods, and outstanding war leaders occasionally ruled over several islands, but information is sparse concerning these matters. Few Portuguese and Luso-Africans were permitted to reside among Bijago, and neither they nor others who traded in the archipelago recorded much concerning their experiences, or related many details to other people (Mota 1974).

European accounts stereotype Bijago men as concentrating their energies in making war, constructing *almadias* (large dugout craft used in raiding expeditions), and drinking palm wine—leaving cultivation, house building, and other tasks to women. Bijago women allegedly encouraged male combativeness and daring by the practice of refusing to marry men who had not proven themselves valorous in warfare (Valdez 1864, 1:375). The era of slave raiding ended during Mãe Aurélia's lifetime, as the British Navy gradually suppressed slave exports from the Upper Guinea Coast. Indeed, Mãe Aurélia and Caetano Nozolini were among the last slavers to export captives from the Guinea-Bissau region, their trade continuing into the 1840s.

Though much remains to be learned concerning Bijago history, anthropological studies by Lima and Scantamburlo delineating contemporary Bijago institutions and customs provide valuable insights concerning Bijago practices in past times. Today, Bijago claim descent from matriclans founded by four female ancestors: *Oraga, Orácuma, Ominca,* and *Ogubane* (or *Onoca*). Every village throughout the archipelago belongs to one of the four clans, a diffusion that fosters amicable relations within and between islands and expedites trade, travel, and marital interchanges (Scantamburlo 1978:50; Lima 1947, map facing p. 46). All rights concerning land and religious responsibilities derive from an individual's mother's clan. Village leaders are males chosen by all members of a community; they also are usually outsiders, an attribute that contributes to their ability to mediate conflicts and otherwise act as a neutral party in intravillage affairs. Scantamburlo (1978:51) explains how Bijago society incorporates complementary female and male rights and prerogatives:

> The matrilineal descent principle reinforces the unity of all the Bijagós people, because the four clans are present in all the islands, and also it does not split the land property of the village, which is protected by the institution of the chief, always of the same clan of the village. Virilocal residence [married women live in their husbands' villages], however, keeps the real property of the village and the social structure in the hands of patrikin, reinforcing the importance of the man in the economic structure. This helps to give stability to farming and helps to unify the extended family in spite of divorce and polygyny.

A principal responsibility of the *oronhó* or village head is to preside daily at religious ceremonies propitiating *Orebok,* the guardian spirit of a village, and the spirits of ancestors that dwell in a sacred hut constructed by the older women of the community. These women exercise the crucial responsibility of consecrating a new outsider-oronhó by establishing contacts between him and Orebok and the spirits of deceased ancestors (Scantamburlo 1978:53–59).

Rice is the staple of the Bijago economy. Men prepare the fields, but the demanding eight-month-long cultivation and the harvesting are done by women. Men harvest palm wine and palm oil; they also fish and hunt, but the latter activity has been greatly attenuated in recent times by the hunting-out of game (Scantamburlo 1978:61–62). One may speculate that in past times, when men were preoccupied with warfare, women may have exercised even more important economic and social roles than is now the case. As men's contributions from fishing, hunting, and collecting decreased in times of conflict, women's cultivation of rice and other foods must have become relatively more important, indeed crucial in times of shortages, when inter-island exchanges and commerce with the mainland were curtailed. And one may suppose that appeal to, and dependence on, supernatural forces increased in such troubled times, and in this sphere women exercised an important, if not a preponderant role.

It seems hardly coincidental that Mãe Aurélia and Mãe Julia possessed such influence during a transitional period of Bijago history, a time when the suppression of the slave trade and the arrival in West Africa of increasingly lethal European weaponry inhibited Bijago raiding and presaged Portuguese conquest and colonial rule. Mãe Aurélia and Mãe Julia may perhaps be regarded as precursors of another woman who allegedly did rule the island of Orango: "Queen" Pampa. Pampa Kanjimpa reportedly succeeded her father, Bankanjapa, as ruler of Orango when the latter died without sons or brothers to succeed him. Pampa was renowned for her exercise of spiritual powers and for her longevity, reputedly being 100 years old when she died in 1930.[5]

It is likely that much may be learned concerning "Queen" Pampa's life and times by collecting oral traditions and examining Portuguese administrative records. Such information would provide new perspectives concerning the careers of Mãe Aurélia and Mãe Julia. Another issue that requires systematic investigation is the question of how many captives (with gender and age breakdowns) were absorbed by Bijago communities in times past, and by what social mechanisms.

Whatever Mãe Aurélia's and Mãe Julia's antecedents may have been, they manifestly took advantage of rights, privileges, and opportunities afforded by their ties with Bijago and Papel to achieve positions of considerable wealth and influence. Together with Caetano Nozolini they dominated the commerce of the Geba-Grande area and the Bissagos archipelago. Mãe Aurélia's daughters likewise attained considerable prominence, their careers similarly exemplifying shrewd manipulation of men and circumstances during changing times in the Guinea-Bissau region.

Mãe Aurélia and Caetano Nozolini

Mention of Mãe Aurélia's name in Portuguese sources is invariably linked with that of her business partner and husband Caetano José Nozolini (1800–1850), a Cape Verdean army officer from the island of Fogo. Together they formed an African–Cape Verdean alliance that supplanted the African-Portuguese alliance of an unknown (possibly Papel) woman and the Portuguese trader Joaquim António de Mattos.

Caetano Nozolini's father was an Italian mariner, André José Nozolini, who sometime during the 1790s married Maria do Monte Henriques, daughter of a prominent landowning family on Fogo. Caetano was the couple's second son; the first-born, José, made his career on Fogo while Caetano sought his fortune in Guinea.[6]

The Cape Verde Islands possessed a tripartite social structure dating from the time of the archipelago's settlement in the fifteenth century: a small number of *morgados—branco* (white) landowners and their families; their African slaves, principally derived from the Guinea-Bissau region and neighboring areas; and, thirdly, an increasing number of free and unfree Luso-Africans or *pardos*. Pardos shared the cultural and ethnic

---

5. Bernatzik 1933:182–87. Lima (1947:74) alludes to Pampa, Aurélia, and Julia, but asserts categorically that Bijago customs prohibited women rulers. For discussion of women's roles in Bijago society, see Lima 1947:74–79 and 140–41 (note 9); and Scantamburlo 1978:46ff.

6. Barbosa (1956?); I am indebted to Deirdre A. Meintel Machado for the foregoing information.

heritage of both Europeans and Africans, although social and economic realities constrained people of mixed descent to emulate the behavior patterns of the dominant branco (though over time, not-so-white) ruling oligarchy.

One or several morgado families controlled affairs on each island of the archipelago, virtually without influence or interference from the Portuguese army officers and officials appointed to govern the Province of Cabo Verde and Guinea (the archipelago plus the trading establishments in the Guinea-Bissau region). For most of the nineteenth century, governors received virtually no funds or other support from the chronically bankrupt Portuguese treasury, and they could raise only derisory amounts of revenue from the province in the best of times—which is to say when the archipelago of Cabo Verde was not afflicted by one of its frequent periods of drought and famine conditions. Governors consequently lacked the wherewithal either to win or to compel the support of the leading inhabitants of Cabo Verde and Guinea. Condemned to impotence by such penury, governors routinely confirmed the most influential morgado of each island as military commandant and, insofar as possible, ignored affairs in Guinea, leaving matters to such influential persons as Caetano Nozolini. Governors usually ensconced themselves and their retinues of officials and hangers-on at Praia on the island of São Tiago, and seldom visited other islands of the archipelago; and prior to the mid-nineteenth century, only one governor visited Guinea, and he fled there after being driven from office.

The proud morgado families of Cabo Verde intermarried amongst themselves, except when they could co-opt Portuguese or other Europeans who might frequent the archipelago as officials, traders, or mariners. Sometimes branco families admitted *degredados*, men exiled from Portugal for criminal behavior, including illicit political activities. Some of the political exiles were well-educated members of the middle class, skilled artisans, or otherwise estimable persons. Marriage alliances with branco families provided Portuguese exiles and foreigners with access to the limited opportunities the archipelago possessed that were not directly controlled by the governor and Portuguese officials. Sometimes, but rarely, branco families admitted pardos who either had somehow acquired wealth, most likely from trade with West Africa, or otherwise possessed unusual attributes and potential.[7]

Thus Caetano Nozolini's parvenu father was acceptable to the branco families of Fogo, and it appears that he married well. A good deal con-

7. The foregoing is derived from numerous sources. Most important are Carreira 1972, ch. 10, and Machado 1978:53ff. For the Cabo Verde–Guinea economic and social nexus, see Brooks 1980b:2–4 and *passim*.

cerning his family connections and something concerning his own precocious talents may be deduced from Caetano Nozolini's spectacular rate of promotion in Fogo's militia, an almost infallible index to a branco family's status and "clout" on an island, if not always to an individual's military skills. Nozolini joined the militia as a private on May 15, 1815, five days before his fifteenth birthday. The *following day,* May 16, 1815, he was promoted to *cabo* (corporal). Less than five months later, on October 1, 1815, he was made *porte bandeira* (flag bearer), and six months later, on April 25, 1816, he was promoted again, to *alferes* (second lieutenant). *Tenente* was something of a hurdle: Nozolini was not promoted to lieutenant until April 2, 1823. He was made *capitão* (captain) two years later, on March 12, 1825, apparently not long before he began active service in Guinea.[8] Although Nozolini could scarcely have merited such extraordinarily rapid advancement, his career is evidence that he possessed unusual leadership qualities and other capabilities—all of which must have persuaded Mãe Aurélia of his potential as a partner, for successful nharas were astute in selecting men who would be of greatest advantage in their commercial affairs.

Information is lacking as to the date when Nozolini began military service in Guinea, or whether he had begun his commercial career before leaving Cabo Verde. Service in Guinea combined with trade offered one of the most promising avenues to wealth for enterprising Cape Verdeans of all military ranks, but especially for officers. Officers generally could peculate in various ways, and the income thus gotten could be invested in commerce. Soldiers received meager pay, which sometimes was not forthcoming for months or even years at a time. Whether officer or soldier, they collaborated in trade with African and Luso-African women. Depending on a man's resources and capabilities he might attract a nhara as his partner, or perhaps a young woman seeking her first alliance. Officers' and soldiers' involvement in commerce was expressly forbidden by regulations, which in Guinea were routinely ignored.

Nharas and Their Retinues

Mãe Aurélia shared with Caetano Nozolini her personal abilities, influence, and experience. She also provided a large retinue of relatives, domestic slaves, and *grumetes* (African mariners and other hired skilled employees). Whether one were a ruler, trader, religious leader, or war captain

8. Barcellos 1911, 5:2; and information recorded in A.H.U., Guiné: Caixa 22 (1825–29). Eventually, in 1842, Nozolini obtained a commission as a lieutenant-colonel in the regular army. The year of Nozolini's birth is recorded variously in documents. The memorial in the Bissau cemetery erected by his daughters gives his dates of birth and death as May 20, 1800, and July 11, 1850.

in West Africa, power and influence ultimately depended on the number and capabilities of people one could mobilize. This was of critical importance in the Guinea-Bissau region during the first half of the nineteenth century, for the area was rife with warfare, slaving, and pillaging. Control over the woodlands and savannas of the interior was contested between the Mandinka of the Kaabu Empire and Fula supported by the Fula almamate of Futa Jallon. The situation was more complicated in the coastal and riverine areas, where in addition to competition and warring between Papel, Balanta, Biafada, and Bijago, there was sporadic conflict between Luso-Africans, Cape Verdeans, Portuguese, and other European and Eur-African traders who competed for commerce in slaves, wax, ivory, and other commodities.

The principal trading centers in the coastal-riverine areas were the arenas of three cooperative and competitive groupings: (1) traditional rulers and their coteries of notables; (2) Luso-Africans who were born in Guinea and had close kinship and commercial ties with local African elites; and (3) Portuguese and Cape Verdean officials, soldiers, and traders who might or might not have kinship affiliations with local Luso-Africans and Africans. Learning how individuals in each of these groups cooperated and competed with others is crucial to understanding historical developments in the Guinea-Bissau region, but difficult because Portuguese documents inevitably portray a one-sided and frequently grossly distorted accounting of events—when they record anything at all.

During the nineteenth century, officials who reported from Guinea, and to a considerable extent those who kept private accounts as well, were influenced to depict conditions as officials in Portugal believed (or pretended to believe) them to exist. Like other European powers in Africa, the Portuguese government made extravagant claims concerning its control of territory and influence over African rulers and societies. In the Guinea-Bissau region Portuguese claims were based on long-standing residence at two *praças* (fortresses), Cacheu and Bissau, and their *presidios* (dependent garrisons of soldiers). In the 1820s, when Nozolini arrived in Guinea, the praça at Cacheu had a detachment of soldiers at Farim at the head of navigation on the Cacheu River and at Ziguinchor at the principal crossing point along the middle Casamance River; while Bissau administered a detachment at Geba, located at the head of navigation of the Geba River (see map 15.1).

The strength of the "fortresses" and garrisons was much touted by imperial-minded Portuguese, but a sham. Except for the praça at Bissau, which was constructed in the eighteenth century with strong stone walls (at the price of several thousand lives and continuing Papel enmity), the settlements in Guinea bore little resemblance to what existed in the imaginations of Portuguese who had never been to Guinea. Cacheu's defenses

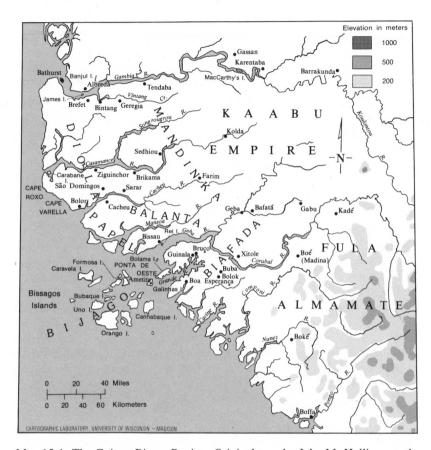

Map 15.1. The Guinea-Bissau Region. Original map by John M. Hollingsworth.

consisted of rotten and indefensible wooden palisades, and the *baluartes* (bastions) there and at Farim, Ziguinchor, and Geba were no more than mounds of dirt (mud in the rainy reason) with a few rusted and unserviceable cannon. They were garrisoned by a rabble in rags living in shambles of barracks or in African dwellings.

Most of the Portuguese soldiers stationed in Guinea represented the dregs of the Army, culled from regiments in Portugal, and culled again from the São Tiago garrison. Many were degredados. Likewise, many of the Cape Verdean militiamen sent to Guinea were criminals and misfits. As the century wore on, more and more of the soldiers were Guinea-born, mostly Luso-Africans it would seem, probably in many instances the offspring of soldiers and local women.

Officers and men shared the same iniquitous neglect by their superiors in Cabo Verde and Portugal. Conditions in Guinea were insupportable for many Portuguese, who succumbed to malaria, dysentery, and other diseases with scant or no medical attention. Commandants' pleas for money and materiel to repair barracks and officers' quarters, for new weapons and replacement parts, and so on, generally went unheeded by governors of the province and authorities in Portugal; but when supplies were forthcoming, they were almost invariably diverted to private use. Pay was continually in arrears, sometimes for years at a stretch, and was never specie. The military was paid either in *cedulas,* next-to-worthless paper money issued by governors of the Province of Cabo Verde and Guinea, or in commodities produced in the Cape Verde archipelago: *panos* (cotton cloth), tobacco, and aguardente, all generally of the poorest quality. Commandants and senior officers arrogated what they wanted for their illegal private commerce, sparing little for junior officers and virtually nothing for soldiers. Goaded beyond endurance, soldiers sporadically mutinied, sometimes incited to revolt by junior officers; but most of the time the garrisons languished in torpid squalor with the men resigned to their fate.[9]

Jehudi Ashmun, Agent for the American Colonization Society's Liberia settlement, excoriated the conditions he observed at Bissau during a six-week stay in May–June 1824:

> The whole number of convicts, all of whom are enrolled on the garrison books, and compelled to do the duty of soldiers, attached to Bissao and its dependencies, is about 250. Half of these are from Lisbon—the balance, coloured people and negroes, from the Cape Verde Islands. The whites, being of the most degraded class of the vicious, in an old European city—long accustomed to punishment, disgrace and guilt—and enervated by an unnatural climate—are perhaps of all the human race, the most depressed, spiritless and refuse. Considered as animals, the veriest reptiles are their superiors. Many are afflicted with incurable and loathsome diseases, the consequences of their present and former dissoluteness—all have been transformed to cadaverous spectres, by sickness. Ignorant, despairing, unprincipled, if they have not energy sufficient to commit crimes, they have scarce a restraining motive remaining to save them from wallowing in the most swinish vices. (1827:75–76)

Debauched and diseased, "not one in ten" of the degredados from Portugal survived a year in Guinea. Ashmun (1827:74–75) commented:

> They receive from the Portuguese Government a miserable monthly allowance of Tobacco, Rum, and other articles suitable to barter with the natives for Yams, Rice and Fish—amounting in all to about 3 dollars per man. And out of this pittance they must feed, clothe, medicate and content themselves as they

---

9. The foregoing is based on information in A.H.U., Guiné: Caixas 15–23 (1794–1834), and Cabo Verde: Pastas 54–66 (1834–56), excerpts of which are published in Barcellos 1905, vol. 3; 1910, vol. 4; and 1911, vol. 5.

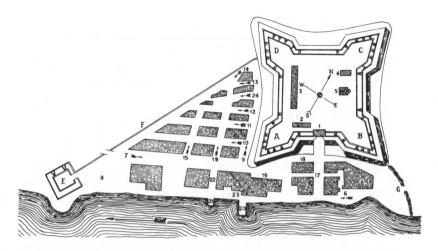

Figure 15.1. Plan of the Praça of José de Bissau.

1 Governor's residence
2 Dilapidated officers' quarters
3 Dilapidated soldiers' barracks and
  military hospital
4 Powder magazine
5 Chapel
6 Rua da Praia/Beach Street
7 Rua de S. José
8 Largo da Fonte de Pigiguite/Pigjiguiti
  Spring Plaza
9 Rua do Fosso/Moat Street
10 Rua do baluarte de Bandeira/Flag Bastion
   Street
11 Rua do General Bastos
12 Rua Nozolini
13 Rua do baluarte da Balança/Balança
   Bastion Street
14 Rua da Tabanca/Stockade Street

15 Travessa de Igreja/Church Street
16 Largo da Feira/Market Square
17 Largo da Mãe Julia/Mãe Julia Place
18 Rua de Alfandega/Customhouse Street
19 Travessa Larga/Wide Alley
20 Caes Nozolini/Nozolini Wharf
21 Molhe Barros/Barros Pier
22 Calçadinha do Banana/Banana Alley
23 Travessa de Botica/Pharmacy Alley
24 Rua do Governador Polaco/Polish Governor Street
A Flag Bastion
B Poama Bastion
C Onça Bastion
D Balança Bastion
E Fort Nozolini
F Stockade
G Poama Palisade

can. Woe to the wretch that falls sick. He is carried off alive to death's ante-chamber—a building constructed of mud and stone, covered with thatch, floored with earth, and having neither bedstead, table, chair, stool nor blanket in it! It is misnamed a hospital. I visited it last Sunday with the commandant of the place. About thirty miserables lay stretched on the ground, with nothing under them but a thin mat—and are abandoned without nurse, medicine or physician to almost inevitable death. I urged, insisted upon the addition of some little conveniences that could be supplied without expense—almost without trouble—but was coldly given to understand that 30 multiplied by three, is 90 dollars a month—and that this sum [times] 12, is 1080 dollars per annum, which would be saved the revenue of his most faithful Majesty, by having the hospital in its present state, every month in the year!

The commandant referred to by Ashmun was Joaquim António de Mattos (discussed below). Conditions did not improve in the decades following Ashmun's visit. Figure 15.1 depicts the praça at Bissau in 1852; numbers 2 and 3 read: "Dilapidated officers' quarters"; "Ditto soldiers' barracks and military hospital." To be sure, not all Portuguese degredados succumbed to disease and deprivation. Survivors might be promoted through the ranks to positions of command. Some managed to return to Portugal by various means. But for the great majority of Portuguese degredados, banishment to Guinea was tantamount to a death sentence.

Official reports substantiate the accounts of visitors to Guinea: fortifications were in chronic disrepair, if not in ruins; barracks and other buildings lacked roofs or were otherwise uninhabitable; regular maintenance of cannon was neglected so that the barrels rusted beyond repair and the gun carriages rotted, and so on—this in a land with ample resources of timber, stone, and mollusk shells that could be burned to make lime for mortar, and where skilled African smiths, woodworkers, and other artisans might be hired or purchased as domestic slaves, which private traders did to supply their needs.[10]

In the circumstances, there was no Portuguese "power" in Guinea such as was asserted in nineteenth-century Portuguese writings. The vaunted praças and presidios existed on the sufferance of African societies who wished to engage in commerce with Portuguese, Cape Verdean, and Luso-African traders, all of whom were circumscribed as to where they might reside, trade, and travel. Mandinka never allowed Portuguese or Luso-Africans access to the caravan routes connecting interior markets. And while Papel and Diola for several centuries permitted them to use overland routes connecting the Geba, Cacheu, Casamance, and Gambia rivers, such travel was progressively limited during the eighteenth century. By the beginning of the nineteenth century, Portuguese and Luso-Africans were "encapsulated": they were restricted to travel and trade along the rivers of the Guinea-Bissau region, but not permitted to travel overland between them (Brooks 1980b:13–17).

Only rarely do Portuguese sources acknowledge the payment of rents and presents to the African rulers who guaranteed the security of the trading communities and could enforce these and other demands by means of trade stoppages, intimidation and harassment of individual traders, and threatening to cut off supplies of food and water, set fire to tinder-like dwellings during the long dry season, or initiate armed conflict.[11] In times

10. Compare Ashmun (1827) with Barreto (1843) and excerpts of official reports published in Barcellos, vols. 3, 4, and 5.

11. The freshwater sources for both Cacheu (the spring-fed Bouganbor streamlet) and Bissau (Pidjiguiti Spring) lay outside the praças and were controlled by African landlords

of crisis, the "defenses" of Portuguese settlements in Guinea were not fictive "fortresses," but the mediating abilities of the resident Luso-Africans, Cape Verdeans, and the few Portuguese who had kinship affiliations with local Africans. When fighting could not be avoided for whatever reason— and most often the reason appears to have been ignorance and pretension on the part of newly arrived Portuguese military officers unfamiliar with local realities—it was the armed retinues of relatives, slaves, and grumetes belonging to traders such as Mãe Aurélia, Mãe Julia, and Caetano Nozolini that were relied on, not the rabble in the garrisons. In any event, armed conflicts seldom lasted for long before the interested parties convened for mediation and reconciliation so that commerce might be renewed for the benefit of all.

The grumetes mentioned above were men hired from African seafaring societies, such as Papel and Biafada in the Guinea-Bissau region. Grumetes manned trading craft, performed ancillary skilled occupations such as boat building and repair, and served as compradors at trading establishments among African societies. There were grumete communities attached to all the European and Eur-African trading settlements along the Upper Guinea Coast and Senegambia, and leading traders relied on dozens of grumetes to carry on their businesses and, if necessary, defend them. Command of a large and reliable force of grumetes was a Mãe Aurélia–Nozolini "trademark."

The usual circumstance at each praça and presidio was that the leading trader, not infrequently the commandant, appropriated the bulk of commerce by whatever means, leaving other traders to contend for the remainder. Sporadically there were vicious conflicts between traders competing with each other, or defending their collective interests against encroaching European, Eur-African, and African traders from the French commercial sphere to the north of the Guinea-Bissau region or the English trading sphere to the south.

The murder of the French trader Dumaigne (see below) provides a documented instance of the intimidation and violence that generally went unrecorded in European sources. Rarely mentioned in documents, but no less feared than physical attacks, were poisonings and recourse to magical forces, or rumors of such activities. In these turbulent and dangerous times the people of the Guinea-Bissau region—Africans, Luso-Africans, and

---

down to the nineteenth century (the lower reaches of the Cacheu and Geba rivers are brackish, hence the water is not potable). At Bissau, Fort Nozolini and the *tabanca* (stockade) enclosing Pidjiguiti Spring and extending to the terrain controlled by the praça were constructed on Caetano Nozolini's initiative during the 1844 conflict discussed below (see map 15.2: E, F, and 8). Remarkably, the most celebrated event at the outset of the war of liberation is the August 3, 1959, "Pidjiguiti Massacre" in which soldiers killed and wounded scores of striking longshoremen and sailors assembled in Pidjiguiti Square.

Portuguese alike—sought the protection of the powerful leaders in any area, whoever they might be, African rulers or Luso-African, Cape Verdean, or Portuguese traders associated with nharas and who possessed large entourages of armed followers. For Bissau from the latter years of the 1820s onwards, Mãe Aurélia and Caetano Nozolini, plus Mãe Julia, commanded the most powerful forces in the community. This was recognized by all the inhabitants of the trading community and the praça, including the commandant of the praça (when it was not Caetano Nozolini himself).

Mãe Aurélia and Caetano Nozolini vs. an Unknown [Papel] Woman and Joaquim António de Mattos

The leading trader at Bissau when Nozolini arrived in the 1820s was Joaquim António de Mattos ([1788]–1843), a Portuguese who had risen from customhouse clerk in 1805 to become acting commandant of the praça by 1818. Details are lacking, but Mattos apparently owed much of his success to an African wife, about whom nothing is recorded other than passing mention by Gaspard Mollien, a French explorer who visited Bissau in late 1818. Mollien (1820:327) described Mattos as a commanding personage who possessed "immense" wealth. At the time of Mollien's visit, a dispute between Mattos and the Papel ruler of Bissau had caused, or contributed to, a serious breach in relations between the praça and trading community on the one hand and the Papel on the other. Mollien does not relate the nature of the dispute, but his description of its resolution is very informative concerning Papel-Portuguese relations and the mediating role exercised by Mattos's wife, a role exercised by nharas generally.

> [Mattos] having ordered two pieces of cannon to be pointed towards their villages, the Papels forbade their wives to carry anything to the market of Bissao, so that the settlement was soon in a state of famine: the people were reduced to the necessity of eating all the cassada which grew in the gardens of the inhabitants. At last, a council assembled at the governor's house, and the affair appeared of so much consequence, that all the Portuguese attended. The governor thought proper to make the first advances. His wife (who was a Negress) was sent to the Papels; the conferences which she held with King Joseph (almost all these people have assumed Christian names) were completely successful and they agreed to an interview for the purpose of concluding peace. (Mollien 1820:337)

Mollien recounts the meeting of the Papel ruler and Mattos, the latter's distribution of brandy to the assembled crowd, and the celebrations following the peacemaking. Mollien sententiously concludes, "By such acts of weakness, the Portuguese have contrived, without having recourse to force, to win the attachment of all the Negro nations that surround them" (338–39).

One may speculate that the decline of Mattos's ascendancy at Bissau may date from his marriage in 1820(?) to Maria do Carmo Pusich, daughter of António Pusich, governor of the Province of Cabo Verde and Guinea. So far as is known, Maria do Carmo remained with her parents at Praia during the early period of their marriage and did not join Mattos at Bissau. Mattos's marriage to an outsider, however, may have contributed to strains in his relations with the influential nhara and her relatives which opened the way for Mãe Aurélia and Caetano Nozolini (with Mãe Julia's support) to challenge him in the mid-1820s. Moreover, Mattos's fortunes were adversely affected in May 1821, when his father-in-law, Governor Pusich, was deposed by a "popular uprising" at Praia on behalf of Portugal's revolutionary 1820 Constitution—an uprising that was orchestrated by Manuel António Martins, the power-broker of the archipelago during the 1820s and 1830s. Martins subsequently allied with Mattos against Nozolini and Mãe Aurélia, but too late to arrest their consolidation of power at Bissau (Barcellos 1905, 3:272–77).

In contrast to Mattos, Nozolini remained married to Mãe Aurélia and eventually remarried her in a Christian ceremony as well. In doing this Nozolini broke from the usual pattern of Cape Verdean (and Portuguese) traders, military officers, and officials who married and raised families with African and Luso-African women according to local custom, but remained *solteiro* ("single") insofar as the Catholic Church was concerned so that they might contract marriages when they returned to the Cape Verde Islands. In this and other ways, Mãe Aurélia and Nozolini established a strong and enduring alliance that enabled them to pass on to their children much of their wealth and influence.

In large perspective, Mãe Aurélia's and Nozolini's successful supplanting of Mattos represents the replacing of a Portuguese-African nexus at Bissau by a Cape Verdean–African nexus that would be largely maintained until the beginning of the colonial period. Until the 1880s, the principal challenge to Cape Verdean and Luso-African traders came not from Portuguese rivals, but from French trading interests based in Senegal. From the 1830s onwards, French, Franco-African, and Senegalese traders increasingly encroached into the Bissau trading sphere of the Geba and Grande rivers and the Bissagos archipelago. Their growing influence is evidenced by one of the marriage alliances of the children of Mãe Aurélia and Nozolini (see below), as well as those of other Luso-African families at Cacheu, Ziguinchor, and elsewhere in the Guinea-Bissau region.

Years of Ascendancy at Bissau

Mãe Aurélia's and Nozolini's rise to power may be dated from the May 1826 revolt of the praça's garrison. In December 1825, Captain Domingos Alves de Abreu Picaluga, a Portuguese army officer with no previous service in Guinea, succeeded Mattos as commander of the praça. Mattos was absent from Bissau the following May when the soldiers mutinied, led by several officers and the chaplain. A British man-of-war came to Picaluga's assistance, but it appears that it was Nozolini commanding a force of sixty Papel grumetes who played the most important role in suppressing the revolt and restoring order. Picaluga was afterwards removed from command, and Mattos returned to stabilize the situation before turning over command in 1827 to another Portuguese officer, Captain Luiz António Bastos. Bastos and his successor, naval lieutenant Francisco José Muacho, could not exercise the same authority as Mattos had before them, and it is evident that during this period Nozolini and Mãe Aurélia consolidated their position as the leading traders at Bissau (Barcellos 1905, 3:349–50; Owen 1833:152–53).

Something of the influence Mãe Aurélia and Nozolini achieved is evident from a report made by Sir Neil Campbell, the governor of Sierra Leone, following a visit to Bissau in June 1827, shortly after Muacho had assumed command of the praça. Campbell learned that Nozolini had prevailed on Bastos to furnish official papers certifying that captives shipped to the Cape Verde Islands were "domestic slaves," thereby preventing their seizure by British warships attempting to enforce the Anglo-Portuguese treaty for the suppression of the slave trade. One shipload of slaves dispatched to the Cape Verde Islands included "61 Nozollinos," allegedly members of Nozolini's (extended) family (P.R.O., Campbell 1827). Campbell's revelations, together with other intelligence concerning the slave trade at Bissau and Cacheu, provoked the British government to demand an investigation. The desultory and inconclusive inquiry that followed, as well as others in years following, were of little consequence in deterring the slaving activities of Mãe Aurélia and Nozolini, or those of other traders operating in the Guinea-Bissau region.

The 'clout' that Nozolini and Mãe Aurélia exercised with successive Portuguese governors of the Province of Cabo Verde and Guinea may be appreciated from a major setback they experienced in 1835 when Nozolini was driven from Bissau by the French Navy. The crisis resulted from the murder in February of a Senegal-based French trader named Dumaigne. Dumaigne was known to have pressed Nozolini for the repayment of debts, but the provocation that led to his assassination by grumetes in Nozolini's employ was that Dumaigne was engaged in salt trade with Balanta living along the Geba River, thereby transgressing the monopoly exercised by Mãe Aurélia and Nozolini.

French traders and officials in Senegal demanded that Nozolini be brought to justice, but Nozolini and Mãe Aurélia effectively blocked the investigation instituted by the governor of the province. Among other acts of intimidation, the grumete who had stabbed Dumaigne met an untimely death, an act which rumor attributed to Nozolini ridding himself of a witness who might testify against him. Nozolini left Bissau for the Cape Verde Islands before a French warship arrived in December 1835. The French commander compelled Joaquim António de Mattos, commandant of the praça and Nozolini's longtime rival, to sequester Nozolini's and Mãe Aurélia's property. No specie was found, but hides, rice, wax, and livestock worth more than ten thousand francs were seized to compensate Dumaigne's heirs. The officers of the praça and traders at Bissau drew up a formal protest against the French ultimatum and exactions as a face-saving gesture, but it may be supposed that Mattos for one experienced little anguish seeing his rival despoiled and humiliated.

Nozolini was arrested and for a time incarcerated at Praia, but all charges against him were subsequently dropped, and he returned to Bissau not long after the French warship departed. Although the affair cost them considerable wealth, Mãe Aurélia managed affairs to maintain their power base at Bissau, which remained as strong as ever, if not stronger, in the years following (Barcellos 1910, 4:98–107, 123). Indeed, such was acknowledged by the governor of the province on the occasion of another crisis at Bissau some seven years later. In November 1842, shortly after Nozolini had departed for Portugal on business matters, arbitrary actions by the ignorant new commandant at Bissau aroused the grumete community to attack the garrison and lay siege to the praça. Governor Francisco de Paula Bastos dispatched such reinforcements and supplies as he could spare from Cabo Verde for the besieged garrison, plus advice concerning persons of influence in Guinea who could be of assistance in settling the conflict. These included Joaquim António de Mattos of Bissau, Honório Pereira Barreto of Cacheu, and Mãe Aurélia, whom the governor characterized as "the woman who administers the trading firm of Caetano José Nozolini, . . . who is greatly respected by Africans" (Barcellos 1910, 4:311).

Mãe Aurélia's influence is easier to document for Bissau than for the Bissagos archipelago. Mattos long benefited from close personal and commercial ties with Damião, the principal Bijago ruler on Canhabaque, while Mãe Aurélia's (and Mãe Julia's) influence centered on Orango, the southernmost island in the archipelago. To what extent Mattos's and Mãe Aurélia's spheres of commercial influence reflected political or social divisions among Bijago remains to be studied. One factor seems evident even though documentary evidence is lacking: Mãe Aurélia and Mattos probably encouraged Bijago to attack rival traders. French, Franco-African, and Senegalese traders long feared to trade in the archipelago despite their attraction to its commercial prospects. Following Mattos's death at Bissau in December 1843, Mãe Aurélia and Caetano Nozolini monopolized the commerce of the archipelago.

During the 1830s, Mãe Aurélia and Nozolini developed plantations on the western side of the fertile island of Bolama. They were among the first entrepreneurs in the Guinea-Bissau region to cultivate peanuts for export. In this they followed the pattern of other slavers along the Upper Guinea Coast, which was to use captives to cultivate peanuts, coffee, rice, and other crops for sale to "legitimate" traders while awaiting opportunities to sell them to slave vessels. Their slaving operations extended to the Nuñez River, along which they had European agents and African compradors established in factories (Brooks 1975:46–47; Hawkins 1980, ch. 3; Carreira 1981:42).

Bolama's relatively accessible location provided an opportunity for the officers of the British antislavery squadron to strike at their longtime antagonists. In December 1838, a landing party from the brig-of-war *Brisk* carried off 212 slaves from Ponta de Oeste, besides seizing a schooner, *Aurélia Felix* (presumably named for Mãe Aurélia). The vessel was laden with salt and was eventually released at Freetown for lack of evidence to condemn it as a slaver, but the captives aboard were not returned nor any compensation paid. The *Brisk* raided Bolama again in April 1839, inflicting additional property losses that caused Mãe Aurélia and Nozolini to curtail their operations on the island for a time thereafter (Barcellos 1910, 4:253–58; Walter 1947:68–69; Valdez 1864, 1:367–68; Carreira 1981:33).

Although Nozolini and Mãe Aurélia experienced sporadic harassment and on occasion considerable financial losses during the 1840s as a consequence of the activities of the vessels of the antislavery squadrons, in one incongruous set of circumstances they benefited greatly from the protective deployment of warships. In September 1844, an ignorant and insensitive newly arrived Portuguese officer insulted the Papel ruler of Bissau, thereby igniting a four-month-long conflict during which many grumetes joined Papel in pillaging traders and laying siege to the praça. French, British, and American warships converged on Bissau to defend the praça and the property of the trading community. American involvement was extremely expensive in lives. Commodore Matthew Perry of the American squadron dispatched the sloop-of-war *Preble* to Bissau acting on information that there was some $40,000 worth of American property in the praça—most of it advanced on credit to Nozolini. The *Preble*'s stay at

Bissau for several weeks cost the lives of sixteen men, plus other sailors incapacitated by malaria.

Nozolini and Mãe Aurélia followed their usual practice during times of conflict: they recruited additional grumetes. By the end of the conflict they had an armed force of some 150 Papel and Balanta, for which Nozolini subsequently claimed substantial compensation from the governor of the province (Barcellos 1911, 5:25ff.; A.H.U., Cabo Verde 1845: Pasta 60; Wright 1973:91–92).

Mãe Aurélia's Children

Mãe Aurélia and Caetano Nozolini are known to have had four children who survived past infancy: a son and three daughters. Information concerning their careers and marriages provides valuable clues concerning their parents' social status and changing commercial relationships in West Africa.

Caetano Nozolini, Jr., was sent to France for education, and afterwards participated in the family's commercial affairs. Following his father's death in July 1850, he continued the family business under the name of Nozolini Junior and Company with, one may suppose, continuing guidance from Mãe Aurélia. To date, it is not known whether Caetano, Jr., married or had children (Barcellos 1910, 4:160; 1911, 5:150).

The three daughters married able and enterprising men, who doubtless sought thereby to establish family ties with the influential parents. These men contributed significantly to the family's continuing prosperity and influence during the 1850s and 1860s.

Eugenia, the eldest (?) daughter, married Dr. António Joaquim Ferreira, who in 1844 was appointed to administer the Bissau hospital. Eugenia's dowry included the settlement of Ametite on the northwest corner of Ilha de Galinhas in the Bissagos archipelago. Dr. Ferreira established a convalescent center there for patients from Bissau which became known as *Casaria* ("group of houses"). He planted coconut palms at Ametite, reportedly the first place they were grown in Guinea. Exploiting his family connections, Dr. Ferreira became a leading trader at Bissau by the 1850s, doubtless a much more remunerative activity than practicing medicine. In 1850 he represented the firm of Nozolini Junior and Company in negotiations with the government of the province. Three years later, he and another trader were awarded the contract to construct a new customhouse at Bissau. Dr. Ferreira died sometime afterwards (1853–54?), at which time his widow reemerges in Portuguese sources and shows herself to be her mother's daughter (Barcellos 1911, 5:25, 156, 264, 266; 1912, 6:60, 226, 279).

Following her husband's death, Eugenia Nozolini Ferreira lived at Ametite, managing a trading establishment and plantations cultivating rice and peanuts. Her domestic slaves wove and embroidered cloth, working in large buildings which had been constructed in times past to house captives held for shipment. Eugenia also had a factory at Boa Esperança ("Good Hope") located at the mouth of the Grande River, where there were large stands of valuable hardwoods. Her children continued to operate the trading and agricultural establishment at Ametite until at least the 1860s (Barcellos 1912, 6:26, 42, 60, 62; Thompson 1858/1969:89).

A second daughter, Leopoldina, married Adolphe Demay, a Franco-African trader from Gorée who settled at Bissau in the latter 1840s. Demay's residence at Bissau is a token of the changing times, for in the 1830s and previously Nozolini and other Bissau traders had used every means to exclude rivals. Encouraged and protected by French naval officers, French, Franco-African, and Senegalese traders made increasing inroads into Luso-African and Cape Verdean commerce in the Casamance in the 1830s, and southwards along the Upper Guinea Coast during the 1840s. Intimidation and violence as means to drive away rival traders were no longer feasible after Dumaigne's murder in 1835, so Mãe Aurélia, Nozolini, and Leopoldina may have decided that the family's interests (and Leopoldina's) were best served by the traditional African landlord-stranger strategy of co-opting a capable stranger-trader by a marriage alliance.

However Leopoldina's marriage with Demay was arranged, Demay's commerce throve, and one may assume that Leopoldina's and her family's interests were also well served. Not the least of Leopoldina's assets was that she was heir to her father's commercial establishment and exclusive trading privileges in the Corubal River (Nozolini had obtained the latter in 1843 from the Biafada ruler). Besides trade at Bissau and in the Corubal River, Demay had a factory called "Monte Napoleão" in the Grande River, also part of Mãe Aurélia's and Nozolini's commercial sphere. Demay exercised an important role for French and Senegalese commercial interests in the 1850s and 1860s by supplying reports on trade and other matters to French naval officers and colonial officials in Senegal. For several years in the 1850s he served as a commercial agent for the American consul at Praia in the Cape Verde Islands.[12]

12. Barcellos 1911, 5:270; 1912, 6:62, 198; Brooks 1970:197–98; and Valdez 1864, 1:347. Both Leopoldina Nozolini Demay and Eugenia Nozolini Ferreira are named among the eleven "senhoras principaes" identified by Valdez (1864, 1:353) when he visited Bissau in 1852.

Gertrudes Aurélia Nozolini, a younger daughter born on Bolama in 1835, married a doctor, José Fernandes da Silva Leão. Like Eugenia's husband, Dr. Leão became associated with family business interests. In 1856 he offered the services of the firm's domestic slaves to construct a new hospital. He participated actively in government affairs at Bissau, and continued to do so after Gertrudes's death in 1863.[13]

Many aspects of Mãe Aurélia's life history are poorly documented in European sources or must be derived from what is known concerning her alliance with Caetano Nozolini. Nonetheless, her importance in the history of the Guinea-Bissau region is incontestable, and one may anticipate that significant additional information may be obtained from traditions concerning her and individuals associated with her—and concerning the many other influential women of the Guinea-Bissau region.

To date, historians and social scientists interested in the Upper Guinea Coast and Senegambia have undertaken relatively little research focused on family histories and the collection of genealogical records. This is surprising, given the extraordinary interest West Africans have in their families' heritages. One may confidently predict that such studies will bring to light a wealth of information concerning all aspects of West African societies and cultures. Such research will also provide much new information concerning women's roles in past times, especially in commerce.

Glossary

aguardente: sugar cane brandy.
almadia: dugout craft carved from a tree trunk.
baluarte: bastion, rampart.
branco/a: white person
cédula: certificates of public indebtedness; paper money.
degredado/a: criminal banished from Portugal.
Eur-African: person of mixed African and European ancestry, e.g. a Luso-African, Franco-African, Anglo-African, etc.
grumete: African hired as a seaman, comprador, or skilled artisan.
Luso-African: person of mixed African and Portuguese descent.
mãe: mother; a title of respect.

13. Barcellos 1912, 6:64, 156, 165, 172, 195, 254). I am indebted to Padre Henrique Pinto Rema for furnishing me with information from the tombstone of Gertrudes Aurélia Nozoliny Leão at Bissau. Note that *Nozoliny* is the preferred spelling in the Cape Verde Islands. I wish also to thank Deirdre A. Meintel Machado for providing me with valuable information concerning members of the Nozoliny family in the last quarter of the nineteenth century; space limitations precluded its presentation in this paper.

morgado: landowner in the Cape Verde archipelago; the eldest son, who was heir to an estate; such as estate.
nhara: from *senhora;* woman of wealth and influence.
pano: cotton cloth comprising several hand-woven strips sewn together.
pardo/a: person of mixed African and European descent, e.g., a Luso-African; brown or dark in color.
praça: fortress, stronghold; public square, plaza.
presídio: military garrison.
prêto/a: an African; black or dark in color.
solteiro/a: unmarried person.

References

Unpublished Sources

A.H.U.: Arquivo Histórico Ultramarino, Lisbon.
 Cabo Verde, Pasta 55: Governor Joaquim Pereira Marinho to Ministro e Secretario d'Estado dos Negócios da Marinha e Ultramar, May 13, 1837.
 Guiné, Caixa 22: "Informações da guarnição da praça de Bissau, 1829–1830," January 1, 1830.
Hawkins, J. B. 1980. "Fula, Balanta, Papel, and Portuguese Relations in Guinea-Bissau: Fulbe Expansion and Its Impact, 1850–1900." Ph.D. dissertation, University of California, Los Angeles.
Machado, D. A. M. 1978. "Cape Verdean-Americans: Their Cultural and Historical Background." Ph.D. dissertation, Brown University, Providence, R.I.
P.R.O.: Public Record Office, London.
 Sierra Leone, C.O. 267/89: Governor Sir Neil Campbell to Lord Bathurst, July 1, 1827.
Scantamburlo, L. 1978. "The Ethnography of the Bijagós People of the Island of Bubaque, Guiné-Bissau." M.A. thesis, Wayne State University, Detroit.

Published Sources

Academia das Ciências de Lisboa. 1976–. *Dicionário da Língua Portuguesa.* Lisbon.
A[shmun], J. 1827. "Bissao." *African Repository and Colonial Journal* 3:73–78.
Barbosa, F. J. [1956.] "Notas genealógicas da Ilha do Fogo." *Revista Portuguesa.*
Barcellos, C. J. de S. 1899–1912. *Subsídios para a história de Cabo Verde e Guiné.* 6 vols. Lisbon.
Barreto, H. P. 1843. *Memória sobre o estado actual de Senegambia Portugueza, causas de sua decandência, e meios de a fazer prosperar.* Reprinted in *Honório Pereira Barreto* (Bissau, 1947), ed. J. Walter. Lisbon.
Baumann, H., and D. Westermann. 1962. *Les Peuples et les civilisations de l'Afrique.* Paris.
Beaver, P. 1805. *African Memoranda.* London.

Bernatzik, H. A. 1933. *Äthiopen des westens; Forschungsreisen in Portugiesisch-Guinea*. Vienna.

Brooks, G. E. 1970. *Yankee Traders, Old Coasters, and African Middlemen: A History of American Legitimate Trade with West Africa in the Nineteenth Century*. Boston.

Brooks, G. E. 1975. "Peanuts and Colonialism: Consequences of the Commercialization of Peanuts in West Africa, 1830–1870." *Journal of African History* 16:29–54.

Brooks, G. E. 1976. "The Signares of Saint-Louis and Gorée: Women Entrepreneurs in Eighteenth-Century Senegal." In *Women in Africa: Studies in Social and Economic Change*, ed. N. J. Hafkin and E. G. Bay. Stanford.

Brooks, G. E. 1980a. "Artists' Depictions of Senegalese Signares: Insights Concerning French Racist and Sexist Attitudes in the Nineteenth Century." *Genève-Afrique* 18:75–89.

Brooks, G. E. 1980b. "Perspectives on Luso-African Commerce and Settlement in the Gambia and Guinea-Bissau Region, 16th–19th Centuries." Boston University African Studies Center Working Paper No. 24.

Carreira, A. 1972. *Cabo Verde: Formação e extinção de uma sociedade escravocrata (1460–1878)*. Lisbon.

Carreira, A. 1981. *O Tráfico de escravos nos rios de Guiné e Ilhas de Cabo Verde (1810–1850)*. Lisbon.

Greenberg, J. H. 1963. *The Languages of Africa*. Bloomington, Ind.

Lima, A. J. S. 1947. *Organização económica e social dos Bijagós*. Bissau.

Mahoney, F. 1965. "Notes on Mulattoes of The Gambia before the Mid-Nineteenth Century." *Transactions of the Historical Society of Ghana* 8:120–29.

Mollien, G. T. 1820. *Travels in the Interior of Africa, to the Sources of the Senegal and Gambia*. London.

Monteiro, J. M. de S. 1853. "Estudos sôbre a Guiné de Cabo Verde." *O Panorama*. 10:50 *et seq.*

Mota, A. T. da 1974. "Actividade marítima dos Bijagós nos séculos xvi e xvii." Separata do Volume 3 *In Memoriam António Jorge Dias*. Lisbon.

Murdock, G. P. 1959. *Africa: Its Peoples and Their Culture History*. New York.

Owen, W. F. W. 1833. *Narrative of Voyages to Explore the Shores of Africa, Arabia, and Madagascar*. 2 vols. London.

Thompson, G. 1858/1969. *The Palm Land of West Africa, Illustrated*. 2d ed. Cincinnati and London.

Valdez, F. T. 1864. *Africa Occidental; Notícias e considerações*. 2 vols. Lisbon.

Walter, J. 1947. *Honório Pereira Barreto*. Bissau.

Wright, D. R. 1973. "Matthew Perry and the African Squadron." In *America Spreads Her Sails*, ed. C. R. Barrow, Jr. Annapolis.

16 *Bruce L. Mouser*

Women Slavers of Guinea-Conakry[1]

Along the rivers of coastal Guinea-Conakry, a number of women were active participants in the slave trade during the late eighteenth and early nineteenth centuries. Among the more prosperous women slave traders were three who became as well known to champions of the anti–slave trade movement as they were to ship captains plying the coast. These women were Betsy Heard of Bereira on the Bereira River, Elizabeth Frazer Skelton of Victoria on the Rio Nuñez, and Mary Faber of Sangha on the Rio Pongo. Their commercial and frequent political successes resulted in part from the unique status in local and long distance trades given to resident slave traders, whether men or women. The backgrounds and trade experiences of these women exemplify changes which affected commerce and traders during the latter part of the slave trade era and demonstrate the varied opportunities and roles possible for some women in this trade.

Successful women entrepreneurs along these rivers were not unusual on the windward coast at the time. Perhaps the most famous of the early women traders was Bibiana Vaz of Eur-African ancestry who operated out of Cacheu on the Cacheu River during the seventeenth century (Rodney 1970:209–10). Bibiana Vaz had married a Portuguese captain, Ambrosio Gomez, and had drawn into her commercial empire other Luso-Africans who proclaimed a brief republic in 1684. Less spectacular but certainly

1. I am indebted to the University of Wisconsin–La Crosse and the American Philosophical Society, who sponsored my research in Sierra Leone and European archives during the 1979 spring semester. I also wish to acknowledge the assistance of several colleagues who read various drafts and recommended changes, some of which I have incorporated. The map was drawn by George N. Huppert of the University of Wisconsin–La Crosse Geography Department.

320

more visible were the women traders of Gorée and Saint Louis, some of whom were of Eur-African descent, others of indigenous background (Brooks 1976:22, 29, 40). These African traders, the *signares,* attached themselves to European traders or civil servants for the purpose of obtaining commercial and political advantages as well as social status. Europeans were attracted in turn by the expert knowledge and the ties to the local market which these "culture-brokers" represented. Europeans also were drawn by the chance to escape from the tedium of life on the coast and by the desire to establish a household, if only for a short period. Such a system of "mutual concubinage" benefited both parties. The women traders described in this paper were related in time and circumstances to others on the coast, but they also were products of varied conditions, in respect to both time and place.

Betsy Heard of Bereira

The earliest of the subjects of this paper and perhaps the most accommodating of the three to indigenous political elites was Betsy Heard of Bereira, who was born c. 1759 of mixed African and European descent. Her father probably was attached to the Liverpool entrepôts on the Iles de Los, a group of islands located a little over two miles off Cape Sangara (Conakry). English merchants from Liverpool, like others before them, had found the islands an ideal place to warehouse merchandise which they then carried coastward and retailed in local markets lining the coastal rivers or sold to traders who came from the coast to the islands (Golberry 1803, 2:168–72, 191–94; Mouser 1981:6–9). Heard was born of a liaison which her father established with a local woman. Although the circumstances of this particular relationship are unknown, it was common along these rivers for European traders to arrange a tenancy agreement with a local landlord for the use of land for a factory or trading post (Mouser 1975:429–30; Conneau 1976:106–15).[2] This agreement involved a record of fees, range of mobility, and expectations required from the "stranger" and a corresponding agreement by the landlord to protect property and rights of inheritance. As often as not, the landlord arranged for a daughter by a slave wife to marry this new stranger. This arrangement provided the landlord with an informant who kept him abreast of events at the factory, and at the same time guaranteed that any children would have minimal political or inheritance rights among indigenous peoples. Although Betsy

2. See also Bangura 1971–72:99–101 for a Marxist interpretation of tenancy arrangements along this coast. Bangura correctly observed that the definition of stranger as "foreigner" applied to African outsiders as well as European outsiders.

Map 16.1. Coastal Guinea-Conakry. Original map by George N. Huppert.

Heard was freeborn by virtue of her father's status, her minuscule matrilineal ties did not afford her the security of land and/or people who would
claim her as kin.

Heard was born at an important time in the history of this section of the
windward coast. Many local towns of the coast between Cape Sangara
and the Sierra Leone River by 1750 had become important terminals for
trade caravans from Mandinka peoples in the Upper Niger and from the
Fula of the highlands of the Futa Jalon. An Islamic holy war in the Futa
Jalon which began in 1725 and which continued for a half century had
kept a steady stream of captives flowing coastward and enriching the purses
of landlords and merchants alike (McGowan 1978:29, 36, 103–5). In mid-

century, however, the holy war itself spread coastward into the area south of Bereira through the agency of Mandinka settlers in Moria who were influenced by the religious fervor in the interior (Bright 1802:88). Bereira, where Heard lived, was basically a Susu town which had continued to follow traditional religious practices and to recognize the proprietary rights of traditional landlords in the area. In 1770, however, the Morians and their Fula allies seized Bereira in a holy war and were partially successful in forcing its population to convert to Islam. From 1770 onward Bereira was considered half-Susu, and its people often found themselves precariously perched between warring factions, established families, and age-old antagonisms resulting from the religious war which had changed its character.

Leaning to her father's side, Betsy Heard had little option but to enter the life available to outsiders like herself. Heard's father provided her with the necessary commercial training by sending her to England, where she remained for several years. Most likely she lived in or near Liverpool, where the number of male and female African students fluctuated between fifty and seventy annually. The Africans learned reading, writing, mathematics, and, of course, religion. Primarily, though, they were there "to learn Sense and a get a good Head" (Matthews et al. 1788). Students went to England at their parents' initiative, but there were also Englishmen who recognized that this experience provided English commerce with more secure contacts on the coast. Among those Eur-Africans studying near Liverpool in 1788 were a son of a principal chief in the Sierra Leone River, John and James Cleveland of Bananas Island, John Holeman of Bence Island and the Iles de Los, William and John Bottle of Rio Grande and the Iles de Los, Emmanuel Gomez of Bakia in the Rio Pongo, Andrew White Conta of Bereira, Thomas Williams of the Iles de Los, and William Jellorum Fernandez of Bramaya on the Dembia River. On the basis of this enumeration alone, the ratio of males to females studying near Liverpool must have been very high. The education of Africans or Eur-Africans near Liverpool gave Liverpudlians significant advantages over competitors. One contemporary noted that schooling provided contacts on the coast who had studied the technology of Europe, indulging the preferences of Europeans for trading with people of familiar lifestyles. Some Europeans resident on the African coast, however, opposed the practice of sending daughters and sons to England, charging that Africans in England learned too much pride and "an increased love of Idleness and Pleasure" (B.M., Matthews 1788). One writer suggested that a school be set up in the West Indies instead, perhaps to keep Africans from accumulating too many habits of the English gentry.

This milieu, then, was the one in which Betsy Heard came of age. The precise circumstances of Heard's return to Africa are uncertain, but clearly she inherited the property and position of her father at Bereira as well as his involvement in the slave trade. By 1794, Betsy Heard was well enough known on the coast to be noted specifically in the Sierra Leone Company Report (1795:76) as a successful slave merchant who had studied in England. Adam Afzelius (1795–96:52–58), botanist of the company at Freetown, described her as something of an expert on native medicine.

Betsy Heard both achieved her greatest commercial and political influence and decided to retire during the decade 1800 to 1810. Employees of the Sierra Leone Company who visited Bereira in 1802 described it and the neighboring area in some detail. Richard Bright used Heard's factory as his headquarters while he was in Bereira and in his report noted that her house was furnished in the European style. Her commercial power at Bereira and along the coast was considerable. In addition to operating trading vessels which plied the coast, she owned the principal wharf at Bereira. Long-distance traders from the Futa Jalon, the Upper Niger, and the headwaters of the Sierra Leone River frequented her factory. In 1801, for example, such a large group arrived and demanded customary hospitality that her financial resources were nearly exhausted before local headmen rescued her with contributions of rice with which to feed her guests. On another occasion, Richard Bright (1802:66–71, 90–91), an agent of the Sierra Leone Company, borrowed trade merchandise from Heard's store, further attesting to her commercial acumen along the coast. By 1807, she had built a new house. And Englishmen now were describing Bereira in terms normally reserved for the more important political centers of Wonkapong and Forekaria. At the same time, however, her monopoly at Bereira was under challenge from competition by two other traders: Mrs. Williams and Mrs. Crowdson. The Sierra Leone Company and the Church Missionary Society frequently sent teachers to Bereira where they were politely received and billeted by traders and chiefs alike (Bright 1802:94; Afzelius 1795–96:37; C.M.S., Renner 1807). Missionary Peter Hartwig (C.M.S., Hartwig 1806) lived in or near Bereira from 1806 to 1814 and described Betsy Heard in most flattering terms.

Although Heard's political influence was strong early in this decade, her exact status in local and regional politics is less than clear. For example, in Bereira itself there were four quarters (Ta Fori, Tutta Di, Maligia, and Contaar), none of which belonged to Heard. Yet, whenever emissaries from surrounding towns came to Bereira, they inevitably sought out her factory. In one instance, when traditional gifts were distributed to headmen and other political elites at Bereira, she also received a share. Neighboring headmen brought her gifts, a clear indication of the wide respect for her wealth and for her effective sociopolitical status, if not actual position (Bright 1802:71, 91).

Perhaps even more interesting than her unofficial but probably important role in internal Bereira politics was the role she played in regional conflicts. From 1800 to 1807, for example, the Sierra Leone Company and certain chiefs in Moria, Sumbuya, and Moricania had been in dispute over the role which a few Morian chiefs had taken not only in the Nova Scotian insurrection at Freetown but also in subsequent wars between the company and neighboring Temne peoples. King Tom and several Nova Scotian rebels had taken refuge in Moria following those wars, and the company wanted them turned over for trial. In this instance, Betsy Heard acquired great influence by playing a mediating role between the parties. Sattan Tumani, ruler of Moria, turned to Heard first when it became clear both that a controversy between Moria and the Sierra Leone Company was escalating and that she was the person best qualified to mediate, to act as broker. Other headmen and chiefs accepted her position on the understanding that as long as discussions between Moria and the Sierra Leone Company were peaceful, a woman could participate and play a principal role. Should they change to a war palaver, however, the proceedings would then become man's business. Heard thereafter engaged in "shuttle diplomacy," interceding between parties, recommending compromises, and translating proposals. Respected by all parties concerned, including the company, Heard apparently retired from active participation in the slave trade after the 1800–1807 negotiations. Once the dispute between the company and the chiefs was resolved, Heard's name seldom appeared in Sierra Leone records, save for an unusual report in 1812 (C.M.S., Renner 1812) that she had borne a male child at the Church Missionary Society mission in the Rio Pongo, a highly unlikely event since she would have been more than fifty years old at the time.

Elizabeth Frazer Skelton of Victoria

Very much in contrast to the experiences of Betsy Heard were those of Elizabeth Frazer Skelton. Skelton was born in 1800 to John Frazer at Bangalan town on the Rio Pongo. Frazer, an American tailor of black American and Caucasian descent, arrived in 1797 at Freetown. The Company refused him permission to settle there, believing him to be a slaver (H.L., Macaulay 1797). Frazer subsequently moved to the Rio Pongo where he found a sizeable trading community and a willingness on the part of chiefs to welcome another outsider to the trading system. The Rio Pongo, like the rivers to the south, had its headwaters in the highlands of the Futa Jalon, and it served as a path for caravans bringing slaves, ivory, gold, rice, hides, and other products to trading posts along the coast. European and other outsider merchants, besides engaging in slave trading, made arrangements for land and trading factories with local landlords, and perhaps obtained wives, in much the same manner as fifty years earlier in

Bereira (Mouser 1973:45–64). The Iles de Los continued to warehouse products for the coastal trade, although Freetown and the Sierra Leone Company increasingly sought to capture that market.

The unique character of the Rio Pongo trading community was owing to the large number of its participants and the lifestyle which they established in the area. By 1800 nearly two dozen Europeans were living along the Pongo's banks. Three of the local chiefs, William Jellorum Fernandez, Emmanuel Gomez, and Fantimani, had lived near Liverpool and inevitably were linked to the Liverpool merchant system centered on the Iles de Los. The practice of sending daughters and sons abroad also had affected traders here, most notably John Ormond of Bangalan town, whose son John was in England in 1800. John Frazer had at least four wives at Bangalan. Only four children were listed (Elizabeth—b. 1800; Helen—b. 1806; Mary Anne—b. 1803; and Nancy—n.d.), but it is reasonable to speculate that more existed (C.M.S., Butscher 1811; Walker 1845:363). Assuming that some traders had no wives and others had more than Frazer did, Europeans and their spouses perhaps numbered more than eighty, and children at least twice that many. There was strength in numbers, as the chiefs soon would learn.

Life on the coast at the turn of the century was not without its pleasures. A typical factory or trading post was built above the mangrove line and often was made of brick. One at Bashia was a two-storied brick building with a large courtyard where caravans could rest during the night. Each commonly had a corral, called a *barracoon* on this coast. Here market slaves were chained, awaiting the arrival of a slave ship from the Americas. The ground floor served as a warehouse for merchandise, the second floor as living quarters (C.M.S., Butscher 1809). If the trader had multiple wives, the family compound expanded so that each wife could have her house in the fashion typical of the locality. Wives often were schooled in proper European etiquette, and served meals Western style with customary European food and utensils (H.L., Macaulay 1796). Tales of the "debauch" abound for this coast, however, and perhaps serve only to illuminate the type of person attracted to this trade and lifestyle in the first place. Joseph Hawkins (1797:155–57), clerk on a slaver which visited the area in 1795, described a feast that concluded a purchase between his captain and local merchants.

> They [the traders] come to the table nearly intoxicated, and before dinner is completed, they become downright drunk. . . . The coarse jocularity of destroying their apparel or wasting the food, is their amusement; while the most exquisite viands are wasted without utility, and the appetite being palled by superabundance, loses all its value but that which gratifies the vanity of the

provider, by indulging the waste and absurdity of his guests. After the wine has circulated freely, the meats are even occasionally dashed about at the heads of the best humored, or most patient of the company, and the empty dishes, plates, and tables are demolished to shew the spirit of the party, and the lengths to which they could carry a joke.

Growing up in this environment, Elizabeth Frazer enjoyed benefits not available to Betsy Heard. For example, when missionaries from the London-based Church Missionary Society arrived in the Rio Pongo in 1807, they proposed to establish missions and schools for the children of chiefs and asked the chiefs for land. Fernandez of Bramaya and Fantimani of Cano-fee, both of whom had lived in or near Liverpool, realized the commercial benefits to be derived from such schools. Together with several equally astute slave traders, they provided the missionaries with land and a brick building. The fact that a year later, 1808, England declared slave trading illegal seemed to bother them little, for the benefits of schools outweighed the presence of slavery opponents in their midst. During the next ten years, several hundred children of chiefs and traders received schooling in reading, writing, mathematics, and religion, tools generally useful in all forms of trade. John Frazer in particular supported the schools, to which he sent Elizabeth and three other daughters, all of whom were baptized. After 1817 Elizabeth went to England, where she studied for four years, and apparently spent some time in France before returning to West Africa. By the time of her return, Elizabeth was fluent in French and English and was schooled in the proper English graces (Ware 1842–43/1965:303–4).

Upon her return to the Rio Pongo, where her father enjoyed commercial success, Elizabeth met William Skelton, Jr., a Eur-African. They were married on July 24, 1826. Skelton was born in 1794 at Kissing in the Rio Pongo to William Skelton, Sr., a European who operated an important trading factory until his death in 1805. Skelton, Jr., did not attend the mission schools established in 1807, suggesting his earlier departure for Liverpool where he remained until 1811. When he returned to Kissing, he discovered that his deceased father's fortune had vanished. Skelton, Jr., therefore, took employment as clerk to Samuel Samo, a newly arrived English trader who had factories at Charleston in the Rio Pongo and on the Iles de Los (Anon. 1813a:19). In 1812, Skelton testified in British court proceedings against Samo and other slavers in the Rio Pongo, not because of his opposition to slave trading but rather to gain favor with the English at Freetown and to establish himself as an important person in the river's commerce (Anon. 1813a:16–17; Anon. 1813b:78). This maneuver, however, was not productive, for Skelton remained a minor figure in the river's trade for the next decade, during which he maintained a small factory at Kissing where he was associated with Thomas Curtis. Perhaps it was at this time that Elizabeth first met her future spouse, before she left for England and the traditional studies abroad.

The 1826 marriage between William Skelton and Elizabeth Frazer provided an excellent opportunity for both to start anew. Elizabeth and William moved to the town of Kanfarande in the Rio Nuñez and built a trading post which they called Victoria. With slave trading now illegal for English and American subjects on the coast and with the Rio Pongo under increased scrutiny by the Royal Anti–Slave Trade Squadron, Victoria came to serve initially as a conduit for slaves transported by canoe or overland from the Rio Pongo to Bissau in Portuguese territory to the north (Méo 1919:282).

Perhaps Victoria had begun as little more than a branch of the Curtis empire of factories, but the Skeltons soon made it something special. Two daughters, Emma and Mary Anne, were born in and after 1828, and Elizabeth and William gave them the equivalent of an education abroad at Victoria. Later visitors were indeed surprised that both girls were fluent in French (Ware 1842–43/1965:303–4). Victoria also became an important factory site in its own right. As the first post located near the river's mouth, Victoria became familiar to captains who came there as a place to secure a pilot to lead them through the river's channels. The Skeltons therefore became well known on the coast and naturally profited from this contact, especially when trade began to shift from slave to legitimate and from British to French and when command of the French language became so crucial to their continued success. The degree to which the Skeltons were engaged as middlemen in the slave trade is unclear, but it must have been substantial. Repeated charges against the Skeltons and their partner, John R. Sergeant, a Barbadian operating a factory nearby, commonly were voiced at Freetown, and in 1832 and 1833 Sierra Leone officials launched raids against Victoria, searching for slaves. Although they located none, they did find records which implicated the Skeltons. Sergeant left the river soon thereafter (P.R.O., Findlay 1833).

The 1830s and 1840s were important years in the commercial success of the Skeltons. The addition of steam-paddle vessels to the British Squadron and the arrival of merchants whose interests were primarily in legitimate products such as coffee, rice, groundnuts, and hides spelled the end of the slave trade in the Nuñez and accelerated the Skeltons' transition to legitimate commerce. They maintained commercial and political ties with the Curtises of Kissing who, by this time, also were serving as advisors to the Kati rulers of the lower Rio Pongo. In January 1843 Elizabeth received word of the death of her father, who apparently had moved to the United States, and notification of her inheritance, which included the proceeds of "an estate in Florida." This news came only a few days before the death of her husband on February 10, 1843 (Ware 1842–43/1965:309).

Called Mammy Skelton after the death of William, Elizabeth continued to operate the Victoria factory as well as other factories upstream, in the company of other active women traders. The slave trade was over in the Nuñez, however, and Elizabeth now consolidated her influence along the coast. On August 11, 1846, daughter Mary Anne married Joseph Richmond Lightburn, member of the important Lightburn/Gomez family in the Rio Pongo. This marriage alliance and interlocking commercial arrangements with the Curtises and with Benjamin Campbell maintained the Skelton name in prominence into mid-century (Brooks 1970:203).

Mary Faber of Sangha

Very different from the two examples of women slavers cited above, and perhaps more interesting as a personality, was Mary Faber of Sangha on the Rio Pongo. Mary Faber was described in 1838 (P.R.O., Doherty 1838) as a Nova Scotian from Freetown who had married Paul Faber, an American ship captain. The details of Mary's birth and her marriage to Faber are unknown, but the opportunities for courtship between a Freetown resident and a Pongo-based slaver were present at the time. Assuming that Mary was born to Nova Scotian settlers at Freetown at the turn of the century, she would have been approximately ten years of age when the Church Missionary Society opened its schools in the Rio Pongo in 1807–8. Among the more than two hundred "scholars" who boarded at the schools before their closing in 1817 were numerous girls from Freetown, one of whom might have been Mary. The baptismal list of 1815, for instance, identified thirteen girls named Mary or Maria, some of whom had come from Freetown (Walker 1845:267–72). Letters and journals written by the mission teachers (C.M.S., Renner 1814), moreover, contain occasional references to girls who left the schools to marry classmates or others along the river. Such descriptions always emphasized the need to move the school to Freetown where such temptations would be removed.

Paul Faber was an excellent suitor for a young Nova Scotian woman who was, as events later proved, both ambitious and enterprising. Faber had arrived in the Pongo area around 1809, at the end of the American embargo and as soon as the slave trade revived. In addition to a return of prosperity in the Pongo, Faber also found a commercial hierarchy in the process of generational change. Several of the older established traders, among them William Skelton, Sr., mentioned above, had died or left the river. By 1809 leadership was passing to newcomers like himself who organized trade in a more structured and monopolistic fashion. Among these were Samuel Samo, William Wilson, John Ormond, Jr., and Styles Lightburn (Anon. 1813a:19–20; Anon. 1813b:78).

The early role which Faber played in this arrangement is unclear, but as a ship's captain he may have been primarily engaged in transporting slaves to the Americas, where as late as 1816 he maintained contacts with the Havana-based firm of Antonio de Freres and Company (Howland 1816–17/1965:81, 92).[3] An Admiralty report (P.R.O., Admiralty 1839) identified him as still carrying slaves from Africa to Cuba in 1839. Faber's first confrontation with British authorities at Freetown came late in 1811 when the ruler of the Rio Pongo, representing a faction which opposed the monopolistic group listed above, accused Faber of complicity in the seizure of the Colonial sloop *George* (C.M.S., Renner 1811). That ship had attempted to curtail slavers in the Pongo in September. A year later, William Skelton, Jr., and others testified that Faber had shipped slaves in 1811 and 1812 (Anon. 1813a:16–17; Anon. 1813b:78).

Following a brief absence from the river after 1812, Faber had returned to the Pongo by 1816, and maintained his principal residence there until his death in 1851. Whether Mary married him before he left in 1812 or after he returned in 1816 is unclear. The decade and a half from 1816 to 1833, however, was an important period in the life of the Fabers. Having established a factory at Sangha in the Bangalan branch of the Rio Pongo, the Fabers enjoyed the protection of John Ormond, Jr., chief of Bangalan town and considered the most powerful trader and chief in the upper river at the time. Ormond had allied himself with the Fula upcountry and, supported by that alliance, governed the Bangalan branch as separate from the Susu and the Kati family–controlled areas of the lower river. During this period Faber carried slaves to the Americas, while Mary remained at Sangha where she maintained the family business and gave birth to a son, William (P.R.O., MacCarthy 1820). The decade of the 1820s, however, was a difficult period for slavers in the Bangalan branch. The Royal Anti–Slave Trade Squadron focused surveillance on the river and raided Faber's factories in the upper river several times searching for slaves available for shipments to the Americas (Ward 1969:88–89).

Separating market slaves from locally used laborers became increasingly difficult for squadron captains after 1826, because slavers, including the Fabers, began to construct coffee plantations which conveniently served as concealment for continued slaving. In 1827, one captain reported that Ormond owned between 5,000 and 6,000 plantation slaves, none of whom could be clearly identified as marketable (P.R.O., Campbell 1820). By 1827 the Fabers had more than 6,000 coffee plants in the ground at a

---

3. The editors of *New England Merchants* correctly observed, however, that Howland's Jacob Faber may have been a different person altogether.

plantation located above Lisso on the Fatala branch of the Rio Pongo and were exporting local and upcountry-grown coffee through Freetown merchants to British markets. By remaining in a subservient relationship to Ormond, the Fabers improved their position and share in the continuing slave trade and expanded with slave plantation labor into coffee production as well.

Following the death of John Ormond, Jr., in 1833, his brother William Ormond became chief of the Bangalan region. William did not have the stronger character or abilities of his brother. These weaknesses eventually produced a power vacuum in the upper river and brought families who had cooperated under Ormond into open conflict. For five years, however, Mary Faber of Sangha, Bailey Gomez Lightburn of Faringuia, and Chief William Ormond of Bangalan provisioned slavers according to a quota arrangement similar to the practice established earlier by John Ormond, Jr. Then, in October 1838, Mary Faber abruptly discarded the arrangement and provisioned a slaver with a cargo totally from her own stock (P.R.O., Doherty 1838; P.R.O., Admiralty 1839).[4] Ormond retaliated by stealing a large number of Faber's slaves, and the Ormond and Faber forces prepared for war. Bailey Lightburn, an important trader in her own right but one who had to exercise caution because of her subservient position, remained neutral, at least temporarily.

As the dispute between Mary Faber and William Ormond escalated, other circumstances brought a major alteration of politics in the upper river. In the early stages, when it appeared that warfare might actually break out, two traders from Freetown, who were resident in the river and who had refused to buy and sell slaves, met with William Ormond and convinced him to return Faber's slaves.[5] This only served to prove to Mary Faber, however, that Freetown was attempting to intercede in the dispute and that Freetown merchants expected to play an active role in the upper river thereafter. Consequently, Mary now portrayed herself as representing the "Native" faction against the "Mulatto" or Freetown-oriented group. With the apparent acquiescence of the Fula governor, Mary initiated hostilities by looting the stores of legitimate Freetown traders in the area and by blockading the river between Bangalan and Sangha. Ormond retaliated by stopping river traffic below Sangha. With trade in the upper river ended, the Fula intervened, deposed Ormond as chief of the district, and appointed a new Fula governor at Bangalan. Two years later, William Ormond died. With no capable successor to maintain Bangalan, the center of trade in the Bangalan shifted to Sangha, with Bailey Lightburn also

---

4. Unfortunately the only reports of this incident come from Benjamin Campbell, who was married to a daughter of Bailey Lightburn and was an adversary of Mary Faber.

5. Benjamin Campbell was one of these.

enjoying commercial success at Faringuia (Bandinel 1842/1968:296). Mary now was protected by a resident Fula governor and clearly had become the most powerful trader in the upper river. Her husband, Paul, is rarely mentioned in the sources after the mid-1830s.

The forceful imposition of a Fula presence in Bangalan in 1838, and the rise of Mary Faber with Bailey Lightburn's assistance, rekindled antagonisms between the upper and lower river chiefs and traders and eventually led to new warfare. For nearly a century the Susu and Kati rulers of the lower river had recognized Fula suzerainty and the technical right of the Fula to reject or concur with local elections of chiefs. Before 1838 the Fula were always distant enough that their interference was rare. After 1838, however, the Fula were less than fifteen miles from the Susu capital of Thia. The death of King Yati Yende Kati in 1838 and a contested chieftaincy election between one faction, supported by lower river traders and chiefs, and the other supported by Faber, Lightburn, and the Fula, led to an invasion of the lower river by the private slave armies of Faber and Lightburn. Their forces sacked the Susu capital. The Fula deposed Culom Kati, who had ruled for four years, enthroned their and the Faber candidate, Bala Bangu Kati, and moved the capital to Boffa, away from Thia and the influence of the lower river traders (P.R.O., Macdonald 1852; Arcin 1911:142–43; Saint-Père 1930:137).

With legitimate traders removed from the Rio Pongo and the lower river chiefs and traders intimidated by a Fula presence at Boffa, Mary Faber, as well as others in the upper river, enjoyed unparalleled prosperity in the 1840s. No new legitimate traders entered the river's commerce during this period, and those families already established avoided the new competition which occurred along the neighboring rivers. Another change bringing success to established families was a transformation of many traders from outsiders into headmen or chiefs, thereby allowing them to escape customs and anchorage duties normally charged strangers in the river. For a time, a drop in the prices paid for coffee brought concern to traders, but increasing demands for groundnuts by the French led Pongo traders to change from coffee to groundnuts (Lysaght 1849:29–31; Arcin 1911:142). Leading the shift to groundnut production were the matriarchs of the Faber and Lightburn families, whose sons, William Faber and Styles Lightburn, Jr., began to assume more prominent positions among the river's elites. William Faber, operating large plantations in both the Sangha and Lisso area, became headman of Sangha after his father's death in 1851, and continued to ship slaves as late as 1860 (P.R.O., Macdonald 1850; P.R.O., Fitzjames 1860).

The decade of the 1850s opened with promise of continued prosperity and increased influence for Mary Faber and her family, the Lightburns, and even for traders in the lower river, where a Fula regent kept watch over Bala Bangu Kati at Boffa. While the Pongo had escaped intervention from either Britain or France thus far, neighboring rivers to the north and south were less fortunate, and the Pongo's time was at hand. In 1852, officials from Sierra Leone arrived at Boffa with a request that Bala Bangu Kati sign a treaty formally ending the slave trade, guaranteeing protection of property belonging to Sierra Leone traders who might venture into the river, and permitting an agent of the British government to establish an official residence at Boffa. Initially Bala Bangu Kati hesitated, but, sensing no opposition from the Fula regent or Mary Faber, he signed the treaty on January 17, 1852 (P.R.O., Macdonald 1852).

For Mary Faber, the treaty of 1852 became a rallying call once again for military cooperation among upper river chiefs and traders. This placed the "Native" faction against those of the lower river, who, she believed, had acquiesced to Sierra Leone and outsider trading interests. Faber also was convinced that the lower river traders, or "Mulatto" faction, were attempting to use this new treaty to remove the Susu of the lower river from Fula suzerainty. A large army of slaves from Faber's and Lightburn's plantations gathered at Dominguia and, joined by slave armies of other plantation owners, invaded the heartland of Susu country. The lower river chiefs counterattacked with great force, turned the invasion into a rout, and both captured and burned Sangha before being repulsed at Faringuia. Only then did Fula soldiers arrive and intercede to protect their allies in the upper river (Arcin 1911:142). Although skirmishes continued into 1855, the war was a defeat for the Faber family. After 1852, Faber regional political influence diminished, although the Bangalan branch of the Rio Pongo continued to be shared by the Faber and Lightburn families. Whether in consequence of this defeat or for other reasons, Mary Faber after 1852 assumed a less visible position in the river's life. This change was so pronounced by 1857 that a missionary then visiting the river identified Mary as simply matriarch of the family and William Faber as "Ali of the King of the Fullahs" (*Fallangia Mission* 1858:13). The Faber commercial empire meanwhile expanded in the Bangalan and Fatala branches, where it maintained large groundnut plantations into the mid-1850s (*Pongas Mission* 1862:17–19; S.P.G., Phillips 1860).

Conclusions

These narratives clearly portray phases in the slave trade, pressures which affected all slave traders regardless of sex, and ways that women became successful as slave traders. Although the experiences and circumstances which characterized the rise to power were different in detail in each case, several common themes are sufficiently present to explain how it was possible for such women to become successful slave traders.[6] Heard, Skelton, and Faber were all born free of traditional responsibilities to extended families or lineage and held marginal positions in coastal society. Heard and Skelton, for example, were born in the rivers where they later became successful, but both had European fathers who had married local women. Assuming that European fathers acquired wives as gifts from "landlords" in the traditional fashion, their wives either would have been slave women, and therefore without local rights or privileges, or daughters of slave wives who enjoyed minimal rights. As offspring of such parents, Heard and Skelton were free but were also with few family obligations on the mothers' sides. Faber was even more of a "stranger" to the Rio Pongo by virtue of her Nova Scotian background. Her obligations, to the degree that she had them, would have been at Freetown where her parents had been black settlers from North America. It is doubtful that Faber's obligations extended beyond her parents and herself.

Freedom from lineage and family obligations and corresponding freedom from the restrictions of local women's societies meant that Heard, Skelton, and Faber were able to seek out economic alternatives not available or permitted to local women. The traditional domain of women along the coast had included the house, the fields, and the wells: the care of babies, preparation of food and fetching of water, and conduct of local markets (Gessain 1963:23). Heard and Skelton could be a part of this domain, but because of their marginal status they lacked the economic security which family ties and levirate would give in difficult times. To obtain economic self-sufficiency and security and to escape those restrictions attached to women as a caste, they were forced to lean "to their

6. In a recent article, Levine (1979:21–36) developed a new typology for classifying the intentions of strangers and responses of hosts. These include six types of role—guest, sojourner, newcomer, intruder, inner enemy, and marginal man—and Levine suggests that there would be different relationships depending on whether the unit of analysis was a collectivity or the individual. Such relationships for the individual as well as the group, moreover, would change over time. Sacks (1974:212–13) and Dunbar (1975:48–49) interpret the traditional position of women as approximating a caste into which one is born. Interaction between European or outsider men and local women involved mobility, cross-caste expectations, and the evolution of a new class, but always at a subservient level to men. Paulme (1963:12–14) seems to align with the latter interpretation, noting that in the Futa Jalon men treat women as "tenants" and husbands regard wives as "strangers," at least until they pass childbearing age. Whether the women described in this paper fit the definition of newcomer, marginal man, inner enemy, or separate caste, it does appear that one could be born into the group as well as move into it through marriage. "Neither here nor there," these women were, nevertheless, prominent and successful members of the group to which they belonged on the coast. See Mouser (1980) for an analysis of the opportunities available to Mary Faber as a marginal person and as Big-Man as defined by Howard (1972) and Thayer (1978).

father's side," to identify primarily as traders by occupation. (Faber's circumstances, different in this regard, are discussed below.)

At first glance it might appear that only persons such as Heard and Skelton could enter coastal trade in this fashion, but such was apparently not the case. Nineteenth-century literature of Guinea-Conakry contains the names of several African women traders who took European names and operated factories along the rivers. In some cases, the husbands are easily identified; in others they are not. Perhaps customs similar to those governing the signares of Senegambia prevailed in this area as well, with women free to establish liaisons with Europeans. Chiefs may have given girls of slave descent to strangers who departed after a short time, leaving behind wives who kept their names and a new status in the river's trade. Another possible reason for the emergence of prominent women traders is that women who settled in towns were looked down upon and considered as tainted and undesirable (Van Allen 1976:38). Even in Freetown, women who failed to conform were "seen as belonging to the other side, 'the male side'" (Steady 1976:234), a status allocated to women such as those described above. Caught in the same constraints as Heard and Skelton, these women had little option but to seek their economic security in the same fashion.

Another theme common to the biographies of Heard, Skelton, and Faber is the importance of education and experience in dealing with Europeans. Both Heard and Skelton had lived in England for several years and during that time acquired tastes different from those of the coast. Both had factory houses furnished in the English fashion and served meals to Europeans in the English manner. The factories of both became mandatory ports-of-call for important European visitors, and this contact undoubtedly increased their volume of trade. That both could speak English was an important asset, and Skelton's fluency in French became increasingly crucial as trade shifted in the Rio Nuñez. Growing up at Freetown and perhaps in the Church Missionary Society schools in the Rio Pongo, Faber also learned English, as well as mathematics and bookkeeping skills useful to trade. Balancing their "Western" education, which made them acceptable to European visitors, was their knowledge of African practices and languages, which kept them from making uncorrectable errors with their hosts. As intermediaries in the slave trade, these women could engage in local as well as long-distance trade and represented something different from the usual for male slave ship captains or caravan leaders who frequented factories along the coast.

To ascribe their success to their status as "ladies," however, would be incorrect. Each of these women was an astute person who was present at the right time and under the right circumstances. Heard inherited economic position and kept it going with her own abilities. At the turn of the century, she became a mediator between chiefs and the British and was principal agent in the "peace palaver," a laudable role in any age. This position gave her political and economic influence unusual for the time. The successes of Skelton and Faber, in contrast, were aided by the fact that there was an "alter" (Van Allen 1976:33) involved in each case. Both raised families while their husbands established businesses. Of the two, Skelton perhaps came closest to the status of "lady" when she served as a shrewd hostess to visiting Europeans. When her husband died in 1843, she kept the Skelton commercial fortune intact, evidence of her prior experience in trade. The marriage of her daughter to the Lightburns of the Rio Pongo further testified to her political and economic astuteness. Mary Faber's life with Faber was different from that between the Skeltons. Faber was often away from the coast, and while raising her family, Mary Faber also assumed total responsibility for the business. She was careful to court the favor of the right persons at the right times, and during the 1820s and 1830s enjoyed great success. In the 1840s and 1850s, by shifting and adjusting alliances with the Fula and by firm control of her family, she guided the Faber fortune to its greatest height.

In one sense it is ironic that African women became principal agents in the slave trade between Africa and the Americas. Many of these women were apparently of slave descent and perhaps should have turned from the trade with disdain. But, deprived of the opportunities and privileges available to women who could participate fully in the local markets and of the security which full membership in the host society would have provided, these women turned to that profession which had given their mothers security, an affiliation with stranger societies and with the goods which strangers were seeking at the time, slaves. This position of intermediary in trade between Europeans, hosts, and African strangers gave these women extraordinary influence in the commerce of the rivers of Guinea-Conakry during the early nineteenth century.

References

Unpublished Sources

Bangura, M. 1971–72. "Contribution à l'histoire des Sosoe du 16ᵉ au 19ᵉ Siècle." Diplome de fin d'Etudes Superieures, Institut Polytechnique Gamal Abdel Nasser, Conakry, Guinea.
B. M.: British Museum (Library), London.
    Matthews, J. Letter, March 22, 1789. ADD Mss 38416.
C.M.S.: Church Missionary Society Archives, London.
    Butscher. Letter, June 30, 1809. CA1/E2.
    Butscher. Journal, October 22, 1811. CA1/E2.

Hartwig. Letter, October 16, 1806. CA1/E1
Renner. Letters, March 11 and April 21, 1807. CA1/E1.
Renner. Letter, October 30, 1811. CA1/E2
Renner. Letter, March 1, 1812. CA1/E1.
Renner. Letters, February 12, 1814, and June 24, 1814. CA1/E3 and CA1/E4.
Howard, A. M. 1972. "Big Men, Traders, and Chiefs: Power, Commerce, and Spacial Change in the Sierra Leone–Guinea Plain, 1865–1895." Ph.D. dissertation, University of Wisconsin, Madison.
H.L.: Huntington Library, San Marino, California.
Macaulay, Z. Journal, April 1, 1796.
Macaulay, Z. Journal, July 29, 1797.
Macaulay, Z. Journal, January 24, 1798.
McGowan, W. F. 1978. "The Development of European Relations with Futa Jallon and the Development of French Colonial Rule, 1794–1897." Ph.D. dissertation, University of London.
Mouser, B. L. 1980. "Women Traders and Big-Men of Guinea-Conakry." Paper presented at the African Studies Association Conference, Philadelphia, 1980.
Mouser, B. L. 1981. "Iles de Los as Bulking Centre in the Slave Trade, 1750–1800." Paper presented at the African Studies Association Conference, Bloomington, Ind., 1981.
P.R.O.: Public Record Office, London.
Admiralty. March 19, 1839. CO267/155.
Campbell, July 28, 1827. CO67/82/confidential.
Doherty. December 10, 1837. CO267/148.
Findlay. March 20, 1833, and March 4, 1833. CO267/114 and CO267/119.
Fitzjames. August 8, 1860. CO267/267.
MacCarthy. May 27, 1820. CO267/51.
Macdonald. November 4, 1850. FO84/788.
Macdonald. February 17, 1852. CO267/227.
S.P.G.: Society for the Propagation of the Gospel Archive, London.
Phillips, A. April 1, 1860. E-6/1115–35.

Published Sources

Afzelius, A. 1795–96/1967. *Sierra Leone Journal, 1795–1796.* Edited by A. P. Kup. Uppsala.
Anon. 1813a. *The Trials of the Slave Traders.* London.
Anon. 1813b. Review of *The Trials* by "A Gentleman . . . at Sierra Leone." *Edinburgh Review* 21:72–93.
Arcin, H. 1911. *Histoire de la Guinée Française.* Paris.
Bandinel, J. 1842/1968. *Some Account of the Trade in Slaves from Africa.* London.
Bright, R., 1802/1979. "Journal of Richard Bright." In *Guinea Journals: Journeys into Guinea-Conakry during the Sierra Leone Phase, 1800–1821,* ed. B. Mouser. Washington, D.C.
Brooks, G. E. 1970. *Yankee Traders, Old Coasters, and African Middlemen: A*

History of American Legitimate Trade with West Africa in the Nineteenth Century. Boston.

Brooks, G. E. 1976. "The Signares of Saint-Louis and Gorée: Women Entrepreneurs in Eighteenth-Century Senegal." In *Women in Africa,* ed. N. J. Hafkin and E. G. Bay. Stanford.

Conneau, T. 1853/1976. *A Slaver's Log Book.* New York.

Dunbar, R. A. 1975. "Female Liberation as the Basis of Social Revolution." In *Voices of the New Feminism,* ed. M. L. Thompson. Boston.

Fallangia Mission: Quarterly Paper for July, 1857. 1857. Barbados.

Gessain, M. 1963. "Coniagui Women (Guinea)." In *Women in Tropical Africa,* ed. D. Paulme. Berkeley.

Golberry, S. M. X. 1803. *Travels in Africa Performed during the Years 1785, 1786, and 1787.* Trans. W. Mudford. London.

Hawkins, J. 1797. *A History of a Voyage to the Coast of Africa.* Troy, N.Y.

Howland, G. 1816–17/1965. "Captain George Howland's Voyage to West Africa, 1816–1817." In *New England Merchants in Africa,* ed. N. R. Bennett and G. E. Brooks. Boston.

Levine, R. N. 1979. "Simmel at a Distance: On the History and Systematics of the Sociology of the Stranger." In *Strangers in African Society,* ed. W. A. Shack and E. P. Skinner. Berkeley.

Lysaght, T. 1849. "Report on the River Nunez, Its Trade and Resources." *Journal of the Royal Geographical Society* 19:29–31.

Matthews, J., J. Penny, and R. Norris. 1978. Letter of April 16, 1788. In *Report of the Lords of the Committee of Council . . . relating to Trade and Foreign Plantations.* Great Britain, Privy Council, London.

Méo, Docteur. 1919. "Etudes sur la Rio-Nunez." *Bulletin du Comite d'Etudes de l'A.O.F.* Paris.

Mouser, B. L. 1973. "Trade, Coasters, and Conflict in the Rio Pongo from 1790 to 1808." *Journal of African History* 14:45–64.

Mouser. B. L. 1975. "Landlords-Strangers: A Process of Accommodation and Assimilation." *International Journal of African Historical Studies* 8:425–40.

Paulme, D., ed. 1963. *Women in Tropical Africa.* Berkeley.

Pongas Mission Annual Report for 1862. 1862. Barbados.

Rodney, W. 1970. *A History of the Upper Guinea Coast, 1545–1800.* Oxford.

Sacks, K. 1974. "Engels Revisited: Women, the Organization of Production, and Private Property." In *Women, Culture and Society,* ed. M. F. Rosaldo.

Saint-Père, J. H. 1930. "Petit historique de Sosoos du Rio Pongo." *Bulletin du comité d'etudes historiques et scientifiques de l'Afrique Occidentale Française* 13:26–47.

Sierra Leone Company. 1795. *Substance of the Report of the . . . Sierra Leone Company . . . 1794.* Philadelphia.

Steady, F. C. 1976. "Protestant Women's Association in Freetown, Sierra Leone." In *Women in Africa,* ed. N. F. Hafkin and E. G. Bay. Stanford.

Thayer, J. S. 1978. "Some Remarks on Informal Social Networks among the Soso of Sierra Leone." *Africana Research Bulletin* 9:44–66.

Van Allen, J. 1976. "African Women, 'Modernization,' and National Liberation."

In *Women in the World: A Comparative Study,* ed. L. B. Iglitzin and R. Ross. Santa Barbara.

Walker, A. 1845. *Missions in Western Africa among the Soosoos, Bulloms, etc.* Dublin.

Ward, W. E. F. 1969. *The Royal Navy and the Slavers.* New York.

Ware, E. R. 1842–43/1965. "Enoch Richmond Ware's Voyage to West Africa, 1842–1843." In *New England Merchants in Africa,* ed. N. R. Bennett and G. E. Brooks. Boston.

17 *Edna G. Bay*

Servitude and Worldly Success in the Palace of Dahomey[1]

Recent studies of slavery in Africa have unquestionably enlarged our understanding of the productive and reproductive importance of nonfree persons and their varying social and political statuses in precolonial societies. However, scholars have seldom differentiated between the experiences of men and women as slaves. When distinctions are drawn, women are generally assumed to have played roles narrowly limited to childbearing and the performance of domestic tasks. Suzanne Miers and Igor Kopytoff, for example, suggest that a female slave's status and activities differed little from those of a wife. Moreover, they assert that "An acquired of her mate . . . and thereafter she could achieve little worldly success on her own" (1977:28–29). According to Miers and Kopytoff, worldly success and achievement under conditions of slavery accrued only to men, or to women fortunate enough to have won the esteem of a well-placed mate. Thus male "'Slaves' . . . served as ministers of state and counselors, as soldiers and commanders, as governors of provinces, as trading agents, and, in the case of women, as favored wives" (1977:28).

Data from the kingdom of Dahomey not only do not corroborate Miers and Kopytoff's assertions about women, but on the contrary, show that many women of slave origin did in fact amass considerable wealth and rise to positions of responsibility, power, and honor. In precolonial Dahomey, women slaves might serve as ministers of state and counselors, as soldiers and commanders, as governors of provinces, as trading agents,

1. This paper is based mainly on archival and field data gathered in 1971–73. I am grateful to the Foreign Area Fellowship Program which supported this research, the initial results of which were incorporated in my Ph.D. dissertation (1977).

and as favored wives. Moreover, evidence from neighboring areas and from the Yoruba states in particular suggests a pattern of utilization of female as well as male slaves in positions of trust and authority (Oroge 1971). In each case the route to success was through service to a ruler.

In the precolonial Fon kingdom of Dahomey the greatest opportunities for worldly success for slave or free women occurred through membership in a complex institution at the heart of the state structure, the royal household. For convenience I shall use the terms "royal household" or "palace" to refer generally to this institution that in fact was housed in a series of palaces located at strategic points throughout the kingdom. Central to the organization was Simboji palace in Abomey, behind whose massive clay walls resided in the nineteenth century an estimated 5,000 to 8,000 *ahosi*, the "wives" or dependents of the king.[2] The palace inhabitants, who comprised roughly 15 percent of the capital city's total population, included war captives and slaves purchased abroad, daughters of the king and female descendants of his lineage, and women and girls recruited from all the lineages in the Dahomean state.

An institution controlled by the monarch but directed by itself, the nineteenth-century royal household was central to the political, administrative, military, and religious life of the kingdom. Auguste Le Hérissé, who perhaps understood the kingdom and its history better than any other European to this day, described the palace as "the pivot of political life . . . a 'miniature replica' of the kingdom in its entirety" (Le Hérissé 1911:26). The palace organization worked to maintain and extend the political power and control of the monarchy. It absorbed or distributed the bulk of female slaves brought to Dahomey. It reinforced and augmented the material well-being of the kings and, through human reproduction, its members enlarged the royal family and the household's own permanent slave population. Effectively a cross section of the socioeconomic strata of the kingdom, the heterogeneous makeup of the palace meant that the whole nation participated in the royal household, at the same time that it was controlled by it.

The palace organization developed gradually out of the structure of the polygynous household in Dahomey. For the sake of simplicity, this paper will discuss the royal household as it existed in the late nineteenth century when its population was at its height, numbering as many as 8,000 persons (Le Hérissé 1911:27). Although the legal and social standing of women who entered the king's service varied widely, a fundamental distinction of

2. The term *ahosi* can refer to male or female dependents of a monarch. In fact, a very small portion of the ahosi were male eunuchs. They are usually said to have been palace guards, though at least one high court office, that of male *Tononu*, was regularly held by eunuchs. Unlike eunuchs in the Yoruba states and elsewhere, the roles and activities of Dahomean eunuchs were very circumscribed. See Burton 1864/1966:140–41.

residence in the palace gave all nonroyal women there a status so unlike any other that contemporary Fon informants sometimes refer to them all as having been "slaves." All were legally wives (ahosi) to the king, and the language and institutional structures of the common polygynous household were employed to describe their duties. Yet the analogy with common marriage was limited, for although at least some ahosi were allowed to remain in contact with their families, all lacked the most fundamental protection of common marriage, the right to divorce. The king's service was life-long; an ahosi could never, as could wives of common men, repudiate her husband and return to her father's home. Beyond this single limit to the rights of all ahosi were wide variations in their individual legal statuses.

All persons in the kingdom could be broadly categorized as royal (ahovi), commoner (anato), or slave (kannounnon). The slave status included only persons not born within the borders of Dahomey, that is, brought into the state against their will through purchase or war. Anyone born of commoner or slave parents within the kingdom was considered anato (commoner), even though, as will be seen, certain commoners were subject to forms of perpetual servitude. Moreover, commoners whose parents were both slaves appear to have suffered at best a lower status than those anato with one or both Dahomean parents (A.N.S., "Rapport . . . Allada").[3] The barriers between the categories of royal, commoner, and slave were rigid. In the words of one Fon scholar, "one was born and one died ahovi, anato, or kannounnon" (Glélé 1971:8).

An individual's legal status thus was inalterable. Rank was not. A complex hierarchy of positions within the palace was accessible to women of all three legal grades. At the hierarchy's apex were opportunities for women to exercise power and authority, to make and influence policy, and to gain honor and wealth. Though obviously only a tiny fraction of ahosi could reach such levels, slave women clearly had access to high office. Because women of slave status were sometimes made queen mother, the highest office in the kingdom after that of the monarch himself, the possibility of worldly success for a slave woman was in practice *greater* than that for any man of comparable background. This paper will attempt a broad reconstruction of the political and economic functions and importance of common women, Fon and foreign, slave and non-slave, at various levels within the palace. Because their prerogatives and status differed markedly

3. Some persons born of slave parents in Dahomey, for example, became *glesi*. *Glesi* were farmers who were directly attached to royal estates granted by the king to "great cabeceers, village chiefs, and the mothers of kings." The glesi were not owned by the titled person who profited from the land they worked. Their children became glesi after them and did not become, as would have been normal for a slave owned outright, members of the lineage of the person who controlled them (Le Hérissé 1911:57).

from those of commoners, I will exclude from this discussion all ahosi of royal blood, including kings' daughters and sisters who at various moments held important positions within the palace hierarchy.

Fon Social Organization

Central to an understanding of the royal household of Dahomey is a consideration of two pervasive traits of Fon social organization: doubling or duality, which I shall here call mirroring, and hierarchy. Doubling, of titles, functions, and even institutions, was noticed by virtually all European visitors to precolonial Dahomey, and has been nearly universally discussed by twentieth-century scholars of the state. Examples abound of a constant pattern of pairing: male and female, right and left, royal and common, living and dead. But on closer examination the contrasts are not dual, but multiple: for example, the male ministers of state are divided into two complementary groups, at the right and left hands of the king, both of which are duplicated by sets of female ministers in the palace, and echoed again by male and female sets of commanders of the right and left wings of the army. The king himself is doubled by his queen mother; by the kings who reigned before him; by his *tohossu,* a deformed sibling literally returned to the waters of a sacred marsh at birth; by a distinguished forebear who provided him a name and eternal spirit; and in the nineteenth century, by his own self as prince.[4] In none of these pairs are the members either exactly the same or exactly opposite. In this sense, the term "mirroring" better expresses the relationships among contrasting elements in Fon social and political structures.

"Mirroring," in its usual metaphorical sense, is used to speak of identical pairs. But in reality, a mirror always distorts. Depending upon the quality and form of its surface, a mirror image may darken, deform, or otherwise modify the object reflected, in part or whole. Two or more mirrors placed at angles reflect multiple, but differing images. Similarity is evident in such multiple reflected images, but absolute identity is always absent. In an analogous way, a sense of the appropriateness of constant contrast seemed to pervade Fon ideas of social organization.

As noted above, the palace itself was a kind of microcosm of Fon society as a whole, a predominantly female institution within yet apart from Fon society. It was mirrored again in the court of the queen mother, whose retainers duplicated on a smaller scale the offices of the king's retinue. On a structural level, the palace mirrored the administrative organization of the kingdom as a whole. Every office within the kingdom was held jointly

---

4. Erroneously called the King of the Bush, this imaginary being was conceived and first honored by King Gezo (1818–58). See Bay 1979.

by two persons, an official (usually male) outside of the king's household and a woman within the palace. The women holders of office had functions corresponding to those of the persons outside; thus the women who were principal ministers of state, for example, performed their appropriate governing functions within the palace, were present at court when their male counterparts reported to the king, and actively participated as members of the state council in the making of national policy decisions. The mirroring was carried to its logical extreme: one European visitor, made a prince by King Glele in 1871, reported that a woman inside the palace received similar rank and title (Skertchly 1874:457); others noted that women representing state prostitutes were mirrored, too, by women of the same rank in the palace (Burton 1864/1966:335; Skertchly 1874:316).

Hierarchy characterized all forms of social organization—the Fon lineage, village government, chapter houses of the gods, and of course the court. From queen mothers down to the lowest slave, from lineage heads down to the youngest wives in a compound, Fon individuals were set in a strict ordering of authority and rank. Hierarchization was so deep a trait that a European missionary resident at Dahomey well after the conquest marveled at finding "everywhere a hierarchic society, well ordered and disciplined: masters and servants understand their duties and rights" (Hazoumé n.d.:33). Even today the Fon underline the appropriateness of hierarchic institutions by asking "Are we in Adja country, for all the stools are at the same level?" (Glélé 1974:29), a rhetorical question that refers to the material symbols of rank in precolonial Dahomean society.

Rank and function for women in the palace, then, were affected horizontally by the principle of mirroring and vertically by hierarchy. Hierarchy guaranteed a strict ordering of rank while mirroring insured the broadest range of ranks that reflected the extremes of social stratification in the kingdom as a whole. Women were initially placed in the palace hierarchy according to the rank they and/or their lineage held outside, their age, their beauty, and their manner of recruitment to the institution. Yet rank was not wholly fixed. In theory at least, a woman, slave or non-slave, might through meritorious service to the king rise to a position of great trust, responsibility, and honor.

Recruitment to the Palace

The female population of the king's household was augmented in three ways: by the incorporation of slaves captured outside Dahomey, by the addition of women from lineages within the kingdom, and by the natural increase of women already within the palace system. Unfortunately, there is little available evidence of how many women entered the palace service annually or of the proportions among them of slave and nonslave origin.

Warfare, and the concomitant capture of slaves, were annual activities in nineteenth-century Dahomey. An integral part of the ceremonial cycle, war mirrored *hwe tanu,* or Customs, the annual period when, theoretically, all Dahomey gathered in the capital to take part in ceremonial activities that ensured the continued well-being of the monarch and nation. Male and female court officials each year assumed warrior titles in yet another form of the rhythm of contrast in Dahomean life.

The palace organization played a central role in the housing, feeding, and ultimate disposal of literally thousands of war captives. At the end of each campaign, the king ceremonially purchased all captives.[5] In time they would be redistributed: as gifts and rewards to loyal subjects, including the male and female warriors who initially captured them; as workers on royal plantations, and prior to the mid-nineteenth century, as captives sold into the overseas trade; as sacrifices made during the annual hwe tanu cycle of ceremonies in honor of the ancestors; as soldiers enrolled in the king's standing army; and as members of the royal household.

Women born in Dahomey might become palace residents through several means. As early as the 1720s, agents of the king reportedly went out to seek ahosi from among the citizenry of Dahomey. A mid-eighteenth century source reported that every family in the kingdom was required to give the king a daughter as tribute (Smith 1744/1967:201). By the nineteenth century, a court official named the *Kpakpa* was responsible for recruitment within Dahomey (Le Hérissé 1911:78). Prior to marriage, every young girl was brought before the king's representatives, who visited each village in the kingdom at three-year intervals (Mattei 1890:179; Barbou 1893:30).[6] Because census figures were kept by the palace organization, the Kpakpa and his officials knew the approximate number of young girls to expect in every household. Girls judged suitable for the king's service were taken. A girl's lineage notified the ancestors of her marriage to the king, and gifts were offered the family in the name of the monarch. In theory, these girls were not allowed to return home for visits, and their

---

5. Robin Law (1977:561–62) summarizes the evidence for the king's "purchase" of war captives.

6. Both Richard Burton (1864/1966:256) and J. A. Skertchly (1874:454–55) claimed that the nineteenth-century kings had all Dahomeans bring their young daughters before them at court. However, such an event, which obviously would have involved a very large gathering, was not seen at first hand by either observer, and was not cited by other travelers; furthermore, it is not described by modern informants. I suspect, therefore, that informants of the two Englishmen were speaking figuratively of the activities of the *Kpakpa* as king's representative.

families were not supposed to seek them out at the palace (interviews: V. Kinhwe, December 22, 1972; Y. Soude, July 11, 1972).

A lineage head might offer a daughter, one who was, in the words of Fon informants, "fat and beautiful," to the king. Girls admitted to the palace service in this manner were allowed to visit their families on ceremonial occasions, and were not placed on the lowest levels of the palace hierarchy. The presentation of a daughter to the king reaffirmed lines of authority and obligation, and held out the possibility of wealth if the girls performed well in service. However, the giving of women to the king was limited to relatively wealthy lines, for granting a daughter to the palace does not appear to have exempted lineages from the visits of the Kpakpa. A poor or small family could ill afford the loss of bridewealth and of a female laborer that went along with giving up a daughter, especially since it risked losing more daughters through direct recruitment.[7] A rich lineage, on the other hand, would give as many daughters as possible, for it could hope to see its women on the higher levels of the palace organization, thereby enlarging its own ability to influence the monarchy. A prominent Whydah family, for example, is said to have presented seven fair-skinned daughters to King Glele (1858–89) alone (interview: C. Dosso-Yovo Loko, November 14, 1972).[8]

Women were also sent to the palace for various forms of misbehavior. A. B. Ellis claimed that prior to the reign of King Gezo (1818–58) all the women soldiers were criminals. Their "crimes" consisted of being adulterous wives or "scolds" (Ellis 1890:183). An 1843 visitor was told that the king's residence at Allada was ". . . a house of discipline for adulterous women. When an influential man has gripes against his wife, he complains to the king of Dahomey who has her locked up for the rest of her days to work for his profit" (de Brue 1845:58).[9] Thomas Birch Freeman claimed that daughters and female slaves, as well as wives, could be sent to the palace if they were "badly behaved and unmanageable" (M.M.S.:326). Others cited general criminal activity, including stealing, as a reason for sending wives to the king (Burton 1865:406; A.A.V.)

7. In the nineteenth century, lineages were further subject to the call-up of both women and men for war campaigns.

8. Bulfinch Lamb, who was held captive by King Agadja in 1724, was well aware of the benefits to be gained by presenting a woman to the king, and pleaded to the commandant of the English fort at Whydah that "If there is any Cast-off Whore, either White or Mullattoe, that can be persuaded to come to this Country, either to be his Wife or else practice her old Trade; I should gain his Majesty's Heart entirely by it . . ." (Smith 1744/1967:183).

9. See also Auguste Bouët 1852:42. Both G. de Wailly (1890:392) and Burton (1864/ 1966:257) claimed that one-third of the soldiers of the standing army had previously been married.

A woman might fall under the control of the palace not only through insubordinate or criminal activity, but through some shortcoming of the head of her *hwe* or household. Important or powerful persons were especially susceptible to accusations of disloyalty, which could result in the destruction of their households and the entry of their wives and daughters into the palace as *hwemesi* (literally, compound member in a subservient position). Bulfinch Lamb described these falls from favor in the early eighteenth century: "The King's Wives are the Executors of his Sentences, and 'tis merry enough when a Grandee has offended the King, 3 or 400 of them are sent to the Offender's House, which they immediately strip and level with the Ground" (Smith 1744/1967:206).

A third group of palace inhabitants was born into the system. Likely the smallest of the three sources of women for the king's household, they included both daughters of the king and girl children fathered by others but born of mothers belonging to certain classes within the palace. The origins of the latter will be discussed in more detail below.

Ahosi were drawn, then, from among Dahomeans as well as from neighboring areas. Because they were recruited from all levels of society, palace women formed a powerful centralizing force within the kingdom. Most lineages could point to at least one daughter within the palace structure. Depending upon the rank and position such a woman achieved, her lineage could reap the advantages of gifts of slaves, land, women, and sinecures. More important, the lineage heads could enjoy a direct communications link with the very center of power in the kingdom, the palace at Abomey.

Female slaves were additionally a vital channel of cross-cultural influence. Religious practices can often be traced to women integrated into Dahomean society through the palace organization. A prime example is Hwanjile, the Aja captive who became queen mother to King Tegbesu, and who introduced the major deities Mawu, Lisa, and Age into the Fon pantheon of *vodun* or gods. Yoruba cultural institutions, so evident in twentieth-century Dahomey, seem to have been established in large part through the impact of the presence of large numbers of Yoruba-speaking women as wives in leading Fon families. For example, a Muslim Yoruba wife in the lineage of the descendants of King Agonglo established a branch of the family that practices Islam and is referred to as "Yoruba" (interview: M. Gnimavo, September 10, 1972). Abomeans commonly credit Yoruba wives with the establishment in Dahomey of the *kutito* society of the dead, the Fon equivalent of the Yoruba *egungun* (interview: A. Feliho, May 20, 1972). Many of Dahomey's greatest *bokonon* or diviners were royal descendants who learned Fa (Ifa) divination through relatives in their mothers' families (interview: L. Agoliagbo, September 7, 1972).

Production and Reproduction

Upon entry into the palace, new ahosi were given specific ranks and duties. Like wives in common polygynous households, palace women were expected to work for the welfare of their husbands and to undertake production activities for their own independent benefit. Yet in a situation where clear distinctions were not drawn between the king's household and the state, ahosi became by definition part of the royal administration. Literally hundreds of offices and occupations, most of them mirroring common wives' usual economic activities, were carried on by ahosi in the name of the king.

Labor-intensive palace industries generally complemented the work of laborers, male and female, on the king's and on his clients' farms. The king's household processed palm oil and carried it some ninety-five kilometers to the port of Whydah, manufactured pottery and other clay products, helped create the uniforms worn by 2,000 or more women warriors, and processed food for war and ceremony. Storage within the palace was itself a monumental task by the nineteenth century. In addition to the fresh foodstuffs and currency paid as tax, palace women were responsible for the vast royal treasury of gifts and imported goods. The royal ceremonial cycle, doubled in length by the innovations of Gezo, presented enormous problems of organization and management. Food had to be collected and prepared to feed literally thousands of persons over several weeks; treasures had to be removed from storage and refurbished, and women organized and trained for long processions, dance and military displays, and ancestral rites. Wartime required other preparations. Women fighters needed to be trained and ready for combat. Female as well as male spies carried out reconnaissance missions to neighboring areas. Other women were sent out to seduce men, denounce them for having intercourse with ahosi, and then see that they were enrolled in the army as punishment (Maire 1905:51; Le Hérissé 1911:72).

Certain women worked to cure ill ahosi; others assured the spiritual health of the palace inhabitants through appropriate offerings to gods and ancestors. At the palace hierarchy's apex were sacred women who formed the link between the kingdom as a whole and the ancestral spirits. Others in high office directed the palace industries and advised the king. The work of some women was public—the English visitor Frederick Forbes (1851/1966, 2:86–104), for example, described long public debates at court. Others' functions were shrouded in mystery—no one could touch or even speak directly to the women called *kposi*, a title naming those who were wives or dependents of the leopard-founder of the royal lineage. Some high-ranking women could make loans to persons outside the palace. Women on lower levels strung cowries for currency; the palace's smaller number of cowries per string guaranteed a royal profit. In brief, the economic, political, and spiritual functions of the ahosi were many and various. Taken together, they were meant to maintain and enhance the monarch's material and spiritual well-being and to ensure his domestic control and ability to protect and expand the state's boundaries.

But not all palace economic activity was directed towards the enrichment of the king and state. Like common wives, slave and Dahomean ahosi were permitted to own personal property separate from their husband's control. Each woman was expected to work for herself as well as the king. Some carried on occupations apart from their palace duties. A woman responsible for sweeping and cleaning the king's reception area, for instance, might weave mats to sell in the small market adjacent to the palace walls. Some of the palace industries were designed so that the king and the women could divide the profits of the women's labor. The cowrie-stringers, for example, who made shorter strings for their monarch's use, were permitted to keep a portion of the shells as payment for their work. The descendant of one ahosi recounted that Gezo had set her ancestor up in Whydah with 333 slaves: "If a stranger came and he needed a woman, he could come to her house and find one. If strangers came and gave money, she would send it to Gezo. The children born in her house belonged to her" (interview: Avloko, February 27, 1973). A small number of high-ranking women were able to enrich themselves and their paternal families by the judicious use of human labor and natural resources given them by the king.

The organizational structure of the palace recognized and encouraged the ahosi's productive activities for the benefit of the king and themselves. It also aimed to control their reproductive functions to several ends: to ensure that candidates for heir were without question fathered by the king, to encourage the undivided loyalty of the king's closest advisors, to reinforce strictly military goals among the women soldiers, and to enlarge the number of women permanently attached to the palace. Control of women's reproductive functions appears linked to two values in Fon society, the desire for children on the one hand, and the popular belief, on the other, that a strong mother-child bond was antithetical to the interests of the patrilineage. Whether or not a woman was allowed to bear or continue to bear children was directly related to her rank and occupation within the palace. For the sake of analysis, women's functions within the king's household can be divided into three broad categories: the elite, the army, and the serving classes. Women of the elite and the army controlled the productive and to some extent the reproductive activities of the third group, the serving classes.

The elite included both women who could become physical wives of the king and all officeholders and titled women. The potential sexual partners of the king were estimated at about 1,000 women (Le Hérissé 1911:26).[10] The majority probably were slaves, for sources consistently underline a preference for slave, or at least common, women on grounds that they were more trustworthy and faithful (Glélé 1974:156; A.N.S., "Rapport . . . Abomey"). Youthfulness and beauty are claimed to have been criteria for placement among the physical wives. Some had previously been married, as evidenced by several well-documented cases in which Dahomean princes had older half-brothers born before their mothers entered the palace.[11] Their progeny were fairly numerous. Biographical data on princes serving as administrative officers in the twentieth century indicate that Glele fathered some 129 children who grew to maturity. Gbehanzin, whose reign lasted less than four years (1890–94), was credited with seventy-seven daughters and sons (A.N.B.). Male children remained in the palace until age seven or eight, when they were sent to live in the households of other members of the royal lineage. Daughters remained more closely linked to the palace, leaving at marriage but often returning for varying periods of time.

Other members of the elite included women with religious duties associated with the well-being of king and state, and all those with titles and functions paralleling the secular administration. Evidence is ambiguous as to whether or not a woman might simultaneously hold an office and be a physical wife of the king. The sacred kposi and *dadasi*, women with ritual roles, were definitely celibate. Some women in the higher ranks—ministers, high household officials, and the like, are known to have had children by the king, possibly before they were promoted to high office. However, a pattern had been established by the nineteenth century in which no woman with a living male child held high office or an advisory position close to the king. Justification for such a policy may be found in the frequently related story of a wife of King Agadja. Entrusted with the security of the royal treasury, this ahosi tried to bribe representatives of the Oyo empire to help make her son the Dahomean king (Anilo G. 1946:49; Cornevin 1962:107). The story may be apocryphal; the lesson was not. In a kingdom where the officially named heir invariably was challenged and often failed to win the throne, and where candidates for king needed the support of the king's household, successful bids for the throne became based on alliances between ambitious princes and powerful palace women. Kings could hope to control the succession process by choosing as their closest

10. P. Labarthe (1803:122) reported an estimated 800–1,000 physical wives at a much earlier period, the third quarter of the eighteenth century.

11. Examples include Hwanjile, the queen mother of King Tegbesu; Sophie, a Eur-African woman previously married to a French trader at the coast; and the mother of Oua-nilo, the only son to accompany King Gbehanzin into exile after the French conquest.

female advisors women who at the least did not have natural sons that they wished to place in their husband's royal sandals.

Elite women with lower-level official responsibilities, however, may have shared the king's bedchamber. New ahosi, perhaps including those women presented as gifts to the monarch by wealthy lineages, would have been given such lesser offices; others of the new ahosi remained among the elite women only until they were presented as wives to high-ranking commoners and princes. Some of the girls drafted into the palace service would have been placed among the elite wives, too, for placement of girls recruited by the king's Kpakpa reflected the socioeconomic position of their own lineages. According to J. A. Skertchly, the king "selected the most promising of the children of the upper ten, and created them officers, while the lower orders were dubbed soldiers, and the children of slave parents became the slaves of the Amazons within the palace" (1874: 454–55).

Elite women were carefully guarded from contacts with men other than the king. Though some ahosi could move relatively freely in and out of the palace, the elite women were among those whose path outside the palace walls was cleared of men. All men were required to leave the road and to avert their gaze when groups of ahosi moved about town or country. Members of Forbes's expedition in 1849 were forced to wait outside a city gate for three-quarters of an hour one morning, and on another occasion were told not to venture into the western areas of Abomey, for 4,000 ahosi were going out to bathe (Forbes 1851/1966, 2:71). Edouard Foa described the passage of wives of Fon chiefs after the French conquest: " . . . the wives of the king or of chiefs cry continuously in the streets, Ago! Everyone gets out of the way and sometimes when the street is narrow they step into the houses in order to let them pass. . . . The women avoid crowds; but, when they go to the market, a void opens around them, which proves how much people fear the anger of their husbands" (1895:245).

The rationale for the seclusion of elite women is obvious. A son born to a physical wife through an adulterous relationship would have raised the question of the paternity of virtually all the monarch's offspring, including the heir himself. Also among the elite were high-ranking women cognizant of certain state secrets; the king undoubtedly would not have risked their sharing confidences with lovers.

The second major category of positions within the palace was that associated with the army of women. Though women had been fighters for Dahomey from as early as the 1720s, the women's army was not made a permanent force until the reign of Gezo (1818–58). Roughly one-quarter of the palace population in the nineteenth century were warriors. They appear to have been drawn mainly from among young captives, *soudofi,* who could be trained from an early age into the fierce loyalty characteristic of the finest soldiers (Glélé 1971:85; Laffitte 1873:88–89). Others, perhaps as many as a third of the soldiers, were taken from among the so-called criminal element, those women who for various reasons—adultery, bad temper, or stealing—were judged by husbands and families too strong-willed to be tolerated (de Wailly 1890:392; Burton 1865:406). Some of the Dahomean girls drafted by the palace were placed among the soldiers. Occasionally, women from among the soldiers were presented to persons at court as rewards from the king.

Though the kings could and did occasionally take a soldier as a lover (Burton 1865:406; Hazoumé 1925), warriors within the palace were in theory held to strict celibacy. Pregnancies among the soldiers would have been at best an inconvenience to their carrying out of professional duties. It was presumably to discourage sexual activity that a few pregnant warriors were executed from time to time while the great majority were punished by enrollment in the Gate-opening Company, "a corps exposed to the hottest fire and the brunt of the battle" (Skertchly 1874:359). Nevertheless, reasonably large numbers appear to have borne children by fathers other than the king. Both Burton in 1863 and Skertchly nearly ten years later found evidence that large numbers of soldiers became pregnant through forbidden liaisons (Burton 1864/1966:166; Skertchly 1874:359).

The third and possibly largest group of palace residents was that in the serving classes, both Dahomeans and slaves. Under less physical seclusion than higher-ranking wives, many among them appear to have had relative freedom to move in and out of the palace. Many would ultimately be offered by the king to visitors at court or to Dahomeans as rewards for faithful service. In a society where large numbers of dependents were a mark of prestige that represented labor for the creation of wealth, control over persons, and control over nubile women in particular, was an invaluable gift. Women granted by the palace were particularly welcomed, for not only did their recipient gain a wife without the expense of bridewealth, but he or she also received heightened social status as a person directly honored by the king (Aguessy 1970:77–78).

Many women of the serving classes were granted to elite women, to women warriors, or to princesses as personal servants. One source, for example, reported that all of the soldiers had at least one servant, and another source that some controlled as many as fifty (de Wailly 1890:391; Burton 1864/1966:123, n. 7). The highest-ranking elite women might control numbers of servants and slaves. Daughters of the king were given what was effectively a human dowry, a household of female slaves and servants who moved from the king's palace to the princesses' marital residences.

Control over the reproductive potential of serving women differed depending upon their status as slave or Dahomean commoner. If slaves were given as gifts, they became the personal property of their palace mistresses, who could use them as personal servants in the palace or send them outside to their own or their families' compounds to work. Palace women could arrange liaisons for their slaves, or marry them to men under their authority. Children born of such unions became in turn dependent upon their mothers' owner, the palace woman, and were part of her family.

Other women, perhaps originally of slave background, fell under a form of perpetual servitude. The kings granted the use of women called *gandoba* to titled ahosi in the palace. The gandoba were considered to be attached to the office, not to the individual who held it. Children that gandoba bore were divided; sons became members of the patrilineage of the person to whom the king had awarded the gandoba's services; daughters were integrated into the palace as gandoba themselves (Le Hérissé 1911:223). Because the gandoba were not under the full legal control of the palace wives to whom they were granted, they could be retaken by the king at any time, and were thus an effective means of assuring a palace woman's continued loyal service to the monarch.

Hwemesi, women who were forced to enter the palace because of a crime attributed to their lineage head, were also granted to persons inside and outside the palace. All children borne by hwemesi belonged to the lineage of their guardians, no matter who the natural father might be (A.S.A., Peines). The

Women on the lower levels of the palace, then, were used not only as servants for persons favored by the king. A recipient of a palace serving woman could enlarge her or his personal estate by the addition of human labor potential: in the case of a slave, with a woman and all the children she bore, in the case of a gandoba, with male children only, and in the case of a hwemesi, with children of both sexes. The king's largesse, initially a reward for meritorious service, was thus expected to be repaid with continued loyalty and, in the case of gandoba, with female replacements for the woman lost.

Loyalty, Reward, and the Exercise of Power

The women of the palace, by contributing to the material and political well-being of the monarchs of Dahomey, were a central element of the king's power. The administration of a complex state system such as Dahomey's required multiple offices and correspondingly provided multiple opportunities for individuals and factions beyond the king's control to reap benefits from the exercise of the king's delegated authority. From the monarch's point of view, the ahosi served as a kind of counterweight to the potential influences of powerful male officeholders outside the palace as well as to the dangers of male rivals from within the royal lineage itself.

Like eunuchs in other state systems, the ahosi were trusted in large part because they occupied an anomalous position in the society as a whole. As women, the ahosi could mirror but never replace and hence never threaten male positions and prerogatives in family or state. Ahosi of slave origin, since they were without patrilineal ties in Fon society, were a step further removed from the male-defined norm.

In patrilineal and virilocal Fon society, women were full members of the patrilineages of their birth. They enjoyed rights of participation in lineage affairs, had special prerogatives in lineage-centered religious activity, and expected at death to join their patrilineal ancestors. Yet in practice, women appear to have been considered, even in their own patrilineages, as less central to the lineage than their brothers. Though women could and did head compounds, popular attitudes suggested that it was only the male members who comprised the core of the patrilineage. Ambivalence in attitudes towards women corresponded to comparable contradictions in images of slaves and highlighted ironies in the life patterns of both.

At base, the argument that the legal status and behavioral expectations of slave and woman were similar has validity for precolonial Dahomey. A Fon woman left her father's home at marriage and lived as a stranger in another lineage's compound. In a strictly legal sense, a woman had no choice in the selection of the lineage or the man to whom she would be married. Two factors distinguished a slave from nonslave wife: 1) the lineage of the husband owed nothing to that of the slave wife, nor was it obliged to allow her to carry out responsibilities to her family, and 2) a slave wife had no recourse if mistreated, for she could not leave and return to her father's home. However, depending upon the treatment that a woman received in the household of her husband or master, the realities of daily life might be little different regardless of whether or not she was legally a slave. Significantly, a 1904 survey of slavery in the Allada region found that of the slaves freed by the French conquest, most men returned to their home areas, but nearly all of the women slaves remained (A.N.S., "Rapport . . . Allada").

Ambiguous attitudes of contempt and admiration were associated with both women and slaves. Women, on the one hand, were despised for being weak, deceitful, and treacherous; even the women warriors boasted that "we are men, not women" (Forbes 1851/1966, 1:23). Yet women were honored as mothers, eagerly sought as indispensable wives, and everywhere named to positions parallel to men as a matter of course. One man provided the following etymology for the Fon word for woman, *gnonnu:*

> *Gnon* means "to know" and *nu* means "to drink"; thus *gnonnu* literally means "to know how to drink." A woman, like water, is a precious commodity and

men must know that they can't take too much of it. A man must not abuse a woman because a woman doesn't belong to him. Women are for everyone. If you take a wife today she's for you, but when you die she'll go to another. Use a woman with moderation. Know that you can't drink the full bottle; you must conserve some of the contents. (Bay 1977:21–22)

Slaves, too, were to be despised, even if they attained high rank. A praise song to Zoindi, the queen mother to Glele, chastizes those who have intrigued against her and who have taunted her with being a slave (E. d'Almeida, pers. comm.). Yet popular belief held that among palace women slaves were most trustworthy, commoners next, and descendants of the royal line last (A.N.S., "Rapport . . . Allada").[12] A slave was nothing, but a slave was by definition more trustworthy than the king's own kinsmen. A woman was an object of contempt for male-dominated Fon society, and a woman slave was subject to scorn on two counts.

From the monarch's perspective, then, the ahosi were outside a male-centered system. They could be offered and could exercise great power, for in their individual lifetime their wealth and influence were dependent upon the king's continued support. The female ahosi, and the slave ahosi in particular, were valuable because as women they could be directly controlled by the throne. One might, therefore, interpret the palace as a system that grossly exploited the productive and intellectual resources of the vast numbers of its female inhabitants. Moreover, one could argue that, by denying to their patrilineages the women's presence and productive potential, the palace organization represented a massive exploitation of the monarch's Dahomean subjects and a destructive drain on the resources of the kingdom's neighboring peoples. A close look at the evidence, however, suggests that the ahosi might as easily be seen as the exploiters rather than the exploited.

The king's household was indeed the center of power in Dahomey. As an institution, it managed vast resources, distributing or investing them for the king and his ahosis' gain. Its female inhabitants supervised public assemblies; they participated in policy formation and were instrumental in its implementation. They represented the king throughout the nation and acted in his name. Perhaps most important, the palace organization controlled access to the monarch himself. Only rarely were outsiders to the palace able to speak directly to the king. Private audiences always included two or more ahosi. In short, the king and his ahosi were tied together with links of mutual dependence through which individual women in the palace could gain and exercise great influence.

---

12. The suspicion of women of royal descent is generally associated with the fact that they were granted sexual freedom.

For the thousands of girls and women who became ahosi, there was initially no great honor attached to entry into the palace service. A large number, perhaps the majority, were of course slaves, forcibly brought from their homes in neighboring areas. Others were sent to the palace in disgrace, or wrenched away from their homes as part of the king's triennial draft. Though a woman's family might gain some prestige by her entry into the king's household, young women themselves undoubtedly faced the king's mysterious city with foreboding.[13] Once inside, strong negative and positive incentives worked to integrate women into the household and to ensure their loyalty to the king.

As noted above, a woman remained in the palace service for life unless the king (upon recommendation of his women advisors) chose to grant her to someone as a gift. There was little hope for escape. One late eighteenth-century European visitor witnessed the public execution of five slave women who had escaped to their own country but had been sought out and recaptured (Dalzel 1793/1967:171–72). Large numbers of female war captives were set aside for sacrifice at annual ceremonies and were never integrated into the palace service. But additional women were also drawn from the palace, and sacrifice was clearly used as a punishment for recalcitrant ahosi (Le Hérissé 1911:180). Up until the mid-nineteenth century, too, the secret sale of palace women at Whydah, or their drowning in the sea, was another form of punishment, one that in at least a few cases was used to rid the palace of women whose power was perceived as a threat (Snelgrave 1734/1971:101–6).

On the other hand, women who gave outstanding service and loyalty to the king and remained in his favor were rewarded with titles and material gifts that included slaves. Women in the warrior and elite groups in particular could expect to rise in rank and responsibility. Stories of the exploits of fighting women and the honors given them were common (Duncan 1847/1967, 1:234; Forbes 1851/1966, 2:90). One detailed account collected by Paul Hazoumé in the early twentieth century is an excellent example. A slave woman from the Holli country (near the border with present-day Nigeria) was captured as a child and raised as a warrior. She distinguished herself in battle by killing a man and was given cloth and cowries as a reward. King Glele then made her pregnant, asking her not to admit that he was the father. The woman, Tata Ajache, subsequently resisted both social pressures and physical beatings to force her to reveal the name of her lover. In the end, Glele gave her a praise-name that alluded to her fidelity, transferred her to the ranks of the elite, and presented her with a house, baskets of cowries, beads, cloth, and two female slaves

13. See comments, for example, by Melville J. Herskovits (1938, 1:339) and Paul Hazoumé (1938:130–31).

(Hazoumé 1925). The story of Tata Ajache is revealing of the attitudes of the Dahomean monarchs. Valor in war was important, but unquestioning loyalty to the king was even more richly rewarded.

High court officials, male and female, were awarded royal titles along with gifts of land, palm trees, and control over numbers of persons. Each had the right to trade at Whydah, trade that could and did include the sale of slaves. Palace women entrusted such trade negotiations and the management of their properties to subordinates (interview: R. Aho, January 21, 1973), most likely members of their patrilineages. Though a woman remained in the palace for life, the properties that she acquired through the king's service (like the personal belongings of any wife) were considered her own. Palace women's titles and property were inherited by female patrilineal relatives. Thus a woman who rose to high office directly enriched her lineage.

Yet to argue that the threat of annihilation coupled with the promise of material riches were the sole factors motivating the ahosi is to ignore the fact that the palace was indeed the political and economic nerve center of Dahomey. An esprit, an elitism, a sense of participation at the pivot of power in the kingdom seem to have pervaded the palace atmosphere. Prestige, honor, wealth, and the exercise of influence were within the reach of clever and ambitous women there. Intrigue was a constant. A woman could build alliances with more powerful mentors in the ranks of the ahosi. She could use serving women granted to her use to build up her own resources and to develop alliances with persons outside the palace. Women clearly risked and gained much as they moved up or down the palace hierarchy, working both for the king's benefit and for the achievement of their individual ambitions.

Because the processes of decision-making within the palace took place within the seclusion of its walls, and because activity in the interior was deliberately shrouded in secrecy, it is difficult to distinguish with precision which women wielded influence and the manner in which they worked. Offices and officers can be named, but their rank in the palace hierarchy and the specific instances where they made a mark on Dahomean history can rarely be discerned. Moreover, the status of an individual high-ranking woman, whether slave or Dahomean, is seldom clear. Despite these difficulties, sources on precolonial Dahomey are replete with examples of the public effects of the private activities of powerful women in the palace. Moreover, the patterns of accession to the office of queen mother, to be discussed below, strongly suggest that many of the women near the apex of power in Simboji palace were of slave origin.

Several examples suffice to suggest why outsiders to the palace feared and respected the king's women. Little could be gained without their active support or at least their acquiescence. Again and again, modern informants as well as the accounts of travelers stress the importance of reaching the king through his women, and the dangers of arousing their enmity (Dalzel 1793/1967:211; Bouche 1885:344; M.M.S.:311; interview: V. Kinhwe, March 23, 1973). At public audiences, the interior of the palace was physically divided from outsiders by a line of mid-ribs of palm branches stretched across the open courtyard. Outsiders to the palace, including the king's male ministers and all foreign visitors, were forbidden to cross the line. The king remained secluded on his royal verandah while a group of women, the *daklo,* transmitted all messages between the king and outsiders beyond the palm line. An incident witnessed by J. A. Skertchly in 1871 underlines the potential in this system for manipulation and control of the monarch and his public. All court officials were required to be present at all times during the long days of public sessions associated with the annual ceremonial cycle. But on a particular day, the male treasurer was called before the king and was discovered to be absent. The unhappy official was found and immediately imprisoned, and released only when it was revealed that he had in fact asked the king's permission to retire. A daklo had given a false assent in the name of the king (Skertchly 1874:375). Unfortunately, Skertchly never learned who was guilty of conspiracy against the king's treasurer, or why.

An earlier traveler, Archibald Dalzel, recorded a more serious incident of palace intrigue in the late eighteenth century:

> It happened during that epocha, that a dangerous female conspiracy had been formed against the liberties of the people. Some of the ladies of the seraglio, who bore evident marks of gallantry, having been questioned concerning their paramours, named upwards of *one hundred and fifty* men, belonging to some villages in the neighborhood of Calmina [Cana]. These were all sold, although most of them were afterwards found to have been innocent, by the confession of a woman who discovered the plot. (Dalzel 1793/1967:211)

Certain high-ranking ahosi had recognized and public rights to influence decisions of state. Two councils advised the nineteenth-century kings of Dahomey. The smaller was composed of the monarch's major ministers. Because the male ministers' ahosi counterparts were required to be present with them at court, the female ministers were clearly involved in the inner council deliberations. Very likely it was these women that E. Chaudoin described when he asserted that: "The king's women play a considerable part in the politics of the country; they attend council meetings, their opinions have great weight with the king. They are the ones who refresh his memory on certain facts and prompt him on his addresses or speeches to the chiefs and to the people" (Chaudoin 1891:269–70). In mid-nineteenth century, Thomas Birch Freeman similarly reported that judicial appeals from districts were heard in Abomey by a council that included chief ministers of the state and "the leaders of the Amazons." According to him, the women's influence was preponderant, "it being a leading feature of Dahomean polity that in the counsels of the King the female sex have the ascendent" (M.M.S.:311).

A larger and more public council existed that appears to have included hundreds of state officials. Meeting each year during the period of the annual ceremonies, this grand council provided a kind of open forum for discussion of questions of general importance to the nation. Women officials were active participants in the debate (Forbes 1851/1966, 2:86–104; Skertchly 1874:276–77, 444). One mid-nineteenth century observer claimed that in council "the Naies, or King's women, have the first vote: they also enjoy the privilege of imposing a fine on any courtier who is so ungallant as to oppose their vote" (Valdez 1861, 1:339).

Certainly of equal importance were the numerous informal occasions where those few most trusted women witnessed the making of decisions. Europeans and Afro-Brazilian traders, for example, were often received in private audience. T. B. Freeman especially enjoyed his nighttime meetings with King Gezo, during which he conferred with the king in the presence of "two or three favorite wives" and the king's second male minister (M.M.S.:285; see also Skertchly 1874:432). Obviously, we cannot know the extent to which the various kings consulted their closest ahosi, nor the nature of the advice they sought. However, the women's presence at important deliberations, coupled with informants' testimony that certain individuals were "advisors," provides evidence for their influence. Private audiences would have been a likely channel for the exercise of female power, a reasonable counterpoint to the well-documented occasions when their voices were heard.

Queen Mothers and the Royal Succession

The careers of the women who became queen mother, or *Kpojito*, to the Dahomean monarchs perhaps best illustrate some of the patterns of advancement in the palace and the implications of the achievement of high rank for individual slave and common women and their lineages. The greatest possible reward for a palace woman was the opportunity to become the queen mother, the highest-ranking office in the kingdom save that of the king himself. The term *Kpojito*, inaccurately translated as queen mother, means literally "she who places the leopard on earth," a reference to the totem of the royal lineage. The evidence strongly suggests that the Kpojito was rarely if ever the natural mother of the king (Bay 1977:231–34). No queen mother could be born of any branch of the royal family; most if not all appear to have been slaves. Yet each established an estate and family line that was supported by subsequent monarchs and survived intact into the twentieth century.

The selection of a queen mother was normally made shortly after the installation of a king. Not only did the king and queen mother in some sense rule together, but in some cases the pair appear to have worked together to win their offices. Obviously, more highly placed women within the palace structure had the greatest potential for aiding a promising prince. Ambitious royals probably sought alliances with trusted, influential, and similarly ambitious wives of their father, women who could help advance the political career of a man. A case in point is the story of the keeper of King Agadja's treasury (p. 350) who sought to place her candidate on the throne. According to a Portuguese priest present in Abomey in 1797, King Agonglo was poisoned by a woman who expected to reign as queen mother with her co-plotter, Prince Dogan, as king (Pires 1957:70). Several traditions tell how Hwanjile, the Aja slave who became queen mother to Tegbesu, used her supernatural powers to protect the young prince, enhance his reputation, and secure the throne from the heir apparent (interviews: Yomana, June 6, 1972, and Hwanjile, April 30, 1972; Dunglas 1957, 1:146–47). Visesegan, the powerful favorite of Glele, attempted to seize power for her protégé, Sasse Koka, but was thwarted by supporters of Gbehanzin (A.N.F.).

Even in cases where a single woman was not clearly involved in a succession struggle, a prince needed the support of palace women generally to assure success in his attempt at the throne. The key to securing power was possession and control of the central Simboji palace. Obviously, when possession of the entourage of the deceased monarch was a central element in effective control for a would-be king, the assistance of women within the palace could determine the success or failure of a candidate. Through the appropriate contacts near the king, a prince could hear of the death of the reigning monarch, could know when and where to make his play for power, and might even hope to hurry the demise of his predecessor. Attempts were often made to keep the actual death of the king secret until the recognized heir or another powerful candidate could take physical control. For example, a brother of Gbehanzin, present when Glele died, sent word to nearby Cana for the crown prince. While waiting for Gbehanzin to arrive, he decapitated a young ahosi witness to prevent news of the monarch's death from reaching others (Dunglas 1957, 3:20). King Tegbesu is said to have raced to the palace on hearing of his father's death elsewhere (interview: Yomana, June 6, 1972). And Dogan, the prince named in the poison plot against Agonglo, arrived at the palace with a force of over 300 persons on the morning of the king's demise (Pires 1957:71). The women warriors, too, could be a significant factor, for they tended to support those holding power. Gezo, for instance, met heavy resistance from Adandozan's ahosi at the time of his 1818 coup. Later, however, when he was enthroned, he was able to stave off an attack by a rival thanks to forewarning by a woman soldier (Hazoume 1938:78, 189).

All of the queen mothers came from frontier areas, regions that the kings were in the process of trying to integrate more closely into the kingdom. For example, before the mid-eighteenth century, Dahomean expansion was directed toward areas to the south and west of Abomey. Adonon, queen mother to the conqueror of Allada, came from the village of Wassa, some twenty-five kilometers southeast of Abomey, while Hwanjile, her successor, was originally from Aja country southwest of the capital city. By the latter part of the eighteenth century, the attention of the Fon had been turned north and east; Mahi and Yoruba peoples became the object of war. Similarly, King Kpengla's queen mother traced her family to Mahi country. It is probably no accident that Agontime, Gezo's queen mother, was from Tenji, a town on one of the two major roads to Agonli, the Yoruba enclave between the Zou and Weme rivers. Though some disagree about her exact origins, Glele's queen mother Zoindi appears to have come from deep in Yoruba country. By the time Gbehanzin succeeded to the throne, the seriousness of the French threat at Cotonou was well recognized. His queen mother was a woman from the town of Abomey-Calavi, a key juncture on the route north from Cotonou.

These coincidences of origin underline a number of patterns noted elsewhere. First, they hint that all of the queen mothers could indeed have been slaves, since most of their home areas were not a part of the kingdom at the period when they themselves entered the palace service. They suggest that numbers of women were being captured and integrated into the king's household. Moreover, they indicate that some slave women were able to rise within the palace hierarchy. Whether the queen mother worked directly with a prince or not, she would have been a relatively high-ranking individual in the king's household. Finally, the geographical location of the queen mothers' homes suggests that consolidation of power in frontier areas was a deliberate policy carried out in part through the contacts provided by these highly placed women. Queen Mother Hwanjile's village of Home, for example, which became a major center in Aja territory, was apparently first integrated into Dahomey at the time of the reign of her reign-mate Tegbesu. Chiefs of the region were appointed from Abomey; a palace built by Tegbesu for Hwanjile at Ajahome was undoubtedly an additional reminder to local people of the power of their Fon neighbors (A.S.A., Situation). Dalzel similarly reported that the people of Mahi country, "in order to live on peaceable terms with Dahomey, claimed kindred with Adahoonzou [Kpengla] whose mother was a Mahee woman" (1793/1967:165).

The Kpojito are remembered as persons of great wealth, richer "than any of the brothers or sisters of the king" (interview: V. Kinhwe, December 22, 1972). They controlled large numbers of slaves and other dependents, palm groves, and farming villages. Like the king, the queen mothers received Fon girls annually to serve in their palaces. Dahomeans presented daughters to them, and they in turn presented women as gifts to men (A.S.A., Résident). A queen mother's material wealth and title were inherited in perpetuity by female descendants of her patrilineage. Normally titleholders appear to have had diminishing impact on subsequent reigns. For example, a king's ministers undoubtedly left a legacy of substantial wealth that may have helped other members of their lineage maintain a degree of influence in political affairs. Successive monarchs, though, do not appear to have selected their own closest officials from among the ranks of titleholding families. Thus, the centers of policy-making were a step further removed from a given titleholder with each successive reign.

Queen mothers, however, appear to have continued to play relatively active roles near the center of power. Kings were obligated to maintain their estate, and the queen mothers, like other influential persons during a king's reign, demonstrated their loyalty by offering contingents of soldiers for national campaigns. A Kpojito's privileges continued in perpetuity; hence a series of small queen mother courts existed, with that of the most recent queen mother enjoying the highest prestige. All the queen mothers appear to have acted as intercessors with the kings, both giving refuge to and pleading on behalf of Dahomean subjects (interviews: V. Kinhwe, December 22, 1972, and A. Glele, October 26, 1972). Evidence suggests that certain Kpojito, in the persons of replacements through perpetual kinship,[14] were able to wield a strong influence on later reigns. Adonon reigned as queen mother to both Akaba and Agaja. It is possible that the power she gained as Kpojito to Akaba enabled her to help Agaja wrest power from Agbo-Sassa, a rival candidate to the throne. Some sources credit Adonon with having presented Hwanjile, the slave woman who became Tegbesu's Kpojito, to Akaba as a wife (interview: S. Glele, July 29, 1972; Herskovits 1938, 2:104).

Once installed, the queen mother apparently had opportunities to wield real power in conjunction with the king. Several traditions recount the settling of old scores by Kpojito who bore long-standing grievances against particular individuals. More important, though, was the queen mother's potential for exercising authority over religious life in the kingdom. The cults of the various popular gods (vodun) were not under direct royal con-

14. Perpetual kinship refers to systems in which a direct descendant of a titled person takes his or her ancestor's name, title, and social identity. Kinsmen bear the same relationship to the replacement that they did to the original titleholder. See Bay (1977:61–62) and Vansina (1966:27).

trol, and the royal dynasty made numerous attempts to bring them more closely under royal authority. A major ministry, that of the *Ajaho,* was created to supervise the activities of the cults. Disputes involving adepts of the cults were judged by the Ajaho, but appeals were made to the queen mother for the reigning king, with final appeal to the king himself (Le Hérissé 1911:133).

A queen mother could succeed in wielding more than just judicial power over the cults. The career of Hwanjile, the Kpojito to Tegbesu, suggests that a queen mother could actively work with the king toward the consolidation of political power within the kingdom through a restructuring of cult life. A major effort toward religious reorganization in Tegbesu's day was directed toward the establishment of new "popular" vodun, nonroyal deities who would remain under the permanent control of Hwanjile herself. The early years of Tegbesu's reign saw threats of coups by two of the king's brothers and their supporters. In order to ensure the king's position, Hwanjile took over the direction of powerful vodun in Dahomey. According to an account recorded by Herskovits:

> During the reign of Tegbesu there was great unrest among the princes, his half-brothers, who coveted his throne. A number of them and their retainers were eventually sold into slavery—to the New World. To allay the disaffection of the people who were being swayed by the priesthoods of the autochthonous gods to resist the monarch, his mother, herself a priestess of Mawu-Lisa, persuaded Tegbesu to cause the cult to be brought to Abomey, and under the aegis of the powerful gods of the Sky to cement his rule and gain the spiritual submissions of his subjects. (Herskovits 1938, 2:104)

Though traditions differ over precisely which vodun were brought to Abomey through Hwanjile's influence, she is known to have had direct control over three central deities: the creator couple Mawu and Lisa and their offspring Age. Hwanjile's descendants continued to direct Fon cult life and reign through perpetual kinship as Kpojito. The eighth Hwanjile of the line was still living at the cult center at Jena, just outside the walls of Simboji palace, at the time of my 1972 field research.

Conclusion

If the office of queen mother of Dahomey represents the apex of power, influence, and wealth that was available to a woman of slave origins, the structures of the palace as a whole comprise the entire range of roles possible to slave women in the kingdom. The palace mirrored Dahomean society as a whole, an institution within yet separate from the social and political structures that it reflected. Like the personal loyalty expected by any husband of a wife, the personal loyalty of the ahosi, slave and commoner, was used by the kings to offset the potential influence of those officeholders necessary to the administration of the state. The monarchs recognized the value of their ahosi as producers, reproducers, and managers of royal affairs. They used them as an avenue of communication and integration for the kingdom as a whole. At the same time, the ahosi could use their own central position to build up personal estates and enhance or establish their own positions within their patrilineages. Within the palace organization itself, the higher-ranking women effectively controlled to their own and to the king's benefit the production activities of the female serving classes.

Within these broad general parameters of the palace population as a whole, the ahosi of slave status faced more extreme possibilities for success and failure. At worst, they could be condemned as offerings to the royal ancestors and publicly executed with dozens of other hapless victims of the royal expressions of piety. On the other hand, with few direct ties to the family of their birth, and no ties to lineages already in influential positions within the kingdom, they could be considered more trustworthy than women of common or royal status. Slave ahosi clearly had everything to gain and nothing to lose by their initiatives within the palace system. Advancement in the king's household was in part based upon merit. By dint of hard work and an astute understanding of the politics of the palace organization, women could hope to rise to positions where their earned rank and wealth could overshadow their slave status. Moreover, in a society that was both expansionist and eclectic, slave women at the center were able to be instrumental in the integration of foreign peoples and cultures into the Dahomean universe.

Glossary

ahosi: dependent of the king; wife of the king.
ahovi: literally, child of the king; royal descendant of either sex.
Ajaho: minister responsible for religious cult activities.
anato: commoner.
daklo: court official (female) who communicated between the king and outsiders during public audiences.
gandoba: dependent person attached to a royal office.
hwe: household.
hwemesi: dependent of a household destroyed by the king.
hwe tanu: "Customs," the annual royal ceremonial cycle.
kannounnon: slave.
Kpakpa: court official who recruited women for the king.
Kpojito: literally, she who places the leopard on earth; queen mother.

kposi: literally, wife or dependent of the leopard (refers to the founding of the royal lineage); a woman of a class of sacred women in the palace.
vodun: deity.

References

Oral Sources

L. Agoliagbo, Abomey, interview on September 7, 1972.
R. Aho, Abomey, interview on January 21, 1973.
Avloko, Whydah, interview on February 27, 1973
A. Feliho, Abomey, interview on May 20, 1972.
A. Glele, Abomey, interview on October 26, 1972.
S. Glele, Abomey, interview on July 29, 1972.
M. Gnimavo, Abomey, interview on September 10, 1972.
Hwanjile, Abomey, interview on April 30, 1972.
V. Kinhwe, Abomey, interviews on December 22, 1972, and March 23, 1973.
C. Dosso-Yovo Loko, Cotonou, interview on November 14, 1972.
Y. Soude, Abomey, interview on July 11, 1972.
Yomana, Abomey, interview on June 6, 1972.

Unpublished Sources

Bay, E. G. 1977. "The Royal Women of Abomey." Ph.D. dissertation, Boston University.
Glélé, P. K. 1971. "Le royaume du Dan-hô-mĩn: Tradition orale et histoire écrite." Paper on deposit in the Archives Nationales, Paris.
Oroge, E. A. 1971. "The Institution of Slavery in Yorubaland with Particular Reference to the Nineteenth Century." Ph.D. dissertation, University of Birmingham.
A.A.V.: Archives du Service Historique de l'Etat Major de l'Armée, Vincennes.
Relation anonyme de l'expédition du Dahomey, Dahomey, Carton I.
A.N.B.: Archives Nationales du Bénin.
Contrôle des Chefs, Abomey et Allada.
A.N.F.: Archives Nationales de France, Section Outre-Mer.
M. Béraud au Résident de France aux Etablissements du Golfe de Bénin, March 12, 1891, Dahomey III, Dossier II.
A.N.S.: Archives Nationales du Sénégal.
Rapport sur l'esclavage dans le cercle d'Abomey, February 10, 1904.
Rapport sur l'esclavage dans le cercle d'Allada, February 8, 1904.
A.S.A.: Archives de la sous-Préfecture d'Abomey.
Peines disciplinaires et conciliations, October 20, 1906.
Résident d'Abomey au Gouverneur du Dahomey, October 8, 1904.
Situation politique et administrative, July 1924.
M.M.S.: Methodist Missionary Society Archives, London.
Thomas Birch Freeman, untitled typescript, Biog. W. Afr. 5, Stack QI.

Published Sources

Aguessy, H. 1970. "Le Dan-Homê du XIXᵉ siècle: était-il une société esclava-giste?" *Revue française d'etudes politiques Africaines* 50:71–91.

Barbou, A. 1893. *Histoire de la guerre au Dahomey*. Paris.

Bay, E. G. 1979. "On the Trail of the Bush King: A Dahomean Lesson in the Use of Evidence." *History in Africa* 6:1–15.

Bouche, l'Abbé P. 1885. *La côte des esclaves et le Dahomey*. Paris.

Bouët, A. 1852. "Le royaume de Dahomey." *Illustration* 20:39–42, 59–62, 71–74.

Brue, A. de. 1845. "Voyage fait en 1843 dans le royaume de Dahomey." *Revue coloniale* 7:55–68.

Burton, R. 1864/1966. *A Mission to Gelele*. London.

Burton, R. 1865. "The Present State of Dahome." *Transactions of the Ethnological Society of London* 3:400–408.

Chaudoin, E. 1891. *Trois mois de captivité au Dahomey*. Paris.

Cornevin, R. 1962. *Histoire du Dahomey*. Paris.

Dalzel, A. 1793/1967. *The History of Dahomy*. London.

Duncan, J. 1847/1967. *Travels in West Africa, in 1845 and 1846*. 2 vols. New York.

Dunglas, E. 1957. "Contribution à l'histoire du Moyen-Dahomey." Parts 1, 2, 3. *Etudes Dahoméenes* 19, 20, 21.

Ellis, A. B. 1890. *The Ewe-Speaking Peoples of the Slave Coast of West Africa*. London.

Foa, E. 1895. *Le Dahomey*. Paris.

Forbes, F. E. 1851/1966. *Dahomey and the Dahomans*. 2 vols. London.

G[   ],A. 1946. "Histoire des rois du Dahomey." *Grands lacs* 88, 89, 90:43–56.

Glélé, M. A. 1974. *De Danxome*. Paris.

Hazoumé, P. n.d. *Cinquante ans d'apostolat*. Lyon.

Hazoumé, P. 1925. "Tata ajachê soupo ma ha awouinyan." *La reconnaissance Africaine* 1:7–9; 2:7–8; 3:7–8.

Hazoumé, P. 1938. *Doguicimi*. Paris.

Herskovits, M. J. 1938. *Dahomey, An Ancient West African Kingdom*. 2 vols. New York.

Labarthe, P. 1803. *Voyage à la côte de Guinée*. Paris.

Laffitte, A. 1873. *Le Dahomé*. Tours.

Law, R. 1977. "Royal Monopoly and Private Enterprise in the Atlantic Trade: The Case of Dahomey." *Journal of African History* 18:555–77.

Le Hérissé, A. 1911. *L'ancien royaume du Dahomey*. Paris.

Maire, C. 1905. *Dahomey*. Besançon.

Mattei, C. 1890. *Bas-Niger, Bénoué, Dahomey*. Grenoble.

Miers, S., and I. Kopytoff, eds. 1977. *Slavery in Africa: Historical and Anthropological Perspectives*. Madison.

Pires, Padre V. F. 1957. *Viagem de Africa em o reino de Dahomé*. São Paulo.

Skertchly, J. A. 1874. *Dahomey As It Is*. London.

Smith, W. 1744/1967. *A New Voyage to Guinea*. London.

Snelgrave, W. 1734/1971. *A New Account of Some Parts of Guinea and the Slave Trade*. London.
Valdez, F. T. 1861. *Six Years of a Traveller's Life in Western Africa*. London.
Vansina, J. 1966. *Kingdoms of the Savannah*. Madison.
Wailly, G. de 1890. "Un régiment sacré." *La nouvelle revue* 63:390–94.

INDEX

Abolition: of slavery, 9, 16, 17 and *n*, 18, 19 and *n*, 52, 77*n*, 112, 113, 122, 125, 126, 127, 153, 155, 156, 157, 220 and *n*, 221, 227, 228 and *n*, 230, 242, 243, 248, 265, 266, 288; of slave trade, 3, 10*n*, 17, 72, 163, 220 and *n*, 221, 230, 265, 281, 300, 327, 328

Abomey, Kingdom of Dahomey, 341, 347, 351, 359, 360, 361, 363

Abortion, 10*n*, 39, 52, 53, 106, 107, 109

Accra, Ghana, 7, 15, 220 and *n*, 221–42 *passim*

Adukwe (female slave), 7, 11, 16, 52, 230–41; as Zama Damasoni, 231, 232

Advice of Mwana Kupona upon the Wifely Duty, 122

Adzo (Ewe slave), 7, 8, 239, 243, 244

Affonso I (king of Kongo), 166

Afute (owner of Adukwe), 233, 239

Afzelius, Adam (botanist), 324

Agadja (king of Dahomey), 346*n*, 350, 360, 362

Agonglo (king of Dahomey), 347, 360

Ahafo, 15, 16

Aja (ethnic group) of central Sudan, 347, 360, 361

Akan (ethnic group) of Ghana, 221, 224, 229, 231*n*, 234

Alima River, Kongo, 99, 100

Allada, Dahomey, 46, 284*n*, 346, 354, 361

Alldridge, Thomas (British official), 282, 284, 288

Álvares d'Almada, A., 44

Álvares, Manuel (Jesuit), 44

Ambriz, Angola, 175, 176

Angola, 36*n*, 39, 40, 42, 96, 167, 175, 252

Anlo (ethnic group) of Gold Coast, 243, 244

Anloga, 243

Antonio de Freres & Company, 330

Arnot, F. S. (missionary), 249, 252*n*, 262

Asante, Ghana, 15, 221, 224 and *n*, 230 and *n*

Asere, 233, 237

Ashmun Jehudi (agent in Liberia), 306, 308

Assimilation of slaves, 6, 7, 8, 13, 36, 50, 56, 57, 67 and *n*, 149, 221, 226, 229, 230, 239, 241. *See also* Slaves, Incorporation of

Azande (ethnic group) of central Sudan, 152

Baadadhiki (manumitted slave), 126

Bakangai (Zande ruler), 152*n*

Bakongo (ethnic group) of Zaire, 160–79

Balanta (ethnic group) of Guinea-Bissau, 304, 312, 315

Baluchi, 112

Bamako (ethnic group) of Sudan, 69*n*, 83*n*

Bamana (ethnic group), 57

Bambara (ethnic group) of Mali, 81

Bamileke (ethnic group) of Cameroon, 8, 14

Bamum (ethnic group) of Cameroon, 54, 60, 63

Ban Bondo Bondopio, 286

Bangalan, Guinea-Conakry, 325–33 *passim*

Bangba (ethnic group) of central Sudan, 150

Bangwa (ethnic group) of Cameroon, 7*n*, 8

Bantu (ethnic group) of Cameroon, 260

Barreira, Baltasar (Jesuit), 43

Basel (missionary society), 222

Bashia, Guinea-Conakry, 326

Bastos, Francisco de Paula (governor of Cape Verde), 313

Bastos, Captain Luiz Antonio (Portuguese army), 312

Baule (ethnic group) of Ivory Coast, 9, 15

Beledugu, 76

Belgium, 95, 155, 253, 256, 259, 260

Bemba (ethnic group) of Zambia, 248

Benin, 46

Bereira, Guinea-Conakry, 320–26 *passim*

371

JACKET DESIGNED BY ED FRANK PRODUCTIONS
COMPOSED BY GRAPHIC COMPOSITION, INC., ATHENS, GEORGIA
MANUFACTURED BY THOMSON-SHORE, INC., DEXTER, MICHIGAN
TEXT AND DISPLAY LINES ARE SET IN TIMES ROMAN

Library of Congress Cataloging in Publication Data
Main entry under title:
Women and slavery in Africa.
Includes bibliographies and index.
1. Slavery—Africa—Addresses, essays, lectures.
2. Women—Africa—Addresses, essays, lectures.
3. Slave trade—Africa—Addresses, essays, lectures.
I. Robertson, Claire C., 1944–. II. Klein, Martin A.
HT1321.W66 1983   305.5'67'096   83-47769
ISBN 0-299-09460-X